LETTERPRESS
REVOLUTION

LETTERPRESS REVOLUTION

The Politics of Anarchist Print Culture

KATHY E. FERGUSON

DUKE UNIVERSITY PRESS
Durham and London
2023

Printed in the United States of America on acid-free paper ∞
Designed by A. Mattson Gallagher
Typeset in Adobe Caslon Pro, Grotesque MT Std, Poplar Std,
and Rosewood Std by Westchester Publishing Services

Library of Congress Cataloging-in-Publication Data
Names: Ferguson, Kathy E., author.
Title: Letterpress revolution : the politics of
anarchist print culture / Kathy E. Ferguson.
Description: Durham : Duke University Press, 2023. |
Includes bibliographical references and index.
Identifiers: LCCN 2022035602 (print)
LCCN 2022035603 (ebook)
ISBN 9781478019237 (paperback)
ISBN 9781478016595 (hardcover)
ISBN 9781478023869 (ebook)
Subjects: LCSH: Anarchism—United States—History—20th century. |
Anarchism—England—History—20th century. | Press, Anarchist—
United States—History—20th century. | Press, Anarchist—
England—History—20th century. | Radicalism and the press. |
Anarchafeminism. | Women's bookstores. | BISAC: SOCIAL
SCIENCE / Media Studies | HISTORY / Modern / General
Classification: LCC HX828 .F45 2023 (print) |
LCC HX828 (ebook) | DDC 320.5/7—dc23/eng/20221121
LC record available at https://lccn.loc.gov/2022035602
LC ebook record available at https://lccn.loc.gov/2022035603

Cover art: Typefounder's cut with an eighteenth-century
American printing press and slogan. Early nineteenth century.
As used for a printer's emblem by Eberhardt Press, Portland,
Oregon. Image source: GRANGER Historical Picture Archive.

For Gili, Oren, and Ari, as always
And for the scholars who will be coming

CONTENTS

PREFACE

In the late 1970s, a small anarchist group called Free Association organized itself in Albany, New York. We wrote and published our own journal, *Mutual Aid Alternatives*. This project was suggested, as I recall, by David Wieck, a senior member of Free Association and a philosophy teacher at Rensselaer Polytechnic Institute in Troy. He was a longtime anarchist teacher and activist: he had been a conscientious objector during World War II and a member of the editorial board of the anarchist journals *Why?* and *Resistance*. Also part of the group was David Porter, a historian of anarchism who edited an important collection of Emma Goldman's letters on the Spanish Revolution, *Vision on Fire*, and another learned volume on French anarchists' relations to Algerian anticolonial politics, *Eyes to the South*.

Neither I nor, I suspect, the other (then) young members of Free Association had any idea at the time that Wieck and Porter were initiating us into an anarchist practice with a long and vigorous history. Ernesto Longa's monumental annotated guide, *Anarchist Periodicals in English Published in the United States, 1833–1955*, includes publication information on ninety-two of the best-known English-language journals during the period. Many hundreds more were published in other languages and other places during the fertile period of anarchist organizing from the Paris Commune to the Spanish Revolution. American studies scholar Andrew Cornell writes in his history of US anarchism, "Newspapers and journals served as de facto political centers—means of grouping anarchists by language and strategic orientation. Publishers of periodicals routinely sponsored lecture series and distributed books and pamphlets by mail. Typically, editors were revered figures who wrote much of the copy and doubled as powerful orators."[1] Historian Kenyon Zimmer summarizes succinctly, "It would be difficult to overstate the functional importance of newspapers in the anarchist movement."[2]

Of course most political movements have their publications, but anarchists were unique. When new socialists came to town, they typically subscribed to the existing high-profile national publications such as *The Masses* (17,000 subscribers), *The Forward* (270,000 subscribers), or *Appeal to Reason* (762,000 subscribers).[3] When new anarchists came to town, they started their own journals, as well as exchanging publications with those already in existence. Consequently, even though there were many more people who called themselves socialists in the United States than called themselves anarchists, the anarchist movement gave birth to a remarkable number of publications, each a center of a radical community, usually with a small print run (a few thousand, commonly) but inviting an intense engagement.[4] Debates over what kind of journal to produce frequently resulted in the creation of a new journal, as Alexander Berkman's militant labor journal *The Blast* branched off from Emma Goldman's *Mother Earth* in 1916. Similarly, the then-weekly London journal *Freedom*, after extensive debate in the early 1960s, added a monthly journal, *Anarchy*, to its roster without abandoning its weekly publication.[5] Journals proliferated because they were vehicles of political self-creation. In his account of late twentieth-century anarchism, John Patten quips, "A Spanish saying goes that if you find two anarchists you'll also find three newspapers."[6] Art historian Patricia Leighten reports that in 1905, "there were 452 separate anarchist publications appearing in France."[7] It is unlikely that the writers and producers of the 452nd journal said to themselves, "What France needs is another anarchist journal." Much more likely, they were driven by their own need to create and to be created by making a journal. Journals did not just report the anarchist movement; they *were*, in large part, the anarchist movement.

Each of those hundreds of publications required one or more printers. Most of the journals were produced on letterpress machines by compositors and press "men" who were part of, or at least sympathetic to, the anarchist movement. While a few journals were printed in job shops (commercial establishments), many more were printed in the living rooms, basements, or out-buildings of the homes, offices, union halls, schools, and community centers of local anarchist groups, often on presses that had been passed down from one radical establishment to the next, cherished, even treated as something like colleagues in the movement. Local activists, many of whom were not trained printers, often helped in the printing process, as well as the writing, editing, assembling, and delivering of the publications. They often lived and worked in close proximity to the presses. While media theorist Lisa Gitelman, in her analysis of writing machines in Thomas Edison's era, remarks, "the clatter of the printing press [was] outside the experience of most individuals," that would not have been the case for many anarchists.[8]

It is this dynamic, powerful, multidirectional relation of letterpress technology to the printers, the archivists, the writers, and the anarchist movement more generally that interests me here. It was unfortunately not always so: I have come to see the production of *Mutual Aid Alternatives* fifty years ago as a neglected opportunity for political growth. Not only did the younger members of Free Association lack knowledge of the radical print history of anarchism, we also lacked even an iota of interest in how *Mutual Aid Alternatives* was printed. The physical production of the journal seemed both irrelevant and insignificant, compared with the content. There were likely anarchist print shops in existence then, as there are now, but it never occurred to us to seek them out. For young radicals who prided ourselves on dismantling prevailing dualisms and grounding theory in practice, we were dismayingly inattentive to a practice that was right under our noses. Indeed, it could have been right in our hands.

So, with apologies to David Wieck and David Porter for taking so long, this book examines the history of anarchist print culture in the United States and Great Britain to glean insights that can be useful to radical politics today. I aim to take up media theorist Jussi Parikka's challenge to "imagin[e] new histories of the suppressed, neglected and forgotten voices of media history" in order to articulate the political potential in the "regimes of sensation and use" that emerge from the interactive relations of presses, printers, publications, and reading publics.[9] Parikka finds much of the literature in media archaeology lacking "strong articulation of politics in the context of the techno-epistemological research," and he challenges media archaeologists to combine careful, accurate attention to specific media with greater analysis of circulations of power and expressions of agency.[10] I am also inspired by the story of learning to write a book about a treasured political movement from within the energies and struggles of that movement, as told by feminist writer Kristen Hogan. Her remarkable account of the feminist bookstore movement enacts what she calls "a methodology of learning and of building relationships to interrupt systems of oppression, not thinking just about my story or this moment, but thinking about the vital life of our interconnected stories and envisioning a just world."[11] The vital life of anarchism's interconnected stories makes its appearance in printeries and archives, journals and correspondence, skilled bodies, curious and brave ideas. I regret the lost opportunity of participating in the making, not just the writing, of *Mutual Aid Alternatives* because I suspect that a significant source of political energy was lost. Understanding that omission could be key to facilitating its reemergence in the present and the future.

While working in the anarchist collection housed in the Library of Congress a few years ago, I was stunned to come across a copy of our modest little journal. It was included in the materials bequeathed to the library by noted historian of anarchism Paul Avrich. Avrich was the grand old man of anarchist scholarship in the United States. Like the Joseph A. Labadie Collection at the University of Michigan, the Joseph Ishill Papers at Harvard, and the International Institute of Social History in Amsterdam, the Paul Avrich Collection reflects a lifetime journey through anarchism. David Wieck, David Porter, and Paul Avrich were of the same generation of radical scholars, the kind with patience, curiosity, and long memories. Their legacies link us, today, with earlier anarchists and the remarkable movement they created. It's never too late to learn.

ACKNOWLEDGMENTS

The older I get, the longer it takes me to write books. While I'd like to think that I'm getting better at it, I'm certainly not getting faster. Yet that slower pace has allowed me to linger in libraries, archives, printeries, and conversations with friends and colleagues, both old and new.

Allan Antliff, Martyn Everett, Judy Greenway, and Barry Pateman have provided sources, answered questions, and shared enthusiasms about anarchism for many years. I am fortunate to know them. The support of Courtney Berger, my editor at Duke University Press, and the wise and thorough recommendations of two anonymous readers have been extraordinarily helpful.

Through the good graces of weekly meetings of the William Morris Cup Society, Jon Goldberg-Hiller and Noenoe Silva have read chapters and discussed ideas through the pandemic and no doubt beyond. The other William Morris Society, the one in London, allowed me to learn about Morris in his home space and to try my hand at Morris's magnificent 1835 Albion press. My thanks to them both.

Tuti Baker, Jane Bennett, Katie Brennan, Cindy Carson, Carol Cohn, Kitty Cooper, Kennan Ferguson, Steve Ferguson, Jairus Grove, Nicole Grove, Kahala Johnson, Steve Johnson, Ryan Knight, Sankaran Krishna, Lori Jo Marso, James Martel, Annie Menzel, Kevin McCarron, Davide Panagia, Michael Shapiro, Suzanne Tiapula, and Liz Wingrove have generously discussed anarchism and printers with me for many years. I am especially grateful to Cindy, Carol, Kitty, Suzanne, and Liz for housing me while I explored archives and printeries near them.

Many letterpress printers have enriched my understanding of their craft. Peter Good, printer of the *Cunningham Amendment* in Bawdeswell, England, opened his home to me, introduced me to other printers, and was unfailingly generous in sharing his knowledge of printing and of anarchism. Others who shared their time, their insights, and their histories include Jules Remedios Faye, Stern and Faye Printers, Mount Vernon, Washington; Nick Loring, the Print Project, Shipley, England; Michael Coughlin, printer and bookmaker, Minneapolis, Minnesota; Rob and Kim Miller, Tribune Showprint, Muncie, Indiana; and the following printers, all in Portland, Oregon: Eric Bagdonas, Stumptown Printers; Joseph Green, Jeff Shay, and Connie Blauwkamp, C. C. Stern Type Foundry; Ali Cat Leeds, Entangled Roots Press; Charles Overbeck, Eberhardt Press; and Ruby Shadburne, Ruby Press. Richard Schofield has been generous in answering printing questions. The Ladies of Letterpress put on a splendid annual conference.

Thanks to Steve Izma for sending me his copy of Charles Overbeck's beautiful book *The Tramp Printers* when I was desperate to see it and couldn't find a copy. Thanks to Duncan Dempster and Anne Bush, colleagues in the Department of Art and Art History at the University of Hawai'i: Duncan explained and demonstrated various presses, while Anne shared her knowledge of William Morris. Thanks to Shaun Slifer for sharing his research on Ross Winn, and Jessica Moran for sharing her research on *The Firebrand*, *Free Society*, *Mother Earth*, and *The Blast*. Thanks to Marcus Rediker for his extraordinary class on writing history from below. Thanks to Markus Faigle for translating Rudolf Rocker's essay on Joseph Ishill into English and for sharing my delight with Rocker's elegant prose. Thanks to Nicole Riché for fascinating conversations about her great aunt, Bertha Johnson. Many, many thanks to students in my anarchism seminars for their curiosity and engagement with ideas.

Robert Helms in Philadelphia has generously shared his comprehensive knowledge of Voltairine de Cleyre, and together we were able to confidently attribute the anonymous social sketch "Between the Living and the Dead" to de Cleyre. It was a delightful surprise to encounter the descendants of Eliezer and Dina Hirschauge: his grandson Orr Hirschauge in Tel Aviv and his son, Orr's father, Menachem Hirschauge, on Kibbutz Ruhama. Their memories of Eliezer and Dina enriched my understanding.

In his history of British anarchism, John Quail writes movingly about his pursuit of anarchist publications, "following fugitive odd copies from library to library." Quail marks the feelings of being both overjoyed and overwhelmed "when the raw documentary stuff of history is confronted, [and] a welter of fragments, stories, biographies, movements, concerns and events burst over the historian."[1] And over the political theorist as well. Many, many thanks go to the librarians, archivists, and local historians whose combination of knowledge, accessibility, and good humor made my research possible: Susan Halpert and Emily Walhout, reference librarians at Houghton Library at Harvard University; Julie Herrada, curator of the Joseph A. Labadie Collection at the University of Michigan; Aryn Orwig at the Hillsboro Public Library in Hillsboro, Oregon; Emma Sarconi and AnnaLee Pauls in the Department of Special Collections at Princeton University; Kathy Shoemaker, reference coordinator, Research Services, Rose Library at Emory University; Neil Weijer, curator of the Harold and Mary Jean Hanson Rare Book Collection at the University of Florida; and many librarians at the Library of Congress in Washington, DC, the British Library in London, the Mitchell Library in Glasgow, the Mile End Library at Queen Mary University of London, and the International Institute of Social History in Amsterdam. Librarians at the University of Hawai'i at Mānoa have found ways to maintain research access during the pandemic. The good folks at the Woodstock Historical Society in upstate New York showed me the site of Holley Cantine's printery and shared their collection of *Retort*. Mary Rhodes, Matt Rose, and others at the Halsway Manor National Centre for Folk Art, near Taunton, England, shared their records as well as the paintings they hold by Lily and Arthur Gair Wilkinson. Clare Debenham and Ron Marsden, in Manchester, England, allowed me to spend many charmed hours in their collection of anarchist material.

Sister Mary Catherine Perry, Dominican Monastery of Our Lady of the Rosary, in Summit, New Jersey, generously shared her memories of operating Ishill's press. Kitty Cooper took me to meet Frances Solokov, a.k.a. Vi Subversa of the Poison Girls, in Brighton, and we spent two lovely days learning about the London journal *Freedom* from Frances's memories. Mary Baldridge shared her memories of Holley Cantine, including his lousy but enthusiastic trombone playing.

My thanks to writers and activists in the Protect Mauna Kea 'Ohana for permission to use their work: Māhealani Ahia, Emalani Case, Noelani Goodyear-Ka'ōpua, Kawena'ulaokalā Kapahua, J. Kēhaulani Kauanui, Bryan Kamaoli Kuwada, Kamakaoka'ilima Long, Yvonne Mahelona, Jamaica Heolimeleikalani Osorio, and No'u Revilla.

As always, sharing life with Gili, Oren, and Ari Ashkenazi is the best thing that ever happened to me. Our beach friends, especially Markus Faigle, Louis Herman, and Jeannette Koijane, join us in weekly Kaimana Beach picnics, Sunday dinners, and holiday gatherings. Weekly dinners with Jairus, Nicole, Oona, and Scout Grove, along with Sandy and Leia, share intellectual, emotional, and culinary sustenance. Beach picnics and meals on the lanai with friends and family have made the pandemic livable.

Lastly, I want to recognize the other scholars of anarchism who gathered at the Labadie Collection to participate in a symposium on Emma Goldman, marking the 150th anniversary of her birth: Ania Aizman, assistant professor of Slavic languages and literatures at the University of Michigan; Tom Goyens, professor of history at Salisbury University; Rachel Hui-Chi Hsu, visiting scholar in the Department of History, Johns Hopkins University; Anna Elena Torres, assistant professor of comparative literature at the University of Chicago; and Kenyon Zimmer, associate professor of history at the University of Texas at Arlington. You are the ones Agnes Inglis was anticipating: you are her scholars who will be coming.

INTRODUCTION

Anarchist Letters

In a letter dated January 14, 1945, the anarchist letterpress printer Joseph Ishill, from his printery in a lovely wooded area of New Jersey, wrote to the anarchist librarian Agnes Inglis in the archives of the University of Michigan Library:

> My mind is full of ideas for the future. I intend to be quite active again after the war. I have too many important items which struggle to be born, or better expressed: to be put in clear print so that others might enjoy reading them. One particular plan I have in mind is to start a periodical devoted exclusively to *letters* only; letters as yet unpublished which are of great historical value to our movement of the past, and which will serve as source material for future historians, biographers, etc....I intend to call this periodical *Life in Letters*, with an appropriate subtitle to follow which would explain the tendencies and aims of such an unique publication. There is room for such an expression and I am the man for it. I do not know why, but that's how it is.[1]

This letter is part of a vigorous correspondence between Ishill, widely known as "the anarchist printer," and Inglis, who organized the Joseph A. Labadie Collection of radical literature at the University of Michigan. While this planned periodical did not materialize, Ishill did succeed in publishing dozens of letters in other collections. He was the printer as well as the editor and sometimes the writer of these publications.

Ishill's enthusiastic missive to Inglis brings together three distinct notions of the term *letter*: a printer's sort—that is, a small metal or wooden block carved on one side with the lines, curves, and dots that make up graphic symbols representing sounds in speech, as in the letter *a*; a written communication between people, as in Ishill's letter to Inglis; and a manner of learnedness, as in *arts and letters*. Struggling with dark times, Ishill was nonetheless "full of ideas for the future." He understood that writing is part of activism, that literary artifacts can "struggle to be born," and that ideas need to be put into "clear print so that others might enjoy reading them." He had faith that written correspondence among radicals is "of great historical value to our movement of the past" because it can inform and inspire the present and future. He had sufficient bold humor to assign himself the job: "I am the man for it. I do not know why, but that's how it is."

Ishill and Inglis were two of many energetic points of connection among people, places, and things creating the anarchist movement in the United States and Great Britain during its classical era, roughly from 1870 to 1940.[2] Anarchism is a philosophy and political practice that rejects centralized, hierarchical authority—including states, churches, corporations, patriarchies, and empires—and works to create egalitarian relations in which individuals cultivate their freedom while organizing themselves into voluntary, self-governing communities. It shares with Marxism its historical critique of capitalism but rejects both parliamentary reform and revolutionary political parties that would control the state on behalf of the workers. Anarchism overlaps with feminism in their common investment in intersectional thinking and suspicion of hierarchy, including patriarchal marriage and family; it shares anticolonialism with indigenous political thinking; it places high value on freedom of expression, as do free thinkers and civil libertarians; and it overlaps with radical ecological thinking in developing participatory relationships with other species and the natural world.

From the Paris Commune to the Spanish Revolution, the anarchist movement was one of the strongest movements for radical change in the world. Historian Kenyon Zimmer estimates that there were tens of thousands of anarchists in the United States from the 1880s through World War I, and they "remained a significant—though largely forgotten—element of the American Left up to the Second World War."[3] While reliable estimates of anarchists are difficult to secure, given their lack of a central organization, anarchism was also a robust part of the British Left and was similarly fueled by large numbers of immigrants as well as a significant domestic contingent. In the exasperated estimate of Marxist historian E. P. Thompson, there was a vexing "rash of Anarchism" throughout England:

> In the next few years [after 1891] a rash of Anarchism was to appear in one major city after another. It took all sorts of shapes and colours: there was the sober group around Kropotkin and Edward Carpenter, which published *Freedom*; there was the studious and restrained old friend of Morris, the tailor, James Tochatti, who lived at Carmagnole House, Railway Approach, Hammersmith and who (after 1893) edited *Liberty*; there was the old Autonomie Club, in Windmill Street, where foreign refugees hatched real conspiracies: the Jewish Anarchist Club in Berners Street; the Scandinavian Club, in Rathbone Place; the Christian Anarchists, the Associated Anarchists, the Collectivist Anarchists, Socialist Anarchists, the followers of Albert Tarn and those of Benjamin Tucker. Papers, published on blue paper, red paper, and toilet paper, ranged from the *Anarchist, Commonweal, Alarm* and *Sheffield Anarchist*, to the *Firebrand, Revenge, British Nihilist* and Dan Chatterton's *Atheistic Communistic Scorcher*.[4]

While Thompson was irritated by the anarchists' unwillingness to become proper Marxists, in fact anarchists created schools, unions, birth control clinics, libraries, independent communities, and above all publications that had a significant impact on their participants as well as the surrounding society into which their influence seeped. It seems incongruous today, when *anarchy* typically is taken to mean chaos and disorder, yet respected scholars including Benedict Anderson, James Scott, and Catherine Malabou have all paid attention to anarchism's global influence and political promise.[5]

This book investigates anarchist print culture in the English language in the United States and England from the Paris Commune to the Spanish Revolution (roughly 1870–1940), while also consulting contemporary letterpress printers who continue the technologies and politics today. My main argument is this: anarchist print culture thrived through a dynamic combination of media technology, epistolary relations, and radical scholarship. It is gathered together by assemblages of three distinct kinds of letters—graphemes, epistles, and learning—into what Gilles Deleuze and Félix Guattari call a "fragmentary whole."[6] Each kind of letter circulates through the anarchist movement, shaping and being shaped by one another. They can be thought of as nodes in anarchist assemblages, relay points opening into sprawling communities of reading and writing that have characteristic modes of producing, practices of distributing, and habits of consuming written texts. Creating and circulating their publications through a process that directly embodies their ideas—combining physical skill, intellectual insight, artistic creativity, comradely engagement, and egalitarian labor practices—was a powerful source for the political energy sustaining anarchist communities. Radical politics today can learn from earlier anarchist successes in combining material, semiotic, and social relations to build alternative forms of public life.

Studying past anarchist print culture requires a combination of methods. Listening to past anarchist voices detectable in scattered collections of rare publications and correspondence is a project that has taken me to archives in the United States, Great Britain, and the Netherlands. I want to know what their print culture meant to them. Jay Fox, a printer who lived in the anarchist community in Home Colony, Washington, is probably representative of most anarchists when he describes his goal succinctly as "to get our ideas before the public."[7] At the same time, I want to take advantage of hindsight to speculate on how our understanding today might usefully exceed theirs without violating it. Certainly, anarchists were devoted to spreading their ideas. Having a press and being a printer were means to that end, a way to be sure of having a voice for anarchist ideals. Yet that does not mean they were *only* a means to an end: there are also immanent political and aesthetic values in anarchist print culture, suggesting intrinsic worth not reducible to achieving an external goal.[8] The large number of papers is often dismissed as merely a reflection of anarchists' obdurate factionalism: every tendency needed its own paper so as to tightly control the editorial line. Yet while obduracy and factionalism were never in short supply, I think there was more to it than that—an "underside" of the print culture that has a perhaps unintended but still potentially powerful message for us today. By reverse engineering the anarchist movement, so to speak, filaments of media, genre, and knowledge that lie underarticulated in anarchists' own self-accounting can become manifest. Toward that end, I've also added interviewing to my tool box, because there is a resurgence of the seemingly obsolete medium of letterpress printing today, and these printers' reflections enrich our understanding of its political potential.[9]

We can think of Ishill, Inglis, and thousands like them who wrote, spoke, and organized anarchism as, in Deleuze and Guattari's language, key operators and connectors in anarchist assemblages. Assemblages, Deleuze and Guattari tell us, are heterogeneous processes rather than fixed structures. They enable phenomena to emerge, flow, gain or lose momentum, rupture, transform, or subside. Each node or link connects horizontally to other linguistic, organic, and material sites, "establish[ing] connections between semiotic chains, organizations of power, and circumstances relative to the arts, sciences, and social struggles."[10] Political theorist Jane Bennett turns to Walt Whitman's poetry to theorize these flows: "'Influx and efflux' invokes that ubiquitous tendency for outsides to come in, muddy the waters, and exit to partake in new (lively/deathly) waves of encounter. The process might also be called Impression-and-Expression, Digestion-and-Excretion, Immigration-and-Emigration—different names for the in-and-out, the comings and goings, as exteriorities cross (always permeable) borders to become interiorities that soon exude."[11] Assemblages *assemble* us with our companions: we take in, we give out, we dwell in constitutive encounters of various contact zones. We can to some degree cultivate or rebuff contamination from other operators. We are, as Bennett concludes, "continuously subject to influence and still managing to add something to the mix."[12]

Cultural theorist Manuel DeLanda usefully explores practices of impression and expression within assemblages by focusing on multilevel processes of interaction among "inorganic, organic, and social" elements.[13] He calls attention to recurrent patterns of repetition and innovation, "*the pattern of recurring links*" issuing in complex feedbacks and feed forwards.[14] These emergent processes are characterized, he argues, by a certain *density* (the presence or absence of connections), *strength* (the frequency and quality of interactions), and *reciprocity* ("symmetry or asymmetry of the obligations").[15] Assemblages operate as sites of memory and solidarity (which means they can also produce forgetting and disintegration). Assemblage analysis requires a great deal of close-up work: DeLanda insists that to do an assemblage analysis, we have to "giv[e] the details of every mechanism involved."[16]

I am not the first to recruit the concepts of assemblage theory to the study of anarchism. Benedict Anderson traces the "vast rhizomal network" of global anarchism from some of its active nodes in the Philippines.[17] Constance Bantman argues that anarchist assemblages were central to the movement's operation but generally overlooked by both radicals and academics: while anarchists failed to set up an international organization, despite efforts from the 1880s to the 1910s, she documents the "informal militant networks [that] proved far more congenial to anarchist militancy."[18] Pennsylvania anarchist Bertha Johnson used the language of filaments to express the workings of networks and connectors in anarchist assemblages.[19] A collection of essays on anarchist geographies develops "anarchism as a transnational movement based on networks and cosmopolite circulations of ideas, publications and militants."[20] In that collection, political scientist Carl Levy calls on "ground-level social history" to understand anarchism because that's where the action is: "Anarchism became flesh and punched over its weight, through global syndicalism, in counter institutions such as free schools and social centres, and in the tissues of diasporic and immigrant communities."[21] In that same collection, historian Andrew Hoyt focuses on interactive networks of relations to sketch an anarchist publication's transnational reach.[22] Latin American studies scholar Kirwin Shaffer's rich analysis of anarchist networks in the Caribbean recommends developing analyses of the nodes and the relations among them "as thickly and simultaneously as possible."[23] My goal is to further develop this line of thinking and to portray what DeLanda calls "*the actual mechanisms*" in the "*pattern of recurring links*" in order to theorize the production of the anarchist movement through the assemblages constituting its print culture.[24]

Given their respective lifetimes of creating, circulating, and preserving anarchist writings, Inglis's and Ishill's physical presences and social relationships were essential connectors in anarchist assemblages. Their work, and comparable labors by hundreds or thousands of other similarly situated people, marked particularly dense, strong, and reciprocal nodes within their movement; they were key operators within the anarchist assemblages. Accordingly, in this book, luminaries of the movement such as Peter Kropotkin and Emma Goldman take a back seat, while the political communities that the less well-known members built are featured. Kropotkin and Goldman would have approved of this move, since both of them regularly called attention to the central importance of the movement's lesser-known participants. In *Memoirs of a Revolutionist*, Kropotkin wrote about his work in Siberia: "The constructive work of the unknown masses, which so seldom finds any mention in books, and the importance of that constructive work in the growth of forms of society, fully appeared before my eyes."[25] In a letter to the US anarchist journal *Free Society*, Goldman wrote, "I have long come to the conclusion that it is not through speaking [that] we will ever change conditions; and that those who arrange things, who work quietly, who are ever ready to comfort, to cheer, to urge on, to dissuade, have done more for the cause than speeches or speech making."[26]

In his memoirs, English activist George Cores, a shoemaker from Leicester, echoed Kropotkin and Goldman on this score: "Most of the work which was done was due to the activities of workingmen and women, most of whom did not appear as orators or as writers in printed papers" but who did the necessary work of production, distribution, and organization.[27] The famed socialist printer William Morris, beloved by anarchists for his melding of work, craft, and art, similarly acknowledged the work of the rank and file in his poem "All for the Cause":

> Named and nameless all live in us;
> one and all they lead us yet.[28]

To apprehend the anarchist movement *as a movement*, a vital assemblage of open-ended networks that are fluid, dynamic, and entangled requires finding access to the marks and traces that the "named and nameless" leave behind.

Anarchist communities usually organized around their publications, and they needed printers and presses as much as they needed writers, editors, translators, distributors, archivists, and readers. Zimmer has collected publication and circulation information for 274 anarchist publications produced in the United States between 1880 and 1940.[29] Hoyt estimates there were as many as 500 anarchist publications in many languages in the United States during roughly the same period.[30] Historian Morris Brodie points out that, while the number and circulation of journals decreased in the late 1920s to mid-1930s, they blossomed again in the late 1930s as interest in the Spanish Revolution grew.[31] The first thing that an emergent anarchist group usually did was launch its own journal, rather than join an existing publication. The nascent FBI, always helpfully on the lookout for radical voices, counted 249 radical periodicals in the United States in 1919. Attorney General A. Mitchell Palmer, in a letter to the US Senate asking for stronger antianarchist legislation, was alarmed at this robust circulation of words: "These newspapers and publications, more than any other one thing, perhaps are responsible for the spread of the Bolshevik, revolutionary, and extreme radical doctrines in this country."[32] In Britain, also, the police and Parliament mobilized to decry anarchist influence and warn of its dangers.[33] The anarchist papers that so alarmed the authorities were available by subscription and could also be accessed in selected taverns, stores, community centers, cafés, and even worksites. In his study of the *Chicagoer Arbeiter-Zeitung*, for example, Jon Bekken found, "Saloons promoted themselves by advertising that they had the latest radical papers from Chicago, Milwaukee and New York for patron's reading."[34] The Yiddish-language journal studied by Bekken had an impressive circulation of 13,000 copies daily in 1880, rising to 26,980 in 1886.[35] Other journals more commonly had circulations of 3,000–5,000 or less, although the sharing of publications among friends, families, and coworkers made their readership substantially larger.

Not just the content of the journals but the printers and presses that made them, and the activists who collected, distributed, and retained them, beckon for attention. Borrowing from cultural theorists Stefano Harney and Fred Moten, we can see anarchism as a kind of undercommons, an example of communities that "study without an end, plan without a pause, rebel without a policy, conserve without a patrimony."[36] Anarchist journals did not simply convey information about their political movement; they created that movement, constituting and expressing anarchist lifeworlds in the process of calling for them. Anderson has taught us that "communities are to be distinguished, not by their falsity/genuineness, but by the style in which they are imagined."[37] He famously calls our attention to the role of regularly reading newspapers in creating communities: "The significance of this mass ceremony . . . is paradoxical. It is performed in silent privacy, in the lair of the skull. Yet each communicant is well aware that the ceremony he performs is being replicated simultaneously by thousands (or millions) of others of whose existence he is confident, yet whose identity he has not the slightest notion."[38] While members of the much smaller reading audience for anarchist publications often knew each other, shared their journals with friends and family, and read them aloud around supper tables, Anderson's basic point nonetheless applies to the creation of anarchist reading publics. Yet we need to go beyond his argument to see that not just the consumption but the production, circulation, and conservation of texts also produces communities, and the materiality of bodies, presses, and documents participates actively in that production. In their media practices, which gave pride of place to printers, presses, and publications, anarchists may have implicitly identified a constitutive condition of possibility for the flourishing of radical political communities in our time as well as theirs.

Chapter Summaries: Three Kinds of Letters

Each kind of letters—graphemes, epistles, and learning—circulates through the anarchist movement, shaping and being shaped by one another. All three connotations of *letters* are present in the etymology of the term, from the Latin *littera* or *litera*: "C. 1200, 'graphic symbol, alphabetic sign, written character conveying information about sound in speech,' from Old French *letre* 'character, letter; missive, note,' in plural, 'literature, writing, learning' (10 c. Modern French *lettre*), from Latin *littera* (also *litera*) 'letter of the alphabet' also 'an epistle, writing, document; literature, great books;

science, learning,' a word of uncertain origin."[39] All three layers of letters are constituted relationally. They emerge out of prior relations, everchanging material and semiotic flows. We manage the relations by separating and naming the parts (the task of subsequent chapters), but in our political thinking, the relations need to come first. All letters are sites of the entanglement of people, things, and meanings, durable but also fragile. It's not just that they have a lot in common but that they are wound together from the get-go. They can be thought of as different literary artifacts or media practices: physical and linguistic objects and processes that constitute meaning through human connections, material arrangements, and symbolic practices. Their agency—that is, their ability to act and be acted on—is distributive in the sense that it is spread across the surfaces of things, moving in multiple directions, resonating in ways that can make new things happen. They are actants in the sense explored by Bennett: they have the capacity to affect and be affected, to intervene and make a difference.[40] One does not, strictly speaking, cause another, but they move each other in their collaborations. Literary scholar Laura Hughes neatly expresses the shared liveliness of literary artifacts: "They cross limits between animate and inanimate matter, between archives and authors, between moments of creation and consultation. What is *vivant* about the artifact is not solely the material content, nor any textual content, but the unexpected connections made possible between artifacts, across collections."[41] Each kind of letter is a site of entanglement where patterns of accidental as well as intentional interaction produce emergent effects. Each node, borrowing from Anna Tsing's analysis of a different sort of assemblage, is an "affect-laden knot that packs its own punch."[42]

Chapter 1 examines the work of presses and printers. Interactions among the sorts (little blocks of type inscribed with letters or other shapes, including blanks), paper, ink, the press itself, and the body, mind, and heart of the printer, as well as the work of the writer, editor, and the larger environment, all fold together to create the culture of printedness in anarchism. Sorts can be thought of as grammatical or compositional as well as material—they are the alphabetic characters that represent in written form the sounds of spoken language, carved onto a wood or lead block. Sorts have to be gathered, organized, and applied with ink onto a surface to constitute printing. The face is the raised letter, punctuation mark, fleuron (small image separating entries in a text), or colophon (printer's emblem) on one side of the sort. The sorts are organized in large subdivided boxes called type cases. Standing in front of the type case, the compositor assembles the sorts on the composing stick, upside down and backward, using blank slugs and leads to properly justify each line. The composed lines of type are deposited on a galley, a shallow tray with one open side. When the galley is filled, a proof is pulled, proofread, corrected, then locked into place and sent to the pressroom for production. The final step is to put the publication together in the bindery.

Anarchist presses were often located in the homes, editorial offices, or community centers of the movement, so the sights, smells, and sounds of printing were part of ordinary life. Presses were often passed down from one publication to another. In designing and producing texts, printers brought together art and craft, mental and manual labor, individual skill and collective self-organization of labor. The best-known of the printers were formally trained in their craft and were nearly always loyal union members. Others volunteered and learned on the job. Printers and presses participated in assemblages of brains, bodies, and machines that generated the energy needed to make anarchism happen. As with their schools, unions, bookstores, and independent communities, anarchist publications practiced what they preached: creating the society for which they longed through the process of calling for it.

Chapter 2 investigates epistolary practices among anarchists, concentrating on exchanges among those who print, write, and archive anarchist material. Just as many anarchists were global travelers, they were also global epistolarians, generating and maintaining webs of relationships that built their movement. Correspondence, usually moving between two persons, is a collaborative affair, as each correspondent's expectations and contributions shape those of the other correspondent. In the dynamic narrative life of vigorous correspondence, the writer and the receiver continually change places, negotiating gaps in time and space, expressing themselves, and gaining impressions from the exchange. In archived collections of correspondence, researchers become external readers who are brought into the flow and can gather elements into unexpected patterns through the expanded temporality of the archive.

The liveliness of the exchanges does not end when the publications or correspondence is initially distributed. The anarchist movement cherished its writings and took steps to share and preserve them, to retain them for the future and to ensure that anarchist histories would not be written primarily by their enemies. The tradition of anarchist libraries is global, including collections in Argentina, Canada, Mexico, Spain, Switzerland, the United Kingdom, the United States, and many other countries. Historian Jessica Moran notes that these voluntary institutions are not minor clerical operations or vanity projects but rather are "sites of resistance, consciously made."[43] Historian Marianne Enckell cleverly coins the term "anarchive" to talk about these typically self-financed collections that operate with voluntary labor: "There are perhaps more archivists at heart among the Anarchists than in the great institutions."[44] Anarchives are also spaces for conversation among anarchists and other radicals, who connect to each other and to their radical past, and who anticipate a radical future, by moving among the collection's artifacts and by making their appearances among them. Each item, each encounter, lights up the webs of association within which they emerge. The constant flow of scholars through the hold-ings opens up the trajectories and connects the relay points in fresh ways. Anarchism's reading publics were also participants in, rather than passive recipients of, the movement's print culture: readers wrote letters, poems, and essays; exchanged publications among themselves; and preserved their collections for unknown futures.

Chapter 3 examines practices of radical study in anarchist publications. Adapting the analysis of the Black undercommons by Harney and Moten, I look at anarchists as a kind of "fugitive public" engaged in creating knowl-edge outside the usual purview of educational institutions.[45] They created an anarchist undercommons, a world in which domination and hierarchy made no sense. Chapter 3 addresses the intellectual and political content of the publications and their likely lines of reception with readers. Sometimes writers and editors addressed current struggles, keeping readers abreast of strikes and rebellions, or disputes with social democrats, communists, liberals, spiritualists, suffragists, or other political groups with whom anarchists quarreled. Sometimes past moments of insurrection, especially the Paris Commune and the Haymarket events, were revisited. Frequently journals republished classic works by respected writers, especially Kropotkin, Mikhail Bakunin, or Leo Tolstoy, often in serial form, encouraging read-ers to return again and again to pick up the threads and participate in the unfolding of their movement's big ideas. Inspirational poems, exchanges with readers, announcements of events and other publications, and reports of local activities stimulated readers' investments in the energies and identi-ties of the movement.

In addition, some anarchist writers, nearly all women, developed creative mixed genres of writing to invite readers into a radical thought-space. For example, "social sketches" are short writings combining elements of a short story, including characters, setting, and drama, with the lively images and evocative language of a poem.[46] Think pieces are short writings that combine elements of an essay and a letter, directly addressing readers about a shared problem that requires their collective attention. These writings are generally less invested in instructing readers and more intent on drawing them into a reflective space. They are anarchistic not just in their content but in the manner of their engagement with readers.

Chapter 4 concludes the book by reversing the old stereotype of anarchism as a nice idea in theory but one that could never work in practice. Instead, I suggest the opposite: the theory needs some work, but the practices have much to offer. Chapter 4 turns to new materialism and intersectionality, especially Black history and theory, to expand classical anarchism's theoretical reach while invoking three recent or current political movements to illustrate the continuing vitality of its practices.

While Harney and Moten's account of Black radical study inspires my analysis of anarchism's creation of knowledge, the conceptual proximity of the two fugitive publics, Black and anarchist, raises some questions that are uncomfortable for anarchism. The main figures in classical anarchism have often been called out for their lack of attention to Blackness; as African American literary scholar Marquis Bey states succinctly in *Anarcho-Blackness*, they "didn't really talk about Blackness, were not really concerned with Blackness, didn't bring Blackness to bear on their thinking, and didn't think that Blackness's specificity demanded attention."[47] While charting Black anarchism or anarcho-Blackness is far beyond the scope of this book, strengthening anarchist theory requires understanding how anarchism's historical neglect of Blackness came to be and how it did its work in the journals I am investigating. How could a political theory and movement that was ruthlessly critical of all power relations nonetheless fail to analyze relations between Black and White people as a specific vector of power? In chapter 4, I consider four possible explanations for anarchism's analytic failure regarding the politics of the color line. First, the Left's widespread tendency to fold all exploitation into the category of "wage slaves" developed no language to analyze the lives and legacies of actual slaves. Second, a lack of historical curiosity framed racism more as a psychological prejudice than a social structure and process emergent over time. Third, the priority anarchists gave to writing may have caused them to overlook other forms of expression. And fourth, anarchists may have prematurely dismissed Black politics as too reformist, too Christian, or not sufficiently revolutionary. Realizing anarchism's promise of vigorous intersectional thinking requires careful attention to how this silence around Blackness was produced and how it can be contested.

New materialist thinking about lively matter enables my analysis of presses and printers, missives and correspondents, publications and readers. In light of the importance of doing and making things together in shared physical space in the classical anarchist movement, I conclude that contemporary political movements could benefit from enhancing the shared materiality of their politics. Chapter 4 looks at three current or recent movements that have a strong element of "thing power"[48]—the agency of food and foodshares in the global antimilitarist movement Food Not Bombs; of an encampment and repurposed road for the Native Hawaiian movement Protect Maunakea 'Ohana; and of books, bookshelves, and booklists in the feminist bookstore movement. Each of these activist examples suggests an empowerment that comes from working closely with nonhuman things as actants, capable of affecting and being affected within relationships.

How Do Letters Act?

How do these three connotations of the word *letters*—graphemes, correspondence, and radical study—work together within the context of anarchist print culture? Assemblage encounters are indeterminate, so there is no fully predictable interaction that is on call, yet there are possibilities that emerge within their entanglements. The *letters* Ishill set on his composing stick, the *letters* he exchanged with other anarchists and printers, and his scholarly attainments as a *man of letters* connect in three ways.

Creativity

First, letters are sites of creativity, where political energies interact with one another. They host an excess of unruly possibilities over any particular realizations. Political theorist William Connolly explores the ways that creativity exceeds our intentions while animating our desires: "When creative freedom is under way in an unsettled context we may find ourselves *allowing* or *encouraging* a new thought, desire, or strategy to crystalize out of the confusion and nest of proto-thoughts that precede it. An agent, individual or collective, can help to open the portals of creativity, but it cannot will that which is creative to come into being by intending the result before it arrives. Real creativity is thus tinged with uncertainty and mystery."[49] Each kind of letter—print blocks for the physical production of text; correspondence with comrades; and radical scholarship—draws on past practices without being controlled by them or necessarily destined toward a fixed end. Connolly calls this uncertainty "a fecund zone of indiscernibility" in which liminal contacts among elements and spontaneous incursions in untried directions invite something fresh and new to be born.[50]

When Ishill wrote to his friend Rudolf Rocker, a bookbinder by trade who became one of the leading intellectuals of the anarchist movement, about his exciting plan for a bibliography of Rocker's work, he was making plans for that which could never be fully planned because the doing of the work generated unexpected gaps and invited new twists that rebounded back on the actors and the materials. Ishill wrote to Rocker,

> My own idea is a bit more interesting and quite original for up to now no one has attempted such a plan, though I must admit that such a form is by far more complicated, both typographically as well as editorially, and yet I hope it will present itself more satisfactorily, both to the eye and mind. How can I explain this to you in a few words what I mean by a *new form!*—for typographically speaking it is quite an intricate job in the arrangement of various sizes of types and characters, which will play an important role throughout, not to mention spacings. To appreciate such a style or form one will have to see it first when it is finally put into print.[51]

Ishill understood himself to be reaching for something that had no obvious precursors: "No one has attempted such a plan." He recognized that the creation of the typography and the content was daunting, and he fumbled to find a way to express his plan: "How can I explain this to you in a few words what I mean by a *new form!*" He was aware that the book itself is an actant in the process, a participant that engages them rather than passively receiving their attention: he hoped it would "present itself more satisfactorily, both to the eye and mind," which meant that it may also fail to do so. And the whole thing was not fully available yet to Rocker or to Ishill, because "to appreciate such a style or form one will have to see it first when it is finally put into print."

Chicago anarchist Lizzie Holmes was similarly insistent that the movement flourished best when she and her comrades cultivated creativity, not just devotion to preexisting ideas. Recognizing that anarchists tend to reiterate their main principles over and over, she asks for more: "Why not wonder a little of what we are going to think, when we are free to think whatever we wish?"[52] Holmes is calling on anarchists to create themselves. The work of the anarchist undercommons, to return to Harney and Moten's small book, is never finished because desire is situated and emergent. As Jack Halberstam writes in the introductory chapter of *The Undercommons*, the current system "limits our ability to find each other, to see beyond it and to access the places that we know lie outside its walls." We cannot now articulate a specific agenda for a better society because the process of making change will alter our vision: "We will inevitably see more and see differently and feel a new sense of wanting and being and becoming."[53]

Creative thinking, Connolly rightly insists, depends on "delicate imbalances" among material, semiotic, and social forces where the given is always potentially interruptible by the strange.[54] The combined familiarity and newness that printers may find in setting type and orchestrating ink with paper; that correspondents may find in writing themselves to their comrades; and that writers may find when they organize available ideas, images, and feelings into texts to publish in the movement's many outlets: these, Connolly notes, "stretch and enliven the *receptive side* of our engagements."[55] Holmes and Ishill embedded themselves in what Halberstam calls "the with and for" of anarchism to express and be impressed by its creative flows.[56]

Resonance

Second, the three types of letters resonate with one another, distributing their agency and receptivity horizontally among press technologies, epistolary relations, and knowledge productions. None of them can be said to cause another in a one-way sense—it would be foolish to suggest that printing or corresponding or writing caused people to become anarchists, or that a person's prior anarchism caused them to become printers, correspondents, or writers—but the energetic interrelations among presses, missives, and knowledge practices create expressive spaces where anarchism can happen. There is no clear starting point: printers, correspondents, and writers are always in the midst of things. There are no dependent or independent variables: all the elements are potentially salient with regard to one another. Changes in any one of the nodes can oscillate within others, touch their elements, surge into their interactions in unexpected ways.

Resonance among distinct yet related ideas, affects, beings, and things enables an understanding of agency as distributive, as enmeshed in organic, semiotic, and material tangles.[57] Relations may resonate lightly on some levels and vigorously on others, as appears to be the case with, to take one example, the interactions between Ishill and Thomas Keell, a legendary English printer and editor of the London journal *Freedom*. In some of

Ishill's correspondence with other printers, the writers share experiences and insights about printing, but the available letters between Ishill and Keell say relatively little about printing or presses. Instead, they focus more on distributing the printed material. The two men exchanged many, many publications. Ishill sent Keell the US journal *Road to Freedom*, published in the anarchist community in Stelton, New Jersey, as well as many of his Oriole Press publications. Keell reciprocated with numerous British publications, including *Freedom*. The relentless incursions of fascism in the 1920s and 1930s instigated even more effort toward the publication and exchange of anarchist writings, in an attempt to stay a step ahead of the people who were burning books. In a March 21, 1934, letter to Ishill, Keell lamented the dearth of production of anarchist books in Europe, Alexander Berkman's *Now and After* being the last one. He indicated that historian Max Nettlau's work had been published in Germany, but "all their stock [was] destroyed by the Nazis."[58] When Ishill learned in an August 3, 1938, letter from Lilian Wolfe, Keell's partner, that Keell had died, Ishill and Wolfe continued their exchange of publications, persisting in spreading the effects of their relationships between themselves and the other anarchists who visited their shops and partook of their libraries.[59]

Following the specific surges, retreats, and interminglings within particular relations is necessary for identifying key operators in anarchist assemblages. Calibrating their density, strength, and reciprocity, as DeLanda urges, also entails attending to our own interventions, as our accounts have some sort of impact on that which is already underway. As Bennett explains, we should always expect our "rough schemas" of resonance to surprise us, because "phases overlap, repeat with a difference, arise out of turn, and form feedback loops that confound attempts to identify a clean sequence of cause and effect."[60] Some of these interactive energies are more problematic than others. The prevailing image of anarchists in the broader public view, from the Haymarket explosion to the Black Lives Matter protests, is steeped in violence. Of course, the authorities exaggerate and sensationalize this reputation and often invent it out of whole cloth while masking the much greater state and corporate violence against workers and protesters. Yet taking resonance seriously suggests the anarchists bear some responsibility for the images and affects that their publications and speeches put into circulation. For example, the Vermont- and Massachusetts-based journal *Cronaca Sovversiva* excelled at stirring readers' outrage and desire for revenge, feelings that propelled anarchist attentats: editor Luigi Galleani regularly enthused, "Against violence, violence!"[61] The Chicago *Alarm* and the New York *Freiheit*, among others, engaged in what *The Masses* writer Floyd Dell called "bomb-talking," perhaps mostly to attract attention and cultivate a radical persona.[62] Certainly, most anarchists did not engage in violence, and in fact opposed reckless calls for destruction because they brought down the full force of the authorities on their movement and on the Left in general.[63] Yet regular calls for "propaganda of the deed" to overthrow the oppressors are not innocent of the ensuing violence they might provoke. Unlike Galleani, Emma Goldman, publisher of the New York–based journal *Mother Earth*, excelled at calibrating the line between sympathizing with the avengers of the people—historian Paul Avrich once remarked that "she never met a bomber she didn't like"—and putting into circulation calls for vengeance that could resonate in ultimately destructive ways.[64] Anarchist assemblages, like all assemblages, are not single, consistent plateaus but, as Bennett explains, "living, throbbing confederations that are able to function despite the persistent presence of energies that confound them from within."[65] The confounding energies are not external to the assemblages but are part of the circuits of operation producing tensions and contradictions as well as affinities within the movement.

Collaboration

Third, the three types of letters enable and reflect collaborations among participants, creating communities that combine material, social, and semiotic actors. Connolly explores the sparks of creativity that can fly when people, objects, and thoughts come forth together, *"in the rush of desire forward to consolidation in action."*[66] Of course collaborations can fail or go awry, but they also have the unpredictable capacity to generate something new. Connolly continues, "When we participate in a creative initiative and when we respond to a creative initiative from elsewhere that jostles received assumptions, *we both change the world and become otherwise than ourselves to a large or small degree.* That is the creative potential lodged between the open logic of identity and the evolution of circumstances with which it is entangled. A creative act, even though it may backfire, is an uncanny power that helps to bind us to the vitality of existence itself....Freedom: to be and to become otherwise than we are."[67] Surging forward to become otherwise can be a community-creating process. The tactile and kinesthetic practices of printing, the interpersonal exchange of correspondence, and the larger counterpublic world of writing, circulating, and preserving texts: all are entangled in the surging forward that creates and sustains bonds to cohere a movement over time.

Anarchists excelled at creating practical vehicles for enhancing creative collective life. In his rich analysis of German anarchism in New York in the last two decades of the nineteenth century, *Beer and Revolution*, historian Tom Goyens charts the anarchists' joyous network of dances, picnics, socials, clubs, and other celebratory opportunities. Goyens calls it "picnic culture."[68] It could also be called theater culture, café culture, poetry culture, periodical culture, pamphlet culture, or tavern culture. In the 1930s, New York anarchist Sidney Solomon similarly relished the vigor of anarchism's collaborations: "It was writing and working, it was personal involvement, it was hitchhiking and travel, it was organizing and demonstrating—it was all the energies of our youth."[69]

Of course, the networks were not always successful, and the relations did not always cohere. Anarchists' correspondence is full of complaints and regrets that not enough comrades shared the work. Bohemian writer and editor Hippolyte Havel, speaking to the 1925 anarchist conference in Stelton, New Jersey, about future directions for the journal *Road to Freedom*, complained, "The work always goes to a few comrades. It is always the few who carry on the movement. It is only camouflage of a movement."[70] Keell similarly lamented to Ishill in a letter of January 17, 1928, that attendance at meetings in London was poor and there was little enthusiasm for the work of putting out *Freedom*.[71] Yet the connectivity made available at the annual conferences in Stelton, the regular exchange of letters between Keell and Ishill, and countless other sites for issuing and receiving these regrets were, ironically, a bulwark against them: they generated some needed connective energies to address the lack. Keell concluded with determination, "But we shall not let Anarchist ideas be entirely lost in this country."[72] At that, they were successful.

Yet not all the collaborations were welcome: the very openness and receptivity to new participants that allowed anarchists to invite their audience in also enabled the persistent and disruptive presence of spies and informants. Recall Bennett's comment that assemblages do their work "despite the persistent presence of energies that confound them from within."[73] Anarchist assemblages could be confounded from within by the disabling betrayals of informants. E. P. Thompson reports in his magisterial history of the English working class that anarchist groups were "deeply penetrated by spies."[74] Infiltration by agents provocateur was sufficiently common that British writer G. K. Chesterton's 1908 novel *The Man Who Was Thursday* imagined an anarchist group in London in which every single member turned out to be an undercover police officer.[75] Veteran anarchists developed skills to identify interlopers, but they were not always successful: Goldman was devastated that she welcomed the son of her friend Gertie Vose, an anarchist from Home Colony in Washington State, into the *Mother Earth* circle, only to later find that he informed to the police on their work for the labor men Matthew Schmidt and David Kaplan.[76] Flows of anarchist assemblages can displace as well as create.

Conclusion

Creativity, resonance, and collaboration are more useful ways to understand the significance of anarchism as a movement than are conventional notions of strict causality. It seriously underestimates the importance of anarchism to count only those individuals who at any given time called themselves anarchists and participated directly in the anarchist movement. Anarchism spread along the surface of communities, moving along their capillaries, circulating within their discourses. Printers who weren't anarchists were drawn into the circles of craftmanship and artistry that Morris, Ishill, Joseph Labadie, and other exemplary anarchist printers inspired. Correspondents who weren't anarchists exchanged letters with Ishill, Goldman, Rocker, and Inglis, among others, widening the circuits touched by anarchist epistolarities. Readers who weren't anarchists were drawn to anarchist publications, venturing outside their comfort zones and perhaps carrying fresh ideas back with them. Historian Constance Bantman's accounts of French anarchists in London around the turn of the twentieth century, for example, note that leading figures such as Kropotkin, Louise Michel (a leader of the Paris Commune), Augustin Hamon (editor of *L'Humanité nouvelle*), Jean Grave (editor of several influential journals, including *Les Temps Nouveaux*), and Charles Malato (respected writer for numerous journals) were highly regarded outside anarchist circles and thus able "to mobilise some non-anarchist acquaintances in support of the cause."[77] Similar resonance is suggested in the subscription list for Goldman's journal *Mother Earth*, which included civil libertarian Roger Baldwin, feminists Alice Stone Blackwell and Charlotte Perkins Gilman, and socialist Helen Keller. These allies could be pressed into service on specific occasions, such as the campaign to protect Goldman's comrade Alexander Berkman from extradition to California in 1917, where he would have faced the death penalty for his work on behalf of labor leader Thomas Mooney, falsely convicted for the 1916 San Francisco Preparedness Day bombing; or the struggle to free antiwar protesters after World War I; or the campaign to allow Goldman back into the United States in 1934. Anarchism enabled a resonance that exceeded its specific parts, an interactive energy that touched many relationships and shaped many events.

It is possible to think of these letter effects separately, but they always work together: creativity/resonance/collaboration. The fertile relations knitting together letterpress printing, epistolary relations, and radical scholarship in the anarchist undercommons may help us today as we face problems that were already familiar to Ishill and Inglis: failing democracies, rising fascism, brutal inequalities, continuous war. In his 1933 anthology *Free Vistas*, Ishill decries the "national megalomania" growing around him and puts his hope not in "the cultivation of 'isms'" but in an aesthetic politics of resistance: "Now more than ever is it necessary to weave the fine fibers of sensitive and sympathetic mentality in an ever increasing circumference to hold delicately and tenderly an ailing universe. Dark forces are abroad."[78] Ishill could have been speaking of our time as well as his own.

My exploration of the anarchist movement of the past raises a critical issue for radicals today: if letterpress printing, epistolary relations, and radical scholarship played the role I am suggesting in creating and sustaining the anarchist movement, then contemporary activists need comparably lively sites in which material, social, and semiotic practices come together to generate worlds. I am not insisting that the relations among printers, presses, publications, and readers are the only candidates for this productive role. There could be other material technologies engaged with semiotic practices and social relations within radical communities. Anarchism's vibrant history leads me to conclude that we need to make things together, to express as well as be impressed by our relationships with things.

1
PRINTERS AND PRESSES

Joseph Ishill ends his beautiful book on Havelock Ellis by recalling how he decided to make the book:

> When I first conceived the idea of issuing this book I was nailing the last few rows of shingles on the roof of my small bungalow. It was during one of those hazy mornings which envelop everything in a strange glamor as of some resurrected biblical Orient. The mist from the mountains on one side blended with the new green of the weeds on the other. I was restless between an intoxication with beauty on one side and an intense desire to do something concrete with my hands, on the other. Each blow of my hammer evoked an echo as if some god had wakened just to yea-say my work. It was just that sort of sweet and mellow morning when one is completely absorbed in exalted things and yet still has a hankering after the little dear tasks of daily life. I felt free and accountable to no one. And I was filled with a stinging delight to think that I could dream and still retain the cunning of my hands.[1]

To dream and to retain the cunning of his hands—Ishill's work challenges the separation of art and craft at the level of the body. Reflecting back on his decision to create the book on Ellis, Ishill connected the beauty of his surroundings with the energy of his labor. Unlike the ugly, confined shop where he learned to print as a youth back in Romania, his printery on the bottom floor of the small bungalow he built for himself and his family near Berkeley Heights, New Jersey, is light and pleasant, surrounded by flowers, meadows, groves, and mountains. Ishill links the sublime with the everyday: the "strange glamor," "intoxication," "hankering," and "exalt[ation]" are set in sweet proximity to the "little dear tasks of daily life." Ishill builds his printing on his freedom from the exploitation of the job shop—"I felt free and accountable to no one"—and his capacity to act, to build things, as well as to partake in the "sweet and mellow morning." He cherishes his own power, which might even awaken a sleeping god to bless his work.

Ishill treasures the "stinging delight" that came from the capacity to "dream and still retain the cunning of [his] hands." His hands are not simply tools of his brain—they, too, reason; they possess their own ingenuity. His reflections on printing anticipate French philosopher Jacques Rancière's argument about "two kinds of gestures" in painting and photography: "For the art of the camera to be recognized as art, the frontier between the artistic and the mechanical had to disappear. For it did not simply oppose the inventions of art with the automation of the machine. More deeply it separated two types of bodies and two ways of using one's body. . . . The gap between the two kinds of gestures had to be filled in."[2] The frontier between art and craft poses a similar challenge between two kinds of bodies, two kinds of gestures. Skilled printers fill that gap: they learn to think with their hands.[3] Unlike in his paid job, where he was reduced, in Rancière's pointed phrase, to "skilled hands following instructions," in his own printery, Ishill's labor is not exploited; his active participation in the flows of beauty and meaning into which he enters is not compromised.[4] The common distinction between art and craft contains implicit class and gender hierarchies: art is typically positioned as higher, greater, extraordinary, and male, while craft is lower, lesser, ordinary, and female. For William Morris, Joseph Ishill, and Jo Labadie, who could be thought of as the fine printers of anarchism, that distinction is part of the system they want to overthrow—it is a "ready-made thought."[5] It gets in the way of imagining and enacting a different creativity, a different order. Rancière concludes, "Social revolution is the daughter of aesthetic revolution" because changes in the assemblages of sense perception, emotional range, and intellectual discernment offer conditions of possibility for changes in social arrangements.[6] Morris, Labadie, and Ishill enabled the frontier between art and craft to recede; they filled in the gap with their own bodies, their own creative labor. Modestly though Ishill usually presented himself, he loved his dreams and equally loved what his hands could do.

While Ishill was widely known as "the anarchist printer," there were in fact hundreds of anarchist printers.[7] In her study of anarchism before World War I, historian Barbara Tuchman muses briefly over this intriguing pattern: Did a lot of anarchists become printers? Or did a lot of printers turn to anarchism?[8] Tuchman does not speculate further on the questions she poses, and no one has picked up the trail since she published her book in 1966; however, there are patterns of creativity, resonance, and collaboration among anarchist printers, presses, publications, and reading publics that open up largely unexplored dimensions of radical politics.

Anarchist communities were grounded in what media theorist Friedrich Kittler calls "print-based media ecology."[9] Publications were the heart of anarchist communities. Certainly public oratory, mass meetings, labor organizing, and the creation of alternative institutions were also central to anarchist politics, yet these too were usually associated with their accompanying publications. The radical movement for birth control, for example, had the *Birth Control Review*. The anarchist schools were accompanied by the *Modern School Magazine*, which anarchist teacher and editor William Thurston Brown characterizes as "*the most beautiful magazine of the radical movement.*"[10] The Industrial Workers of the World produced *Solidarity* and the *Industrial Worker*, among other papers. The printers and presses that made these publications were consequently central to the creation of the classical anarchist movement; as Barry Pateman, a historian of anarchism and member of the online anarchive the Kate Sharpley Library, succinctly remarked, "If you don't have a printing press, you don't have a movement."[11] In his widely circulated 1880 essay, "An Appeal to the Young," Peter Kropotkin urged all anarchists to maintain, despite all obstacles, a working press.[12] Contemporary printer Jules Faye recalls that, when she learned printing in the 1970s in San Francisco, she was "smitten by the thought of having the means of production…the tools in our own hands for producing literature or publications or communication of some kind. That was a common feeling among a bunch of us….Now there are laser printers and Xerox and a lot of access…but in those days, to have your own presses…." She concurs with Pateman and Kropotkin: having a press was a necessary part of having a movement at all.[13]

While digital technologies have revolutionized printing, at the same time, the resurgence of letterpress printing in the 1990s, continuing into the twenty-first century, suggests that "laser printers and Xerox" are not satisfying to everyone. Contemporary Portland printer Charles Overbeck at Eberhardt Press notes that "letterpress is enjoying a revival that one

Fig. 1.1. 12 × 18 C&P platen press from Tribune Showprint, Muncie, Indiana. Photograph by Kathy Ferguson. Courtesy of Rob and Kim Miller.

could almost call a renaissance" in university art departments, community centers, and private studios.[14] Neglected old equipment has been saved (such as the noble C&P platen press in figure 1.1), and many shops now have letterpress machines alongside digital technologies. Anarchists figure prominently in the resurgence of letterpress media and other older printing equipment; they find in an erstwhile obsolete technology an opportunity for creative resistance.

The answer to both of Tuchman's questions, I've found, is *yes*—anarchists were indeed attracted to printing, and printers to anarchism. It is not really feasible to discern which came first. But a more pressing question is *how*— how does the craft of printing, and the medium of the press, intersect with the politics of anarchism?

While some scholars and activists have examined the content of the hundreds of anarchist publications that circulated around the globe in that fertile time from the Paris Commune to the Spanish Revolution, little attention has been paid to their form. This chapter addresses that lacuna: it examines the physical infrastructure and media practices of anarchist print culture. The first section investigates the people and presses creating anarchist publications, paying attention to the specific jobs they did and the patterns of gender, training, and occupation structuring the trade. The second section turns to the practices of printing, exploring the sensory traits of the printery, the physical process of setting type, the semiotic architecture of pages, and the labor histories embedded in printing technologies. Of course, these two vectors of print culture are intertwined, but distinguishing them temporally can highlight their specific dynamics. Looking closely, as Lisa Gitelman suggests, at "the specialized labors of printing and the look of printedness" can help us unpack the specific workings of anarchist assemblages.[15] She rightly warns that the concept of print culture can be overly general, functioning as a "gaping catch-all" for vague generalizations about the meaning of printedness. She calls instead for "very specific histories of printing, print publication, regulation, distribution and circulation" in order to establish "local and contrastive logics for media ... meanings that arise, shift, and persist according to the uses that media—emergent, dominant, and residual—familiarly have."[16] Examining anarchist print culture provides an opportunity to ground the meaning of a particular culture of printedness in the politics and technologies of a unique and neglected political movement.

Anarchists aspired to saturate the world with their words. In 1897 Henry Replogle, coeditor of the anarchist journal *Egoism* in San Francisco, announced with satisfaction, "My ideal emitted some years ago that everybody should publish a paper of his own is materializing surprisingly of late."[17] Thomas Cantwell, compositor for *Freedom*, had a similar aspiration: according to pressman Harry Kelly, "Cantwell had a theory that everyone who associated himself with the Anarchist movement should learn to set type, and in this way be able to spread the ideas by leaflets, papers, or pamphlets under any and all circumstances."[18] Replogle and Cantwell came surprisingly close to their goal. There were so many anarchist papers, so many printers and presses, that the printer-press relation saturated the anarchist undercommons as well as spilling out into larger progressive communities. Creativity slumbers within the relations of presses, pages, and printers: as literary critic N. Katherine Hayles indicates, "Materiality thus emerges from interactions between physical properties and a work's artistic strategies." Materiality cannot be entirely specified in advance, Hayles argues, because it "depends on how the work mobilizes its resources as a physical artifact as well as on the user's interactions with the work and the interpretive strategies she develops—strategies that include physical manipulations as well as conceptual frameworks. In the broadest sense materiality emerges from the dynamic interplay between the richness of a physically robust world and human intelligence as it crafts this physicality to create meaning."[19] Hayles could be speaking directly for anarchist presses and printers: presses are located in a rich material and semiotic world; printers use their intellectual, emotional, and muscular intelligence in dynamic interplay with presses to create meaning. Even if they are not themselves printers, anarchists hanging out in printeries, pitching in when needed, are likely affected by the printshop's vitalities in ways that precede and exceed conscious thought.

Media theorist Jussi Parikka recommends studying media ecologies by patiently exploring their specific practices: in his clever phrase, we should "go *under the hood*, so to speak and extend the idea of an archive into actual machines and circuits."[20] The "actual machines and circuits" include presses and their accoutrements, but also the "little optical machines" that Rancière finds at work on the written page. In Rancière's formulation, pages—like performances, films, or exhibitions—are examples of what he means by a scene. Scenes work as little optical machines, weaving together concepts, percepts, and affects. Rancière emphasizes the scene as an active site,

> a moving constellation in which modes of perception and affect and forms of interpretation defining a paradigm of art, take shape. The scene is not the illustration of an idea. It is a little optical machine that shows us thought busy weaving together perceptions, affects, names

and ideas, constituting the sensible community that these links create, and the intellectual community that makes such weaving thinkable. The scene captures concepts at work, in their relation to the new objects they seek to appropriate, old objects that they try to reconsider, and the patterns they build or transform to this end. For thinking is always firstly thinking the thinkable—a thinking that modifies what is thinkable by welcoming what was unthinkable.[21]

Rancière insists that the page is not simply the illustration of an idea because that formulation suggests that the idea is "over there," in the head of the creator, while the page is "over here," passively recording it. Instead, little optical machines are busy: they weave elements, constitute relationships, capture concepts, and modify the thinkable by welcoming the heretofore unthinkable. The page as a scene is the surface on which the printers weave their anarchism. Rancière coins the phrase "little optical machines" to emphasize that the pages are *doing something*. Scenes are not passive vehicles for conveying meaning but are rather sites of activity that can bring in something new, or reposition something familiar, to challenge conventional thinking. Connecting relations among pages, presses, and printers produced strong, dense, and reciprocal nodes in networks out of which anarchist politics and publics emerged.

The Labor of Presses and Printers

Letterpress printers had a monopoly on printing for four centuries and have been much studied. Patrick Duffy notes in *The Skilled Compositor*, "More has probably been written about printing than about any other trade."[22] The craft entails multiple occupations and tasks: Gitelman notes, the printing trades are "an agglomeration of allied specializations that overlapped in some settings but not in others."[23] The 1904 Census of Manufacturers in the United States found 52 percent of the total print industry was newspapers and periodicals; 30 percent was job printing in commercial shops; 11 percent was books and pamphlets; and 7 percent was music, lithography, blank books, and other miscellany.[24] These types of printing overlapped, as Gitelman explains: "Novels were first serialized in the periodical press and then published as books; newspapers could do job printing on the side, and job printers might be hired to print a publisher's books or periodicals."[25] While printing was a skilled trade, printing shops were often dark, noxious, unhealthy places to work and there were high rates of tuberculosis among printers.[26] For those lacking unions, wages were low.

There are three major roles within the letterpress process: typesetter, pressman, and bookbinder. Typesetters, or compositors, organize the sorts in their cases, set the type (upside down and backward) on the composing stick, fill the galley, and lock the chase. Pressmen manage the ink and the paper, pressing the inked surface on the paper (or cloth, bark, or some other receiving surface) to make the legible text. Bookbinders assemble and join the pages. The related job of engraver is also important for publications using wood engraving to create illustrations or dramatic mastheads. In anarchist schools and families, printers were also teachers, passing on the skills to the next generation.

For printers working at the morning daily papers, as recounted in the biography of Detroit anarchist Jo Labadie, work started around noon. First came "throwing in the case"—that is, returning the type set the previous day to the wooden cases. Around four o'clock in the afternoon, the printers began composition, and they worked until midnight or after, often twelve-hour days, in poorly lit, smelly shops.[27] Their wages were calculated through a complex arithmetic based on the letter *m*, the widest in the alphabet, which gave rise to the *em* unit of typographic measurement. Pieces of metal the size of the letter *m* are called *em quadrats* or simply *quads*.[28] The total amount of type set during the work period was called the printer's "string."[29] The work required precision, attention to detail, the ability to read and assemble text upside down and right to left, and the ability to calculate the printer's point system of measurement.

Printers were and are generally a well-read and well-informed crowd. Of course, they have to be literate to do their work. Beyond that, they were often self-educated in literature and philosophy as well as attentive to current events. The "storied self-regard" that Gitelman notes wryly in printers was in part pride that they could view themselves as both workers and intellectuals, even if they lacked formal education.[30] William Morris was exceptional in that he came from a wealthy family and attended Oxford. Ishill educated himself in the anarchist classics and related literature, and he composed lovely books on Kropotkin, Josiah Warren, Morris, Havelock Ellis, Emma Goldman, and many others. Labadie, also self-educated, was deeply influenced by John Stuart Mill, Ralph Waldo Emerson, and Henry David Thoreau, as well as the standard anarchist writers.[31] Retired printer John Edward Hicks recalls many of his colleagues quoting William Shakespeare, Abraham Lincoln, Mark Twain, Edgar Allen Poe, George

Eliot, and the Bible. One itinerant printer quoted Jean-Jacques Rousseau about the virtues of traveling on foot.[32] Articulate and urbane or rough and reckless, printers were among the intellectuals and adventurers of the working class; their manner of living provided a way for workers to be poor with style. In Gitelman's vivid words, "Mental products went through printerdom as through a mold or a lathe or filter, on the way to becoming thinkable by others."[33] Printers and presses did work that was simultaneously aesthetic, political, intellectual, and duplicative; it was work that enabled a great deal of other work to be done.

There was often considerable overlap of jobs in the print industry, especially in the jobs that typically went to men. The compositor was often "sub-editor, proofreader, engineer, press feeder, and solicitor" as well.[34] Journalists often started out as printers; editors drafted printers to report or edit; printers moved up to be successful editors. Many famous writers started out as printers. The more humble printers were proud of the brotherhood they shared with their famed colleagues, and vice versa: Twain, Hicks remarks, was "proud of his ability as a printer."[35] A young printer named Burns Mantle became a highly regarded New York drama critic and "to the day of his death ... carried a paid-up working card in the Denver Typographical Union."[36] Editor and reformer Horace Greeley was president of New York Typographical Union Local No. 6 and famously remarked, "A printer's case is a better education than a high school or a college."[37] This sentiment is echoed in a collected volume of letters, *Composing Room Memories*, by dozens of professional men who started off as printers. Well-known writer and critic William Dean Howells began as a printer's devil (assistant) in an Ohio weekly newspaper office at age nine: he came to the job "with the wish to be a printer because [Benjamin] Franklin had been one, and with the interest of making the office his university."[38] Walt Whitman was a skilled printer who, as a writer, stayed involved in the production process: one scholar notes, "Whitman did not just *write* his book, he *made* his book, and he made it over and over again, each time producing a different material object that spoke to its readers in different ways."[39] The literary successes of former printers elevated the intellectual life of all printers.

Two further jobs were important to the production of anarchist materials: engravers and teachers. Ishill worked closely with several anarchist engravers to create illustrations for his many books. Other printers whose publications were plainer than Ishill's often still needed an engraver to create the mastheads for their journals. Two engravers whose work stands out in anarchist publications are Carlo Abate, who illustrated *Cronica Sovversiva*, and Louis Moreau, who illustrated many of Ishill's publications.[40] A professional sculptor, Abate's labor further crossed the already porous line between work and art that characterized the printer's world. The woodblocks used in engraving were also letterpress plates and "could be locked up with type on any kind of press that printed from raised surfaces."[41] Metal plates were often used as well, especially for mastheads and other headings put to repeated, long-term use. Abate specialized in portraits of anarchist heroes and sketches of anarchist events for the pages of Luigi Galleani's journal. Abate refused to mimic his competitors' style, the new photographic process, and instead retained his own visual syntax, "composed of white-line engraving techniques."[42] During this time, as Andrew Hoyt explains, the struggle between wood engraving and photography was a labor issue; photography hid labor behind the seemingly unmediated image, while wood engraving displayed the process of labor within the product. Abate both literally and virtually signed his work; as Hoyt remarks, Abate "wanted his hand to be seen."[43] Abate's prints were much more than decoration; Hoyt shows they were "tools for imaginatively connecting readers to an internationalist canon of inspiring historic figures, facilitating the formation of a historic narrative based on a subversive identity rather than religion, ethnic heritage, or national citizenship."[44] Abate used lines and contrasts to highlight an anarchist hero's brooding eyes, distinctive profile, or fiery spirit. Readers often cut out the images and saved them, displaying them in their homes. The prints, created by an engraver who left his mark on the pictures that then left their mark on the readers, were nodal points in assemblages linking printer, reader, and tools in an aspiring revolutionary world.

French artist Louis Moreau used similar engraving techniques to Abate's. In his discussion of Moreau's creativity, fellow artist Manuel Davaldès remarks that Moreau "chose wood in order to manifest his love of beauty and his revolt against the ugliness of men and their society."[45] Moreau dug into the wood to produce the startling white portions of the engraving, a process called *champlevage*.[46] The process and the outcome were dramatic: book historian Lorraine Kooistra notes, "Wood-engraved initials and borders are produced out of a binary system of black and white. The extraordinary beauty produced by this linear art is the result of a seemingly infinite number of infinitesimal cuts, of various depths and widths, incised into a small block of wood. Wood engravers work from black to white, cutting away negative space to bring form out of the void."[47] Letters to Ishill from his readers praised the engravings along with the text as expressing the beauty of the work of the hand: for example, R. Austin

Freeman, a British writer, wrote to Ishill that engraving marks the surface of the plates in ways that suit the press's marking of the paper better than a photograph could: "The woodcuts harmonize with the letter-press in a way that no photo-mechanical blocks ever do."[48]

Printers were also teachers. Anarchists often taught their own children to print: Jo Labadie taught Laurance, Joseph Ishill taught Anatole, Moses Harman, editor of the Kansas journal *Lucifer, the Light-bearer*, taught Lillian. In 1938 Ishill proudly sent Agnes Inglis three essays by anarchist Stephen Pearl Andrews that Anatole had produced under his own imprint at the Freeman Press.[49] Edward Fulton, a printer who lived in the midwestern United States and corresponded extensively with Labadie and others, taught both his children. In one endearing letter to Labadie, Fulton apologized for the errors in some press proofs he had sent him, noting they were "mostly set by my children who are just beginning to set type for me. One is aged 16, the other 8."[50] When the Why? group in New York City bought a handpress during World War II, Holley Cantine, who edited and printed *Retort* in Woodstock, came down to the city and taught the young people how to print.[51] Students in the anarchist schools, called Modern Schools, learned typesetting, sometimes writing and printing their own journals. Many of the aging anarchists interviewed by Paul Avrich in the 1960s through the 1990s had attended the Modern Schools, and the practice of setting type was a beloved anchor for their memories. Ray Shedlovsky, later a professional singer, remembered learning from Ishill: "We printed our own magazine. We did everything ourselves—we were gardeners, we were typesetters, we were cooks. We did everything with our own two hands. I remember how I enjoyed setting type."[52] Ishill supervised the children's monthly magazine, the *Path of Joy*. The kids wrote it, set the type, and printed it. Rudolf Rocker commented, "Ishill took great pleasure in this work and considered the result excellent."[53] Later, Paul Scott took on the children's printery, found needed equipment, and assisted twenty enthusiastic children in writing and printing their own magazine, now called *Voice of the Children*. Engraver Carlo Abate was also a teacher; he founded the Barre School of Design to teach drawing, architecture, and sculpting to working-class boys.[54]

Working in partnership with their presses, anarchist printers and engravers were more than the technicians of publishing. They were key operators in the enduring international assemblages of people and materials that made up the anarchist movement. They needed what wood engraver John Buckland Wright called "an acute sensitivity for [their] materials."[55] Printers must come to terms with the distinct qualities of their sorts, ink, paper, and platens, as well as the overall workings of the press and the many factors that affect all these elements, including temperature, humidity, the conditions of storage, and so on. Designer Colin Banks notes that "lead type is intractable and cannot be shrunk or extended or twisted at the command of the computer's mouse. Lead type must be taken for what it is. Lead and wooden letters strike their own kind of impression *into* the paper. Letterpress can transfer a thicker film of ink than the offset printers' blankets and shows minute irregularities of ink-spread, which gives the work of the handpress, in particular, its own character."[56] Ishill's readers were right to note the compatibility of letterpress printing and wood engraving, in that both reveal the unique and active hand of their creators.

Skilled printers talk about their work as having a satisfying movement and rhythm, of being "on the go."[57] The practiced compositor's labor is useful and fast, an effortless flow of letters, words, sentences. Printers describe the loss of that satisfaction as "soullessness."[58] The compositors sociologist Cynthia Cockburn interviewed, who were displaced by computerization in the 1970s and 1980s, grieved in part because the new skills—typing and handling paper—were feminized rather than manly skills. Yet their grief expressed not only residual gender anxiety but also the loss of a relationship that was formative: the press, while not exactly a comrade, was more than a means to an end; it was a participant in a flow of thoughts, feelings, nerves, and sinews.

Peter Good, a contemporary anarchist printer who sets his journal the *Cunningham Amendment* on a handpress at his home in Bawdeswell, England, views his relation to the press as part of his anarchism. The press, he says, is "free." He is "not dependent on big corporate suppliers or technicians to fix computers." Things last: "Just about everything here is built to last decades and decades." The persistence through time of the sorts, composing sticks, rulers, and frames acts on him as he acts on them: they connect him to radical history in tangible ways. Good remarks, about operating the press, "Although it's very structured, there is a tremendous amount of freedom.... Each impression you pull is unique. It changes ever so slightly, miniscule[ly]. It constantly requires labor.... It constantly requires adjustment. There's not that many people you can go to on the outside.... You have to deal with it yourself."[59] Printers composing on the press the words they have assembled on paper, or in their heads, embody the integration of mental and manual labor that anarchists have always praised. Printing expresses the principle of the "transparency of operation and repair" because the function of the equipment is transparent to the printers, so they can undertake repairs.[60] Making the labor process available to everyone undermines the hierarchy of boss and worker. The anarchists' ability to create their publications through a process that directly embodies their ideas—combining mental and manual work and valuing physical prowess, intellectual insight, and artistic creativity—was and is a source for the political energy sustaining anarchist communities. As with their schools, unions, and independent colonies, in their publications anarchists practice prefigurative politics: they bring means and ends together, enacting anarchism in the process of calling for it.

A few anarchists raised questions about the high expectations in their ranks for good printing and skilled printers. The producers of *The Firebrand* in Oregon, researcher Jessica Moran has found, embraced "the unprofessional and unfinished nature of the paper."[61] One of the writer-editors, Viroqua Daniels, defiantly asked, "Shall fear of ridicule for a little BAD English drive us back to our holes . . . ? Come, come, comrades. Think better of it."[62] Yet her need to defend the rough production of *The Firebrand* suggests that other comrades objected to it. Other moves to devalue the contributions of skilled printers to anarchism were generally unsuccessful with their larger audience. When the makers of *Freedom* split over differences regarding World War I, some members, historian Max Nettlau recalled, opposed Thomas Keell's decisions about the journal by devaluing his role as being "merely the printer."[63] A similar conflict erupted in *La Questione Sociale* when a member accused printer Pedro Estevé of improper behavior. Nettlau and others spoke up for Keell, while no less a luminary than Italian anarchist Errico Malatesta defended Estevé.[64] These disputes stand out because they are contrary to the much larger pattern of appreciation and respect accorded to printers and the high regard placed on quality printing.

Skilled printers could play the presses as though they were musical instruments, gracefully holding the composing stick, selecting the sorts one by one, and manipulating the rule to set type. Recalling the artistic performance of a skilled printer, Hicks says that he "played tunes as he handled planer, mallet, and shooting stick, plugged a dutchman here and there in poorly-spaced ads."[65] Eric Bagdonas at Stumptown Printers recalls a visitor observing that Bagdonas's press had become an extension of his body.[66] Ali Cat Leeds at Entangled Roots Press similarly recalls a friend who, watching her print, said, "You look like you are dancing." Leeds reflects, "I wasn't dancing to the music; I was dancing to the press."[67] Describing another printer's skill, Hicks likens it to sign language: "When he hit the case, stick in hand, his movements were something like deaf-and-dumb signs in the air, but a steady, sure motion that never permitted him to miss a letter. It was like clockwork."[68] Reporting on a race among compositors in Boston in 1886, the local papers noted that the winner, George Graham, possessed a "smooth grace" and "beautiful motion," observing that "he seems to be touching the type with the tips of his fingers."[69] The manipulation of the sorts, the organization of sorts onto composing sticks, the transfer of the material to the frame, the application of the ink, the feeding of the paper—these can take on the grace of a song or dance, the press a partner in the performance.

British designer Colin Banks recognizes a parallel between letterpress at the time of Morris, Ishill, and Labadie and letterpress today: he notes that in both eras, small letterpress printers have been key players in resurgences of the craft: "It is often said that the example of the small craft printers rescued the standards of the commercial printing grade in Britain in the first quarter of [the twentieth] century.... Small press work is having a second vigorous flowering [today]."[70] Creativity can emerge from the resonance of relations among presses and their people as they collaborate to make something new.

Union Men and Printing Women

Printers were union men. I am going with the familiar appellation "union *men*" because, while there were a substantial number of women printers, women's entry into the trade and the unions was uneven and highly contested. Most credentialed male printers joined the International Typographical Union, the oldest craft organization in the United States; especially for the tramp printers, Hicks recalls, "the only certain and indispensable possession was the journeyman's card."[71] The *Typographical Journal* in 1889 noted, "There are more typographical unions who owe their inception to the proselytizing efforts of the tramp than to ... all other causes combined."[72] Young Jo Labadie faithfully joined the typographical union in each city he visited, considering his dues "the best investment [he] ever made." His union card "entitled him to assistance in finding a bed, a meal, and a job as soon as he arrived" in a new city.[73] Keell was proud of his lifetime of membership in his union; his beautifully crafted membership cards from the London Society of Compositors are carefully preserved in the files of the International Institute of Social History in Amsterdam. A printer carrying a union card was a "square man." Hicks, who rarely comments directly on the politics of printers or periodicals in his colorful remembrances, notes matter-of-factly, "A square man then was what in this day and age would be designated as a radical."[74] When the union printers went on strike, it was a "square man walkout." Scabs were "rats" or "new hands" and were none-too-gently ushered out of town.[75]

Sometimes union locals owned the presses. In Chicago, for example, the Social Democratic Cooperative Printing Society, made up of members of the Socialist Party, the anarchist International Working People's Association, and Local Typographia 9, owned the facility that printed *Arbeiter-Zeitung*. Local 9 both represented the paper's production workers and held forty-seven shares in the press. Additionally, five of the eight cooperative directors were required to be members of the union.[76]

There have been women in the printing industry since its inception, usually coming to printing through a religious order or through a family business.[77] They were generally in low-wage positions, mostly doing the folding and sewing that constituted "finishing operations" in print shops.[78] Women had little access to the mandatory seven-year apprenticeships, which Cockburn characterizes as "a patriarchal ascendancy that spanned employment and domestic life."[79] Neither were they admitted to most unions or to what Cockburn calls "the patriarchal craft culture" of printing.[80] There were a few notable efforts to bring women into the trade: in Britain, the Women's Cooperative Print Society (later Women's Printing Society) and the all-women Victoria Press made apprenticeships and jobs available to women. Historian Michelle Tusan characterizes the Women's Printing Society as an early "feminist community-based business organization" because the apprenticeships were paid and the workers shared in the profits as well as collecting a wage.[81] After studying at the Women's Printing Society, Elizabeth Corbet Yeats, inspired by Morris and the Arts and Crafts movement's insistence on integrating beautiful, handmade artifacts into daily life, founded Cuala Press in Ireland. Led by Yeats and her talented siblings, including her brother William Butler Yeats, Cuala Press continued into the 1940s and was associated with the Irish Literary Revival. In the United States, there were numerous printeries run by women and there were serious campaigns by US social reformers, including Elizabeth Cady Stanton and Susan B. Anthony, to train women from the garment trades in a semiskilled capacity as typesetters.[82] Dubbed "the petticoat invasion" by male union printers, it ultimately failed because (among other problems) the women were inadequately trained for a job that could not actually be deskilled.[83] Overall, Cockburn concludes, the printers' unions effectively kept women out: they were "organized to exclude women and were not ashamed to say so."[84]

There was a widespread belief among men that women, lacking the needed physical strength, the mental ability to stick with the job, and the "natural temperament" to work with machines, were constitutionally incapable of printing as well as men.[85] Further, the common view held, women should not take away a man's livelihood, should not work in sexually mixed environments, and should not go out at night. Writer and printer Walker Rumble, calling on union records and newspaper reports of the day, summarizes the unions' view: "Women were careless, women lacked patience to decipher badly handwritten copy. Above all, women could not take the routine grind."[86]

Given most anarchists' commitments (at least formally) to equality, one might expect their movement to be a bit more hospitable to women printers. Certainly, anarchist groups could not afford to enforce the gendered division of labor prevailing in the larger printeries, where women usually were confined to feeding the press, collating and folding the papers, and stitching the binding. Anarchist printers of all genders likely engaged in a substantial range of printing tasks as required. Still, women in the anarchist movement who became skilled printers probably learned the craft the way most other women did, from their fathers or husbands, as Lillian Harman did from her father, Moses, on their Kansas farm.[87] Adalgisa Guabello immigrated with her brother Paolo to Paterson, New Jersey, in 1904 and became active in the Italian anarchist movement; she worked in the print shop of her husband, anarchist Alberto Guabello.[88] Emma Langdon was a printer in Colorado in 1903, where she published the Cripple Creek *Daily Record* singlehandedly after the male workers (including her husband) were jailed for criticizing the mining companies; she was later honored by the anarchist-friendly Western Miners Federation.[89]

Other women picked up informal on-the-job training, as Antonia Fontanillas Borrás did in Spain, Helena Born in Massachusetts, and Leda Rafanelli in Italy. Born in 1917, Fontanillas went to work in a lithography studio and joined the Confederación Nacional del Trajabo and the Libertarian Youth. She took her printing skills into the anarchist movement, becoming one of the printers for the underground paper *Solidaridad Obrera* after Francisco Franco came to power. Throughout her long life, she contributed to anarchist publications.[90] Helena Born volunteered in a print shop in Waltham, Massachusetts, for three months in 1890 to learn typesetting, then worked for a newspaper and later a job shop.[91] Born in 1880, Rafanelli went to work in a print shop as a teenager to help support her family after her father was imprisoned. Her biographer Andrea Pakieser writes that Rafanelli learned printing and anarchism together: "Day in and day out, she would stand at the machines and read pages and pages of new material, absorbing the information being conveyed in a variety of subjects and languages, as well as the text's vocabulary, grammar, and syntax as she laid out each word, letter by letter, on the typesetting machine."[92] Rafanelli worked as a typographer for forty years; wrote dozens of books, stories, and articles; and cofounded two "highly influential anarchist publishing houses in Florence and Milan."[93]

Still other anarchist women printers were probably self-taught or combined family and business opportunities with their own initiative. Margaret Anderson, coeditor of the anarchist-oriented *Little Review*, had been a printer.[94] Anarchist Sonya Deanim printed and clandestinely distributed *Frayhayt*, while Brona Greenburg ran an underground press in Warsaw in the 1930s.[95] Teenage sisters Helen and Olivia Rossetti edited and printed *The Torch* in London.[96] Georgia Replogle was coeditor and compositor for the San Francisco–based journal *Egoism*.[97] Lois Waisbrooker edited, wrote, and sometimes set type for *Our Age, Foundational Principles*, and *Clothed with the Sun*.[98] Ethel MacDonald and Jenny Patrick from Glasgow were practicing printers, but it's not clear how they learned the trade.[99]

It is likely that anarchist printeries were more flexible regarding women's participation than their establishment counterparts, but there are at least two famous examples that disappoint feminist expectations. Pierre-Joseph Proudhon, generally thought to be the first person to call himself an anarchist, was a printer who famously decried women's participation in the printing craft or any occupations that disturbed the gender hierarchy he took to be natural.[100] Proudhon was a significant influence on Benjamin Tucker, editor of *Liberty*; Tucker characterized himself as supportive of women's equality, yet he shared Proudhon's contempt for women printers.[101] In 1891 the journal *Egoism* featured an exchange between Tucker and Georgia Replogle, the coeditor of *Egoism* with her partner, Henry. The editors were also compositors.[102] Tucker repeated the familiar charges regarding women's alleged incompetence as printers, while Georgia Replogle modestly asserted (in type set by her own hand) that at least a few women had mastered the trade. She defended women printers' right to equal pay for equal work and praised the quality of their work. The highly respected editor of *Liberty* dismissed Replogle's arguments, maintaining that, "apart from the special inferiority of woman as printer...there exists the general inferiority of women as worker." The curmudgeonly Tucker went on: "Even the skilled women printers, as a rule, show the average woman's lack of ambition, of self-reliance, of sense of business responsibility, and of interest in her employer's undertakings."[103]

Replogle pointed out in reply that in San Francisco, where *Egoism* was produced, 10 percent of the working union printers were women and were paid equal wages; she took this as "strong evidence that at least that fraction of the sex had practically mastered the accomplishment." She drew on her experience in the trade: "So far as personal observation goes, the women seem as useful as the men. They work as steadily, as fast, require no different accommodations, and their product sells for the same price in the market."[104] To my knowledge, Tucker never acknowledged the contrariness of carrying on this surly dispute in the beautifully printed pages of Replogle's journal.[105]

Tucker and the Reploges fell within the strand of anarchism called individualist, as opposed to the better-known collectivist or communist threads. They embraced small-scale private ownership of land and tools, seeing private property on this scale as a vehicle to resist the power of states. Unlike later libertarians, they did not advocate or defend corporate capitalism but insisted that individual ownership provided a safety net for otherwise vulnerable farmers and workers. Nor were they opposed to unions: Georgia Replogle belonged to the Oakland Typographical Union as an "Associate Member" and Tucker generally supported strikes.[106] Yet obviously the two editors' shared perspective on economic matters was crosscut by a clear difference on gender matters. For Tucker, the operations of the market, with regard to women printers, were not relevant, because women's "special inferiority" trumped the working of supply and demand. Tucker can be seen as the pro-market mirror image of the good union men who drew the line at including women; like the supposedly "natural" operation of markets in Tucker's view, the supposedly universal class struggle faltered on the laboring bodies of women printers.

Professionals and Amateurs

Anarchist printers who were formally trained at their work—that is, they went through the lengthy process of apprenticeship to learn typesetting and attain their union cards—often did many or all of the available printing jobs. They were mostly working-class men, and printing was both their livelihood and part of their contribution to anarchism. Nettlau recalls that early issues of *Freedom* were "set by compositors, mostly comrades, who worked often under the stress of really hard circumstances."[107] English printer Thomas Keell (pictured in figure 1.2 in the famous *Freedom* office at 127 Ossulston Street in London) apprenticed at age fifteen, and seven years later he joined the London Society of Compositors.[108] Keell and Detroit printer Jo Labadie typeset other newspapers before Keell took over at *Freedom* and Labadie began writing, printing, and binding his own poetry and short essays, which with characteristic whimsy he called "Cranky Notions." Ishill printed the periodical the *Modern School Magazine* while he was a resident of the anarchist community in Stelton, New Jersey, where he also taught printing; he made his living at a commercial print shop; and he spent most of his evenings and weekends printing books and pamphlets in his home, a lifetime of work that produced over two hundred handset publications, including many anarchist classics that would otherwise probably have gone out of print. Midwestern printer Edward H. Fulton had formal training in his craft. He wrote to Labadie on May 31, 1897, "I see by the sketch of your career that you went about the same route I have gone. Printer, 'tramp,' State Soc[ialist], and lastly, Anarchist."[109] Fulton put out numerous journals, or, rather, one continuous publication with frequent changes of name: *Age of Thought*, *The Mutualist*, *New Order*, and *The Egoist*, among others.

Albert Parsons, one of the anarchists wrongly convicted and executed for the Haymarket bombing in 1886, learned printing and journalism at the *Galveston News* when he was twelve years old, later moving to Chicago and editing *The Alarm*. He joined the typographical union, and according to his brother, he continued his membership until the time of his death.[110] Estevé served his apprenticeship in Barcelona before immigrating to the United States and printing the anarchist journal *La Questione Sociale* in Paterson, New Jersey.[111] Eliezer Hirschauge defied his parents in Poland to apprentice as a printer at the age of sixteen; after immigrating to Israel, he supported his family by working as a compositor while also printing anarchist materials.[112] Max Metzkow apprenticed in his native Germany before immigrating to Great Britain and then the United States. He worked as a compositor for Johann Most's *Freiheit* and Dyer Lum's *Alarm*, and he was active in the typographical union.[113] When anarchist editors mention that they paid, or more often that they failed to pay, the printer, they might have been referring either to an outside typesetter at another shop or to one of their own group who was formally trained and depended on the income for their livelihood.

Fig. 1.2. Thomas Keell (left) and Percy Meachem (right) in Freedom Printery. Publication by Freedom Press, London.

Tramping was a kind of second apprenticeship into the trade. Ishill, Labadie, and Fulton all mention their days traveling the United States as tramp printers. "In those days," retired printer John Hicks recalls, looking back on his own career, "a printer was not a printer—his education was not considered complete—until he had done some wandering. It was the day of the tramp printer."[114] In the early 1890s, printers' union records indicate that two-thirds of the cards issued annually were travel cards.[115] International Typographical Union cards were accepted in the United States, Canada, Great Britain, and other countries.[116] Tramping was useful both to regulate labor and to acquaint journeymen with the many different types of equipment they could encounter.[117] Media historian David Finkelstein emphasizes the significance of the British tramp printers for their "important and unacknowledged roles as key transmitter[s] of knowledge within a global typographical web."[118] While there could be considerable hardship involved—historian Emma Greenwood shows that during hard times, tramping "was far from the emancipating rite of passage" advocates claimed—itinerant printers were "connected by a craft identity" and loyalty to their unions.[119]

Tramp printers often turned down regular employment to wander. Young itinerant printers in the United States were called "gay cats." The stay-at-homes were called "home guards," and their rootedness was often subsequent to a period of travel: "When a printer had finished his term of apprenticeship, he was told to get out and learn something. The style was different in each town and there was much to learn. He took to the road in order to broaden himself mentally and efficiently, or to see the country."[120] Tramp printers often cultivated particular styles: some dressed in sartorial splendor, sporting top hat, formal coat, gloves, and cane, while others, such as the famed Missouri River Pirates, were known for their shabby dress as well as their formidable expertise as they tramped the Missouri River valley.[121] Within anarchist communities, printers of both the rooted and the traveling varieties were generally respected, but within the larger society the tramp printers were the "bad boys" of the profession: heavy drinking and gambling, illegal riding of the rails, and regular visits to brothels were the rule, or at least the reputation. Tramp printers frequently skirted the law, traveling "a couple of inches ahead of the village constable."[122] Tramp printers often carried a bag of type blocks (sorts), a composing stick, or a rule with them. These mobile markers established the individual as part of the general circulation of itinerant printers.

Some of the sleazier hotels, rooming houses, and saloons catered to tramp printers; wanderers lacking the price of a bed often slept on the floor of the printing establishment, with newspapers for mattresses, and were given some money for breakfast by the editor, so the hungry printer could eat before returning to set type. Barbershops often had bathrooms attached, where itinerant printers could leave their laundry on Saturday, have a bath for twenty-five cents, and "be ready for another week."[123] Word of mouth among printers spread the news about receptive establishments. At John Hakle's saloon at Fourth and Ohio Streets in Terre Haute, Indiana, Hicks recalls, "it was only necessary to lay a printer's rule on the bar to get a drink."[124] Jack O'Brien's basement joint in Chicago permitted Hicks to sleep on the pool table, with the proviso that he relocate under the table if a customer wanted to play.[125] Such places were "known from coast to coast" by tramp printers.[126] Word of such establishments constituted part of the effective networks connecting the wandering printers. Sorts were a form of material and semiotic currency for printers: a bag of sorts could, in different contexts, qualify the holder for a job, establish printing credentials, signal union membership, or secure a drink or overnight accommodation at a friendly establishment. Paul Fisher summarizes the tramp printer as "a builder of an industry, an apostle of a union, and a teacher of a craft."[127]

Looking at the profession of printing as a whole, Gitelman concludes that Ishill, Fulton, Hirschauge, and Labadie were unusual: "For a job printer himself to publish something (rather than just print) was atypical."[128] But the situation was somewhat different among anarchists; they often worked in commercial shops to support themselves and their families (which no doubt sharpened their skills) while also serving as editors, writers, and printers for anarchist publications. When Labadie wrote for the Detroit labor paper *The Socialist*, he and his editor Judson Grennell put out their paper in the evenings and on weekends, after leaving their long day's work at a printing job that paid the bills. Ishill commuted to a job shop in New York City for decades to earn enough money to support his family and do the printing he really wanted to do at home. Hirschauge made his living as a job printer in Tel Aviv while writing, translating, and printing anarchist materials, including a pamphlet on Kropotkin and two issues of a journal called *Deyes* (Opinions).[129] Barnett Derzanski, a printer from South Mackney, England, worked a day job printing in English and Russian while in his off-hours he helped Keell to "make up and impose" *Freedom Bulletin*.[130] Georgia Replogle "held a frame" (that is, worked as a compositor) for a daily paper in Oakland, California, while printing and coediting *Egoism*.[131] James and Blanche Cooney set their radical pacifist journal *The Phoenix* by hand at the Woodstock artists' colony in upstate New York and made a little extra money by doing outside print jobs.[132] Fulton usually made enough money at his stationery business to support his family and write and print his journals, but in later years, he lamented that his health did not permit him to fully devote himself to his political work: "You know a paper of my kind depends on the printer. No paper that is worth a cent a year or century can gain enough subscriptions to pay the cost."[133] While in the larger world of job printing there may have been a bright line between authoring and printing, those skills were often combined among the anarchists.

There are other ways in which the work of writing and of printing blurred together. Labadie's granddaughter writes, "By the light of the kerosene lamp, they [Labadie and his partner] stood at a printer's case on the third floor of the Volksblatt building on Farmer Street, writing and typesetting articles simultaneously to save time."[134] Ishill was also able to create his ideas and set his type simultaneously. Pressman Harry Kelly notes that Estevé "was one of those editors, rare if not extinct today, who composed their editorials as they set them in type."[135] Vincenzo Ferrero of *La Protesta Umana* recalls that Italian printer Giuseppe Ciancabilla "could set his articles directly into print without a first draft."[136] Writing and typesetting at the same time, which entails creating the ideas while assembling the words upside down and backward on the composing stick, suggests a daunting collaboration of the printer with the press. Like jazz musicians who compose the music as they play it, these printers improvise hybrid printing/writing. Additionally, even the ordinary work of printers sometimes blurred the distinction between writing text and setting type. Typically, printers set the words written by reporters, writers, or editors; an editor with a "good fist" was one whose handwriting was readily decipherable.[137] But many editors' scrawls required some intervention by the printers, who had to determine what the text *should* say in order to set the type.

Anarchists who were not trained printers often stepped in to assist or even replace those with formal training out of necessity or comradeship. They learned to print on the job. Abe Isaak learned to print while working on *The Firebrand* in Portland.[138] Eugene Travaglio "apprenticed as a typesetter for *Free Society*" in Chicago.[139] When the talented Canadian writer George Woodcock coedited *War Commentary* with Marie Louise Berneri during World War II, he learned to operate *Freedom*'s printing equipment, including the "treadle-operated platen press for small printing jobs."[140] George Cores, an English activist who also learned to print when needed, notes in his memoirs that, in the early years of *Freedom* and *Commonweal*, "some ardent young spirits around Kings Cross, London, yearned to print a paper which would coincide more with the mentality of poor working people such as themselves. They met in a coffee and dining room weekly, and put their shillings into a common fund until they could purchase enough type and other printing accessories. This they did and printed 'The Alarm' which lasted for some months."[141] There were many "ardent spirits" who took up the challenge of printing without training. Some of the big names in the movement put in their time at the printer's case: Ishill reports that, while Kropotkin was in Switzerland, "during the hours when the workers were at rest around their hearths, Kropotkin would begin with a few others to set up the remaining columns of the 'Révolté.'"[142] François Dumartheray, who put out the journal with Kropotkin, recalls that the grand old man of the movement "loved manual, quite as well as intellectual, work. He never wasted a moment at the printing establishment, either as a compositor or handling a little hand press for the printing of our small brochures."[143] Rudolf Rocker, while a trained bookbinder, did not know how to set type until he worked with a printer named Papa Naroditsky on *Arbeiter Fraint* in London.[144] When Naroditsky moved on, Rocker and his companion Milly Witcop Rocker became compositors for their journal *Germinal*. They carried the heavy cases of type up and down four flights of stairs to set the type in their fourth-floor tenement apartment in Stepney Green. Rocker remembers, with satisfaction, "I had learned a little typesetting from Narodiczky, and though I was not very quick at it, I felt capable of undertaking the work. Milly had also learned typesetting, and she managed by herself to set two whole articles in each issue. When I look back at those issues today I find they were quite well set. Of course Milly and I were not professional compositors; we took much longer over our work. But the result was not bad."[145]

Putting out the journals was often a team effort, requiring several people working together to staff the often aged and quirky equipment, learn the needed skills, and put out the paper. These were opportunities to develop comradery as well as craft. When Alfred Marsh was editor of *Freedom*, American anarchist Harry Kelly worked on the London journal for several years as pressman, the job for which he had been trained in the United States. The group combined antiquated equipment from several sources at the *Freedom* office at 127 Ossulston Street, near Euston Station. In the small, sparsely heated two-story brick building, they set type upstairs and printed the paper downstairs. Kelly comments wryly, "The press, if it had not been held over from Gutenberg's time, looked to me as being of no later date than 1820. It was an oscillating press of the Wharfdale type, with neither power attachment nor sheet delivery, though technically it was a cylinder press. Three persons were required to operate it."[146] In his unpublished autobiography, "Roll Back the Years," Kelly describes the process:

> I made ready the forms and prepared the press, a task which always took at least half a day. There were eight pages, which necessitated two forms. When my preparations were completed, some and occasionally all of the others would turn up to help—Marsh, John Turner, Vassily Tcherkesov, an Irish-Welsh woman with a mysterious air whom we called "A.D.," Dr. Max Nettlau of Austria, and Nikolai Tchaikovsky.
>
> My job now was to feed the press. On its side was a large iron wheel with a handle, like that on a country-store coffee-mill, and some of the men would turn this wheel to operate the press, while A.D. took the printed sheets off as they came around. Some of the group would fold the paper, and others would enclose each copy in an addressed wrapper, and attach the necessary postage.[147]

Occasionally outside help had to be called in: "Sometimes we stopped a labourer in the street and hired him at ninepence an hour—that was 50 percent more than the docker's 'tanner'—but that only happened when the others were unavailable. It was very hard work turning the press, and we never tried it unless two or more men were there to take turns."[148] Then they would "relax over a simple but tasty meal" prepared by Frieda Tcherkesov and Mary Krimont, Kelly's partner, who had come to England from the United States. Meanwhile, the compositor readied the next form.[149] Kelly's recollections reveal a great deal of affection for the English journal: "I don't know how many of you have ever been connected with a paper. It is like a baby, and each issue carries with it the responsibilities and joys of a new-born child. After a struggle it comes forth a finished article, and like a winged messenger goes forth to fill with discontent or inspiration people far away whom one may never see." He concludes, "Those were glorious days for all of us."[150]

Cores remembers a similar cooperative arrangement with *Freedom* some years later. In 1931 the journal's treasurer, John Turner (himself a former printer), announced that there was no more money to produce the journal. Cores tells of seeking a way to keep the journal running:

> I had somehow got into close friendly association with John J. Humphrey, an employee of the underground railways, who had a small printer's outfit, with a platen machine. I told him what was on my mind, and the upshot was the "Freedom" appeared the next month as usual, and was produced by voluntary work. Humphrey also provided premises for it by Malden Crescent, N.W. This first issue consisted of four pages, produced by Comrade Humphrey and a nephew of his named Bob Finch, an all-round printing worker, who was employed by a firm in Lambeth. I recognized that these two comrades could not be expected to perform the drudgery indefinitely, and learned by Humphrey's kind permission, to assist in typesetting.
>
> Then I had the good fortune to meet Fred Stroud, who lived at Holloway, a French polisher by trade. I introduced him to Humphrey and he became quite an expert voluntary compositor and machine operator. We published an eight-page paper until August 1936.
>
> I would like to mention that the machine would only print one page at a time, so that an issue of 1000 copies entailed eight thousand impressions.[151]

Talented writer and architect Colin Ward similarly recalls working collectively to put out *Freedom* after World War II: "Most of us knew, or learned, how to mark up material for the typesetter, how to correct proofs, how to paste up the 'dummy' of the paper ready for Mr. Anderson, the elderly compositor, to insert the headlines, and Ben Chandler, the machinist, to print the paper on the very old printing press that Freedom Press had acquired in 1942 when it became hard to find a printer ready to undertake its work."[152]

There are many other accounts of hardworking amateurs, with or without the guidance of a professional, who labored at paid jobs during the day and put out their journals on their own time. Telling the story of the Oregon journal *The Firebrand*, one of the editors, Henry Addis, recounts, "During the entire time of its publication not more than one practical printer was connected with it at any one time, and the greatest portion of the time the work was done by amateurs in the 'art preservative.'"[153] The editorial group of the journal worked in the hop fields, took in washing, and did other day jobs to support their efforts.[154] Similarly, London anarchist James Tochatti reported in the first issue of his journal *Liberty: A Journal of Anarchist Communism*, "Anyone who has had the bringing out of a paper, without professional assistance, can understand how we set our teeth as each trouble turned up. We are not capitalists. Having raked up enough money to buy a little type, and a press, we comrades set to work to learn printing." The editor thanked all the comrades who helped, especially "those who spent Christmas '93 in an extemporized printing den" working "cheerfully and hopefully for the cause."[155] A half century later, Dorothy Rogers wrote to Agnes Inglis about the success of the New York–based journal *Why?* in obtaining a small handpress: "The printing is truly a cooperative venture. We each take our turn in every phase of the work, from buying the materials to putting the finished work together and then breaking down the type for use again.... Some of us have also learnt simple book binding and we now have a few bound copies of the first two volumes of *Why?*"[156]

Other "ardent ... spirits" who "yearned to print a paper," as Cores characterized them, worked under much less felicitous circumstances. Sometimes, printing was just too much trouble: stalwart Scottish activist John Caldwell writes about the point at which the Glasgow group putting out *The Word* gave up setting type. The old machines were hard to manage, and the type was worn: "We were inexperienced, the paper was horrible, the ink was horrible, and it was a rotten job. So we started having *The Word* professionally set up by Walter Nash and Company—during the whole of the war he did it for us, and it cost us a great deal of money. He paged it and set it up, then delivered it to us, and we printed it on our flatbed machines."[157]

Of course, most groups could not afford to outsource the typesetting. Sometimes, they couldn't afford much at all. When Ross Winn in Tennessee became "too sick and too poor to keep up" with the writing and printing of his journal, he turned to fellow printer and editor Jay Fox and asked him to supply subscribers with Fox's journal *The Agitator* to replace Winn's promised publication.[158] In desperation Winn's wife, Gussie, wrote in secret to Emma Goldman, asking for her help. Ross, she said, "would rather starve than beg but he has worked so hard [*sic*] did all the work on The Firebrand by himself only what little I could do."[159] Goldman and friends raised sixty dollars for the Winns in response to Gussie's plea. Rather than using the gift to take care of himself and his family, Ross bought another printing press to continue the work he embraced, in Goldman's words, as "his one supreme passion . . . a paper, to arouse, inspire, and educate the people to a higher conception of human worth."[160] Ross was setting type to put out *The Advance*, his final paper, the day before he died.

London activist Dan Chatterton, nicknamed "Old Chat," mirrored Winn's determination to put out a journal. He sold *The Torch*, *Freethinker*, *Justice*, and other publications at Hyde Park and also produced his own journal, colorfully entitled *Chatterton's Commune: The Atheistic Communistic Scorcher*. His obituary in *The Torch* noted that he suffered from severe poverty and ill health, yet "he wrote, printed and sold this paper without any assistance, without even a printing press; unable even to see the type, owing to failing eye-sight, he was obliged to feel every letter."[161] Forty years later, *Freedom* ran a series on little-known anarchists from the past and reported that Old Chat "was reputed to have collected his type from printers' dustbins, which he set up on his kitchen table, and his wife sat on the forms, in order to get an impression for he had no machine."[162] The appearance of the publication was understandably ragged, "printed rather haphazardly in jumbled type on coarse paper, or more frequently on insubstantial yellow tissue."[163] Fiercely anticlerical, pro–birth control, and at war against the unearned privileges of all elites, Chatterton's publication was eccentric (to put it mildly), but still he garnered respect from other anarchists for his determination.

An even more difficult set of circumstances surrounded the production of *Prison Blossoms*, a small handmade collection of essays, stories, poems, and fables created by Alexander Berkman, Henry Bauer, and Carl Nold from 1893 to 1897 when they were serving time in Western Pennsylvania Penitentiary. "Passing messages from cell to cell via circuitous routes," their later editor notes, "these comrades risked grave retaliation if their clandestine writing was uncovered and they were perceived to be hatching an anarchist plot."[164] Despite these conditions, they wrote sixty booklets, hid them under a floorboard of the prison broom shop, and mailed them via a bribed guard. The handwritten documents were in English and German, three inches by five inches in size, "small enough to elude guards who searched the prison cells where, for the most part, they were composed and hidden."[165] They were even more ragged in appearance than Old Chat's solitary production, with "poor-quality paper, water damage, words almost obliterated by rubbing, ink bleeding through from the other side of the paper, crumbling edges, the hand-stitching of the small pages that sometimes encroached on the writing."[166]

Over and over, the perseverance and fortitude of both the professional and the amateur anarchist printers, and others putting out the journals, is extraordinary. What accounts for this remarkable degree of stick-to-it-iveness for anarchists and their publications? Anarchist political culture was uniformly respectful of written work: they may have been atheists, but they were people of the book. The account most anarchists gave for their indefatigable labors—their devotion to getting the word out—is certainly one aspect of their dedication, but I suspect it is not the whole picture. In addition to their determination to communicate their ideas, which reflects their steadfast commitment to changing society by educating people, I speculate that it was the act of making the journals that helped to produce the capacity to go on. Presses and printers were nodal points in anarchist assemblages; they were participants in what philosopher John Protevi calls the "powers of immanent self-organization and creative transformation" that allowed anarchism to be.[167] Hayles describes this feedback/feedforward loop succinctly: "Obviously artifacts spring from thought, but thought also emerges from interactions with artifacts. Someone starts to make a technical object—a book, say—but in selecting the paper and choosing the cover design, new thoughts come as the materials are handled. Insights are stimulated through touching, seeing, manually fitting parts together, and playing with the materials that declined to come when the object was merely an abstract proposition."[168]

Recall from the introduction how excited Ishill was when he tried to explain his new book idea in a letter to his friend Rudolf Rocker: he had an idea for a new kind of book that would be both typographically and editorially fresh, but he could not know just how the book would act on the reader's "eye and mind" because the making of the book would stimulate new insights that would be unpredictable in their effects.[169]

English printer Peter Good gets at a similar idea when he remarks, "You have to understand the time of letterpress. It has its own duration, its own rhythm." The printer has to attend to the task at hand, as well as the immediate context and the larger context, taking steps, adjusting, moving forward. Good continues, "The machine is giving something. If I'm doing it wrong, it fights back." When something goes wrong, he says, "you are into a struggle....It's only you and the machine that can solve the problem." On the other hand, when the process goes smoothly, all its elements coming together, Good confirms, "the press did a good job that day."[170]

Jules Faye, a printer now living in upstate Washington, continues that line of thought:

> It was like a living being....The presses are people, almost. They have a persona, a personality, they have moods. Sometimes they don't feel like working, even if you do.
>
> There are days when you've done everything, technically, that is required, you've double-checked everything, and the press is just not producing good results. There's just nothing left to fix. It's got to be the press. You take a break, come back the next day, and it's working. What the hell.
>
> I can't explain it. You go to work, but the press is not working.[171]

Anarchist collaborations included such mutual interactions of presses and their people, each efficacious for the other, carrying, in Jane Bennett's words, "the power to make a difference that calls for response."[172] The moments resonate among their elements; everything adjusts. The press-printer relation is a two-way street.

When anarchists were harassed and arrested, their printing equipment was often confiscated or destroyed. After the shooting of President William McKinley in 1901 by anarchist Leon Czolgosz, police raided the offices of *Free Society* in Chicago, arrested editor Abe Isaak and his family along with many other anarchists, confiscated their literature, and "smashed Isaak's printing press."[173] When the police raided the Socialist Labor Party offices in Glasgow, subsequent to the banning of their literature, the authorities took the press's rollers; despite his best efforts, the printer could not replace them.[174] When Lillian Harman, compositor for *Lucifer*, was disturbing the good citizens of Valley Falls, Kansas, by "living in sin" with coeditor Edwin Walker, Walker reported that the town's other paper recommended "that our printing plant be destroyed and we driven from Valley Falls."[175]

The London journal *Freedom* was raided four times during World War I, the authorities confiscating the forms, sorts, type cases, and crucial machine parts as well as the publications.[176] Printer and editor Thomas Keell and organizer Lilian Wolfe were arrested and imprisoned in 1916 for obstructing conscription; historian John Quail notes, "As a result of the raid, printers refused to print further issues of the paper."[177] Other comrades stepped in and put out the journal for several months, but they too were raided and arrested, their press also seized.[178] Journals fought back when their printing efforts were blocked. In its November 1918 issue, *Freedom* reprinted a cheeky letter from Joan Beauchamp, printer of the socialist publication *The Tribunal*, pillorying the magistrates for their persecution of her publication, including raiding the offices, arresting and prosecuting the staff, and destroying the press. Beauchamp readily gave her own location but refused to reveal the whereabouts of her remaining press: "I have a valuable printing press, and in view of the destructive propensities of this freedom-loving Government, I think it advisable not to say where that press is situated."[179] Beauchamp ended up serving two short prison sentences (one with Bertrand Russell) for violating the Defense of the Realm Act. In another instance, the journal of the British Legitimation League, *The Adult*, printed a telegram from its (former) printer, who balked at the radical content of the journal because he feared arrest: "I have just seen the new matter. I certainly cannot print it. The first portion is bad enough, but we are printing that and decline to print more."[180] Incidents such as these mocked the authorities and no doubt also reinforced the importance of having printers in the ranks.

Sometimes vigilante groups attacked presses. When a group of irate citizens described as "a well-to-do crowd" descended on the offices of *La Protesta* in Buenos Aires in 1910, they seized the press, carried it into the street, set it afire, and danced around the flames.[181] Attacks by the state or angry mobs on presses, not just on people or the offending printed matter, suggest a very precise animosity. It was not illegal to own printing equipment. Other relevant objects like pencils, paper, ink, desks, and chairs were not usually confiscated or deliberately destroyed. It is as though the printing equipment could not be divorced from its products, as though the presses too were anarchists. Like editors, writers, and printers, the presses were seized or attacked for what they *did*.[182]

Printers, presses, writers, and readers brought together, in Gitelman's succinct phrase, "enlarged and enlarging constituencies" of anarchism.[183] Writers, editors, illustrators, and printers created the publications; distributors, agents, and readers circulated the works in widening runs; librarians and collectors preserved the work and brought it to the general public. The circulation of anarchist texts, as they were created, read, displayed, discussed, and shared, constituted what Gitelman calls "a drama of shared presence."[184] Disparate elements resonate, interact, and produce something more. Their interactions reveal layers of entanglements that animate anarchist political worlds. The "print-based media ecology," in Kittler's words, constitutes a diffuse technology of anarchist communities, spreading across surfaces, producing feedback and feed-forward loops, enabling something fresh to emerge.[185]

The integration of what Rancière calls two gestures—in this case, bodily practices of craft and art—produces a hybrid "gesturality" that allows concepts, percepts, and affects to be realized together to create new narratives.[186] What Rancière calls an "oppositional community of sense," Stefano Harney and Fred Moten call an undercommons: a place where established closures on thinking, imagining, and feeling are interrupted by different organic, inorganic, semiotic, and social connectors that make fresh intelligibilities possible.[187] Making and circulating journals did more than "get the word out"—it helped to articulate the words, to "provide thinking outside of the conventional modes of recognition that serve entrenched modes of authority."[188] Anarchy became possible.

The Practices of Printing

While technological changes in printing during the late nineteenth and early twentieth centuries, particularly the invention of linotype, changed the profession, many anarchist printers continued their intimate relations with letterpress technology. Historian Alexander Lawson, in his study of compositors, calls the period between the Civil War and the turn of the century a "time of giants" because, as printer and historian Walker Rumble explains, it was "the last time journeymen had control of their craft."[189] The linotype, in their view, was radically changing the printers' workplace, "replacing speed and skill with taste and refinement, and shifting as well the locus of power and prestige from shop floor and union to studio and salon."[190] However, for the numerous small and hardy periodicals published by anarchists, the time of giants persevered and may be making a comeback today.

Although many skilled printers bemoaned the coming of linotype and other automations as destroying both a trade and a way of life, in fact the practice of printing changed little, and then slowly, from the time of Johannes Gutenberg's invention to the post–World War II era. True, the major newspapers were quick to move to linotype following Ottmar Merganthaler's remarkable invention in 1886. This change understandably alarmed printers. John Hicks, in his autobiography of his days as a tramp printer, laments the displacement of printers by typesetting machines as comparable to the interference of barbed wire in the life and work of cowboys.[191] While printers' fears were not misplaced—Horace Greeley's paper, the *New York Tribune*, replaced more than one hundred hand compositors with a mere twenty-eight linotype operators—the printer-press relation hung on.[192] In more remote areas and among smaller publications, linotype was not widely utilized until well into the twentieth century.[193] Freedom Press in London, for example, did not entirely abandon letterpress until after 1964, when it became cheaper to make the change.[194]

Anarchist printers often defied the logic of technological progress for two reasons: financial and political. First, the new technologies were prohibitively expensive for groups with little capital, while the letterpress technology was widely available well into the 1970s. Debates within the journal *Free Society* at the turn of the twentieth century exemplify this situation: editor and printer Abe Isaak regretted the intensive labor required by the letterpress and proposed that the community buy a linotype machine. Isaak, a Russian immigrant from a Mennonite community in Rosenthal (now part of Ukraine); his wife, Maria; and their son Abe Jr. had been the driving force behind the journal, first in San Francisco, then Chicago, and finally New York City. With Abe Jr. leaving the Free Society group to develop his independent career as a printer, his father sought a technological solution to the workload problem. Readers raised questions about who would own and control the machine, but another anarchist printer, Jay Fox from Home Colony, Washington, anticipated other problems. In his reply to the linotype proposal, Fox first voiced agreement with Isaak's goal: "A more concentrated effort [should] be made to get our ideas before the public. And as literature is the great weapon for the destruction of the monster of ignorance, it is the opinion of many that a group should be formed to promote the publication and distribution of literature. It is thought that by such a plan very many who are now inactive would be induced to take more interest in the movement; there being a lot of pessimists, so-called, who from want of a more coherent effort on the part of others neglect the propaganda altogether."[195] But Fox raised financial and technological concerns:

I believe the price of a [linotype] machine is $3,250 which is a very large capital for poor Anarchists to attempt to raise and invest for the mere setting up of a little eight-page weekly, the work of about a day on the machine. And the proposition seems especially funny when we reflect that frequently we are so poor the paper has to be cut down to four pages; still nobody seems to see the joke. If we were publishing a daily paper the idea would be commendable; for then the machine would be kept constantly in use! But will it pay to invest $3250 in a machine and have it stand idle about five-sixths of the time?

True, Comrade Isaak says he would take in work from the outside. Yes, if he could get it. He will find any number of men in Chicago with complete printing plants, Webb and cylinder presses, linotypes, etc., favorably located and possessing the experience and business connections requisite to the publishing, who also "take in work"; and he will find, when he goes "up against them," that these men will be more than a match for him. Once in a while when some radical friend writes a book or pamphlet thru sympathy it might get into the hands of the Anarchist lynotypists [*sic*], but I see no hope for them to compete with the old established houses who know the business so well, and how to get it.[196]

Fox proved correct; the Free Society group could not afford the new technology. The journal had neither the volunteers nor the capital to continue. As announced in the November 26, 1904, issue, soon after the linotype plan was put forward and then abandoned, the journal folded.

The second reason for sticking with letterpress was aesthetic and political: the letterpress appealed politically and artistically to some anarchists for its merger of mental and manual labor, of art, craft, and collective action. The famed editor of the Boston anarchist journal *Liberty*, printer Benjamin Tucker, who so clearly expressed his wholesale contempt for women printers, was equally forthright in expressing his disgust for the new linotype. In fact, he speculated that his demonstration of linotype's hideousness may have been a factor in William Morris's turn to printing. One evening in 1889, he wrote in a letter to Ishill, Tucker took an early linotype sample to a dinner party at the Morris home in Hammersmith, London. At the gathering, also attended by May Morris, George Bernard Shaw, and others, Tucker showed Morris "a thin strip of metal bearing on its edge, as part of itself, my name in the letters of typography." It was made by linotype and given to Tucker by Stilson Hutchins, an American trying to sell linotype equipment in England. "I love to believe that this incident helped induce Morris to champion the cause of artistic printing," Tucker said. He concludes the letter emphatically: "For my part, I *hate* the linotype."[197] Anarchists did not, I think, generally reject the new technologies simply because they were new, but because they were financially impractical and, at least for some, aesthetically incompatible with their politics.

The revered grandfather of radical letterpress printing was the English poet and designer Morris, who considered himself a socialist but was beloved by anarchists for his merger of arts with crafts and his political work to create a society based on liberated artisanship. He was born in Walthamstow, Essex, to a wealthy middle-class family. He married Jane Burden and they raised two daughters, Jenny and May. He is usually described as an amiable, substantial man with an unruly beard and hair and a quick temper. Morris founded an interior design company and is best known today for producing beautiful textiles, wallpaper, stained glass, embroideries, furniture, and other ornamentations. He is credited with founding the Arts and Crafts movement in England and for his activism in the Socialist League. Journalist and printer Frank Colebrook remarked affectionately, in his 1886 lecture to students at a London printing school, "To the larger public the name William Morris stands for a whole-hearted, strenuous, consistent Socialism. He can be dragged about anywhere by any comrade to speak a word for Socialism, for all the world, as a man of war is pulled about by a tug. He will start speaking of the beauty there may be in life to an open-air meeting of six small boys and a policeman."[198]

When Morris established Kelmscott Press in London in 1891, his bold move positioned him at the heart of controversy: Was he revolutionizing book printing, or merely reverting to an obsolete technology? He provoked a fierce debate between two groups his editor characterizes as "apologists for mechanization and advocates of traditional craftsmanship."[199] Morris came to printing relatively late in his life, having already become known as a poet and designer and as a spokesman for a generous and artistic socialism. At the heart of his politics was his insistence that work must be creative:

> A man at work making something which he feels will exist because he is working at it and wills it, is exercising the energies of his mind and soul as well as of his body. Memory and imagination help him as he works. Not only his own thoughts, but the thoughts of the men of the past ages guide his hands; as part of the human race he creates. If we work thus we shall be men, and our days will be happy and eventful. This worthy work carries with it the hope of pleasure in rest, the hope of our

pleasure in using what it makes, and the hope of pleasure in our daily creative skill. All other work but this is worthless; it is slaves' work— mere toiling to live, that we may live to toil.[200]

Morris was appalled at the deskilling of the printers' trade. Typographic designer Frederick Goudy recalled that Morris was "shocked by the vulgar and expressionless quality of the typography of the times."[201] Morris's goal was always to combine beauty and utility, to cultivate an immanent aesthetic in which the beauty of the page arises out of its materials.

British writer and bibliophile Holbrook Jackson commented that Morris "made it possible for a printer to become an artist."[202] In Rancière's terms, Morris bridged the gap between artistic gestures and craft gestures, between creating bodies and laboring bodies. Morris set standards for combining art, craft, and politics that inspired many anarchists. Anarchists claimed him for their own; Nettlau, speaking of Morris's influence on London's primary anarchist journal, wrote that "the example of William Morris, his love of a beautiful free Socialism, has left its mark on *Freedom* to this very day."[203] Art historian Allan Antliff traces Morris's friendships and collaborations with Kropotkin, Elisée Reclus, Jean Grave, Louise Michel, and others who bridged anarchism with Morris's artisanal socialism.[204] Creating their publications through a process that directly embodies their ideas was a source of political energy sustaining anarchist communities. All printers, I imagine, participate in political assemblages of brains, bodies, and machines, but those assemblages are more intense and extensive in anarchist communities, where the linkages of the press, the printers, the publications, and the reading publics were constitutive, not just descriptive, of the politics that held communities together. As with their schools, unions, clinics, bookstores, and independent communities, anarchist publications enacted anarchism as they advocated it.

Printing Sensorium

For many anarchists, the printery was an intimate site: they printed where they lived and wrote. Presses were located in the basements or backrooms of the offices, homes, outbuildings, community centers, or schools of their people. Morris established Kelmscott Press a few doors down from his residence on the Thames River in Hammersmith. The coach house and basement of his home, Kelmscott House, are the site of the William Morris Society today, and they house Morris's 1835 Albion press, still in full working order.[205] The intimacy was often welcome: Ishill wrote to Emma Goldman on July 16, 1930, that establishing his print shop in his home was "a part of [his] dream."[206] Labadie's granddaughter recalls that, in his seventies, at their home called Bubbling Waters, Labadie "reveled in the painstaking process of running the century-old press by foot power, plucking the type, letter by letter from a font drawer, setting a single page at a time because of a shortage of type."[207] Edward Fulton wrote and printed his journals from his home, with the support of a group of friends he often referred to in correspondence as "his boys."[208] After several years of hardship and frequent moves, Fulton secured a "fine cottage" with a furnace and electric lights that could accommodate his press. "Your shop is about like mine," he wrote to Labadie, "only I may have a larger room (20 × 30 feet). You are at the case much. I am [at the case] half the 'idle time' at home."[209]

Tennessee anarchist Ross Winn kept his small hand-operated press in the bedroom he shared with his wife, Gussie.[210] Ross wrote, "I get the paper out myself, working it off one page at a time on a 'Pilot' hand press—devilish slow work it is, too."[211] For many years *Freedom* was printed in the basement of its London offices, where American pressman Harry Kelly recalled "an old world atmosphere about the office and an artistic charm to the people who conduct the paper."[212] The office of *The Firebrand* was in Abe and Mary Isaak's home outside Portland, Oregon.[213] We know that the editors of *Free Society* proofed the paper in their Clinton Park office in San Francisco, because they tell a whimsical story about a breeze coming in through an open window and carrying off one of the proof sheets for Voltairine de Cleyre's translation of French anarchist Jean Grave's book *Moribund Society and Anarchy*.[214] Perhaps they were printing there as well. Holley Cantine and Dachine Rainer printed *Revolt* in a small shed next to their home near Woodstock, New York, much as Peter Good now prints the *Cunningham Amendment* in a small print shop behind his home.[215] The Rossetti sisters printed *The Torch* in their father's home in London. Writing to Ishill on March 14, 1933, book collector Holbrook Jackson commented, "What better work can a man do than build his own house & live in it and to have his printing press near at hand?"[216] While Ishill was probably unique in building his own house, all these printers had their presses near at hand.

Print shops could be gathering places for communities. In December 1908, *Freedom* ran an obituary for French anarchist Albert Libertad, one of the founders of the weekly journal *L'Anarchie* and of the informal local meetings called *causeries populaires*. The writer describes Libertad's pleasant printshop: "A two-roomed shop, door and windows in summer wide open to the street, which forms a quiet corner here...one room full of young compositors at their printing cases, and next to them, near the open door, some young women doing needlework or preparing food with a baby or two thrown in the middle near the table where all the office work is done, literature briskly sent out, etc. The back walls contain the stock of pamphlets, and a collection of advanced books forming a lending library."[217] The *Modern School Magazine* office in the Stelton community, when Ishill printed there, was "editorial office, composing room, and press room all in one" and was "a beehive of activity."[218] Sam Dolgoff remembers that he and his friends were enthusiastically welcomed to the "dingy little loft on lower Broadway near Union Square" where *Road to Freedom* was published.[219] Blanche Cooney, who coedited and set type for the pacifist journal *The Phoenix* in Woodstock, New York, writes in her autobiography, "I learned to set type in the composing stick....The print shop was a gathering place, a clubhouse, a forum. The press hums in a golden hive, pollen gathered far away from the Maverick; the baby sleeps in her basket, lulled by the rhythm....There's the smell of ink, coffee's always on, soup simmers on a hot plate; we're camping in the shop now. Not just anyone can help, we're selective even though it's free and volunteer labor; we learn to weed the casual from the committed, and among the committed, the careless from the precise."[220] John Caldwell's colleague Ethel MacDonald at *The Word* in Glasgow, in contrast, was less sanguine about the printery as a gathering place, warning "hangers-on" not to accumulate underfoot and interfere with the operation.[221] *Freedom*'s notoriously grouchy printer Thomas Cantwell expressed similar reservations: Kelly recalled Cantwell scolding loiterers that "an Anarchist printing office is a place where work has to be done, and that he had neither time nor inclination to indulge in 'hot air.'"[222] Yet the very need to shoo away those who might gather in the printery suggests that folks were likely to do just that. Printers who worked in greater isolation, as did Ishill in his shop in Berkeley Heights, New Jersey, nonetheless were nourished by international networks of participants. Each press had quite a few people with whom to collaborate, drawing writers, compositors, pressmen, binders, sellers, illustrators, and readers together into horizontal chains of associations.

Printeries have their own sensory environment, which contemporary Portland anarchist printer Charles Overbeck sums up as a characteristic "reek and clamour."[223] "The press mesmerizes," comments Allan Runfeldt of the Excelsior Press.[224] There is a sensory draw in the ensemble of surfaces, colors, odors, sounds, and moving parts. Rose Ishill, partner to

Joseph, described the whirr of the press, the pungent smell of ink, and the detectable vibration of the house when Joseph was printing.[225] Similar memories are reported by Sister Mary Catherine Perry, who was the last nun to be trained to operate the press that the Ishills donated to the Dominican Monastery of Our Lady of the Rosary after Joseph died in 1966. Sister Mary Catherine describes the "small *clug, clug* as the wheel turned and the platen hit the chase" and the "*swish, swish*" as the rollers "hit the ink wheel."[226] A poorly maintained press made more ominous sounds: when John Caldwell and Jenny Patrick printed *The Word* in Glasgow in 1937, their "ancient foot-treadled printing press...made a great rumble as it inked, and a thunderous clap as the platen met the typeface."[227]

Printers' ink is bright, viscous, and shiny. Depending on the job at hand, it may be colorful as well as a dramatic black. Metal sorts make a characteristic clinking sound when they are "dissed"—that is, returned to the case in preparation for setting another form. Different weights, weaves, and shades of paper have their particular look, feel, and smell. Several contemporary printers whom I've interviewed are unabashed about their love for the sensory richness of presses:

> *Ruby Shadburne of Ruby Press:* "I love using the presses. I love the feel of the press, the sound of the press. It's really an experience, printing. It's exciting to create something and feel it and look at it and other people are feeling it and looking at it and excited too. The tactile thing—a lot of people have a strong reaction to the cards [she prints]. They say 'Oh, wow.'"[228]
>
> *Eric Bagdonas of Stumptown Printers:* "There's this huge satisfaction in taking the raw materials, the blank paper, and watching the image grow from each pass, each color application, and at the end of the day having this beautiful finished piece."[229]
>
> *Sister Mary Catherine Perry of the Dominican Monastery of Our Lady of the Rosary:* "The rhythm was the part I liked the most. You had to really fall into it to put in the paper behind the guides in the platen and take it out and replace it with a new piece of paper. You really used your whole body when you printed on the letterpress."[230]

Having tried my hand at printing a few times and watched numerous printers at work, I think of printing as something like a cross between chopping wood and playing the piano. It is rhythmic, exacting work, both physically and artistically challenging. It takes years of practice to get good at it. It calls on the printer's whole body. Cynthia Cockburn, who spent a year learning to print at the London College of Printing in order to write about it, specifies the aesthetic and physical requirements of the work:

> [The printer] had to have a sense of design and spacing to enable him to create a graphic whole of the printed page, which he secured through the manipulation of the assembled type, illustrative blocks and lead spacing pieces. The whole he then locked up in a form weighing 50 pounds or more. This he would lift and move to the proofing press or bring back to the stone for the distribution of used type. He thus required a degree of strength and stamina, a strong wrist, and, for standing long hours at the case, a sturdy spine and good legs.[231]

The other side of the brute strength required is the subtlety of touch. Skilled printers develop acute sensitivity to fine differences in the weight and feel of the sorts. Peter Good comments, "When you pick each sort up, you know they're right because you get used to the weight....Picking up a letter, you sort of know straight away [if it's the right one]. They all feel a bit different."[232] It reflects remarkable intimacy with the sorts to register with one's fingertips the subtle differences in weight among them.

Printing is based on routines yet requires frequent adjustment. It requires continuous attention while also encouraging contemplation. Ruby Shadburne comments, "A majority of what I'm doing is constantly adjusting the press." The ink is mixed a little differently each time; the color of the ink and the amount dispersed on the page will vary, as will the needed pressure between the rollers on the plate and between the plate and the paper. "It is constantly changing as you're printing," Shadburne finishes.[233] Good also indicates that he is always thinking about the point at hand as well as looking to the future at the larger process, "adjusting, moving forward." He likened the temporality of the press to the poet Gerald Manley Hopkins's idea of "sprung rhythm." Sprung rhythm is a metrical arrangement in which the number of unstressed syllables in a line of poetry is not predictable; it varies in relation to the force of the stressed syllable, the same way that common speech varies, reflecting the dynamic and diverse qualities different speakers bring to the verse.[234] The relation of the printer and the press is also "sprung"—it varies in relation to the forces of the other participant. "If you invest something it will give something back," Good concludes. "You have to understand the time of letterpress. It has its own duration. It has its own rhythms."[235]

Presses affect the bodies of printers in many ways. Inky fingers and aching muscles are only the beginning. Many printers shared the health problems faced by Labadie due to long hours in poorly ventilated shops, breathing hot air carrying poison from lead type. The foul air in print shops led to rates of tuberculosis among printers that were "twice the rate of the general population."[236] Repetitive stress injuries were common. Cockburn reports meeting elderly printers "whose fingers and thumbs are physically flattened by a lifetime shifting type."[237] Before the imposition of safety protocols, printers were often recognizable by missing fingers, a result of poor timing, sometimes exacerbated by alcohol. In 1935 Agnes Inglis wrote to Ishill about Floyd E. Nimes, an Industrial Workers of the World printer who had helped compose *Solidarity* and was missing "4 fingers and his teeth."[238] Eighty years later, Seattle printer Jules Faye recalls her early years in printing: "If you are preoccupied, tired, angry, you're going to get hurt. It requires a degree of presence. I grew up with a lot of printers who had less than ten fingers."[239] Even with better protective equipment and safety protocols today, repetitive stress injuries, back and knee problems, and smashed hands are common. The physical intimacies of the press can be seductive, and they can also be unforgiving.

Condensed Labor Histories

Anarchist presses often carried the history of the movement with them. Printer Jay Fox originally issued *The Agitator* in 1910–12 from the anarchist colony of Home, Washington, on a press used by Ezra and Angela Haywood to publish *The Word* from 1872 to 1893.[240] After Morris's death, the Guild of Handicraft, another project of the Arts and Crafts movement, purchased some of the magnificent equipment of Kelmscott Press to establish Essex House Press; one of Morris's presses was subsequently purchased by Indian anarchist Ananda Coomaraswamy, who continued publishing anarchist books with his wife, weaver Edith Partridge.[241] The Rossetti sisters' printing equipment for *The Torch* was a "derelict printing press" that had belonged to Joseph Lane of the Socialist League in 1892; when the sisters ceased publication in 1898, the press went to *Freedom* at 127 Ossulston Street.[242] During its long career, *Freedom* was published on a series of cobbled-together presses, including the "already legendary handpress" previously used by German anarchist Johann Most's journal *Freiheit*; after serving *Freedom* for thirty years, the press was purchased by Lilian Wolfe for the Whiteway Colony to provide printing lessons for the children at the colony's school.[243] In 1939, when Glasgow anarchists Guy Aldred, John

Caldwell, Jenny Patrick, and Ethel MacDonald established Strickland Press, they acquired an old press from the Socialist Labor Party.[244] In 1943 a New York group called the Liberal League bought "an old Multilith 1200 press" that Dick Ellington, a mechanic and "excellent typesetter and printer," used to print their journal *Views and Comments*. Several years later the press was sold to the anarchist-oriented *Catholic Worker*.[245]

Contemporary anarchist printers continue to value the fingerprints of past labor on their presses. Nick Loring of the Print Project in Shipley, England, notes, "Some of this type has gone through the hands of other printers for hundreds of years. It can be used again and again ... [and is] holding out to be used for the next generation."[246] Ali Cat Leeds of Entangled Roots Press comments, "I think it's beautiful because a lot of the presses we use have this history to them, there is always a story of where the press went and who built it. I'm in love with presses."[247] Faye reflects on the history of working-class labor when she runs her press: "My work has turned more purely toward love of the physical labor of handling these tools, using these machines, the lineage of workers having done this; everything I own in here belonged to someone before me, and someone before them, and someone before them. I love that lineage.... There is a particular beauty to the work of the human hand. To me the tools radiate that. Making beauty is equivalent in my mind to making peace."[248]

Presses that were not passed down from within the movement were nonetheless typically acquired second- or thirdhand, since anarchists could not afford new equipment. Fortunately for them, the printing trades had expanded so much during the nineteenth century that old and even abandoned presses were abundant.[249] In 1906 Labadie bought an old press, a Washington jobber, on which he and his wife, Sophie, printed unique, small books of Labadie's poetry. The press was older than he was (he was fifty-six).[250] One of the presses used to put out the Glasgow journal *The Word* in 1939 was a Wharfdale quad Crown machine that another paper had acquired in 1864.[251] Dachine Rainer, partner and coprinter with Holley Cantine, recalled that they printed *Retort* with "a Gordon Upright Foot-pedal press which had been obsolete since 1875" that Cantine had found in New York City.[252]

Ishill found one of his presses, a small job press called a "Favorite," abandoned in a wood shed, serving as a home for nesting orioles. He restored the press after nesting season was over and named his printery the Oriole Press.[253] When Ishill was putting together his book on Kropotkin, his little handpress broke down three times, had to be retired permanently, and was "replaced by another old, but larger press which also showed great disinclination to work. But at last strength was conquered by determination."[254] When Paul Scott took on the job of making a print shop and teaching printing to the children at the Stelton Modern School, he similarly scrounged up the needed materials: "I went in search of printing material which I understood was somewhere in the Colony, finding it finally in Wally's chicken house—the most godawful assortment of mixed fonts any printer was ever confronted with. The type cases had been used as a breeding place by mice, and wasps, spiders, mud-daubers had contributed liberally of their industry, in addition to accumulated dust and dirt from the nearby road."[255] The whole lot had to be cleaned, disinfected, and organized. Scott concluded that it was worth it: "I found so much joy in working with these spontaneous, creative youngsters that I could not break away and return to my printing job, and so began an adventure that lasted five short years, which I shall ever regard as the most satisfactory period of my life."[256]

Journals frequently announced "press funds" or otherwise sought donations to enable printing. In the early days of *Freedom*, the editors wrangled equipment via a call for donations of whatever odd bits readers might have sitting around: "All contributions thankfully received. We are furnishing our printing office. We had nothing but type three weeks ago, but one comrade besides some type has given us a couple of cases and a composing stick. Another has sent us chases, others have made us a frame. If friends who happen to have any of the odds and ends needed in a printing office would send us anything they could spare they would be giving valuable help to the paper."[257] The Harmans bought type to print *Lucifer*, and a Prouty power press that could print one thousand impressions per hour, with a loan from their supporters.[258] A Liverpool group announced in *Freedom* that they had a volunteer who would print their planned leaflet for free, and they were raising funds to purchase "a small printing machine of our own."[259] Sometimes the process worked in the other direction: a decade later, a Leeds group offered the use of its print shop to other anarchist groups.[260] Glasgow anarchist Guy Aldred's journal *The Commune* asked for donations to its "Press Maintenance Fund," explaining, "We now own the press and can survive and extend our influence with a little solidarity on the part of our comrades."[261] And so on. Impoverished journals appealed to impoverished readers for support. Miraculously, they often received enough to continue.

At the center of the letterpress printer's work is the *sort*, the small wooden or metal block with the shape of a letter or other signifier on it. British designer Colin Banks explains, "The basic building blocks of printing, whether mechanical or electronic, are the integrity of letter shapes and their good composition into words."[262] Sorts are, taken individually, complex little organizations of matter; the small blocks have twenty-one identifiable parts, including the face (the raised figure on one side of the block), the body or shank, the feet, and the small channel, called a nick, that helps the compositor to position the sort on the composing stick by feel.[263] After each use, the sorts are returned to the large segmented boxes called *type cases* (see figure 1.3), which separate the letters and other symbols, the upper-case and lower-case versions of the letters, and the styles of font, like a busy, crowded apartment house for language. The *composing stick* (see figure 1.4) is the narrow handheld rectangular tool (it looks a bit like a slide rule) in which the sorts are initially assembled, upside down and backward. Once the stick is filled, the composed line of type is transferred to a *galley*, a flat three-sided tray. When the galley is filled, a proof is pulled and proofread, then returned to the compositor, who corrects errors using a pointed steel tool called a *bodkin*. The type is then placed in a metal frame, a *chase*, and locked into place by filling the spare space in the chase with wooden blocks, called *furniture* (see figure 1.5). The *quoin* (pronounced *coin*) is the corkscrew-looking object that expands the blocks to hold the job in place. The completed form is then sent to the pressroom for production, and finally the papers are assembled in the bindery.

Compositors usually hold the stick in their left hand, nestled in their up-curled fingers, the outer end pointed slightly up to take advantage of gravity in holding the sorts in the stick. They select type from the case with the right hand, laying each sort into the stick with the nick facing up, using blank slugs and leads to properly justify each line. The left thumb rests on the last piece of type set into the stick; pressure from the thumb, plus the force of gravity on the sorts, discourages them from spilling out of the stick.[264] Contemporary letterpress printer and book artist Johanna Drucker points out that the unique physicality of this process, in which letters, punctuation marks, spacing units, and so on must be handled one at a time as individual blocks of matter with specific heights, weights, and shapes, requires the compositor to think about "the relation between the formal, visual aspects of typography and the production of meaning

Fig. 1.3. Type case as shown by Duncan Dempster, University of Hawaiʻi. Photograph by Kathy Ferguson.

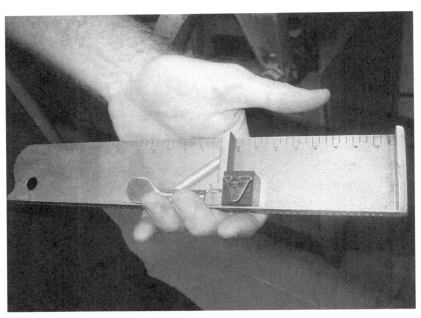

Fig. 1.4. Composing stick as shown by Duncan Dempster, University of Hawaiʻi. Photograph by Kathy Ferguson.

Fig. 1.5. Chase locked up as shown by Duncan Dempster, University of Hawaiʻi. Photograph by Kathy Ferguson.

in the printed text."[265] Letters do not just represent sounds; they are also matter and as matter they command the compositor's attention.

Setting type combines Rancière's two gestures—arranging objects to make shapes and arranging representations to make meaning. Typographer Joseph Green from C. C. Stern Foundry noted that the act of setting type for a poem requires him to think simultaneously as a poet and a designer: "If I'm setting type by hand, one letter at a time, I'm also proofreading that poem, one letter at a time, backwards and upside down. I'm thinking about space, I'm thinking about word choice."[266] Walt Whitman referred to this as "an anticipatory eye": "Having been a printer myself," he told his disciple Horace Traubel, "I have what may be called an anticipatory eye—know pretty well as I write how a thing will turn up in the type—appear—take form."[267] Jules Faye similarly refers to the process of acquiring the ability to sense the ongoing, changing relation between the materiality and the meaning as "developing your eye." The anticipatory eye is not a static assessment, Faye explains, but a process of engagement with the press: "Learning to listen and actually receive can be hard for people....It's critical that you listen to the press constantly. I find that all of my sensory capacities have been heightened from being a printer...[and] that extends into my life outside the shop."[268]

When printers discuss their problems, glimpses of their craft and art come forward because solving problems requires attending to the complex relationality among the elements. Each sort is vulnerable to inconsistencies of height or angle as well as to the consequences of aging, the edges rubbed down with use. Ink easily becomes too thick, too thin, too sticky, too heavy-bodied. If the ink contains too much linseed oil, it will penetrate the paper and blemish the page.[269] Paper can become cockled (wrinkled or rippled) if there is excess ink causing the fibers in the paper to expand while drying.[270] The page can lack proper register if any of the elements are out of alignment. The text is properly registered if the impressions on the page are precisely where and how they are supposed to be.[271]

Ishill's correspondence with other printers sometimes discussed such challenges. In exchanges with Martin Thorn, editor and printer of an anarchist publication called *News of No Importance*, the two printers discussed problems with picking (when the force of the ink film is greater than the surface strength of the paper), burrs (raised edges that make the lines fuzzy), and shellholes (I am not sure what these are, but it sounds like the inner space of letters, called the counterspace, is filled in with too much ink).[272] In contemplating these problems, the printer is confronted with what literary scholar Bill Brown calls "the thingness of objects": "We begin to confront the thingness of objects when they stop working for us: when the drill breaks, when the car stalls, when the windows get filthy, when their flow within the circuits of production and distribution, consumption and exhibition, has been arrested, however momentarily. The story of objects asserting themselves as things, then, is the story of a changed relation to the human subject and thus the story of how the thing really names less an object than a particular subject-object relation."[273] Presses, printers tell us, seldom let printers forget their thingness—presses regularly assert themselves. Attending to relationships with the press, and among the elements of the press, is central to printing. Proofreading, for example, is more than finding and correcting mistakes, because errors are not necessarily discrete items—they can be problems in the *relations* of the letters. For printers, the surface of a page is three dimensional—it has depth as well as length and width. When regarding a printed page in which a few clear letters stand out against a host of blurry ones, an uninitiated observer would likely assume that the blurry letters are the problem. But in reality it is quite the opposite: the clear letters are clear precisely because they stand up too high, keeping the ink from spreading evenly over the surface. Sorts that stand up too high violate the depth of the printed page. The thing that looks correct is actually the error. To take another example, the phenomenon of picking suggests that letterpress printers manage a relation between ink and paper that most present-day vehicles for writing do not require: it is possible for the ink to be too strong for the paper, for the paper to be overwhelmed by the ink. Clearly neither the ink nor the paper could simply be dispensed with; both are necessary to the process, yet they stand in tension with each other. It's the relationship that has to be negotiated. A third example involves calculations of proximity and distance: neighboring elements of a text can grip each other in "friendly strength," or they can crowd each other out of alignment.[274] Jules Faye urges her students to embrace these complexities as life lessons, because they require attention but there is no one clear answer: "There's more than one right way.... I love that.... That's very anarchist.... When I teach, I try to show multiple ways to approach things.... We need to make room for multiple right ways."[275] Having resistance, multiplicity, and the need for negotiation built into the materials themselves suggests political implications: printing could teach printers to hold friction-filled relations together rather than seeking a clear or final resolution.[276]

Little Optical Machines

Printers create what medieval studies scholar Bonnie Mak calls "the architecture of the page."[277] For printers, the page is not just a page; it is a series of possible spaces. Every space on every page is "printed," regardless of whether it has typographical markings on it, in that the printer has to decide how each bit of the surface will be used. Pages "remain persuasive through time," Mak explains, through printers' orchestration of text, images, graphic markers, ink, receiving surface, and blank space: "a changing interplay of form and content, of message and medium, of the conceptual and the physical."[278] Pages host both material and rhetorical strategies; as Mak succinctly insists, the page is "entangled in the story."[279] Book scholars have identified the material surrounding and supporting the main text as the paratext, including the shape and size of the font, title pages, tables of contents, prologues, epilogues, dedications, chapter headings, footnotes, and running headers, "each playing a particular role in mapping out the territory of a literary community linked through its traditions, attitudes and social interactions."[280] The paratext participates with the text in configuring available meanings and inviting and guiding readers through the text's offered terrain. Introductory materials prepare the reader for the coming reading experience; headings and subheadings "punctuate important moments in the story and thereby affect in what manner the treatise will be read"; colophons (the mark of the printer on the final page of a publication, such as Ishill's elegant woodcut images in figures 1.6 and 1.7), fleurons (small images separating entries), signatures, and epilogues "leave a final impression of the text upon the reader."[281]

The spacing of the textual elements is critical: skilled lithographer and graphic artist Ben Shahn, who created a series of drawings protesting the execution of Nicola Sacco and Bartolomeo Vanzetti, writes of learning from his mentor about spacing: "Then he shared with me the secret of the glass of water. 'Imagine,' he said, 'that you have a small measuring glass. It holds, of course, just so much water. Now, you have to pour the water out of the glass into the spaces between the letters, and every one has to contain exactly the same amount—whatever its shape. Now try!'" Shahn continues, "That was it; letters are quantities, and spaces are quantities, and only the eye and the hand can measure them. As in the ear and the sensibilities of the poet, sounds and syllables and pauses are quantities, so in both cases are the balancing and forward movement of these quantities only a matter of skill and feeling and art."[282] In the "minor theme" of the spaces around the letters, which look empty to an outsider, Shahn finds balance, rhythm, and movement that he apprehends with his eye and his hand.[283] Shahn's mentor taught him to imagine the spaces as water; the water is part of the printing in the same way that a pause is part of a poem. "The page," Mak succinctly concludes, "is an expressive space for text, space, and image; it is a cultural artifact; it is a technological device. But it is also all of these at once."[284]

All publications have a particular "look of printedness" to them.[285] They each, in their own way, integrate design with meaning. They are persuasive to their readers by their particular interweaving of text and paratext, their way of building a page. Ishill's pages worked in ways similar to those that political theorist Michael Shapiro finds in the poet Stéphane Mallarmé: "Influenced by musical punctuation, Mallarmé interspersed blank spaces in

Fig. 1.6. Joseph Ishill's colophon of a bird, the Oriole Press, from Rudolf Rocker, *Milly Witkop-Rocker* (Berkeley Heights, NJ: Oriole, 1956), the back page. Publication is held in the Joseph A. Labadie Collection, Special Collections Research Center, University of Michigan Library.

MILLY WITKOP-ROCKER

THIS ESSAY BY RUDOLF ROCKER WAS HANDSET
WITH THE KENNERLEY AND HADRIANO TYPES
DESIGNED BY FREDERIC W. GOUDY & PRINTED
ON SUPERFINE TEXT PAPER.

FRONTISPIECE (DRAWING) BY FERMIN ROCKER.

PRIVATE EDITION PRINTED FOR THE AUTHOR.

June - 1956

Fig. 1.7. Joseph Ishill's colophon of a printer at a case, based on a drawing by Louis Moreau, from Rose Freeman Ishill, *Dream and Advent* (Berkeley Heights, NJ: Oriole, 1929), the back page. Publication is held in the Joseph A. Labadie Collection, Special Collections Research Center, University of Michigan Library.

his poems, making his poetic punctuation mime musical rests."The poems open up to different meanings because they encourage active encounters with the page. Blank spaces are "interruptions that momentarily suspend reception and render the reader a reflective accomplice in the poem's sense making."[286] In the conventional register of printing, blank space, font size, and so on are part of the page layout, just as punctuation is part of grammar. However, page layout and construction, like punctuation, do more than clarify what is already in the text. They knit together some parts and fragment others; they create some rhythms and interrupt others.

Some readers viewed Ishill's generous margins simply as a waste of paper. Writing to Agnes Inglis, Pennsylvania anarchist Bertha Johnson expressed her reservations: "It seems to Emery [her husband] and me that if an idea is important, that *numbers* of copies are more important than *a very few deluxe* copies. Really Ishill's books are so dainty that one hesitates to loan them to anyone, lest they be soiled or lost or mistreated. One wants to put them in a sealed case. He [Ishill] was quite scornful of the five cent booklets of Haldeman-Julius, yet they seem to me to have value, and I have frequently been surprised to find how much some intelligent person of limited means has gotten from them."[287] Anarchist publications, including Ishill's, were always financially precarious, yet he persisted in strategies such as generous margins, numerous blank pages at beginning and end, multiple colors, rich paper, ornamentation, and periodic interruptions of the page. *Freedom, Free Society, Lucifer, Egoism*, and most other anarchist journals were more economical than Ishill's work: like the inexpensive Little Blue Book series put out by Emanuel Haldeman-Julius, which Johnson found valuable but Ishill scorned, they are plainly printed and bound, with little variation of font or margins. They sometimes have eye-catching mastheads or covers but otherwise usually carry few illustrations. The printers completely filled each column and each page, occasionally decreasing the font size to squeeze in the last few lines of an essay. The printing is plain, neat, accurate, and thrifty.

Free Society, for example, engages the reader's eye with a dramatic masthead (see figure 1.8): a sword-wielding figure on a winged white horse, carrying the banner "Humanity," charges into battle with skulking figures marked "privilege," "false doctrine," "bias," "law," and "stocks." The title of the journal is emblazoned on a banner that stretches between "knowledge," "solidarity," "reason," and "peace" on one side and "truth" and "liberty" on the other.[288] The masthead positions the reader to expect to go into battle and to win.

A PERIODICAL OF ANARCHIST THOUGHT, WORK, AND LITERATURE.

Fig. 1.8. *Free Society* masthead, March 30, 1902. Publication held at the International Institute of Social History, Amsterdam.

After the dramatic masthead, the remaining pages are crowded with words. Of course, their content is anarchist; the writings challenge readers to think critically about existing power relations and to transform society, a kind of radical scholarship that I will address in chapter 3. Here I am interested in exploring the political implications of the architecture of different pages. In *Free Society*, the running header is the name of the journal; it reminds the reader of what they seek—a free society. The font is an ordinary serif typeface.[289] The margins are narrow at the top and sides, slightly wider at the bottom. Titles of essays are in bold capital letters in the same size of type as the body of the articles. Each page has three columns, the print justified on both edges. The columns are close together, only two or three spaces between them. Most of the pages are completely filled with words. Small, simple fleurons—three tiny dots or a small circle and two short lines—narrowly separate the articles. The page is all black and white; usually there are no illustrations. On the last page, where subscription information, announcements of lectures, books for sale, receipts of donations, and so on are displayed, narrow vertical lines separate the columns, cramming even more text onto the page.

Freedom has a similar look of printedness (see figure 1.9). The masthead is the title of the journal, standing dramatically alone, in large black letters, sometimes stylized, other times plain and stark but always striking. The running header is the name of the journal in all caps, again reminding the reader of what they seek: freedom. The top and sides of the pages have slim margins, while the space at the bottom is usually a bit wider. Each page has two columns, rather than three, and the titles of the articles are a bit larger, but the format is otherwise similar to that of *Free Society*: the margins are justified on both sides, with a narrow column of white separating the columns of words. It

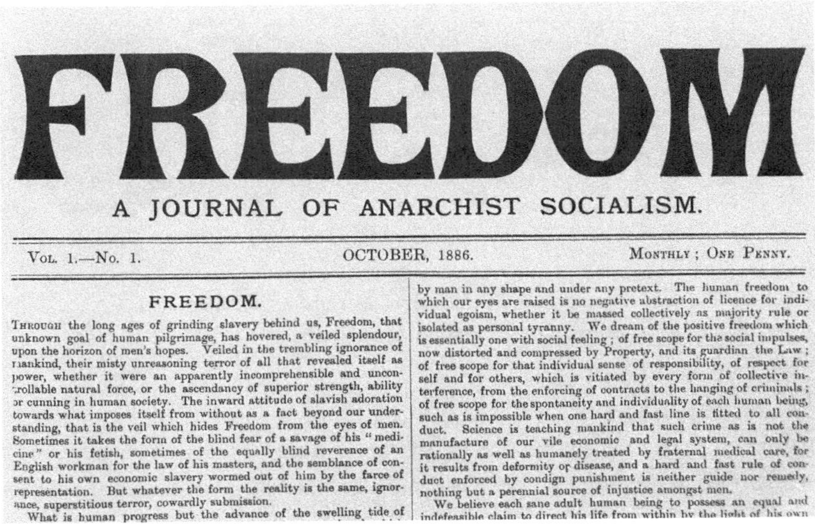

FREEDOM

A JOURNAL OF ANARCHIST SOCIALISM.

VOL. 1.—No. 1.   OCTOBER, 1886.   MONTHLY; ONE PENNY.

FREEDOM.

THROUGH the long ages of grinding slavery behind us, Freedom, that unknown goal of human pilgrimage, has hovered, a veiled splendour, upon the horizon of men's hopes. Veiled in the trembling ignorance of mankind, their misty unreasoning terror of all that revealed itself as power, whether it were an apparently incomprehensible and uncontrollable natural force, or the ascendancy of superior strength, ability or cunning in human society. The inward attitude of slavish adoration towards what imposes itself from without as a fact beyond our understanding, that is the veil which hides Freedom from the eyes of men. Sometimes it takes the form of the blind fear of a savage of his "medicine" or his fetish, sometimes of the equally blind reverence of an English workman for the law of his masters, and the semblance of consent to his own economic slavery wormed out of him by the farce of representation. But whatever the form the reality is the same, ignorance, superstitious terror, cowardly submission.

What is human progress but the advance of the swelling tide of by man in any shape and under any pretext. The human freedom to which our eyes are raised is no negative abstraction of licence for individual egoism, whether it be massed collectively as majority rule or isolated as personal tyranny. We dream of the positive freedom which is essentially one with social feeling; of free scope for the social impulses, now distorted and compressed by Property, and its guardian the Law; of free scope for that individual sense of responsibility, of respect for self and for others, which is vitiated by every form of collective interference, from the enforcing of contracts to the hanging of criminals; of free scope for the spontaneity and individuality of each human being, such as is impossible when one hard and fast line is fitted to all conduct. Science is teaching mankind that such crime as is not the manufacture of our vile economic and legal system, can only be rationally as well as humanely treated by fraternal medical care, for it results from deformity or disease, and a hard and fast rule of conduct enforced by condign punishment is neither guide nor remedy, nothing but a perennial source of injustice amongst men.

We believe each sane adult human being to possess an equal and indefeasible claim to direct his life from within by the light of his own

Fig. 1.9. *Freedom* masthead, October 1886. Publication by Freedom Press, London.

uses a standard serif typeface. Occasional pictures mark the death of an important anarchist, such as Kropotkin in February 1921, or an important event such as May Day, but most issues have no images.

What stands out is what's missing: no generous white spaces to let the text and the reader breathe. No color. Few illustrations. No illuminated, enlarged initial letter at the beginning of the first line to mark the point of entry and draw the reader into the text. No delicate, ornamental fleurons between entries to mark transitions and encourage the reader to pause before continuing. No picturesque colophons at the end to sign off with the printer's mark. Neither *Free Society* nor *Freedom* offers much to invite the eye to wander. They employ a disciplined presentation, suggesting that the same is expected of the reader. Start at the beginning, read to the end, stop. There's really nothing else to do.

This is the page Johnson prefers: it is efficient, it gets the job done, it wastes nothing. It has its own kind of beauty, both in the sweeping mastheads and in the regular competence of the printed text, but the paratext is forbidding. The pages of *Free Society* and *Freedom* constitute the person apprehending the page *as a reader*, as one primarily engaged in processing ideas. Anarchist analysis is offered to readers: they are invited to learn anarchism's history, meet its intellectuals, engage its debates, share its challenges, embrace its hopes. The journals provide a scene in which poor and oppressed people can be intellectuals and rebels; the little optical machines are constituting a community of thinkers and activists among people who have largely been written off by the larger society.

Ishill's pages (see figure 1.10) employ a different pedagogy—they speed up or slow down "the process of reception," in Shapiro's words, to direct readers' attention and cultivate judgment.[290] There are many directions to go in Ishill's publications—they invite wandering, pausing, returning, and skipping ahead. He dramatizes his text to intervene in the readers' practices of recognition; he recomposes elements of situations to make new situations and "redistribute assets" of the discursive formations in which the journal and the people participate.[291] Contemporary anarchist printer Charles Overbeck at Eberhardt Press draws his inspiration from Ishill: "Ishill's typesetting was immaculate," Overbeck observes. "He was one of the great typesetters of all time....He always had big margins on the side and bottom....He wasn't just filling up a page, he wanted it to breathe and be readable."[292] Arrangements of shapes and patterns, text and illustration, colors and tints emerge through engagement with the page and the text. By "re-uniting design and print," Overbeck reflects, "the loop makes things possible."[293]

In a 1929 review of Ishill's book on Havelock Ellis for the *Chicago Evening Post*, critic Llewellyn Jones writes that Ishill's work brings together the collector, "whose fingers are enchanted by the paper and his eye enchanted by the type page," and the reader, "who reads books solely for what he can get out of them."[294] Connecting the collector to the reader, the eye and hand to the mind, Ishill's little optical machines invite creative movement from materiality to meaning and back again. Both the printer creating the page and the reader encountering it are invited into a space where, as Hayles explains, "a literary work mobilizes its physical embodiment in conjunction with its verbal signifiers to construct meanings in ways that implicitly construct the user/reader as well."[295] People may well collect *Free Society* and *Freedom*, too, but no matter how enthusiastic they are about the content, they are unlikely to be enchanted by the page.

Morris and Ishill both give priority to "how two pages looked, when opened, as a total picture."[296] Morris identifies these fundamental elements of the two-page unit that together formed the visual horizon of his printing: "the paper, the form of the type, the relative spacing of the letters, the words, and the lines; and lastly the position of the printed matter on the page." The lateral spacing between words should be "no more than is necessary to distinguish clearly the division into words" and, as Shahn also

⁋ THEY broke the holy covenant sworn by our great teachers with the lowly and disinherited : henceforth opportunism and reform with their accompanying corruption were to be the slogan under which the proletariat was to fight its battle for liberation.

⁋ ALBEIT branded with the stigma of mental and intellectual degradation, these parasitical misleaders had the audacity to denounce every sincere enthusiast and faithful worker for the social revolution either as a confusionist or as an agent provocateur, and to crown their shameful betrayel of revolutionary ideals and sentiments these charlatans in the garb of honest men had the impudence to proclaim themselves as the only true exponent of the revolutionary movements.

⁋ VERILY a cruel joke perpetrated at the expense of the social and artist rebels!

⁋ BUT the days of political quacks and upstarts are numbered. ❦ Today we participate in a renaissance of the revolutionary movement. The idea of social rebellion, sneered at by the narrow-visioned reformer, once more possesses the mind of the proletair— the idea of revolt which is life itself.

⁋ THE new generation finds a-gain inspiration in the life and work of those noble souls who followed in the footsteps of Prometheus. The youth is moved to courageous deeds, thus proving itself worthy of the inheritance left us by the great thinkers in the realm of

CARVED CROSSES

 N the metropolis there is a certain little park hemmed in by a square of houses. I do not know why, at night, I dream of that particular place —I hardly think of it by day. Perhaps it is because, as a child, I was shut out from its supercilious environs since it is exclusively reserved for the aristocratic inhabitants of the square who all have private keys. No plebian may enter. At any rate I often dream of that neighborhood by night, and as if to compensate me for all my wistful and impotent desires to enter during the day, I have free access, in my sleep to every house. Every house. In how many have I already made myself at home —in dreams. And surely peopled them with more fantastic spirits than ever dwelt there in the matter-of-fact day.

⁋ I very rarely choose to enter houses of interesting or picturesque exteriors, for I long to create from outside inwards. It was a dull uninteresting, bare, brownstone house about which my imagination was most prolific. A strait-laced, coffin-narrow, three-storied house about which more than the others, there hung an air of cloistral seclusion.

⁋ Intuitively I felt that this must be a sort

Fig. 1.10. *Open Vistas* 1, no. 1 (January–February 1925): 3. Held in Houghton Library, Harvard University.

learned through his mentor's water metaphor, should be "as nearly equal as possible." Without modest and equal spacing, texts acquire "those ugly rivers of lines running about the page which are such a blemish to decent printing." The margins should be narrowest at the inner side of the printed matter, slightly larger at the top, wider still at the outer edge (called the fore edge), and widest of all at the bottom.[297] The type should not look, as

Morris lamented, as if it is "about to slip off the page."[298] For Morris and Ishill, making beautiful books was a step toward unalienated labor, a way to fight capitalism, as literary scholar Jeffrey Skoblow notes, "to reclaim the thingness of things from the dilutions, adulterations, and abstractions of commodification."[299]

Ishill's look is similar to Morris's regarding the page, but it is sometimes different regarding the type. Ishill too cultivated spacious margins on the right and bottom, modest and regular spacing, rich paper, uniform inking, and crisp, clear type. He too deplored the crowded look, as though the print had gotten too close to the edge of the page and might slide off. Both men frequently made use of beautiful engravings, illuminated capital letters, and lavish ornamentation, yet both sometimes printed more plainly and always stressed that typography should enhance the content of the text, not compete with it. Ishill sometimes made use of what his friend Leonard Abbott called "quaint headlines running across the page," more conversational than the one-word headers in *Freedom* and *Free Society*.[300] Morris's volumes, especially his famous Kelmscott Chaucer, feature "dark and solemn density," while Ishill's pages let in more light.[301] While Morris advocated "firm, clear typefaces ... best furthered by the avoidance of irrational swellings and spikey projections, and by the using of careful purity of line," Ishill's choice of typeface was perhaps a bit more ornate.[302] Among others, Ishill favored the Garamond typeface, which has small serifs (feet at the bottom, flags at the top) on the vertical lines, thickening and thinning strokes on the curves, and small flourishes that might have looked like "irrational swellings" or "spikey projections" to Morris.

Morris and Ishill differed in another significant way: Morris was, in the end, a businessman, and even though he regretted the price, his magnificent books were costly. While he worked, politically, for the liberation of the working class, he sold his radical ideas to those who could pay. Ishill never took money for his publications and only occasionally allowed grateful recipients to donate funds to the next printing. He gave out only originals—there were no copies—sometimes only one hundred printed, sometimes only five. They were original works of art, and people were often astonished to receive them. He sent them to people who asked for them and to people who didn't; he sent them to people who printed or collected books and people too poor to ever reciprocate. When someone wrote to thank him for a book, he often responded by sending another one. The receiver was often stunned at his generosity. He was widely respected both within the anarchist movement and within the larger world of printing; several universities, including

Rutgers and Columbia, arranged exhibits of his work, and he spent a year as the printer in residence at the University of Florida.

Labadie's characteristic look of printedness is quite different from those of Morris and Ishill. He too printed in clear type with even spacing and generous margins on the right and bottom of the page, but his books are frequently tiny, about three inches by four inches, hand-bound with colorful bits of wallpaper for covers. They often contain his poetry or his short, humorous essays called "Cranky Notions." Philadelphia anarchist Voltairine de Cleyre wrote her appreciation to Labadie on September 11, 1905, for a book he sent to her: "I am delighted with the quaint and beautiful little piece of work. Something sings of the old north woods and the nomads thereof when I touch it. Sunshiny days at the tent door, when the light work was done, and all the lazy time in the world to make something for one's own delight. Dear, lost spirit! If we could only charm it back into the hurry-up world again."[303] Labadie (see figure 1.11) was raised largely in the backwoods of Michigan and spent time with the Ojibway community, part of his inheritance on his father's side. He had little formal schooling, but he spoke English, French, and Pottawatomi.[304] His ties to Native American communities and to wilderness living informed his vision of anarchy as voluntary, egalitarian communities in rich natural settings. Whereas Morris's printing deliberately evokes the grandeur of medieval ornamentation, Labadie's calls up, in de Cleyre's words, the nomads of the old north woods. Both men were out of time, and both summoned an anti-industrial ethos to press against capitalist exploitation and state domination. They both suggested that making something beautiful is "one's own delight." One man's work is grand and one is humble, but both were carefully crafted to lift readers' imaginations toward an unalienated world.

Other printers also rejoiced in Labadie's small treasures: Edward Fulton wrote to him, "Your little books are the best in our line."[305] Thomas Keell praised the little booklets: "They were to the point and with a spice of humour which is usually lacking in so many anarchist publications. The Communists sin greatly in that respect."[306] In an earlier letter to Labadie, Keell expressed his desire to create something similar: "It is a good hobby of yours to write, print and bind these writings yourself, and I hope to do something similar some day when too old to look after this office. I also write articles, set all the type of *Freedom*, and have printed it, but now the printing is done by an outside man. I am also editor and errand-boy: a regular Anarchist Poo-Bah! So I guess you and I would hit it well together in a little printing 'drum' of our own."[307] Labadie's dainty, fanciful books

Fig. 1.11. Jo Labadie at about age twenty, wearing a suit. Studio tintype. Held in the Joseph A. Labadie Collection, Special Collections Research Center, University of Michigan Library.

suggest similarities to a book that Whitman once said he longed to make. In her analysis of Whitman's poetic portrayals of subjectivity, Bennett notes that Whitman reportedly expressed a desire to make something like an enchiridion, a small treatise or manual, to be easily carried outdoors: "I have long teased my brain with visions of a handsome little book, a dear, strong, aromatic volume like the Encheiridion, as it is called, for the pocket. That would tend to induce people to take me along with them and read in the open air: I am nearly always successful with the reader in the open air."[308] A "quaint and beautiful" book that "sings" bears a sensory resemblance to a "dear, strong, aromatic volume." De Cleyre imagines that Labadie's book sings when she touches it. Whitman imagines his book would release an attractive fragrance. Both place their little books in the sunshine and the open air, where readers can find delight in things that are dear.[309]

It may sound as though *Freedom* and *Free Society* are the poor cousins of the elaborate volumes by Morris and Ishill and Labadie's dainty, sweet books. Yet I do not think that judgment does justice to the different sorts of gestures, the different little optical machines, that each type of anarchist literature creates. Publications offering more conventional architectures of the page also work as little optical machines, in that they too weave together concepts, percepts, and affects; they too constitute an anarchist readership by the act of addressing it. Each kind of publication takes its own steps toward the anarchist futures it envisions. They each have a version of what book historian Frans Janssen calls "expressive strength": a compelling link between the text's outward appearance and its meanings.[310] Fine printers are creating scenes that close the gap between craft and art; they take a step toward a world in which workers would not be alienated from the product or the process of their labor. Plain printers are creating scenes that close the gap between oppressed people and people who rebel; they take a step toward a world in which no one would rule or be ruled. They each in their own way do what printer and book artist Johanna Drucker says the main text and paratext should do: they each play a valuable role "in mapping out the territory of a literary community linked through its traditions, attitudes and social interactions."[311]

The finely decorated pages of Ishill and Morris, the diminutive pages of Labadie, and the plain, relentless pages of *Freedom* and *Free Society* are all matters of pride and allegiance for many anarchist readers. Each kind of page has a surface that can be experienced as an event.[312] As Gitelman remarks, "Any space within the printed page is—effectively—printed, the result of specific labors in composition, imposition, and presswork. Each specialization of letterpress printing involved a different balance of concerns and a different spatial economy."[313] In the spatial economy of Ishill's work, every detail is attended; editor Leonard Abbott spoke for many readers when he described feeling a "glow of artistic satisfaction" in Ishill's "loving craftsmanship."[314] In the spatial economies of less aesthetically complex anarchist publications, pages are laid out to save on expenses rather than to diversify readerly experience. Yet *Freedom* and *Free Society*, like the work of the fine printers, are also opportunities for readers to encounter anarchism and to recognize themselves in those expressions.

In Ishill's extensive correspondence, other anarchists write over and over of his work in terms of beauty, joy, inspiration, and love. Bruce Calvert, socialist and editor of the *Open Road (Not Everybody's Magazine)*, wrote, "I am happy to see you are still carrying on in the old tradition, still making beautiful things to give away. If there is any higher life than that, I don't know it."[315] Scottish anarchist William Duff noted of Ishill's book *Free*

Vistas, "Every item is perfect.... The courage, patience, labour and craftsmanship displayed ... [These are] books that matter."[316] Herman Frank, editor of the Yiddish-language anarchist journal *Freie Arbeiter Stimme,* wrote of the appreciation of his comrades who "in our very mean civilization, still preserve the faculty of seeing the practical value of all kinds of applied art, particularly in regard to printing and book-binding."[317] Anarchist poet Lola Ridge wrote to Rose Ishill, "The chaste beauty of presentation recalls the early days of printing.... Men were still in love with the new art and willing to take such infinite pains, in execution and design, that each work produced was a creation of beauty."[318] Rudolf Rocker praised Joseph Ishill's contribution to anarchism: "You have demonstrated what a single man with a creative spirit and a natural sense for liberty and beauty is able to do. That is something one cannot buy for money."[319] Van Valkenberg, coeditor of *Road to Freedom,* wrote to Ishill, "I almost envy you the job which must be yours in the knowledge that the creations of your own hands shall endure long after the master shall have laid down his tools to inspire those who are to carry on the struggle to make men and women want to achieve freedom."[320]

Alexander Berkman, editor of *The Blast* (San Francisco) and for many years of *Mother Earth* (New York), could set type in four languages—German, Russian, Yiddish, and English.[321] He never lost the echo of the printery; he thanked Ishill for the "beautiful and splendid work," saying, "I am an old printer myself and I love a book well done."[322] Varlam Tcherkesoff, a Russian exile and writer for *Freedom,* wrote about how Kropotkin would have loved the book that Ishill made for him: "The love and deep appreciation of the anarchist and man Kropotkin which you so evidently are feeling could not have found a more touching proof than this beautiful book. Peter would have handled it with all the fondness of an artistic soul and craftsman which he was besides a revolutionist and scientist!"[323] Max Sartin, editor of the Italian American anarchist journal *L'Adunata dei Refrattari* in Newark, New Jersey, wrote that *Free Vistas* gave him "a sense of joy and content" and that he was "saving the book [*Plant Physiognomies*] for [his] little boy when he will be able to understand it."[324] Henry Rabe, a fruit merchant who became politicized through his encounters with Ishill and other radicals, wrote, "I just wanted to be alone with the book and turn over each page slowly—just to look at it—and resented any intrusion."[325] Rabe (who sent Ishill a case of apples in thanks) took in Ishill's books more as though he were listening to music than reading as it is conventionally understood. Emma Goldman's succinct compliment echoed many other correspondents: "You are the William Morris of the United States, if people would but know you."[326]

And on, and on, and on. There is a near-universal tone of respect uniting Ishill's correspondence (with the exception of an occasional grumpy letter from a commercial publisher arguing over copyright or disgruntled anarchists miffed that they did not receive a text that was gifted to others). Both within the movement and outside it, Ishill's work was honored. Beyond respect, certain words repeat regularly in the letters to Ishill: "joy," "beauty," "inspiration," "love." At first I read these as hyperbole, but the sheer repetition of phrases made me reconsider this too-quick dismissal. Rather than setting them aside as effusive or merely polite, I have come to see them as honest portrayals of the emotional economy of Ishill's work as it circulated within anarchist communities.

Yet anarchist readers did not always expect or require the beauty of fine printing to elicit their approval of a publication well done. Printers' and readers' satisfaction in the ordinary, well-printed page was widespread. When compositor Lillian Harman was jailed for illegally cohabiting with a man, and her father, Moses Harman, had to put out *Lucifer, The Lightbearer* without her, readers complained that his sloppy pages were a poor replacement for her near-perfect printing. A similar complaint was made by Benjamin Tucker against the spelling errors in early publications of his friend Ishill: "My 'printer's eye,' while reveling in the beauties of your work, detects not a few blemishes."[327] Writer and printer Lois Waisbrooker took pride in her printing, even including in the ads for her books a statement that "this book is printed in large clear type and on good book paper."[328] Keell's printing attracted the praise of the prodigious historian of anarchism Max Nettlau, who saw Morris's influence in Keell's "well proportioned aesthetic harmony and beauty which alone really evokes the best that is hidden in man."[329] The editors of *Spain and the World* felt the need to issue "An Apology" when they let down the side: "We owe an apology to our readers, and a special apology to our contributors, for the abnormal number of misprints in the last issue of 'Spain and the World.' Our last issue was produced under even greater difficulties than usual."[330]

I have come to see this pattern as indicative of more than professional pride or readerly impatience with errors. I think it suggests the aesthetic, and thus political, importance of all these publications for their communities. Anarchists were continually framed in popular discourse as dirty, ignorant, ugly, and dangerous, a kind of Othering that combines the usual disdain for the poor with fear of immigrants and of radical ideas in general, along with the unique demonization of anarchy as the absence of all order. English historian John Quail documents many examples of long-running stereotypes of anarchists as violent, conspiratorial, and insane: "The mad professor in *The Secret Agent*, the Anarchists in G.K. Chesterton's *The Man Who Was Thursday*, and the figure in cloak and wide-brimmed hat carrying a bomb marked 'BOMB' in Pip, Squeak and Wilfred cartoons were all variations on the stereotype developed in the early 1890s."[331] Nathaniel Hong finds comparable stereotypes of anarchists in US magazines portraying the "anarchist beast" as "morally adrift, intellectually illogical, religiously unacceptable, medically anomalous, and dangerously unpatriotic."[332] A comic US version was provided by a Philadelphia cartoonist named Walter Bradford, who launched a comic strip called *Fizzboomski the Anarchist* in 1905.[333] Dark and bearded, poor Fizzboomski was always trying and failing at assassinations. The czar was always one step ahead. The dominant register of public reception marked anarchism with alarm, ridicule, and loathing.

Anarchists, in contrast, saw their movement as the expression of a just struggle for their beautiful ideal. I think that anarchists were so heavily invested in their publications not just because the content was right and true but because the texts were small, recurrent sites of beauty and learning, prefiguring the world anarchists were struggling to make. "Art," Rancière suggests, "is given to us through these transformations of the sensible fabric, at the cost of constantly merging its own reasons with those belonging to other spheres of experience."[334] Ishill and Goldman corresponded about art's "transformations of the sensible fabric," when art "merges its own reasons" with anarchism. Goldman wrote, "I am so thoroughly in agreement with you in your idea that artistic effort ultimately benefits humanity, if only in the sense that it creates a new vision—it enriches the language with new images—it reawakens the love of beauty."[335] Anarchist printers and their comrades transformed the sensible fabric of anarchism's undercommons, merging printing's aesthetic practices with anarchist arguments and visions. Some texts primarily invited readers to learn, to encounter ideas that could change their lives, change the world. Other texts invited readers to imagine, to attend to how the text acted on them and how they might emerge from the encounter changed. Anarchists' fiery, revolutionary publications embodied their determination to struggle. Their aesthetically pleasing publications embodied their beautiful ideal. Anarchism became intellectually satisfying. Anarchism became beautiful.

Printers merge the aesthetic and the political: they dream, as Ishill said, and still retain the cunning of their hands. While the stock image of the bearded, black-clad, bomb-toting anarchist prevails in the public eye, a more representative figure for the classical anarchist movement would be the printer, composing stick in hand, standing in front of the type case, making and being made by the material process for producing and circulating words.

2
EPISTOLARITY

In a letter to Rudolf Rocker on October 15, 1953, Joseph Ishill described his next plans to create "things which are close to my heart and which I would like to shape with my mind and hands."[1] He longed to publish collections of letters from his friends Havelock Ellis and Emma Goldman.[2] Joseph commented on their value to the anarchist movement: "I consider these letters a fountain of rebellious expression, like a burning torch in a world of darkness and confusion."[3] While these were personal letters that he cherished, he was certain that their rebellious energies would also illuminate the larger, desperate world.

Joseph had a great deal of material to work with, because anarchists wrote *a lot* of letters. While anarchists are not unique in this regard—cultural theorist Margaretta Jolly observes in her study of feminism that "letters are a staple of any political movement"—anarchists are particularly prolific epistolarians.[4] During the classical anarchist movement from the Paris Commune to the Spanish Revolution, a remarkable global epistolary communications network linked many hundreds or thousands of individuals, publications, and institutions. Goldman is probably the best known of these, as her letters are more widely available than most. Historians Richard and Anna Maria Drinnon estimate that Goldman wrote over two hundred thousand letters in her lifetime.[5] There are two published editions plus a hefty four-volume collection of materials and a vast digital archive, all edited after her death.[6] Yet this prodigious output differs in degree rather than in kind from that of her comrades. The archives that collect, catalog, and make available the written record of anarchism and anarchists contain many, many thousands of letters as well as journals, manuscripts, photographs, pamphlets, posters, and other records. Anarchists wrote letters to each other, to allies and adversaries outside their movement, and to their journals, which often featured letters from readers on the back pages. Ink was "life's blood" for both anarchist publications and anarchist letters. Anarchists wrote themselves into their politics.

This chapter and the next switch from a focus on media to analyses of genre. Following Lisa Gitelman, I am approaching genre not as a set of rules governing the production of a type of literature but as a dynamic relationship between the creators and receivers of political messages and the larger discursive regime within which they appear. In Gitelman's charming example, genres are "like words hidden in a random grid of letters." It is possible to pick them out through their contrasts to the patterns and noise around them; they emerge "amid a jumble of discourse because of the ways they have been internalized by members of a shared culture."[7] Recognizable genres have productive power: they express and are impressed by what Jacques Rancière calls the "distribution of the sensible": "the system of self-evident facts of sense perception that simultaneously discloses the existence of something in common and the delimitations that define the respective parts and positions within it. . . . The distribution of the sensible reveals who can have a share in what is common to the community based on what they do and on the time and space in which this activity is performed."[8] The distribution of the sensible allows some concepts, percepts, and affects to rise to the level of intelligibility, while others linger in a jumble of incomprehensible noise. Our share of what is common includes our at-home-ness with the genres of our community. Genres are both "out there" and in us, and that is why they can do important political work.

The next chapter explores anarchist arts and letters, examining types of radical study appearing in anarchist journals. This chapter focuses on written interpersonal communication. All letters entangle material and discursive elements: they are things, and they are about things. Sociologist Liz Stanley provides a useful and fluid idea of letters, in the sense of missives, as a genre: "Letter writing and correspondences involve a theatre of usage, for although there are indeed conventions about the form that letters take, these provide a loose shape rather than being determining, and the letter-writing practices that result are performative and emergent and often play with 'other' genres or indeed shade into these."[9] Following Gitelman and

Stanley, I set aside the idea of hard-and-fast formal structures and instead appreciate "letter-writing *practices*...[that] are indeed emergent, relational and change over time."[10] The classical anarchist movement in the United States and Great Britain was, in Stanley's evocative term, a vigorous epistolary theater of usage. Anarchists' extraordinary chains of communication were not just *about* anarchism; they were *part of* anarchism.

Political theorist Elizabeth Wingrove, in her study of letters from prisoners of the ancien régime, usefully reflects on changing intellectual engagements as her relation to prison-based epistolarity evolves. She started out looking for information in the prisoners' letters, just trying to "figure out what had happened."[11] However, she discovered that sustained encounters with letters can encourage a different reading practice: "It became clear somewhere along the line that I had started to read them as political theoretical texts," she noted, rather than simply as data.[12] Like Wingrove, I started out modestly, reading anarchists' letters to learn what the writers and recipients had done in the anarchist movement. Eventually, I noticed a different reading practice had crept in, attending not just to what the people did but to what the letters themselves were doing, as texts.

While letters of prisoners to authorities are situated very differently from letters of activists to one another, the basic scholarly opportunity is similar: the letters do not just report information; they do interpretive work, creating (or sometimes failing to create) patterns of interaction and modes of address that invite, as Wingrove concludes, "a fruitful rethinking of our relationship to texts."[13] Letters can be sites of creativity, where writers and readers generate, or sometimes erode, selves-in-relation as they emerge into unknown futures. Chains of letters can resonate among themselves, and with other political practices, producing networks of influence or disruption. Letters can be sites of collaboration, both within the epistolary exchanges themselves and in the planned or disputed projects about which correspondents write. The anarchist movement writes itself in layers of written transmissions, in which many activists corresponded, over and over, often for decades, with their comrades. The accumulated weight of the "epistolary record that remains for *post hoc* scrutiny" is, again using Stanley's lively vocabulary, the anarchist epistolarium.[14]

The conditions of possibility of this theater of usage are found in the anarchist "distribution of the sensible," the dynamic assemblages that allow people and things to "have a share in what is common to the community" during their time, in their place.[15] Epistolary relations by themselves do not "cause" anarchism or vice versa. Lots of people write letters, and it doesn't make them anarchists; nor does an affiliation with anarchism necessarily produce an epistolary urge. Yet networks of epistolary relations interwoven with letterpress media and radical scholarship resonate together, creating and being created by one another. There is no obvious starting point for these relations; rather, there are moving layers of connectivity. As political theorist Maria Tamboukou succinctly explains, "Unlike closed organisms, structural systems and fixed identities, assemblages do not have any organizing centre; they can only function as they connect with other assemblages in a constant process of becoming."[16] Sprawling networks of material and semiotic elements offer possibilities of creativity and collaboration. They give rise to the anarchist undercommons.

This chapter looks closely at two bodies of correspondence that serve as key operators in the anarchist epistolarium.[17] Following philosopher Manuel DeLanda's theorizing of assemblages, these bundles of letters are *dense*, in that they host many exchanges; they are *strong*, in that the interchanges are relatively cohesive and extensive; and they are *reciprocal*, in that the participants eagerly called and responded to one another.[18] First is the exchange between printer, editor, and writer Joseph Ishill and his friend Rudolf Rocker, a bookbinder, labor organizer, and intellectual leader of the movement. The Rudolf Rocker Papers at the International Institute of Social History (IISH) in Amsterdam contain many hundreds of letters, fifty-eight of which were written to Rocker between 1924 and 1958 in Ishill's tiny, precise handwriting.[19] The Joseph Ishill Papers in the Houghton Library at Harvard, similarly rich with over forty boxes of correspondence, contain fifty-eight letters from Rocker to Ishill, all neatly typed, usually about four pages long. The file culminates with a clipping of Rocker's obituary from the *New York Times* on September 11, 1958.

Second is the exchange between the first curator of the Joseph A. Labadie Collection at the University of Michigan, Agnes Inglis, and two sisters, Bertha Johnson in Pennsylvania and Pearl Johnson Tucker in New York, France, and Monaco. The sisters collected and dispatched numerous publications and documents to Inglis for inclusion in the collection. The Johnson sisters descended from a radical family: their grandfather Moses Hull was a well-known spiritualist and advocate for the rights of women, farmers, and workers. Pearl was the companion of printer and editor Benjamin Tucker; the couple possessed a significant anarchist library despite the devastating fire that destroyed Benjamin's New York warehouse in 1908. Bertha also had a substantial library of radical material inherited from a family friend and from her neighbor Belle Chaapel. The sisters organized their extensive accumulations of anarchist literature, exchanging with other individuals and contributing to the Labadie Collection and to other libraries. The vast Labadie Collection contains 238 letters from Bertha to Agnes, spanning two decades, nearly all neatly typed; 74 letters from Agnes to Bertha, often long and chatty; 54 letters from Agnes to Pearl; and 81 letters from Pearl to Agnes in Pearl's steady, legible hand. Agnes's outgoing letters were nearly always typed carbon copies. Occasionally Agnes wrote to Pearl and Bertha together. Additionally, Bertha wrote to her sister nearly every day.[20] It appears that Bertha first contacted Agnes on March 16, 1933, explaining that she had inherited a library and, as she had no children to leave it to, she would like to donate the materials to the Labadie Collection when she was done with them. Many letters among the women describe the materials sent and received, culminating unceremoniously with Pearl's death in 1948 and Agnes's death in 1952. Bertha lived until 1958. There are also numerous letters to Bertha in which Agnes recounted letters she had written to other correspondents, perhaps in an effort to assuage Bertha's feeling of isolation by bringing her into a larger conversation.

These bodies of correspondence often reference each other, intersecting in a larger network rather than standing as discrete exchanges between separate individuals. It is an artifact of the archiving system that the two bodies of correspondence appear as separate. The writers all knew each other, often mentioning other letters and visits in their correspondence. Since each reader in an epistolary exchange (including those who read the letter after it has completed its initial circuit) is also enmeshed in other partnerings, other patterns, energies can flow in multiple directions. Tamboukou sketches the emergent connections: "Politics, ideas and practices *become* in the process of their entanglements and intra-actions with other ideas, conditions, and practices. In forming relations of interiority among themselves, but also in connection through relations of exteriority with components of other assemblages ... [relations are] complex, fluent and in the process of becoming other."[21] While other entanglements haunt the exchanges, I foreground these identifiable bodies of correspondence to sketch a ground for theorizing the epistolary dimension of anarchist print culture. Some of these letters may rise to the level of the "burning torch" that Ishill envisioned to cast out the darkness of his time. Others are occupied with more mundane tasks of planning and executing projects, forging and maintaining relationships, and surviving hard times. Yet "ordinary" letters also can ignite or receive sparks of the sort that animate political movements. Wingrove emphasizes the dynamic call of letters: a letter "calls its addressee into speech, into a dialogue that creates or sustains an interlocutory relationship comprised of, for example, rule, debate, love, or friendship (or again, fails to do so)."[22] Letters have a characteristic temporality: literary scholar Elizabeth MacArthur characterizes epistolary narratives as "generated forward"—that is, implicitly moving into the future when the letter will be received and answered. Letters, MacArthur continues, "privilege the energy that propels them" and create meaning by writing into the future without knowing how the stories will turn out.[23] The energy that propels them is both personal and political. The unfinished quality of both interlocutionary relations and political movements can, Tamboukou suggests, become an advantage, creating sense out of "an agglomeration of epistolary stories that are incomplete, irresolute or broken."[24] Since the writer can always receive, or at least hope for, another response, a different response, something new is possible.

Further, this chapter reflects on the archival work needed to encounter anarchists' letters and manuscripts in the Ishill Collection, the Labadie Collection, and the IISH. Considering the relation of researchers to collections introduces another layer of analysis of specific encounters with anarchist histories. The location of a cache of letters, in relation to the location of the investments recounted and produced in those letters, suggests a geographic dimension to epistolary archives. Individuals' letters, and the archives that shelter them, continue to act as loci of transmission of anarchist politics. Ishill, Rocker, Inglis, the Johnson sisters, and hundreds of other anarchists have left behind chains of correspondence that, while sometimes "incomplete, irresolute or broken," as Tamboukou comments, are often strong, dense, and reciprocal, as DeLanda requires. By inquiring into the political life of their correspondence, I aim to expand our understanding of the circulations of anarchist texts to include epistolary manifestations and thus deepen our understanding of how anarchism happened.

Meeting Joseph Ishill (1888–1966) and Rudolf Rocker (1873–1958)

Ishill and Rocker were lifelong anarchists who contributed substantially to the intellectual and aesthetic practices of their movement. They were both engaged in the production of knowledge as intellectual work (writing, researching, and editing) and physical labor (printing, binding, and distributing written material). They were widely recognized as influential within the movement during their lifetimes but are relatively unknown today. They met a few times in person: Rudolf visited Joseph in the summer of 1926 and again in late 1952 or early 1953. Joseph mentions meeting Rudolf's partner, Milly, at Mohegan in 1943, so he must have visited the Rockers at the anarchist colony. I do not know if there were other face-to-face encounters, but they conducted the bulk of their long relationship through correspondence.

While there were hundreds of anarchist printers, Ishill was widely known as the anarchist printer. He was born in Romania, where he apprenticed to a print shop at age fourteen. While still a boy, he met some anarchists in his home country and became interested in the ideas of the movement. He immigrated to the United States in 1909 and soon after married Rose Freeman, who became an accomplished poet and translator. They joined the anarchist colony in Stelton, New Jersey, in 1915, where Joseph built a cottage they named "little Nirvana," rescued an old printing press from an outbuilding, and taught printing to enthusiastic students in the community's school, based on the educational philosophy of Spanish anarchist Francisco Ferrer. There Joseph printed the *Modern School Magazine*. When Rose and Joseph left Stelton, they moved to Berkeley Heights, New Jersey, where Joseph built a cottage outside town with a basement printery named Oriole Press. Joseph supported his family for many years by commuting two hours each way by train to a job in a commercial print shop in New York City. On his own time, he printed more than two hundred books and pamphlets by and about anarchists and others he deemed worthy for their contribution to freedom, including Peter Kropotkin, Élisée and Élie Reclus, Benjamin Tucker, Emma Goldman, and many others. He also developed unique technologies of typesetting and printing that both created and expressed his politics, as described in the previous chapter. Art historian Jacques Mesnil concludes, regarding Joseph, "He organizes the spiritual composition of [the books] as he organizes their material composition; he solicits collaborations and chooses the text with as much care and in the same spirit as the type characters. These books are his life."[25] His work was exhibited at several universities, and in the mid-1960s he spent one year at the University of Florida as their printer in residence. Photographs of Joseph as a young man show a dapper, clean-shaven man with a heart-shaped face and thick head of hair. Louis Moreau's woodcut (see figure 2.1) portrays him in dramatic black and white hand-cut lines. His young wife, Rose Freeman Ishill, was described by Bertha Johnson as a delicate woman with bright eyes and a mass of dark curly hair.[26] They had three children: Oriole, Anatole (also a printer), and Crystal.

Fig. 2.1. Joseph Ishill, woodcut by Louis Moreau (1934). From Manuel Devaldès, "Louis Moreau," in *Free Vistas*, vol. 2, ed. Joseph Ishill (Berkeley Heights, NJ: Oriole, 1937), 320. Held in Houghton Library, Harvard University.

While there were many thousands of Jews in the anarchist movement, Rocker was widely known as the anarchist rabbi. (Ironically, he was not Jewish, although Ishill was.) Rocker was born into a progressive Catholic family in Germany. His father was a lithographer and his uncle, a typographer. Rocker became a bookbinder. He traveled extensively through Europe, learning about socialism and anarchism, before immigrating to London's East End, where he became a beloved leader of the Jewish radical community. He rose to prominence as a writer, editor, and labor leader. He learned Yiddish and edited as well as set type for the anarchist journals *Arbeiter Fraynd*, *Germinal*, and others.[27] He and his companion, Milly Witcop, who had immigrated to London from Russia, had one son, Fermin, who became a lithographer and noted painter. Fermin described his beloved father as a strong, stoutly built man with glasses and a thick mustache, in his later years sporting a trim beard, and his mother, Milly, as a striking olive-skinned woman with thick hair coiled on top of her head in two long braids. Photographs of Rocker (see figure 2.2) reliably portray

Fig. 2.2. Rudolf Rocker, *Testimonial to Rudolf Rocker, 1873–1943* (Los Angeles: Rocker Publications Committee, 1944), front page. Held in the Joseph A. Labadie Collection, Special Collections Research Center, University of Michigan Library.

him as a man of dignity and learning. Milly was also active in the anarchist movement, as was her sister Rose. Rocker had an older son, also named Rudolf, from an earlier relationship in Paris.

Rocker smuggled the manuscript that became his best-known book, *Nationalism and Culture*, out of Nazi Germany in 1933, escaping with little more than the book and his life while the fascists burned his library of five thousand books.[28] Rudolf and Milly moved to the United States and lived for many years in the anarchist colony Mohegan in upstate New York. Rudolf was one of the revered intellectuals of the movement, the best known of the five individuals discussed in this chapter. He published extensively on anarchism and syndicalism in many languages and was a popular lecturer on the radical circuit. Long after he ceased supporting himself and his family through bookbinding, Rudolf, Fermin reports, never stopped dreaming of resuming his trade or loving the shape of a book in his hand.[29]

Both Ishill and Rocker came from poor families and lived in economically marginal circumstances for all of their lives. Both were polyglots who lived global lives and struggled with the unsettled circumstances of immigration: Rudolf was imprisoned in England during World War I as an "enemy alien," and Milly was jailed for associating with an enemy alien and for opposing the war. Rudolf was selected as leader by the jailed exiles; he helped the prisoners organize to improve their conditions, negotiated with the authorities, served as counselor and adviser, and conducted regular lectures on historical and literary topics. When he was released, "a profound sadness could be felt in the assembly"; the other prisoners lined up to shake his hand and sing a farewell song.[30]

After moving to the United States, he and Milly were plagued by uncertainty regarding needed visa extensions.[31] Despite his prodigious publications, Rocker received little financial compensation for his writing. In contrast, Ishill had a more stable if modest income for many years as a job printer; however, he used much of his income to print anarchist materials that he seldom sold but instead freely gave away. After being fired from his job of thirty years at a New York City print shop, Ishill had trouble finding work because he was an immigrant and lacked needed certifications to qualify for many printing jobs, despite his worldwide reputation as a skilled printer.[32] He supported himself and his family in later years by freelance printing. Like Rudolf and Milly, Rose and Joseph were sometimes too poor to heat their home, pay medical bills, or afford transportation.

Both men were known by their friends and comrades to be modest and generous souls whose lives were devoted to the anarchist movement. Ishill's students write warmly of his artistic genius.[33] Rocker fondly calls Ishill "a Mensch who lived fully immersed in his work."[34] Ishill praised Rocker as "a shining beacon" carrying "the torch of liberty and enlightenment," bringing "treasured light" to the world.[35] Rudolf's daughter-in-law Ruth Rocker affectionately characterized her husband's father: "Very few people quarreled with Rudolf. People who couldn't talk to each other got along with him. He brought out the best in them."[36] Ishill was less charismatic than Rocker, more introverted, but charming in his own way. He loved the outdoors. In an article about Ishill in the local paper, a reporter explains why both his press and his older daughter are named Oriole: "The name was suggested by birds he found nesting in an abandoned printing press in a tool house on the Stelton farm where he once lived. Some of his best work has been done on that same press, which he restored with painstaking care when the nesting season was over."[37] In her tender poem "To Joseph Ishill," Rose pictures her partner as her "solitary, deep-souled friend."[38]

Both men wrote unusual autobiographies: Rocker's son Fermin quipped that his father managed to write "2000 pages of memoirs about everyone under the sun except Rudolf Rocker."[39] Like Rocker, Ishill seldom wrote about himself, but he compiled and printed an enormous book that was actually (and fittingly) a bibliography of the Oriole Press (1953). Rocker called the story of the press a "majestic, richly illustrated volume of almost 500 pages and an outstanding masterpiece of typographical aesthetics."[40] Readily mixing his own life with the life of his press, Ishill referred to the achievement as "chiseling my own tombstone."[41]

Rocker and Ishill's correspondence is characteristically warm and became increasingly intimate over time. Letters' opening paragraphs always included mention of Milly and Rose. Rose was often ill, and Joseph confided his worries to Rudolf; Rudolf and Milly grieved with Joseph, hopeful of finding additional medical assistance and concerned for both Joseph's and Rose's health as the toll of caring for Rose became increasingly debilitating for Joseph.[42] When Rose was better in 1954, Milly's health had become poor, so the Rockers visited California to escape the harsh, cold winters in the Mohegan colony.[43]

As time passed, the letters included more comments on aging and on the precious value of time and the ability to work. Updates and encouragement on projects followed, including those by the two correspondents and by others in the anarchist movement, mixed in with general observations on the state of the world. Rudolf's letters often culminated with hope: "But men like we have never to give up any hope, because to give up the last hope means to give up oneself, and that we shall never do."[44] Trying to cheer Joseph, Rudolf stressed both his personal regard and his friend's importance to the anarchist movement: "I love you as a human being and have the greatest admiration for the wonderful work you have done in all these struggling years. Such a work will never be forgotten, and you have no reason to become pessimistic."[45] They shared their fears and forebodings. They supported one another. "I was never afraid of death," Rudolf wrote, "but I would not like to waste my later years, useless and becom[ing] a burden to myself."[46]

In November 1955, Rudolf wrote to his "dear old friends Rose & Joseph" that Milly had died. His suffering saturates the page: "My soul is bleeding."[47] Now it was Rudolf's turn to draw strength from Joseph. In 1956 Rose was again very ill and had lost much of her vision; Rudolf sympathized and recalled his wretchedness when Milly was suffering, gasping for breath at the end of her life, and he could not help. The men were bitter about their losses, but they never stopped trying to carry each other. After Milly's death, Rudolf lived with his son Fermin and his family; he reported to Joseph that he kept up a positive demeanor so as not to be a further burden to his son, but to Joseph he revealed his despair. The men exchanged writings and photographs. They aged together. They gave each other courage. Their letters stand out in the anarchist epistolary network because of their volume, detail, and reciprocity of communication. In their relations to themselves, each other, and the larger anarchist movement, there are patterns of expression and reception that can help us make sense of anarchist politics.

Meeting Agnes Inglis (1870–1952),
Bertha Johnson (1880–1958),
and Pearl Johnson Tucker (1879–1948)

Agnes Inglis was born into a large Presbyterian family of Scottish descent in Detroit. Early photographs (see figure 2.3) show a slender, serious young woman with wavy brown hair, who became gaunt and silver-haired as she aged. Inglis was the only one of the five anarchists examined in this chapter who was not exposed to radical ideas as a child. She explained in a letter to Industrial Workers of the World activist Ralph Chaplin and his partner, Edith, who, like Inglis, worked for amnesty for political prisoners after World War I, that reading Emma Goldman's essay "What I Believe" challenged her conservative religious upbringing: "E.G.'s 'What I Believe' started me on the path of Anarchism, I was so astonished that that bad notorious woman believed in so beautiful a world—right here on earth! A world without poorhouses and jails. I thought you had to die and go to heaven for such a place."[48] In her unpublished autobiography, Inglis recalls the effect of Goldman's words: "Out there in the bungalow among the hills and flowers of Ann Arbor surrounded by beauty, yet conscious of squalor and poverty and little children doomed to make artificial flowers in cellars, I re-read it. It was astonishing. I have to say it burned my fingers to hold the book."[49]

After working for a time in settlement houses, Inglis became active in the Industrial Workers of the World and the anarchist movement. For several years she organized Goldman's and Alexander Berkman's talks in Detroit

Fig. 2.3. Agnes Inglis, Abbot Academy, age twenty. Held in the Joseph A. Labadie Collection, Special Collections Research Center, University of Michigan Library.

and Ann Arbor and also worked to protect immigrants from deportation and to secure amnesty for political prisoners during and after World War I. Years later she recalled the thrill of sitting with Labadie and Berkman at a Detroit restaurant, singing revolutionary songs. She went home to Ann Arbor for the night, then returned to Detroit to pick up Berkman: "I arrived as the dawn was breaking and walked through the sleeping town. But I was walking into a new life—into a life that had Pitchfork Henderson in it and Ernest Schleiffer and Gordon Cascaden and Emma Goldman."[50]

In 1924 Inglis discovered that the extensive donation of anarchist materials made to the University of Michigan by her friend Labadie was languishing in a locked cage, and she essentially launched an anarchist incursion into the university's library. She took on the job of organizing the materials and making them available to the public. She poached furniture and supplies from other departments in the library, worked without pay for most of her career, and succeeded in large part because the higher administration was not paying attention. She curated the Labadie Collection for nearly thirty years, expanding its holdings many times over. Inglis's work was widely recognized among radicals, to the point that Ishill suggested renaming the collection after her, a move she did not pursue. Current curator Julie Herrada notes that Inglis was able to extend the collection because she had "a large network of activists" and credibility with radicals who were "typically dubious of institutions."[51] Inglis was able to live as a full-time activist and then as a volunteer librarian thanks to a stipend from her older brother James, a conservative businessman who nonetheless supported Inglis's life's work.[52]

The correspondence between Agnes Inglis and the Johnson sisters is a treasure for researchers because the women's relationships were primarily epistolary. Their letters often spell out details that correspondents with a face-to-face history would not have needed to mention. Bertha Johnson is the least well-known individual of the five discussed in this chapter, because the work of collecting, organizing, and distributing the movement's written material was (and is) much less recognized as political than was writing or speaking.[53] Pearl Johnson Tucker is better known, but again not so much for her work on the movement's written legacy, more for being the companion of Benjamin Tucker. Agnes and Bertha did not meet face-to-face for many years, and then only twice: in 1937, Agnes visited Bertha on her farm, and in late 1948 or early 1949, Bertha traveled to Ann Arbor to visit Agnes.[54] While Pearl often expressed her wish to visit the collection, Agnes and Pearl never met face-to-face; however, their epistolary relationship, while less intimate than that of Bertha with the Ann Arbor librarian, was both cordial and practical.

Bertha sent Agnes a photo in 1933 (see figure 2.4), when it appears that their correspondence began, and described herself as five feet tall, 110 pounds, "broad shouldered, full busted and deep chested." She had gray eyes and "medium brown hair with coppery glints and fast getting grey." She gave Agnes a glimpse of her temperament: "Emery says, 'you have appraising eyes,' and even my baby pictures look that way."[55] In contrast to the sturdily built Bertha, Pearl (see figure 2.5) was described as delicate. People used to say to Bertha about Pearl, "Your sister looks like a piece of Dresden china."[56] The two sisters were close friends and allies their entire lives—Pearl commented to Agnes that "one could not have a more devoted sister than she is to me and *always* has been since I can remember!" even though they were quite different in character.[57] Bertha described them this way: Pearl was industrious, "ultra-conscientious ... less spontaneously merry than I, but perhaps evener tempered.... Her disposition is almost saintly, and mine isn't. But I get along averagely well with folks I like. I try to have as little to do with others as possible, lest I get irritable at them."[58] The tone of their correspondence suggests that Pearl was more prickly and judgmental than Bertha, but that was not how Bertha perceived her.

The sisters were raised in a radical family, and they knew many other anarchists, suggesting the truth of the saying (attributed to Virginia Woolf) that if you meet one radical, you meet all the radicals. "How these radical friendship lines do cross!" Bertha exclaimed to Agnes in a letter of April 1, 1934.[59] The sisters knew printer George Schumm and his partner, writer Beatrice Schumm, of New York City, and George recommended Pearl to his friend Benjamin Tucker for a job in Tucker's bookstore. Pearl became Benjamin's secretary and later his companion. After the disastrous fire that destroyed most of Benjamin's books in 1908, he and Pearl moved to France, where he had always intended to retire. Bertha speculated that their relation changed from a work relation to a romantic one because "their mutual grief over the fire, well it seemed to reveal them to each other."[60] They had one child, a daughter, Oriole. Agnes observed that having a family changed Benjamin. She commented to Pearl, "I think that you came in then and the baby came—two experiences he had never had before and he felt the luxury of having a home and people who loved him near him. It rested him. After all one can't fight wind-mills forever."[61] Pearl homeschooled Oriole, who described her mother as "a born teacher and psychologist" (in contrast to her less communicative father).[62] Benjamin wrote to Joseph Ishill from Monaco, "Our third-floor apartment commands a glorious view of sea and sky and gorge & mountain, all close at hand, and immediately surrounding an active civilization. Awaiting the good things in store."[63] By all accounts they had a good life abroad, with Benjamin's inheritance and Pearl's thrifty management providing financial security that the others often lacked. Pearl wrote to Bertha that she dreaded the thought of returning to America, but when Benjamin died in 1939 and world war loomed in Europe, Pearl and Oriole came back to the United States.[64] Pearl lived for a time with Bertha on the farm in Pennsylvania that Bertha's husband, Emery Andrews, had inherited.

The sisters were well connected in the anarchist movement prior to corresponding with Agnes. They knew the movement's respected poet and

Fig. 2.4. Bertha Johnson, August 7, 1920, age forty. Held in the Joseph A. Labadie Collection, Special Collections Research Center, University of Michigan Library.

thinker Voltairine de Cleyre, the printer and sex radical Lillian Harman, and many, many others. The older feminist, spiritualist, and anarchist writer Lois Waisbrooker was a good friend of Moses Hull, the sisters' grandfather. Millie Baginski, sister of printer George Schumm and partner of editor Max Baginski, was "a darling old lady and a close friend" whom the sisters had known since childhood.[65] Bertha lived for a time with Pearl and Benjamin, and she hotly defended Benjamin against frequent assaults on his character: while many people thought him cold and rigid, Bertha affectionately described him as "humorous, kindly, non-invasive, gentle, *most dependable* about doing whatever he sets about."[66] Bertha knew the writer and editor Leonard Abbott and fondly remembered that she once taught him how to soft-boil an egg.[67] While they considered themselves more individualist than communist anarchists, the sisters liked and respected Goldman, whom Bertha described as "a small, plump, german-housefrau type, with soft, wavy golden hair ... always hospitable, serving Russian tea, in glasses, and making everyone at home, in her tiny top floor flat in a poor section of New York, 'Miss Smith' on the name plate at the letter box."[68]

In contrast to Bertha's cheerful and often philosophical reflections, letters from Pearl to Agnes are more like lengthy working documents, describing Pearl's collection and documenting material sent to the Labadie Collection and elsewhere. Agnes described Pearl as "a most painstaking and accurate

Fig. 2.5. Pearl Johnson Tucker, 1925, age forty-six. Studio portrait by George Berger, Nice, France. Held in the Joseph A. Labadie Collection, Special Collections Research Center, University of Michigan Library.

scholar."[69] Yet there was room in the letters for personal messages and concerns, as well as an increasing amiability over time; Pearl's sign-offs mutated from the initial formal signature to "Love, Pearl." Both sisters reveled in the anarchist networks they shared with Agnes, who did not grow up in radical communities but met many progressives when they visited the Labadie Collection. Bertha wrote, "The endless chain of fellowship is a source of satisfaction to me." Bertha described the assemblage of relationships with the striking term *filament*: "you and Alice [Furst] and the dear Ishills and the filament reaching out to your friends and my friends."[70] A filament, appropriately, can be a flexible carbon or metal thread that conducts electric current, or it can be a long, thin, organic fiber that is part of a plant or animal. *Filament* is a good image for the connecting material—organic, inorganic, semiotic, and social—that branches across the anarchist landscape, connecting people and things in horizontal relations. Exchanging letters and publications; requesting, receiving, reading, acknowledging, and sharing materials; watching the histories of their movement become concrete in their hands and under their eyes; these archival matters, repeated and appreciated, again and again, create a kind of intimacy. Borrowing communications scholar Cait McKinney's observation of later feminist information activists, the women "carved pathways through information," which were also pathways through the anarchist movement, that others might follow.[71]

In hard times, the correspondents kept each other going. When possible, they shared financial resources: Agnes and Pearl both sent money to Bertha when the situation on the farm was desperate, and many comrades tried to help Joseph although he often rebuffed their efforts.[72] Through their epistolary relations, they nurtured friendships, exchanged photographs, shared news of family and friends, dissected relationships, analyzed politics, rejoiced in beauty, regretted illnesses and hard times—together. As with the body of correspondence between the two more famous men, the correspondence among these women reveals layers of entanglements that animate anarchist political worlds.

Hot Spots in the In-Between

Letters are a unique written form. When considering novels and essays, readers rightly ask whether the example in our hands is a *good* one, but we seldom question whether novels and essays as a type of writing have worth. Letters, in contrast, are challenged and defended at the level of *genre*. Tamboukou aptly summarizes debates between those who dismiss letters as "overwhelming, fragmentary, unfocused and idiosyncratic" and those who see them as useful "documents of life."[73] Sociologist Ken Plummer, for example, finds that "letters are not generally focused enough to be of analytic interest—they contain far too much material that strays from the researcher's concern."[74] Liz Stanley, in contrast, finds that the traits that lead critics to dismiss letters are exactly what is interesting about them "as analytic problematics": letters are dialogical (constructing relationships out of written exchanges), perspectival (changing according to the position in space and time of recipients and other readers), and emergent (coming into meaning as a process, with "their own preoccupations and conventions and indeed their own epistolary ethics").[75] Tamboukou agrees that letters are fragmented yet finds that trait valuable in enacting a meaning-making process in which "unforeseeable relational narratives" unfold.[76]

While literary critics are likely to analyze letter-based fiction and social scientists more often examine real-life correspondence, Elizabeth MacArthur's influential text *Extravagant Narratives* connects the two through their shared dynamic, open-ended form. Participants become "co-authors of a narrative in which they, or rather epistolary constructions of themselves, also play the leading roles."[77] The traits of openness and coauthorship are central to the roles letters play within anarchist collaborations, because those traits contribute to the weaving of connections out of which comradeship and collaboration can emerge. This emergent coauthorship can expand to include the contributions of readers other than the intended recipients: letters can be dialogical not just between sender and receiver but between the letter and any reader. When Ishill envisioned creating new collections of letters "with [his] mind and hands" to share epistolary sparks of rebellion with other readers, he was imagining not simply that readers would connect with individual letter writers but that they would find entry into anarchism via those letters.

The dialogical emergence of letters within relationships makes them useful points of entry into assemblages. Letters are already, by their structure, in the "in-between." Their unfocused quality can ironically allow for an unexpected focus to emerge. For example, Agnes, Pearl, and English anarchist Lilian Wolfe wrote letters among themselves expressing anger about the misuse of letters or libraries belonging to anarchists. These incidents, while initially unrelated, emerge through juxtaposition as "minor, even repetitive moments of struggle" that McKinney calls "eventfulness."[78] By themselves they are unsuggestive, but taken together they offer clues about significant investments held by the authors and likely others as well. The first incident is Agnes's uncharacteristic anger at Scottish anarchist Guy Aldred, who edited and helped to print several Glasgow publications, including *The Word* and *Herald of Revolt*. Aldred was widely recognized as a difficult person, so it is not surprising that even Agnes, usually even-tempered and forgiving, also had trouble with him. In a letter to Lilian at Freedom Press in London, Agnes wrote that Aldred had rewritten a letter that Agnes had sent him, adding material she had not included, then published it.[79] Lilian, evidently not surprised, responded that Aldred "gets away with all these horrid things."[80] The second incident entailed a burst of anger from Pearl at Joseph, who was accused by Bertha's neighbor Belle Chaapel of stealing some items from Chaapel's personal library. Chaapel told Bertha, as related in Bertha's letter to Agnes, that Chaapel caught Ishill red-handed, and he blustered that "he meant to pay her" for the books, then fled.[81] While this is an alarming accusation, it is a second- or thirdhand account, and there are intervening circumstances that could mitigate judgment. Bertha describes Chaapel as well meaning but rather out of touch, "like a visitor from another country or planet."[82] In this scene, Agnes tried unsuccessfully to act as peacemaker, while Pearl continued to express her anger toward and suspicion of Joseph for the rest of her life. In the third instance, Lilian expressed anger that the personal library of a comrade, Oscar Swede, a conscientious objector in World War I and a participant in *Freedom* during the turbulent 1930s, had been carelessly handled after Swede's death. The brother of the deceased had evidently broken up the collection, donating some of the books to Oxford and selling others. John Hewitson, a comrade from *Freedom*, found some of Swede's books in a secondhand store. Lilian felt strongly that the collection should have been kept together.[83]

These instances initially caught my interest because the writers came across as uncharacteristically worked up about the offending behavior. They were textual "hot spots" in the sense that therapist Beth Roy identifies: affective pressure points in an exchange that let partially submerged undercurrents emerge.[84] They were certainly not spectacles in any larger sense, yet they clearly stirred these women into intense reactions. They are eventful in that they arise out of and reflect back on the connective filaments of anarchist assemblages, both highlighting what mattered and helping it to matter. Considered within the larger context of anarchist print culture, the correspondents' ire comes into clearer focus: letters and publications were the currency of the movement, its lifeblood. Misrepresenting a letter to an editor or abusing a comrade's collection of literature was a blow not just to the individuals involved but to the movement. Sharing indignation about these misdeeds was a way to address the damage thus caused and to reknit the connections whose integrity had been eroded.

Doubleness and the Desire for Exchange

The anarchist letters examined here have a characteristic rhythm: initial salutations and final valedictions that become increasingly intimate over the years; a first paragraph or two inquiring into the recipient's health and welfare as well as reporting on the health and well-being of the writer and their loved ones; a portion that is, so to speak, "conducting business," including plans for projects, fund-raising, speaking tours, collections, and publications; a portion discussing the political situation, including exchanges and exhortations about the anarchist movement, news and gossip about absent comrades, and reflections on how best to live through the times at hand. First paragraphs often include an apology for not having written sooner, suggesting that both parties expect and value a regular exchange. When both correspondents are printers, reflections about and queries into the printing process are sometimes part of the business at hand.

Literary theorist Janet Altman uses the concept of epistolarity to sketch a framework of reading that works from letters' formal properties to the meaning they can create.[85] Letters, she suggests, have a dynamic narrative form that makes them identifiable as letters. First, there is their characteristic doubleness in people (there is always a writer and a recipient); second, there is a spatial gap between the locations of the participants; and third, there is a temporal gap between the writing and the receiving of the missive. Altman succinctly summarizes this as "I/you, here/there, now/then."[86]

The doubleness of the participants is marked by ritualized forms of address for greetings and farewells. At first the salutations and valedictions in the Rocker-Ishill letters display an Old World formality: "Dear Mr. Rocker," "Sincerely, Joseph Ishill." Over time these "gestures of self-definition" become more informal and affectionate: by the 1950s, they signed their letters, "Always your old friend and comrade, Rudolf," and "Your devoted friend, Joseph."[87] A similar process emerges across the two decades of correspondence among Johnson, Tucker, and Inglis. Full first and last names give way to "Dear Agnes," "Love, Pearl," and "Lovingly, Bertha." These rituals of opening and closing help to "make sense of the span" covered by the exchange as a whole.[88] Altman suggests that the "individual sign-off" helps us to decode the dynamics that enable the correspondence to emerge: "To ask how narrative ends is to ask what makes it proceed; a close look at the dynamics of epistolary closure should reveal many of the forces that generate letter narrative in the first place."[89] Unlike memoirs or essays, in which the addressee could be anyone, anywhere, letters invite writers to "map [their] coordinates—temporal, spatial, emotional, intellectual"—in relation to the recipient of the message.[90] Salutations and valedictions are the places where writers greet their correspondents and bid them farewell. I speculate that the increasing intimacy of these correspondents, their emergent love (and willingness to express that love) for one another, was both productive of and haunted by their love of anarchism. The rise of fascism, the immense losses of two world wars, and the suffocating repression of the Cold War were devastating blows to the anarchist movement. All of these correspondents were from the older generation, born in the nineteenth century. They believed that they were watching their movement die as they felt their own deaths approaching. They both expressed and displaced their hopes for political change within their regard for one another.

There is a "desire for exchange" that is an implicit grounds for what Altman calls "the epistolary pact": each letter invites a response (or, in the case of a break in a relationship, discourages a response) from a specific reader.[91] Agnes's letters often begin, "Let's have a visit! Where shall we begin?"[92] She had the ability to conjure people into an exchange by her detailed and enthusiastic mode of address. While most writing hopes for an audience, letters are founded on the double expectation that there will be an audience and that the audience will become the writer: "Such reciprocality whereby the original *you* becomes the *I* of a new utterance is essential to the maintenance of the epistolary exchange."[93] Altman aptly calls epistolary discourse "a reversible medium" because "the *you* of any *I-you* statement can, and is expected to, become the *I* of a new text."[94] Since a new response may be coming, as Tamboukou explains, the reader has a prominent role in each writing:

> The epistolary experience is thus a reciprocal one: through the epistolary act, the reader is actively invited to contribute to the story by responding to it, but since they can always get a new response from their addressee, correspondence as a relation is inherently open. In this light, the epistolary story is always, already incomplete and this openness is its sine-qua-non condition and not a defect, in the Aristotelian narrative configuration of beginning-middle-end. If epistolary stories are always relational, then the subject positions that their characters can occupy either as readers, or writers, or both, are always, already relational as well as vulnerable and therefore political in the Arendtian sense: they depend on each other for their mere survival and they exist through their immersion in the epistolary relationship and from it into the web of human relations.[95]

Agnes excelled at reversibility, at writing in a way that elicited response, both because she was genuinely interested in her correspondents' lives and because so many of them shared her enthusiasm for the work of anarchist remembering. The laconic printer and editor Thomas Keell found himself responding to Agnes's inquiries about the history of *Freedom*, telling her about his work over the years as compositor, business manager, and editor. He ended with, "I have not written such a long letter as this for months, but you seemed to be interested in *Freedom*."[96] Not surprisingly, Keell told his companion, Lilian Wolfe, that he felt as if he knew Agnes, even though they had never met.[97] Agnes succeeded at the task at which, Altman argues, all letter writers strive: to make the missing recipient present by the act of writing. Letters mark an absence, but they create a presence. Stanley observes that letters

> involve a simulacrum of presence by "standing for" or conjuring up the writer: their characteristic phrases or mistakes, their hand having folded the paper and sealed the envelope, or their coffee stains marking the page, all referentially signal "that person." A letter exists because of the absence of the writer and the distance (literal or figurative) between them and the addressee; but the materiality and meaning of letters also conjure up something of the being of the writer. And in doing so, letters have similar effects concerning the relation itself. Indeed they often do so in ways that are more than symbolic (by being an exchange between them) or descriptive (by evoking times and places shared), because correspondents also often incorporate words and phrases in letters sent to them with their replies.[98]

Agnes was aware that her letters could overwhelm recipients. She often gave people permission not to answer, even while reminding them that her letters were both personal "visits" and invitations to contribute to the Labadie Collection. To Roger Baldwin, cofounder (with Crystal Eastman) of the American Civil Liberties Union, Agnes wrote,

> Have you time to peruse a letter? My letters are sort of impositions for they are likely to be real visits once I start. The one redeeming feature about them is they don't come often. I usually plan and think about them for a long time: then the mood comes and off I go! But I am not going to ask for any money or for any thing [*sic*]. I ask for one thing! Literature for the Labadie Collection.
> …Do not answer this, please. It requires no answer and I'd rather feel free to write it—wanting to—and not have any answer at all. One should be free to write. I would like it so much better to be free to write and not to be expected to answer. Then when necessary to have an answer one can get one.[99]

To the elderly printer Max Metzkow, who had been a compositor on *Freiheit* in 1888 and had known many of the leading English and US anarchists, Agnes wrote, "If you do not feel like answering this, it will be all right, but I want you to know you are recorded and will not be forgotten by the future generations who study the movement."[100] Metzkow did sometimes complain that he was too tired to write, that Agnes's enthusiasm wore him out: in one irascible and bemused letter, he pleaded with her, "Dear Friend Agnes: Do not think so much at me!"[101] Yet in the end her determined search for anarchism's rank-and-file activists did him, and the movement, a lot of good: "I always thought that my life here has been very dull," Metzkow wrote to Agnes, "but now my remembrance tells me that this is not quite true."[102]

Agnes may have met her match, epistolarily, in Bertha, who reflected on her own process of writing to Agnes as a kind of neighborliness: "It is fun to write to you, because I have no sense of obligation about it, I can write informally, a scrap or a long letter, just as I would run in at the back door of a friend's house, wearing my apron."[103] Bertha valued spontaneity, even while she respected the greater discipline she saw when she compared herself with her sister Pearl: "I can sit down in a railroad station or on a stump in the woods and write a letter. Pearl must have proper conditions. But she would never leave a room unswept or undusted to read a story or write a letter, and I am likely to."[104] Even though Bertha and Agnes had not yet met face-to-face at the date of this exchange, their letters imagine an intimate presence: "If you should drop in this morning I would take you out nutting! If you wanted to go. And if it were cloudy and cold, I would drag down from the attic an old steamer trunk full of pictures, and perhaps you would want some for the collection."[105]

Anarchists writing frequently to their comrades, often over a span of years or decades, were doing more than bringing each individual into their here and now: they were making the anarchist movement present as well. Small wonder that visitors to the Labadie Collection often experienced a sense of displacement, as though they had left the University of Michigan and entered an anarchist world. In an October 3, 1934, letter to Baldwin, Agnes reminded him of his experience reading a letter from the respected poet and writer Voltairine de Cleyre: "And you forgot the world while reading it.... You got the spirit of the Labadie Collection by that."[106] Diva Agostinelli, one of the young anarchists involved with the new journal *Why?* after World War II, wrote to Agnes about finding the collection: "Truly, I felt like someone who has reached an oasis after a trial in a desert. Too many of our libraries, schools and other 'scholarly' institutions are so barren of spirit and awareness of the contribution of the radical thinkers in our social progress."[107] Agostinelli was one of many who craved access to anarchist histories that the Labadie Collection could materialize.

At the same time, epistolary doubleness can separate as well as connect: it is both a bridge and a barrier. As a chain of communication, letters as connectors can emphasize either the distance or the intimacy, the gulf or the power to span it. Letters decrease the distance between writers and readers by crossing it, but they increase it by calling attention to it. They are halfway points that "straddle the gulf between presence and absence" and can move correspondents toward intimacy or indifference, toward transparency or opacity. They can provide, Altman writes, "a portrait or a mask."[108] For example, over time, Agnes withdrew somewhat from her relationship with Goldman. While she continued to share Goldman's politics and admire her contribution to the anarchist movement, she tired of the demands Goldman placed on her friends. Just as Agnes gave others permission to decline to answer her letters, she gave herself permission to withdraw from Goldman's orbit. There was no dramatic break—they continued their correspondence, and Goldman visited the Labadie Collection when she returned to the United States in 1934 on her ninety-day lecture tour—but Agnes gradually came to use her letters to create a bit of distance. She wrote to Baldwin, "Great souls enriched my life. But egos go by the board with me now. I've been fed up by them. I'd rather eat an apple sitting on a stone in the sunshine all by myself, then [sic] have to strain to serve the 'ideal' thru the egos. I feel a good deal like the bishops in 'Joan of Arc' when she asked if she should come back to life again and they said 'Oh, no!' It was easier to put up a table to her memory."[109] Agnes's droll sense of humor created some space between herself and the movement's great heroine: no dramatic break, but a small epistolary side step, constructing more of a barrier, less of a bridge.

While letters are usually between two participants, they nonetheless disturb binary arrangements in some ways. They are similar to a conversation, but neither party can interrupt the other and both must wait to hear the rejoinder they seek. There is certainly interpersonal labor in letters, but there is no immediate "face-work" and it is much easier to simply refrain from answering. Letters are more fixed than spoken utterances, and thus they take a different kind of work to deny or revise.[110] Agnes often enhanced the letter she was writing at the moment by telling the recipient about other letters written recently to other individuals or sending material for comment, so that something like a three-way conversation became possible.

Correspondence is often difficult for researchers to decode because letter writers tend not to include material that is not needed. That is, they don't describe people or places already well known to the participants, unless it is to notify the recipient of a change; they don't recount shared histories unless it is to retell them. This means there is a lot that the external readers don't get, because we weren't in on the correspondents' situations from the get-go. It also means that if the editor or compiler "finishes" them too much, by filling in missing information, we can undermine the ongoingness and lack of closure inherent in the genre.[111] Allowing the openness of letters to stay active is an important aspect of letting epistolary subjectivities move. The specific *I* within a chain of correspondence is not necessarily a stable subject: different *I*'s can emerge with different *you*s. We are always outside ourselves in letters because epistolary texts are always already explicitly in conversation with other texts. Tamboukou offers this colorful observation: "Each letter becomes a graph of the wandering self, and a part of the wider cartography of the correspondence and its epistolary figures."[112] Voices can move into greater or lesser prominence: Altman points out, "It is not necessarily the voice that pronounces 'I' who captures our attention."[113] In the thirty years of letters from Rudolf Rocker to Joseph Ishill, Rudolf's repeated references to Joseph's sorrow and desperation regarding Rose's illnesses are poignant examples of what Altman calls "*you*-oriented letters"; they plummeted me, the external reader, into Joseph's life long before I read Joseph's own words.[114]

The External Reader in the Archive

Altman brings in the concept of the external reader to theorize the position of those who join the conversation after it appears to be complete. While the internal reader is the addressee of letters, Altman defines the external reader as "we, the general public, who read the work as a finished product and have no effect on the writing of individual letters."[115] In my project, I am the external reader of the anarchists' letters, while you are the external reader of what Stanley calls the "ur-letters" produced by my interventions as interpreter.[116] Altman aptly describes the experience of the external reader as "very much like reading over the shoulder of another character whose readings—and misreadings—must enter into our experience of the work."[117] So external readers are active participants in the epistolary process. They read, implicitly, from at least three points of view: those of the writer, the intended recipient, and themselves. External readers are the audience who remembers, who negotiates the story's possible meanings and thus extends the story by attending to its narrative trajectories.

What does the external reader actually do in the archive? Tamboukou's analysis of the relations among external readers, internal readers, and writers is methodologically insightful. In *Sewing, Fighting and Writing*, she enters insofar as possible into the lifeworlds of French seamstresses in nineteenth-century Paris, imagines their struggles, and recalls comparable political circumstances from her experiences in the feminist movement more than a century later. She dwells in the correspondence, holds on to the words that capture her even if she doesn't know quite why at the time: something inchoate is happening, and with patience it may "open up vistas in the reader's imagination, which would later become an element in her grasped unity of prehensions."[118] Including the external reader in archival assemblages as an active node theorizes our participation as constitutive as well as receptive.

External readers often describe archival "finds" as serendipitous, as happy accidents, and my experience suggests that is how they feel. However, Tamboukou rightly asks, what enables serendipity to emerge? What makes this particular passage, this scribbled note, this souvenir, a "find"? She suggests there are "trails of narrative sensibility" where "memory and imagination are brought together in the study and understanding of documents." She is looking at the "process through which both the reader and the story emerge, as intra-actively constituted within the boundaries of the 'narrative phenomenon.'" It is in the entanglement of the reader and the documents that the philosopher Alfred North Whitehead's notion of prehension can emerge, a grasping enabled by certain conditions of possibility, not predictable and not reliably on call, but not random either. We "feel narratives," Tamboukou urges. "We are drawn to certain storylines, topics, characters or themes and not to others." The emotional economy of the archive offers "an uncanny feeling of dizziness or frenziness when you feel you have prehended something in your 'data,' which makes you forget your world and its concerns, whether around or far away from you." From moments of episodic insight, Tamboukou reconstructs a "process of remembering/ imagining" that initiates for the external reader a new research story about to unfold. Archives, Tamboukou says, should be seen as events, emergent moments in processes of becoming, "and the analytical interest should shift from structure to process and narrative force" or, following Whitehead, "narrative energy."[119] Media theorist Kate Eichhorn similarly characterizes archives' narrative becoming as "their remarkable ability to be in time differently—to recognize the past as a way to reinvigorate a beleaguered present and to recognize the future as always already implicated by the pull of the past."[120] As Wingrove found in her study of prison letters in the ancien régime, the texts at hand can mutate in terms of the reading practices they invite or sustain. There is a temporality to archival work, and while "there was not enough time for ruminations while still in the reading room," some elements stand out and clamor for attention.[121]

Returning to my earlier examples of unexpectedly intense anger expressed in letters by Agnes Inglis, Pearl Johnson Tucker, and Lilian Wolfe, what caught my eye, as I reread my notes at a later date, was not the substance of their complaints but the "vibe" in their expression. I had originally made note of these three incidents without any reason that I could articulate— not a great breakthrough but more like, "Huh…What's that about?" Each event lent itself to reframing. In past letters Bertha described her neighbor Chaapel as exasperating and contrary (as well as generous and engaged with the movement). Given Bertha's account of Chaapel as loving but a bit flakey, Pearl had some reason to question the story of Ishill's alleged theft of her books, at least to give him the benefit of the doubt in light of their long family friendship. Aldred's churlishness was legendary, a flaw that might have made Agnes question why she corresponded with him in the first place. Oscar Swede's brother Dorian does not appear to have been active in the anarchist movement—"We are not in touch with Dorian at all," Lilian wrote to Agnes—so he may not have had any idea of the significance of his brother's library in the eyes of his comrades.[122] These "hot spots" clamor for my attention because behind their everydayness is an urgency that seems out of proportion to the events.[123] The incidents seem initially to be unrelated, yet their combined weight issues a kind of invitation: following Tamboukou, they suggest a "narrative sense" that "emerges as an effect of the exploration and indeed juxtaposition of wider collections of letters and bodies of correspondence."[124] I was able to make better sense of them—that is, to bring them to a level of intelligibility that otherwise eluded me—as I reflected on the central importance of letters and publications in anarchist assemblages.

Personal libraries, like presses, were passed down from radical to radical; they came with their histories, which were also histories of the movement. Belle Chaapel inherited her library from her father, the spiritualist and reformer Jay Chaapel.[125] Bertha inherited her library of 1,200 books and trunks of papers and photographs from nineteenth-century sex radicals and labor reformers

Flora and Josephine Tilton, and also from Belle, who at her death left her collection to Bertha.[126] Pearl's library had been Benjamin's. These women kept their materials in their homes. Bertha and Emery Andrews made a library in an old pantry, which Bertha described to Agnes as decorated "with a steel engraving of Thomas Paine, (made by an old Boston radical, and coming to me from Josephine Tilton through Mrs. Denton's hands) as its presiding genius, or patron saint."[127] Bertha reported to Agnes on the pleasure she and Emery got from organizing material for the Labadie Collection: "Since we got our filing cabinet Emery and I have been busy sorting and filing. It is marvelous what a space, 24 inches high, 13 inches wide and 26 inches deep, can absorb, and make order out of chaos. I have looked over such piles of old papers, clipped for you and us, and Pearl, and disposed of useless parts. You will see by some of the dates on your next bundle of 'clips' that it is an aging pile of papers."[128]

Bertha's work in her personal library, reading, organizing, and sharing the material, was a kind of apprenticeship as an archivist. Many of her letters contain an inventory of the books, clippings, photographs, and correspondence that she is sending. Pearl too worked extensively on her collection. Agnes wrote about Pearl's work to French anarchist E. Armand: "She saved the Library but parted with much in the way of extra material and duplicates, and for this reason the Labadie Collection has been deeply enriched. It is deeply enriched both by the literature and also by many notes made by Mrs. Tucker in her correspondence with me. Her notes are the work of a scholar, a most painstaking and accurate scholar."[129] The women's emotional investments in the literature often show in their letters: remembering the destruction of the warehouse by fire four decades earlier, Pearl wrote Agnes, "I still grieve over that trunk of Spooner manuscripts burned in 1908."[130] She wrote, "I am ever grateful to you, Agnes, for the fine work you are doing to keep live the work of those who have gone before and making it possible to revive all pertaining to them for future students."[131] All of the women stressed the importance of retaining the contributions of the less well-known participants in the movement. Agnes wrote to Belle Chaapel, "I get a big satisfaction out of my work, in keeping alive the memory of people who did things but who did not get the credit. It's lovely to secure for them a place in history."[132]

Lilian also was intimately involved with the literature she oversaw. During part of her time in London, she literally lived in the *Freedom* library. She wrote to Agnes about how she spent her Sundays:

I spend the morning here cleaning the shop, office, and library (which is also my room—just a camouflaged bed in it) cook my lunch, eat it (vegetarian of course) then dash along to Hyde Park to sell papers and literature. Back again for a spot of tea and then off to the evening lecture where I am in charge of the literature. Yes—our program is not easy to attain, but I'm convinced it's the real thing and I can't see any sense in working for anything less. Especially as there are so many willing to work for half measures—someone must keep the flag flying for the whole thing.[133]

"Keep[ing] the flag flying for the whole thing" was a process that immersed these women in the printed material of their movement. "The whole thing" could mean both the full vision of an anarchist society and the full range of the movement's work. Libraries and letters melded personal loyalties with political allegiances, constituting as well as reflecting the filaments that Bertha described as running through anarchist assemblages. The offenses (allegedly) given by Ishill, Aldred, and Dorian Swede were greater than any ordinary theft, misrepresentation, or carelessness would have been because the currency of the anarchist movement itself was eroded.[134]

There is undecidability built into the sort of scholarly hunch that I am following here. Scholars of epistolarity caution against attributing too much coherence to a set of letters: bodies of correspondence possess no necessary beginning-middle-end pattern; they offer no pure window to reality; they are by definition unfinished. I could be overinterpreting these incidents that rise up to my attention through the gaps and stutters, willing a truth to arise out of unconnected moments that might reflect no real pattern or be better made comprehensible through some other account. Yet it is precisely such a bringing together of otherwise dispersed bits and pieces into a new alignment that the external reader can offer. "When brought together," Tamboukou suggests, "these fragmented narratives create a milieu of communication where the silenced, the secret and the unsaid release forces that remind us of the limits of human communication, the inability of language and representation to be brought together."[135] In Tamboukou's remarkable analysis of the letters and publications of nineteenth-century French socialist feminists, she models an approach that veers away from the older practice of simply mining letters for data; instead, she urges readers to think about exactly what we are doing when we take letters in their larger context, make connections among letters and collections of letters, and consider problems of their production (including translation and preservation). She encourages readers to avoid reducing letters to tag lines for other purposes, to keep the exchange open by imagining missing letters, and to keep looking for more letters. Aptly quoting Whitehead— "We think in generalities, but we live in detail"—her work seeks the terrain offered by the details and patterns arising from letters in order to make lively generalizations possible.[136]

One of the reasons that women's contributions to the anarchist movement have been underdocumented is that the labor of collecting material and making archives, which has often been done by women, has not been fully counted as political. Sophie Kropotkin assembled the Kropotkin Museum in the newly formed Soviet Union, and Annie Adama Van Scheltema was the first curator at the IISH in Amsterdam.[137] Sophie Labadie, wife of Jo Labadie, carefully saved all of Jo's publications, correspondence, and ephemera to provide the raw material for the initial Labadie Collection. Agnes regularly recognized Sophie Labadie's otherwise unknown work. In a letter of February 22, 1931, Goldman thanked Agnes for that recognition: "I am so glad of what you wrote me about Mrs. Labadie. Nobody ever heard anything about her in the past. In fact we were led to believe that she was rigidly Catholic, opposed to Joe's [sic] friends and his ideas. Fancy her having kept and collected every scrap of historic data and having taken such loving care of it. It is wonderful. Will you remember me to her and tell her posterity will be grateful to her memory for having done such a devoted labor of love?"[138] The point is not just, as the old saying goes, "Behind every successful man stands a strong woman," although that is probably true too. The point is that Sophie was not just "behind" Jo, or Milly "behind" Rudolf, or Rose "behind" Joseph. (Although it does prompt us to ask, is someone "behind" Agnes?) The point is that partnership and comradery can be co-creative and can take many forms. Sophie Labadie was a partner in the archival process through her determined preservation of the materials written, printed, or collected by Jo, as was Sophie Kropotkin in the grand public life of her famous husband. Accumulating and caring for the materials extended the movement's scope, anticipated its shared legacy, and instantiated porous boundaries among participants.

Historically, library work is feminized and thus discounted. As McKinney notes about information activism several generations after these women, it is seen as "gentle work," appropriate for the weaker sex, with their nimble fingers, patient dispositions, and high tolerance for tedium.[139] This sexist reading of archivists and librarians both demeans women and undermines a full accounting of the life of political movements. Assembling, organizing, and sharing a library is not a simple clerical task: it is an active and demanding process of stewardship. Agnes had evidently encountered attitudes devaluing her work, as she wrote rather indignantly to Goldman in 1925, "It's no joke to take all that mass of material and fix it up so students can really use it. It is not a work everyone can do. One has to know the material. People don't appreciate that."[140] These women do more than just preserve the material: they interact with it, bring it to usable order for others, make it theirs so that it can be ours. Agnes came to understand that her work was political; she wrote to Keell, "I had to just think that my work here in the collection was my work for the movement and had to take the place of what I couldn't do."[141] Acquiring, comprehending, and mapping a movement's literature and making it available for future study is not only a record *of* the movement; it is participation *in* the movement.

Tamboukou encourages "epistolary sensibility" that respects letters' necessary incompleteness, the circumstances of their production, and the larger communicative context. This sensibility includes the physicality of the materials and the setting as well. The materiality of letters peeks out in the archive. The surface of a page can arrive creased, stained, or torn; clean or marked by the rusted remains of an old paperclip; durable, flimsy, or near to shattering. Handwriting, like coffee stains on the page or characteristic oddities of punctuation or grammar, comes to invoke "that person" who is being called into presence but will never fully arrive. The difference between typed and handwritten material can make or break the external reader, especially if they are reading many different people's writing in succession. Bertha, thankfully, usually typed her letters, but her preferred mode of writing letters was interrupted in 1941 when her typewriter broke. There was little money available in the household even for necessities, so she wrote her letters by hand for four years. In 1945 her friend Adeline Champney, an anarchist writer in Cleveland, sent Bertha "a portable noiseless Underwood, in fine condition."[142] Bertha went back immediately to typing her letters. I imagine the new typewriter made her archiving work more efficient. As an external reader, I breathed a sigh of relief in returning to typescript, yet there was a further vague presence in that small shift, something more than just my or Bertha's convenience. For people who struggled to make ends meet, a typewriter was a major gift, possibly an act of recognition of Bertha's work for the anarchist movement. The smooth readability of Bertha's typed letters took on a new valence as I imagined the personal and political relationships that may have enabled and been enabled by that act of generosity.[143]

Meaning and Matter

There is a characteristic materiality to Agnes's correspondence: she nearly always made carbon copies of her lengthy typed letters, providing the Labadie Collection with a convenient record of her labors. Carbons have a characteristic look, feel, and smell. Novelist Andrew O'Hagan characterizes them as "old and sweet."[144] Agnes often added a handwritten note on the page to clarify and personalize the record. She made little distinction between letters as personal missives and as professional communication, so her records for the collection and her memories for herself come to the external reader in the reading room as one long, intertwined trail.

Rudolf Rocker also sometimes personalized his records. For example, in the margins of his copy of Keell's obituary in *Spain and the World* in 1938, Rocker wrote that Keell and Harry Kelly were "two of the most practical interpreters of libertarian ideals." Rocker counted Keell a friend; he was grateful for his "friendly care, advice and assistance" and was happy to meet him again in Paris in 1930.[145] Rocker could have been reminding himself in these handwritten notes of his connection with Keell, in light of attacks on Keell during the schisms within the Freedom group during and after World War I. Rocker's handwriting on the newsprint, scribbled in pencil in the narrow margins of the text, brought him to presence for me in the reading room. The text in my hand, bearing the mark of his hand over eighty years ago, shifted in a subtle way. We had read the same obituary, but it was not the same at all: I read it seeking to learn about Keell the famous printer, while Rocker read through his grief at the loss of his friend.

In addition to the materiality of the page, there is meaning to be found or made in the geography of the archive. Again drawing on Whitehead, Tamboukou suggests that the physical location of the archived material in relation to its subject matter can matter. As she says, "Spatial relationships ingress in our modes of knowledge and experience, but we are not always consciously aware of such activities."[146] Tamboukou was working in archives in France, close to the place where the nineteenth-century seamstresses were active and the first feminist publication was created. I was working primarily at three institutions: Harvard, the University of Michigan, and the IISH, and each has its own spatial relationships to its holdings. At Harvard, I worked in the midst of Ishill's legacy: surrounded by forty-three boxes of correspondence, manuscripts, and photographs that Ishill cared enough about to keep, his family cared enough about to donate, and Harvard cared enough about to accept. The Harvard-ness of the archive seeps in: elegant marble stairs, high ceilings, and gracious weekly receptions for visiting scholars echoed Ishill's pride that libraries, especially university libraries, housed his books. He was cognizant that his legacy would be primarily in libraries and very aware that prestigious institutions might well reject his work. Wondering where to deposit the literary items he had collected, he wrote, "I find that most of the important libraries are quite reactionary, especially when there is a question of acquiring some *real* libertarian literature for their libraries."[147] Yet sometimes it can be made to happen: notifying Rudolf in a letter of April 24, 1953, that he had printed Rudolf's essay on the poet and writer Henrich Heine, Joseph wrote, "This literary gem is now part of my humble collection which will someday be deposited with some important University library, either here or abroad."[148] Writing to his trusted friend, he let down his guard against self-pride and boasted that copies of his magnificent bibliography of the Oriole Press would be given to libraries around the world "so that other nations can see the record of my typographical work."[149]

Yet that was not his only reason. Both the scholarship and the politics of the future would be served: "Imagine for a moment what this means when throughout all important libraries and universities, librarians and readers will meet their eyes with names like the Reclus Brothers, Peter Kropotkin, Emma Goldman, Dywer [*sic*] D. Lum, and so many others. It is going to remain a permanent mark in the history of private presses in America and incidentally, some libraries will start on a new hunting for copies of this press."[150] The work of these anarchists in writing, printing, circulating, and collecting the movement's literary history worked as a kind of political "voucher" to the anarchist movement, in Laura Hughes's clever term, "a promise for future goods to be redeemed."[151]

Unfortunately, while bibliographers and scholars of fine print had been contacting Ishill about his work, the anarchist media ignored the exhibit of Ishill's printing at Rutgers: "Our *own* press, little as it is passed my first exhibit in silence! I do not know why they have taken such an attitude toward me. But I don't care. Nevertheless, I was glad that my *libertarian* work was after all presented in a *state* library and appreciated, even when some of the works displayed were decidedly against their ethics and principles."[152] When fellow anarchists withheld recognition of the successful exhibits of his work at universities and public libraries, events that had a high profile in the world of professional librarians, book collectors, and printers, Ishill clearly *did* care. He was discouraged because he wanted his comrades to recognize this aspect of his work for anarchism. Anarchists often judge each other harshly when the establishment offers recognition: there was much criticism of English art critic Herbert Read for accepting a knighthood, for example. (Admittedly, being knighted by the Queen probably entailed more of a compromise with anarchist principles than being recognized for fine printing by Rutgers or Columbia.) But for Ishill, public recognition was not an act of selling out; it was, rather, inviting in. He was pleased that libraries took his books because the visitors to those libraries could read great anarchist literature presented with artistry and love.[153]

At the IISH, visitors are surrounded by the institutionalized memory of the Left. The IISH mandate is to preserve "global labour history." Hundreds of radicals, including Goldman, passed through Amsterdam in the years before World War II, donating their papers as they fled the fascists. The institute's first librarian, Annie Adama van Scheltema, smuggled Mikhail Bakunin's manuscripts out of Austria "just before the Nazis marched into Vienna."[154] There is a conference room named for the anarchist historian Max Nettlau. This independent scholarly institution, supported by state, corporate, and foundation monies, houses a remarkable accumulation of anarchist histories; they have survived being collected, hidden, dispersed, and re-collected; they are available to readers at no charge. Lunch in the IISH café, with its opportunities to meet staff and other researchers, is affordable, and free espresso is available all day.

The Labadie Collection at the University of Michigan is like the Ishill Papers at Harvard in that it is housed at a big American university, one small part of a much larger system of libraries. However, it is like the IISH in that it is devoted to maintaining the history of the Left as told by its participants (except there is no free espresso). The sunny and comfortable reading room on the sixth floor of Hatcher Library is adjacent to the old building where Inglis assembled her materials. If Labadie had not insisted that his literature be donated to the University of Michigan but instead given it to the University of Wisconsin or another institution expressing interest, then Inglis would not have been able to launch her incredible twenty-eight-year career as an anarchist librarian. She was able to show anarchism's own ongoing records to itself, establishing that it had not expired and was capable of resurgence. On any given day, she opened a letter and was greeted with a message, something like this: "Come here, look in this trunk, it's been in my attic." She went, she looked, she gathered, and she reported: "And in that trunk were things! They told a story!"[155] The stories of Inglis's finds become stories of anarchism's finds; her joys leak down to me, become mine as well.

These three institutions are intertwined for external readers of anarchism. The thirty-two boxes of materials in the initial Ishill collection at the Houghton Library at Harvard, plus nine boxes in the first supplementary collection and two boxes in the second, ironically contain almost no letters from Ishill. His own words are largely found in the IISH and the Labadie Collection. The Harvard correspondence is almost entirely from others, written to Ishill. This has the consequence of forcing the external reader at Harvard to get to know Ishill through the eyes of his correspondents. Reading Rudolf's heartfelt concern for Joseph and Rose's health in letter after letter, my own feeling of alarm grew. Rose was ill. Joseph's despair is palpable through repeated expressions of Rudolf and Milly's concern. Rudolf and Milly wrote their hope that Joseph felt better "after all these dreadful years of continual misery and moral depression."[156] Yet I have incomplete information: I don't have the bigger story that they got from occasional face-to-face visits, missing letters, and the larger network of their travel and correspondence. At one point Rudolf mentioned that Rose had "a lack of willpower" and urged Joseph to be strong for her.[157] When I read that Joseph was afraid to leave Rose alone, a cold chill ran through me.

A year later, in cubicle 13 of the IISH reading room, I read the other half of the correspondence. Throughout the 1940s and 1950s, Joseph's letters were filled with despair. Rose had several operations on her back and her eyes, with poor results. He referred to the surgeries that precipitated her blindness as "the great disaster."[158] She was often bedridden and hallucinating from drugs. The children had all grown up and moved away. Joseph was the full-time caregiver and housekeeper. They were isolated in their cottage. No one visited. They had huge medical bills. Joseph wrote, on February 14, 1949, that it had been three years since he'd written or "seen last the face of a loving comrade."[159] He managed to print a few items: an essay by Josiah Warren and a piece that Rocker wrote on Henrich Heine; but he still had more work he wanted to do, and he felt his age: "There are so many things I crave to give expression to before my day is over."[160] The exhibit of his work at Rutgers University was a success. He began work on his cherished bibliography of the Oriole Press, "an enduring memento of our past."[161]

The desperation in these letters is palpable. Reading them in sequence, one after another, shows patterns that the writer and the internal reader, who may go months or even years between letters, may not realize. Nearly every letter starts with an affirmation that Rose was getting better. Yet the accumulated weight of two decades of letters suggests that she was not getting better, that Joseph was trying to comfort either his friends or himself with these empty words. He too had physical injuries and illnesses, but always Rose's need was greater. Even when Rose did really feel better, well enough to visit their adult children, the burden of long-term caregiving was hard to shake: "It almost crushed me to a pulp," he cried out. "At times, I feel quite painful at the heart."[162]

In my IISH cubicle, turning to the letter from Joseph to Rudolf of January 12, 1956, I inadvertently violated the reading room rules by gasping loudly with disbelief. Rudolf was devastated by his cherished wife's death, and he wrote a tribute to her. He asked Joseph to print it. Joseph declined! He said it moved him to tears, "But right now my hands are tied with commercial work from which I extract my living expenses."[163] He also declined to translate it into English, saying his German wasn't good enough.[164] I imagine that I can feel the shock, bracketed by pity, that Rudolf must have felt when he received that letter. It is as though there were still an echo of the jolt of rejection in the aging paper and the familiar, precise handwriting. I am not sure whether I muttered aloud, "NO! This is RUDOLF!" but I certainly thought it, loudly. Perhaps Joseph also shocked himself, because by the end of the letter he was changing his mind: "I would like nevertheless to publish for you some memento in booklet form. Think it over and let me know what you would like me to do for you."[165] But this request is quite beside the point, since his friend had already asked for the thing he wanted. In the next letter in the archive, Joseph has fully changed his mind and was planning "an unpretentious but simple and dignified typographical expression so as to fit into the framework of her life."[166] Looking back, I initially wondered why Joseph didn't just throw away the January 12 letter, once he felt himself changing his mind. He could then have written a cleaner, more loving response to Rudolf's intense bereavement. Rudolf would never have had to feel the pain of Joseph's initial reluctance. But I think my impulse to "tidy up" the communication does a disservice to the epistolary relationship. Joseph came to his change of heart, I imagine, by working through his first impulse, seeing it on the page, and living for a time with the consequences. He did not just change his mind—he wrote himself to a different place.

A different kind of shock ambushed me in the Harvard collection. As an external reader at the middle table in the Houghton Library reading room, I keep turning the pages of Rudolf's letters to Joseph, absorbed in Rudolf's easy and elegant prose. I was drawn into the correspondence in both senses of that word—pulled *toward* it and made, sketched, outlined, or filled in *by* it. The dynamic relation of the "word-when-written" and the "word-when-read" sneaked up on me.[167] At first, the letter of August 6, 1957, seemed little different from those before. Rudolf encouraged Joseph to "bring out your essay on our good old Emma" (which Joseph subsequently published). Rudolf reported that Laurance Labadie, son of Jo Labadie, used to visit him, and sent Laurance's address in Pennsylvania. This was welcome news for me, since it illustrates the epistolary network among anarchist printers for which I was searching. Laurance is a somewhat comic figure in the history of anarchist letterpress printers, since he actually detested printing and wasn't very good at it. His letters are filled with self-deprecating accounts of failures and laments about his inability to match his father's legendary versatility with the press. Rudolf, Joseph, Bertha, and Agnes encouraged the boy, who was often floundering, while Laurance complained about his sorts, press, paper, ink, and the circumstances of printing. I spent several minutes enjoying the next file, which contained photographs, including a lovely sketch of Milly by her son Fermin. Then I picked up the file that appeared initially to be only the next file but turned out to be the last file. It contains a single item: Rudolf's obituary from the *New York Times* on September 11, 1958. This final signing off ambushed me; while I knew Rudolf died in the fall of 1958, I had just read a letter he wrote a few months earlier, and his solid epistolary presence gave me a false sense of ongoingness. I thought we had more time. The correspondence dropped abruptly into silence, as though a door had suddenly slammed shut, leaving me quietly weeping in the archive. As Joseph said, it is quite painful at the heart. I felt Rudolf's death and Joseph's grief as though it were new, as though it were raw, as though it were mine.

Reimagining Bertha and Agnes

Anarchist correspondents brought together "enlarged and enlarging constituencies" of anarchism.[168] Letters are not passive windows to convey messages between actors; the correspondence itself is a reaching, a grasping, and sometimes a losing of connectivities that made anarchism happen. Decades of correspondence do not simply record politics happening elsewhere; the correspondence and the larger epistolarium are part of the politics, part of the glue that held the movement together. Instead of thinking of people, fully formed, who then write letters, we see people becoming subjects within the practices of letter writing. The connections in the latticework of relations resonate among one another and produce conditions of possibility for radical politics.

As the external reader of the body of correspondence between Bertha Johnson and Agnes Inglis, I witnessed another decades-long friendship in which aging radicals, with unflagging political commitments but few material resources, helped and supported one another, largely through their exchange of letters. Yet immersion in the women's epistolary exchange is quite different from immersion in that of Joseph and Rudolf in the sense that there is no dramatic ending contained in the files, not really any ending at all. The letters just stop. The forward-looking orientation that MacArthur attributes to epistolary exchange turns out to be fragile: meaning cannot move toward future reception and response when the chain is broken. There is no final sign-off from Bertha in the archive.

When Bertha began writing to Agnes, she wrote that she could not find work in her chosen profession in the farm community in Pennsylvania where she and her husband, Emery Andrews, had moved. Bertha earned her medical degree from the New York Medical Hospital and College for Women in 1905.[169] She worked in a variety of professional positions overseeing children's health before moving to the dairy farm near Troy, Pennsylvania, in 1924. The farm was the childhood home and the inheritance of Emery. She was the only woman doctor in the area, she told Agnes, and the only woman "queer enough to retain [her] maiden name."[170] She kept up her medical license and paid her medical society dues, even when poverty forced them to give up most subscriptions and all luxuries, as she continued to seek employment.[171] She regularly disparaged the patriarchal attitudes that stood in the way of finding paid work: in one letter she muses on men who think women can't stand the strain of work though women do most of the actual labor, yet "they should not read or write or go to college or address public meetings!"[172] However, even though she volunteered her medical skills when possible, including a stint giving medical exams to the students at the local school, she could not find paid work as a physician.[173]

Without professional employment, she applied herself to the demanding labor of a farm wife while also doing all she could to care for others in their community. The work was hard: "canning fruits and vegetables, saving everything I can, not knowing who may need it next winter. I really like preparation of food, tho much housework does not appeal to me. Sorting and classifying, mending almost hopeless garments, and making something useful out of something useless or worthless arouses my pride in ingenuity, but sweeping and dusting are done only because I hate dirt."[174] She participated in an economy of rural sharing: "I cast my grapes and pears on the waters, and they come back as eggs and squash, and cabbage and tomatoes, etc. Dorothy's mother brought a dozen big eggs. I gave her grapes and pears and she frequently sends me eggs, too large or small or slightly cracked, but fresh."[175] She canned plums, pears, rhubarb, applesauce, carrots, and chard. Friends sent clothing and she found homes for what she and Emery could not use.

She and Emery lived in a sixty-year-old farmhouse on a 260-acre farm: "Our luxury is fine mountain air, our elevation being about 1600 feet, floods of sunshine, beautiful scenery, quiet and isolation."[176] They did not have electricity or modern conveniences until Pearl paid to have the house wired, indoor plumbing installed, and the roof repaired in 1939.[177] They lived on a dirt road with little traffic and looked out over a beautiful landscape: "As we got up and prepared for the day's doings Emery and I have watched a most beautiful sunrise, all the lovely colors, and as we look across the highest hill, it seemed almost like looking over the sea ... smooth and calm near shore, but distant billowy waves."[178]

Bertha held great affection for the farm's plants and flowers, while Emery paid more attention to the animals, tools, and machines. "In the winter," Bertha wrote, "my sunny living room is a regular flower garden which my more orderly neighbors would not bother with. But they are so cheery and I tend them as others do babies."[179] She sent Agnes a beautiful line drawing of her fuchsia plant, which she held up with horizontal strings. Her letters regularly shared the beauty she saw in her world: "A gorgeous crispy morning, a few fleecy clouds in the southern sky, but the northern sky blue as can be. And the varying colors on the hills make a lovely picture. Folks speak of winter as colorless, but they don't half see—browns, greens, gold, blue, rosy sunsets—midnight blue hills—all shades of tan and russet."[180]

The Great Depression was catastrophic for Bertha and Emery, as for many farmers and rural workers. Their survival strategies combined the possibilities of enterprising farm life with the mutual aid of anarchist politics: taking in boarders and "strays"; inviting people to build cabins on their land in exchange for work; trading food and board for labor; sharing bedding with those who couldn't afford coal; mending old clothes and giving them away; selling or trading canned fruits and jellies. The Depression was long and hard in the Pennsylvania countryside. It mercilessly framed their lives.[181]

As the Depression deepened, they feared losing their farm. The sense of anxiety in the letters grows. After the very hard winter of 1935–36, the bank threatened to foreclose on their farm; they sold their life insurance to pay the mortgage and the back taxes and to fix the roof. If Bertha had been able to find work as a doctor, things could have been different. Instead, the situation continued to worsen. They had to sell their herd of dairy cows for beef, which meant their major income was gone. They sold one horse; the other died. They sold Emery's beloved collection of farm machinery and tried for years to sell their farm. "So we just stay on, not knowing what to do, and having no money to do anything else."[182] The debilitating economic catastrophe, her hard personal labor, and her political vision of how people ought to be able to live are all interspersed in her letters with her attention to the natural beauty around her.[183]

While Bertha found joy in farm life, she was intellectually isolated. Her contact with Agnes was, as she said in an early letter, "like fresh waters to a thirsty soul."[184] After more formal greetings and sign-offs in earlier communications, her letters quickly evolve to "Dear Agnes" and "Lovingly, Bertha." In the midst of very hard times, she still found time to go over material that Agnes sent, to write her thoughts, and to continue to organize her own holdings.

Many letters begin with, "I am always so glad to get your letters," or "How often I wish you could be with me." Bertha had an acute memory, frequently helping Agnes identify activists for the collection. She periodically expressed her happiness that Agnes loved her work.[185] As in so many stories of aging radicals, with few resources to spare, they never stopped helping each other. They loved each other. All the letters, even those recounting bitter suffering, are affectionate and engaged. Letters often end, "Love to you always, Bertha."[186]

Eventually Emery and Bertha did sell their farm, some time before July 15, 1945, when Bertha mentioned it in a letter. Emery died on September 27, 1948, after a lengthy illness. Soon after, Bertha visited Agnes in Ann Arbor, and subsequent letters often end with fond remembrance of this visit.[187] She enjoyed finally having a mental picture of Agnes's life. She regularly expressed her gratitude for a full life, rich in memories.

There is no dramatic ending. The final letter in the collection from Bertha to Agnes is dated October 5, 1951, a few months before Agnes's death on January 30, 1952. I don't know what happened to Bertha after that. She died in 1958 in Ossining, New York, at the home of her friend, Beatrice Fetz. Of the five letter writers discussed here, her life was the least documented outside of these bodies of correspondence. Online searching locates a tombstone for Dr. Bertha F. Johnson, shared with her sister Pearl Tucker, in the Granville Center Cemetery in Bradford County, Pennsylvania.[188] In the absence of closure, I'm drawn back to Laura Hughes's characterization of archival time as having the capacity to dilate: "We could also describe research in the archive as the dilation of the present moment into which 'another time, another place'—or perhaps multiple times and places—can flow."[189] In this "dilation of the present moment," time opens up, creating, as Carolyn Dinshaw remarks, "a fuller, denser, more crowded *now*."[190] Temporalities can collide, and it can become unclear what is "forward" and what is "back." Hughes calls this the "expansive instant" of a multiple and dissonant archival present.[191]

In this "expansive instant," I imagine a different ending: Since she often said she wished she and Agnes could be together, why couldn't they? After Pearl and Emery both died in 1948, and Bertha visited Agnes in Ann Arbor, she could have stayed. She had already shown her adaptability by segueing from being a successful doctor to becoming a farm wife and the librarian of a private collection. She might have joined Agnes in her cozy Ann Arbor apartment, raising flowers in the living room and the garden. Both women had had cats in the past. Bertha's cat died when the farm was falling apart. Agnes's cat was, horrifically, bludgeoned to death by an unknown assailant. I imagine them adopting a couple of strays, stretching their modest table to feed two more mouths. Neither woman liked domestic labor, and they would have been happy to forgo sweeping and dusting to read another book or enjoy another lemonade on the front porch. They both could have enjoyed working in the garden. Bertha could have cultivated her cherished flowers and tied up another fuchsia plant with delicate strings. Agnes could have raised pumpkins as she did on the small farm she used to own, where she recounts killing bugs to "make the world safe for pumpkin pie and jack-o-lanterns."[192]

Bertha could have assisted Agnes in the Labadie Collection. Instead of one elderly, dignified, white-haired lady coming to work every day in Hatcher Library, there would have been two. Maybe after Agnes died in 1952, Bertha could have quietly continued; she had, after all, done something like an apprenticeship with Agnes for two decades. She knew the anarchist movement well. She had read widely in both the individualist side of anarchism, as represented by Benjamin Tucker's work, and the communist side, as in Rudolf Rocker's writings.[193] An imaginative library director might have seen the benefit of replacing one aging radical curator with another, to keep the library's connections with activist communities alive.

Bertha ended one letter by quoting a song for Agnes: "When I grow too old to dream, I'll have you to remember; when I grow too old to dream your love will live in my heart."[194] In my dilation of the flow of archival time, their love grows. I imagine them happy living together. They were both generous souls, modest in their needs, quick to share. Perhaps they would get on each other's nerves a bit. Agnes once described Bertha rather uncharitably as someone who "never stops talking," a flow of words that might have irritated Agnes, who had grown accustomed to solitude.[195] Yet Bertha's presence could have filled a deep longing in Agnes, who wrote in a poem entitled "Sunday April 28th 1928,"

> I am neither lonely or unlonely.
> I seem to be beloved and people smile glad-eyed when I come
> But no one loves me with a deep and needing love.[196]

Bertha could have needed her that way, loved her that way. Perhaps it is not a betrayal of epistolarity's mediated intimacy to wish they could have shared a home, a bed, a life.

Days of Futures Past

Many anarchists felt, after World War I, that their movement was dying. It was difficult to keep anarchism alive during the time of deportation, imprisonment, exile, fascist and Bolshevik brutality, economic catastrophe, and war. Rudolf Rocker wrote to James Dick, one of the Modern School teachers, "We have seen another time, a time full with hope and great expectations[;] in one word we lived in a time which is worth longing for, although we know that it belongs already to history."[197] Joseph Ishill wrote to Rudolf about their shared past: "Was all this a dream? Regretfully I must also say: Yes, it was a dream but worth while living for, if all else go to perdition."[198] They were not the only ones: Keell wrote to his friend Max Nettlau on June 2, 1938, "When I think of the dreams of socialists and anarchists thirty or forty years ago and the realities of the present day it seems to me that those who died then cherishing their dreams were the last of that happy race. Today, dreams are no longer possible."[199] Nettlau quoted from Keell's letter in his obituary of "the old compositor" in the July 15, 1938, issue of *Spain and the World*. The sadness in the journal's pages is tangible: grim headlines about the fall of Barcelona and the savage aerial bombing of market towns, stand next to Emma Goldman's obituary of Walter Starrett, her "pupil, comrade and friend," and Nettlau's farewell to "dear old comrade Keell of the Freedom Group."[200]

These political veterans thought they were seeing the end of anarchism, their comrades dying, their revolution dying. Yet, taking a longer view, they misread a temporary decline as a permanent defeat. They neither credited anarchism's continuing presence nor anticipated its return. First, anarchism was not dead. The two women who worked closely with young people, Agnes Inglis and Lilian Wolfe, were understandably more aware of continued anarchist activism. Lilian wrote to Agnes in 1946, "I enjoy life here with the young comrades very much."[201] Lilian noted that Agnes was similarly situated: "It must make life very interesting for you being in touch with so many earnest young Comrades and being able to help them in their researches."[202] Agnes elaborated to Pearl that the American movement was in decline, especially with the loss of the two major journals *Liberty* and *Mother Earth*, but it was not defunct.[203] She saw the US situation as uneven: the Russian and Italian groups, in her view, held together better than the Jewish and the nonimmigrant groups. British journalist Nicolas Walter offers a similar assessment of the anarchist movement in England: after World War I, the movement was "under constant and crippling pressure," but it was "full of energy even at the worst time, and no doubt more research on that period would unearth more evidence."[204]

Ishill, Rocker, Keell, and the others in mourning for anarchism might have taken heart from the work of younger activists and intellectuals. Lillian Kisliuk Dinowitzer ran a progressive nursery from the 1920s to the 1940s and wrote and organized for the movement until her death in 1969. Audrey Goodfriend and Dorothy Rogers created the journal *Why?* in 1942, later changing the name to *Resistance*. They were joined by Diva Agostinelli, David Wieck, printer Robert Bek-Gran, and others. Goodfriend and Dave Koven ran the Walden School in Berkeley. Sam and Esther Dolgoff founded the Libertarian League. Holley Cantine and Dorothy Paul started *Retort* in Woodstock, New York. Writer Paul Goodman, poet Kenneth Rexroth, Catholic anarchist Dorothy Day, environmental anarchist Murray Bookchin, and other political and literary figures aligned with anarchism. Around each of these figures, relationships formed, networks took shape, and anarchism's influence spread across the surface of things. Anarchism intermixed with radical pacifism, antiracism, and the Beat Generation. Out of those fertile encounters, the journal *Direct Action* emerged, as did the City Lights Bookstore, the Pacifica Radio Network, the Libertarian Press, and other organizations. In England, the London journal *War Commentary* morphed back into *Freedom* and brought in younger activists including Marie Louise Berneri, Vernon Richards, Philip Samson, Colin Ward, and Frances Solokov.[205] Alex Comfort and Herbert Read were leading philosophical figures. The older anarchists were too quick to equate their own generation of radicals, remarkable though they were, with the movement as a whole.[206]

Second, they were understandably unable to anticipate anarchism's big comeback in the 1960s and beyond. The view from the first vicenary of the twenty-first century looks quite different from perspectives available around World War II. The New Left of the 1960s and 1970s, the counterculture, feminist, civil rights, and environmental movements, all reflected substantial anarchist influence. Radical bookstores, cafés, schools, clinics, zines, blogs, puppet theaters, art collectives, publishers, and public gathering places exemplified anarchist resurgence. The extensive underground press of the 1960s could be seen as heir to the earlier anarchist print culture, including the Detroit Printing Co-op organized by Fredy and Lorraine Perlman and other activists; Dumont Press Graphix in Kitchener-Waterloo, Ontario; and the Appalachian Movement Press in West Virginia.[207] Hundreds of feminist newsletters, mostly produced by local collectives on mimeograph machines, connected the threads of the women's liberation movement.[208] Further, the counterglobalization movement, the Occupy movement, Indigenous protests and protections of Native land and water, and many other movements for social change have anarchist dimensions to them.

Reflecting on her lifetime of political struggle, civil rights activist Ella Baker said, "Somebody else carries on."[209] Voltairine de Cleyre wrote a similar, if more tart, message to her friend Alexander Berkman soon after he left prison in 1906: "You have brains enough to know that movements proceed even when people are not fizzing like soda water uncorked."[210] Agnes, Pearl, Lilian, and Bertha had a similar conviction that future scholars and activists would be coming. Someone will carry on. This was not blind faith on these women's parts but rather a reflection of their experiences within radical assemblages, where relationships are open-ended processes that invite new elements in. Agnes characterized the Labadie Collection as a place not just holding books but housing "vital, living people because of the material being of the nature it is."[211] The collection invited its visitors as well as its creators into its world.

This is not to say that Agnes was contented with the anarchist movement she saw around her. She looked at the US movement and found it especially wanting for a solid anarchist journal, something like *Freedom*, a publication that would "[let] all expressions be presented and discussed. I like best to have presentations—not as arguments, as we need above all things to learn wherein ideas agree and differ."[212] When Benjamin Tucker and Victor Yarros (an anarchist who had turned to social democracy) got into a heated dispute, Agnes saw a lost opportunity to bring anarchist ideas to a larger public: "I could only have wished that there had been an organ like Liberty so others could have read Yarros' article and Mr. Tucker's reply and then thrashed the matter out and revived all the ideas.... Brought to life the ideas—that, while one hates to admit it, are eclipsed in America."[213]

Meanwhile, the women anticipated new generations who would come. Reflecting her Presbyterian upbringing as well as her love of the collection, and her expectations for future radical politics, Agnes wrote a poem to the Labadie Collection:

TO THE LABADIE COLLECTION:

Gather, dust, and rays of sun-heat beat imperceptible, beat.

And let the unbound wrapped-up volumes of voices of dreamers and world builders keep their silence, and time will leisurely emerge out of space, out of events so measured.

Perhaps no dreamer, no builder of worlds will reincarnate you into his thoughts, his deeds: you may rest for long under the dust, wrapped up in brown paper and tied with string awaiting the judgement day.

But—one day—*that* day—young dreamers, young builders, will untie the strings and unwrap the volumes and they will cry out! They will say "My Brothers! My Sisters!" They will say, "You dreamers, you world-builders!" And they will peruse these old records of voices and they will repeat your words and speak your names.... As, in these volumes, your thoughts and the record of your acts lie in silence, the dawning spirit of the Revolution will sweep on.... It is sweeping on! And your thoughts and your acts—past tho they are—are not lost in it. And this, the record, will ever be beloved.

Signed Agnes Inglis, Summer of 1932, Ann Arbor Michigan[214]

As the scholars who are in the archives now, we can lend ourselves to the sparks currently flying. We can welcome, as Dinshaw counsels, "temporalities other than the narrowly sequential."[215] We may find or make not a resurrection but "another kind of afterlife," with no guaranteed destination but many possible routes.[216]

3

RADICAL STUDY

An unknown correspondent wrote of Joseph Ishill that, in addition to his work as a printer and a correspondent, he was also a "man of letters": "The type, his manner of placing the materials, the ornaments, paper, illustrations, the binding, in a word, all that contributes toward the realization of the beauty in a book, Ishill brings to perfection.... But it must not be believed that he is a simple printer, as he would make one believe modestly in his colophons. No, indeed, he is a cultured soul, a man of letter[s], who selects and comments upon the works and who is in close contact with the most famous writers."[1] The unnamed writer recognizes Ishill's proficiency with all three kinds of letters this book engages: his printing realizes "the beauty in a book," while his correspondence keeps him "in close contact with the most famous writers," and he himself is "a cultured soul, a man of letter[s]." Chapter 1 inquired into the work of Ishill and his comrades as printers, asking what role printers and presses played in the anarchist movement during its classical period from the Paris Commune to the Spanish Revolution. In that chapter I agree with the unidentified writer just quoted that Ishill was not a "simple printer," that in fact printing was not a simple task but rather a formative node in the creative relations of anarchist assemblages. Chapter 2 explores the epistolary practices of Ishill and his comrades, who were knit into expansive circuits of communication with both anarchism's famous writers and less known figures. In that chapter I ask how written correspondence operated within the anarchist movement to express and impress its participants.

This chapter takes up the third dimension of anarchist letters, invoked by the unidentified writer quoted to mark Ishill as a learned person, a person of letters. What does it mean to be an anarchist of letters? What were the characteristic textual practices that anarchists utilized or created, and how did those practices do the work of the anarchist movement?

The classical anarchist movement of the mid-nineteenth to mid-twentieth centuries is known today largely through the work of a handful of thinkers whose writings have remained in, or come back into, print: Peter Kropotkin, Mikhail Bakunin, Pierre-Joseph Proudhon, Max Stirner, Errico Malatesta, Rudolf Rocker, Leo Tolstoy, Élisée and Élie Reclus, Gustav Landauer, Benjamin Tucker, Alexander Berkman, Emma Goldman, Voltairine de Cleyre, Lucy Parsons, and a few others. Other anarchist writings often build on these classic works, commonly stating and restating shared principles of freedom, equality, and justice.

Yet the daily textual labor of the anarchist movement was done far more in the pages of the many hundreds of journals written and published by small local groups around the world than it was in books. At a few cents an issue, journals were more readily available than books. Journals were carried in reading rooms, bars, and cafés; they were shared by subscribers around kitchen tables, neighborhoods, and worksites. In his autobiography Peter Kropotkin, the grand old man of anarchism, challenges researchers to take up these sources because the movement's "small pamphlets and newspapers" reveal its world: "Socialistic literature has never been rich in books. It is written for workers for whom one penny is money, and its main force lies in its small pamphlets and its newspapers....There remains nothing but to take collections of papers and read them all through—the news as well as the leading articles—the former, perhaps, even more than the latter."[2] Historian Morris Brodie aptly summarizes the journals' practical purposes: "to expose the wider public to radical ideas; keep activists in different parts of the country (and, indeed, the wider world) in touch; update comrades with significant (particularly labour) news; and to raise support for various causes—ultimately, to build the movement. They provided a focal point for activity and a means of individual and collective self-expression, through both the editorial process and the submission of articles by activists."[3]

In addition to their greater affordability and their relevant content, the ongoing-ness of the papers was part of their force. Their periodicity brought back readers and collectors—"Here it is again"—and also brought back writers, editors, illustrators, printers, and distributors; regardless of what else was happening, including arrests of people and confiscations of presses, the paper must go on. Former editor of *Freedom* as well as the English journal *Anarchy*, Colin Ward, notes that the continuity is in and of itself important: "There is a value in simply being there. The continued existence of Freedom Press in one form or another, has meant that there has been a clearing house, a permanent address (or a series of them) which has acted as a centre for enquiries about the anarchist press and a permanent stock of anarchist literature."[4] Journals enact as well as articulate an implicit reach for an anarchist future.

This chapter looks for detectable patterns in the content and style of the publications. What were anarchists reading and writing in these journals? What kind of political and intellectual work did those texts do? Jacques Rancière reminds us that the task of accurately representing the subject matter at hand is only the beginning; words acquire their best power "by naming, by calling, by commanding, by intriguing, by seducing [so] that they slice into the naturalness of existences, set humans on their path, separate them and unite them into communities." How did anarchist texts set readers and writers "on their path," so that they could land, as Rancière suggests, "near where the meaning of what has been said must speak"?[5]

In the final chapter I will return to these writings with a different question: How do they contribute, or fail to contribute, to contemporary anarchist theory? It has often been noted that classical anarchism's primary grounding in European class and state analysis tended to push race and gender inquiry to the side.[6] Analyses of sex and gender varied in a predictable way: those journals with more women writers and editors brought stronger feminist direction to the publications. The anarchist journals examined here included relatively few contributions from people of color; analyses of race and racism were generally missing and the specifically racial dimensions of capitalist patriarchy were obscured.[7] In the next chapter I ask how this happened, how a political theory and movement that was so consistently dedicated to freedom and equality could be so inadequate in theorizing race.

In this chapter I look closely at three journals: *Freedom* in London; *Free Society* in San Francisco, Chicago, and (briefly) New York City; and *Mother Earth* in New York City. I am looking for the shared urgencies in the publications, the textual patterns that made anarchism cohere for readers. In this overview of their common elements, I do not venture detailed assessments about the relative strength of the publications or changes in their coverage over time. Ward rightly points out that journals that continue for a substantial period of time are bound to vary in quality, with high points emerging "when the personnel of the moment have been a well-matched team with qualities which complement each other."[8] My analysis provides a snapshot of their characteristic textual elements: What sort of political work did these writings do? How do they become, in Rancière's words, "seeds able to bear fruit"?[9]

Anarchist Worlds of Letters

The world of letters was highly regarded by anarchists, whom one historian refers to as "bookish poor people."[10] The anarchist world of letters was part of the nineteenth- and twentieth-century world of popular learning that Angela Ray and Paul Stob explore in *Thinking Together: Lecturing, Learning and Difference in the Long Nineteenth Century.* They explain, "Despite—or perhaps because of—their ambiguous relationships with established educational institutions, the people and groups who populate this ... [sphere] created their own places, spaces, and discourses for sharing ideas, better understanding themselves and their world, and critiquing the society that surrounded them."[11] While anarchist counterpublics were often under attack by authorities, making them not just another sphere but a beleaguered one, Ray and Stob's overview of the practices of popular learning is nonetheless accurate for the anarchists: "The practices of learning they adopted were consistent with their time but modified to respond to their own circumstances; they blended oral, scribal, and print production, as they debated, lectured, kept minutes of meetings, and wrote letters, diaries, essays, poems, stories, histories, town plans, and geographic texts."[12]

A few anarchists were credentialed professionals—Peter Kropotkin and Élisée Reclus were geographers; Élie Reclus was an ethnographer; Herbert Read was a philosopher and art historian; Max Nettlau earned a PhD in philology before turning to history; Marie Goldsmith and Patrick Geddes had PhDs in biology; Fernando Tarrida del Mármol was a mathematician; and a few others, often editors, were university trained—but most were talented amateurs, driven to learning through love and desire for a different sort of society. Taking anarchists seriously as people of letters requires rethinking conventional expectations regarding who can make knowledge. In her insightful discussion of multiple temporalities in medieval texts, Carolyn Dinshaw builds on the etymology of *amateur*, from the Latin *amare*, "to love": "Clearing space for such amateurs, hobbyists, and dabblers ... [can contribute] to a broad and heterogeneous knowledge collective that values various ways of knowing that are derived not only from positions of detachment but also ... from positions of affect and attachment, from desires to build another kind of world."[13] Like the medievalists Dinshaw studies, anarchists drew on "their affections, their intimacy with their materials, their desires" to create and share knowledge outside the approved realms of professional detachment.[14] They may have done their anarchism in the off-hours, as did Ishill and Jo Labadie, who made their livings as printers in commercial shops; or they may have made a modest living in the movement itself, as did Kropotkin and Rocker; or they may have received adequate resources from family and friends to support their political work, as did Ann Arbor librarian Agnes Inglis as well as Labadie in his later years. Many, like Emma Goldman, combined all three: Goldman worked as a dressmaker and a nurse-midwife in her youth and also supported herself through her lecture tours, her publications, and the patronage of benefactors. Regardless of how they paid the bills, the anarchists who lectured, taught, and organized the movement, as well as wrote, edited, printed, illustrated, translated, distributed, and read anarchist publications, operated vigorously outside professional "regimes of detachment."[15] Like Cait McKinney's "capable amateurs" constructing lesbian feminist archives in the 1970s, anarchists combined "a fearless approach to learning" with a "lack of professional baggage."[16] They freely mixed genres of writing and readily took on tasks such as printing, editing, and archiving that the professional world reserved for recognized experts. People who did the intellectual work of writing or editing for one journal sometimes did the manual labor of distribution for another. Like Dinshaw's medievalists, anarchists were carried into the world not by scientific *detachment* but by devoted *attachment* to the objects of their attention.[17] They are part of what social theorists Stefano Harney and Fred Moten call an "incredible history of study that goes on beyond the university."[18] Taking their contributions seriously broadens the possibilities within which legitimate knowing can happen.

Anarchists of letters participated in the break with the world of capitalist labor that Rancière explores in *Nights of Labor* and *The Philosopher and His Poor*, "a rupture in the traditional division [*partage*] assigning the privilege of thought to some and the tasks of production to others." Rancière continues, "The French workers who, in the nineteenth century, created newspapers or associations, wrote poems, or joined utopian groups, were claiming the status of fully speaking and thinking beings." Rancière finds in working-class archives not evidence of a separate class-based culture but "the transgressive will to appropriate the 'night' of poets and thinkers, to appropriate the language and culture of the other, to act as if intellectual equality were indeed real and effectual."[19]

Disturbances of "the visible and the sayable" that Rancière finds in the "part of those without part" include, adapting Harney and Moten's term, the workings of the anarchist undercommons.[20] In this world, capitalism, patriarchy, colonialism, and the state are not just wrong or harmful, they are unintelligible. Queer theorist Jack Halberstam explains,

> If you want to know what the undercommons wants, what Moten and Harney want, what black people, indigenous peoples, queers and poor people want, what we (the "we" who cohabit in the space of the under-commons) want, it is this—we cannot be satisfied with the recognition and acknowledgement generated by the very system that denies a) that anything was ever broken and b) that we deserved to be the broken part; so we refuse to ask for recognition and instead we want to take apart, dismantle, tear down the structure that, right now, limits our ability to find each other, to see beyond it and to access the places that we know lie outside its walls.[21]

Anarchism refuses the logic of hierarchy and domination, "not to end the troubles but to end the world that created those particular troubles as the ones that must be opposed."[22] Anarchism is not bound by the establishment's demand to have an agenda, to make policy demands, to "check IDs and give advice."[23] Anarchist sites give directions for finding our way to what Harney and Moten call "the fugitive public," where our debts to and with others become our credits, where mutual aid happens:

> The place of refuge is the place to which you can only owe more and more because there is no creditor, no payment possible. This refuge, this place of bad debt, is what we call the fugitive public. Running through the public and the private, the state and the economy, the fugitive public cannot be known by its bad debt but only by bad debtors. To creditors it is just a place where something is wrong, though that something wrong—the invaluable thing, the thing that has no value—is desired. Creditors seek to demolish that place, that project, in order to save the ones who live there from themselves and their lives.[24]

Harney and Moten reverse the poles of credit and debt in order to explode them: they urge us to run from capitalist credit, because it marks our subordination to "universal exchange on the grounds of capitalism": "The hospital talks to the prison which talks to the university which talks to the NGO which talks to the corporation through governance, and not just to each other but about each other. Everybody knows everything about our biopolitics. This is the perfection of democracy under the general equivalent. It is also the annunciation of governance as the realisation of universal exchange on the grounds of capitalism." It is debt, in the reversed polarities of the undercommons, that can be good because it is social. Debt is lodged in our relationships of giving and being given to. It is what anarchists call mutual aid, and it is already here: "The new thing...already lives around and below."25

It is ironic that anarchists are regularly caricatured as lacking the capacity to get anything done, when in fact their enthusiastic amateurism, expressed through self-organization and mutual aid, has resulted in the creation of hundreds of journals, schools, unions, food and housing cooperatives, theaters, bookstores, and independent communities. The stale bromide that anarchism is great in theory but would never work in practice actually has it backward: the theory needs some work, a task this book addresses, but anarchism in practice has been remarkably successful in prefiguring the world it seeks, a world for the part that has no part, for the undercommons:

> Once you start to see bad debt, you start to see it everywhere, hear it everywhere, feel it everywhere. This is the real crisis for credit, its real crisis of accumulation. Now debt begins to accumulate without it. That's what makes it so bad. We saw it in a step yesterday, some hips, a smile, the way a hand moved. We heard it in a break, a cut, a lilt, the way the words leapt. We felt it in the way someone saves the best stuff just to give it to you and then it's gone, given, a debt. They don't want nothing. You have got to accept it, you have got to accept that. You're in debt but you can't give credit because they won't hold it.26

This chapter delves into "the way the words leapt" in the anarchist undercommons, those sites of radical study where there is room for transgressive ways, where, as Harney and Moten rejoice, "you cannot hear them say there is something wrong with you." In these spaces, you can "seek solidity in a mobile place from which to plan, some hold in which to imagine, some love on which to count."27 Anarchist journals came into readers' lives every week or every month, year after year. I imagine subscribers receiving each new issue from the mail carrier, or acquiring it from a vendor, or borrowing it from a neighbor, or picking it up in the reading room, pub, or café: some readers lingering on the poetry; others thumbing eagerly through the pages for updates on strikes, confrontations, and revolutions; others immersing themselves in the newest installment of a serialized column carrying a classic text; still others eager to engage debates within the movement or between anarchists and the factions with whom they did battle. Immigrants might check the international news to learn about events in their home countries. Some readers might linger on the local reports and the personal correspondence in the letters section, looking for news of comrades; still others might be hungry for the fiction; and a few might scrutinize the fundraising reports to check the financial health of the publication. As Brodie says, each of these encounters between reader and text was an opportunity to build a movement. What went on in these practices of radical study? What could readers plan, what could they imagine, what could they love?

Exploring Anarchist Journals

Anarchist journals work in and emerge from their networks of readers and makers. They enable political subjects by their invitations to make new meanings or to solidify or disrupt prior meanings. As a "mode of recognition instantiated in discourse" rather than a preexisting object, they make themselves known through a process of acknowledgment that Lisa Gitelman describes as "collective, spontaneous, and dynamic." She explains that we learn, unlearn, and relearn how to communicate by participating in "ongoing and changeable practices of expression and reception that are recognizable in myriad and variable constituent instances at once and also across time. They are specific and dynamic, socially realized sites and segments of coherence within the discursive field."[28] Creators and receivers of anarchist texts know what they are doing because they participate in the active grasping and assembling of available elements to produce what Rancière calls a community of sense. They are engaging in practices that create a specifically anarchist familiarity, pressing on what can count as common sense to create a new sense that can be shared.

   This chapter takes Kropotkin's advice and explores three anarchist journals—*Free Society*, *Mother Earth*, and *Freedom*—operating during those fertile years between the Paris Commune and the Spanish Revolution.[29] The discussion has three parts. First, I introduce the three journals, giving a brief history of each and looking at their own self-definitions. Second, I sketch some recurrent textual practices in anarchism's world of letters, giving a few examples of each. While there are significant differences among the journals examined here, there are nonetheless some characteristic ways of writing that regularly appear and reappear in their pages. The journals usually contained poetry, analyses of current events and debates, celebrations of landmark struggles, accounts of speaking tours, support for strikes and rebellions, updates on arrests and imprisonments, and shortened versions of classic books in serial form. The authors of these texts, with the exception of some of the poets, by and large write *about* anarchism, in a strong active voice, presenting anarchism's arguments, mocking its opponents, and commanding readers' attention. They are spreading anarchist ideas directly, through the strength of their evidence, their logic, and their ethical persuasion. The journals also reliably offer overviews of local anarchist activities, letters to and from readers, exchanges with other publications, and updates on organizing, publishing, and fund-raising. These reports are more about the organization of participants than ideas; they register the anarchist movement *as a movement*, a participatory space in which readers can also be actors.

Additionally, there are other articles that, while also spreading the word, have the capacity to act differently on their readers. In the third section of the discussion, I home in on two distinct kinds of anarchist texts in order to exemplify an alternative sense-making project. These are more literary, less explanatory texts, nearly always written by women. I'm calling one of these "social sketches," following Italian anarchist Leda Rafanelli; the second I'm calling think pieces.[30] Social sketches and think pieces invite readers to partake in their stories and queries. The writer does not have a strong didactic presence but rather identifies a problem or a setting of shared concern and finds a way through it or offers narrative personae with whom readers can interact. Social sketches and think pieces are not only about anarchism; they are themselves anarchistic. Social sketches combine elements of short stories and poems, while think pieces weave the structure of essays with the personal tone of letters. If, with Liz Stanley, we see intertextuality as the norm for understanding genres, then these small improvisations are not lesser versions of the "real thing" but creative anarchist inventions that invite readers into the intellectual space of the movement, beckoning them to become the readers that the journals need. Anarchists' strategies of creating themselves through texts and publications can help us understand, in Harney and Moten's words, "the way the words leapt" in anarchist worlds of radical study.

Introducing *Free Society*, *Mother Earth*, and *Freedom*

The range of writings found in anarchist journals defies neat summary. Some, like the London journal *Freedom*, saw themselves as the theoretical front edge of the movement. Others, like Berkman's San Francisco–based journal *The Blast*, were specifically aimed at militant labor activism or, like the Kansas-based (later Chicago-based) *Lucifer, The Lightbearer* or *The Adult* in London, at sexual and marital freedom. Still others bridged a variety of political and literary topics, as did Goldman's *Mother Earth*. Some were specifically aimed at an individualist audience, as was Tucker's *Liberty*, while others were strongly communist in orientation, as was *Freedom*, while others, including *The Firebrand* and *Free Society*, gave play to both the individualist and communist threads of the movement. The monthly publications, such as *Mother Earth* and *Freedom*, could not fully keep up with fast-moving current events; to be useful in organizing, the movement needed weekly publications, such as *The Blast*.

I have selected *Freedom*, *Free Society*, and *Mother Earth* for several reasons. They were each well known and generally well regarded within the anarchist movement. They spanned a variety of topics and interests, were attentive to current events as well as historical analysis, and give a sense of the breadth of ideas and events that mattered to anarchists. They by and large live up to the standard set by *Freedom* editor and printer Thomas Keell in the 1920s: "An anarchist journal was intended for serious people in their most serious moments."[31] Largely avoiding empty sloganeering and catchphrases, they were usually well written and make a good read. They typically exhibit the characteristic anarchist disposition that Constance Bantman describes as defiant and irreverent. "The anarchist ethos," says Bantman, "was a mixture of diffidence, provocation, and humour, and a refusal to subject to any form of authority."[32] Examples of anarchists' indefatigable sense of humor range from delightful to poignant to harsh. A favorite of mine comes from the unnamed wit who suggested using Alphonse Bertillon's system for measuring the physiology of alleged criminals on Cecil Rhodes and other powerful men—"It would be of great interest and value for future generations to know the kind of men who came to the top towards the end of this era of capitalism."[33] Two years earlier, the same journal reported on a police crackdown on anarchist publications in France: "The apartments of Elisée Reclus have been invaded and searched. During the search he remained seated calmly at his literary work. 'I am making a good deal of disorder,' says the police agent apologetically. 'It is your trade,' briefly replies our comrade, continuing to write."[34] From irony and satire through sarcasm to unrestrained vitriol, mocking authorities was and is a widely shared anarchist approach.

These journals interacted with each other on many levels. Their links were ongoing and reciprocal, marking each journal as a potent interactive node in anarchist assemblages. When their publication periods overlapped, they exchanged issues. *Freedom*, by then twenty years old, welcomed *Mother Earth*'s inaugural issue in April 1906. Writers and writings from each journal periodically reappeared in the others. Harry Kelly and Voltairine de Cleyre, who regularly contributed to *Mother Earth*, also wrote a column on US anarchist activities for *Freedom*. Essays by Lizzie Holmes (who wrote for the Chicago journals *Freedom* and *The Alarm* as well as the Portland, Oregon–based *Firebrand* before coming to *Free Society*) sometimes appeared in both the London *Freedom* and *Mother Earth*.[35] Books by writers associated with one journal were advertised in the others. The journals were connected behind the scenes as well: Keell's voluminous correspondence includes exchanges with Kelly (from *Mother Earth*'s inner circle) and Abe Isaak (former editor of *Free Society* who moved to Aurora Colony Ranch in California), securing a subscription and sending money for back issues of the London journal.[36] Charmingly, writers and editors from one journal often served as distributors of the others: Goldman (going under the name E. G. Smith) distributed *Freedom* when she lived in Liverpool, while Hippolyte Havel, a member of *Mother Earth*'s inner circle, distributed *Free Society* in Chicago. Philadelphia anarchist Natasha Notkin, to take just one other example, connected the publications by serving as a distribution agent for all three journals, as well as subscribing and contributing money to their campaigns. Lastly, these three publications are explicit and self-reflective about their aims and practices. A look at the editorial self-understanding of *Free Society*, *Freedom*, and *Mother Earth* can clarify the specific reading and writing communities with which each engaged and the goals they pursued.

Free Society

Free Society was published weekly, first in San Francisco, later in Chicago, with a few final issues in New York, from 1897 to 1904. Eight pages when the group could afford it, four pages when costs were prohibitive, the pages were large (about fourteen inches by ten inches) and the price was fifty cents per year. *Free Society* had a circulation of about three thousand in 1898; since anarchists typically shared their publications with others, readership was no doubt larger.[37]

Free Society was a continuation of the Portland-based journal *Firebrand*, which was closed down after a two-year run when the editors were arrested for violating the Comstock laws by publishing Walt Whitman's "A Woman Waits for Me." At a time when most anarchist publications in the United States were based in immigrant communities and published in German, Yiddish, Spanish, Italian, or Russian, *The Firebrand* and its successor *Free Society* were two of the major anarchist publications in English. The leading historian of anarchism in the United States, Paul Avrich, regarded *Free Society* as the "foremost revolutionary anarchist paper in America around the turn of the century."[38] While Isaak is usually identified as the editor, James Morton, Nellie Jerauld, and others also served as editors.[39] The Isaak family printed the journal. Several women wrote for *Free Society*, and letters to and from the editors show a lively engagement with feminist issues.

In her history of the earlier journal, Jessica Moran notes, "By combining the economic and political arguments of anarchist communism with the social and cultural ideas of free love, *Firebrand* and its contributors consciously developed an anarchism that appealed to both immigrant and native-born Americans."[40] *Free Society* continued this combination of communist and individualist anarchism, often called "anarchism without adjectives," as proponents of both threads came to see their arguments as differences within a family of ideas rather than entirely antagonistic positions. The community of sense fostered around *Free Society*, as announced on the masthead, named itself "An Advocate of Communal Life and Individual Sovereignty."[41]

The salutary statement in the first issue states,

> In launching a new paper it is customary to give an outline of its proposed policy. Our policy is and will be to advocate a conformity to common sense without regard to custom, and we shall hold to the right to mind our own affairs without awaiting the consent of any foreign powers or potentates.
>
> Economically we shall advocate voluntary cooperation on a communistic basis.
>
> We have no space to waste on political panaceas, so don't send us any ready-relief-ballot-box plans.
>
> We hope old comrades will dispense with further remarks on this score and with good digestion attending, attack the contents of our publications. In doing so, do not shrink at a word or phrase—investigate, rather, the meaning underlying them.[42]

The announcement sets a tone that is both militant and cheeky. It appeals to a new anarchist common sense, one that defies custom and reaches toward the conditions needed for sharing a new "sensible world in common."[43] The editorial statement identifies the journal as communist anarchist ("voluntary cooperation on a communistic basis") and as radical rather than reformist ("no space to waste on political panaceas"). It is addressing an already existing community ("old comrades") and inviting them to think actively with the journal ("with good digestion attending").

In the summer of 1900, then-editor James F. Morton (identified only by his initials) published a series of appeals to readers that were also reflections on the journal's role within the anarchist movement. In the June 17 issue, he lays out his vision: the paper should be "a weekly missionary" to newcomers, presenting best arguments from "ablest pens"; it should interpret current events with "up-to-date facts and illustrations." Further elements include global news of the movement; personal issues of interest to comrades; reports of lecturers and groups; reviews of important books and periodicals; histories and biographies; and excerpts from other journals "when well-expressed ideas are found worthy of repetition." Diverse styles were important: "We should not fall into a single rut of expression." The paper should include "general literary matter" and other things that "will make our paper attractive to all readers, and thus vastly increase its influence in the movement."[44]

In the next issue, Morton further characterizes the journal's relation to the movement: "Free Society is not the organ of a clique, but the representative of a principle. It belongs to the Anarchist movement, and has no reason for existence, other than the purpose of strengthening that movement in this country. The printed word is the most effective means of reaching the people. A well-sustained paper, kept up to the highest standard, is a tower of strength to any propaganda."[45] In the following issue, he encourages readers to value the "opportunities for associative action" that the journal offers. Morton invites readers to help with circulation of the paper and organization of lecture tours, to educate themselves and share their knowledge with the journal, to do "quiet, persistent, personal work," and to "live your convictions." He stakes the journal's survival on its veracity: "It depends for its success on the truth that is in it."[46] Free Society exemplified practices that made it a significant community of sense for anarchists. The variety of writings, and the strategies of engagement with readers, created reliably readable texts that brought readers in.

Two years after *Free Society* closed, *Mother Earth* began, taking its place as the foremost anarchist journal published in the English language in the United States. Selling for ten cents an issue or a dollar a year, *Mother Earth* was published in New York City from 1906 to 1918 by Goldman, Max Baginski (the first editor), Berkman (the second and longest-running editor), Ben Reitman (Goldman's tour manager), and other writers and editors including Czech anarchist Hippolyte Havel, British-born anarchist-socialist Leonard Abbott, printer Harry Kelly, German Japanese poet Sadakichi Hartmann, Goldman's niece Stella Ballantine, and editor and theater director Eleanor "Fitzi" Fitzgerald. Each of these people was in turn linked to other publications: Baginski also wrote for *The Alarm* and *Road to Freedom*, which Havel coedited; Berkman and Fitzgerald edited and wrote *The Blast*; Abbott and Kelly served as editors of the *Modern School*.[47] Anarchist journals read one another: according to *Mother Earth*'s subscriber list, helpfully retyped by the FBI after its 1918 raid on the journal's offices, over 150 progressive publications from all over the world received *Mother Earth*.

Originally sixty pages, later reduced to thirty pages for financial reasons, *Mother Earth* was nicely printed on quality paper, sometimes with striking cover art by up-and-coming surrealist Man Ray, French poster artist Jules-Félix Grandjouan, and others. The five-by-eight-inch journal was cut to fit into the front pocket of a worker's shirt. *Mother Earth* reached a global reading public of anarchists, feminists, trade unionists, civil libertarians, and progressives of various alignments, not to mention persistent eavesdroppers from various state surveillance agencies. Historian Rachel Hsu characterizes the journal as "the nexus of a hybrid counterculture, surpassing the immediate anarchist movement and making anarchism widely accessible."[48] The subscription list included about three thousand individuals, publications, and organizations.[49] Given anarchists' propensity to share their publications, Peter Glassgold's estimate of a readership as high as ten thousand is not unreasonable.[50] Candace Falk, director of the Emma Goldman Papers Project at the University of California, Berkeley, nicely summarizes the journal as "a visual representation of an intrepid, literate, and enterprising association of anarchists."[51]

The journal's mission was laid out in the first issue: "MOTHER EARTH will endeavor to attract and appeal to all those who oppose encroachment on public and individual life. It will appeal to those who strive for something higher, weary of the common place; those who feel that stagnation is a deadweight on the firm and elastic step of progress; to those who breathe freely only in limitless space; to those who long for the tender shade of a new dawn for a humanity free from the dread of want, the dread of starvation in the face of mountains of riches. The Earth free for the free individual!"[52] On its "sixth birthday," Goldman and Berkman further defined their project: to "create a medium for the free expression of our ideas, a medium bold, defiant, and unafraid," to "serve as a gathering point ... for those who, struggling to free themselves from the absurdities of the Old, had not yet reached firm footing," and to "infuse new blood in Anarchism."[53]

Goldman modeled her journal on the French literary and political magazine edited by Augustin Hamon, *L'Humanite Nouvelle*, which also featured writings by a range of radical intellectuals and activists. Kelly states in his autobiography that *Mother Earth*'s original intention to fully blend political and literary topics was sometimes overrun by the urgent need to respond to pressing events, yet the journal never abandoned its intertwined goals. Many issues were organized around themes, including birth control, freedom of thought, strikes, war, and censorship. The cover of the tenth anniversary issue of March 1915, for example, features a striking drawing by Canadian American illustrator Boardman Robinson of a woman protecting a child while looking over her shoulder at approaching danger. The woman's body curves around the child she is sheltering—her long hair, loose garment, and strong arm, shoulder, and back flow across the page. Since Goldman often referred to *Mother Earth* as her child, it is likely that the cover announces the looming danger of censorship while still striving to nurture the vulnerable offspring whose accomplishments are evaluated and celebrated in subsequent pages. Craig Monk rightly notes that it was a remarkable achievement "to print 138 consecutive issues during a time in American history marked by zealous oppression of unorthodox political thought."[54]

Richard Drinnon, the first major biographer of Goldman, draws this conclusion about her journal: "Over the years *Mother Earth* played a significant role in American radicalism. It acted as a rallying center for isolated individuals, as an outlet for their ideas and feelings, and as a source of support for them in their difficulties."[55] While I concur with Drinnon that *Mother Earth* was an important voice within radical American politics, I want to push his conclusion a bit further. First, the significance of the journal was not limited to the United States, because the networks of circulation among anarchists were transnational. The exchange list included journals in London, Paris, Milan, Havana, Barcelona, São Paulo, Montevideo,

Auckland, Geneva, Alexandria, Lima, Wellington, Canton, Buenos Aires, Santiago, Genoa, Zurich, Malmö, Bologna, Montreal, and Mexico City. Second, *Mother Earth*'s subscription list suggests that many of the journal's readers were not isolated individuals but rather participants in networks of anarchist, socialist, feminist, syndicalist, free speech, free love, and antiwar activism. Even those who lived in geographically remote areas with no immediate community to sustain them found more than a "rallying center" and an "outlet" for preexisting inclinations. Instead, I argue that in *Mother Earth*, as well as the other journals examined here, people found ways to *become* anarchists.

Freedom

Freedom's long life and central role in anarchism make it even more difficult to generalize about than the other two journals. It was newspaper-sized; each issue was four pages at the beginning of its production, with pages added later as finances and available labor allowed. As described in chapter 1, *Freedom* and *Free Society* had a similar look of printedness, while *Mother Earth* was a more elegant production.

Founded by English anarchist Charlotte Wilson, Kropotkin, and other volunteers in 1886, *Freedom*'s monthly publication has been interrupted on a few occasions, notably when its creators split over anarchist support for the Allies in World War I, but it always resumed and continued in paper form until 2014. As of this writing, it continues as a biannual publication in digital form. Editors after Wilson and Kropotkin include the violinist Alfred Marsh, printers John Turner and Keell, and, in the 1930s and 1940s, a new group of young anarchists including Marie Louise Berneri, Vernon Richards, George Woodcock, and Colin Ward.

A long front-page column in the first issue outlines the creators' political vision, including this passage:

> Therefore, we are Anarchists, disbelievers in the government of man by man in any shape and under any pretext. The human freedom to which our eyes are raised is no negative abstraction of licence for individual egoism, whether it be masked collectively as majority rule or isolated as personal tyranny. We dream of the positive freedom which is essentially one with social feeling; of free scope for the social impulses, now distorted and compressed by Property, and its guardian the Law; of free scope for that individual sense of responsibility, of respect for self and

for others, which is vitiated by every form of collective interference, from the enforcing of contracts to the hanging of criminals; of free scope for the spontaneity and individuality of each human being, such as is impossible when one hard and fast line is fitted to all conduct.[56]

Heiner Becker, who edited the strikingly illustrated journal *The Raven* for Freedom Press from 1987 to 2003, reports that *Freedom*'s first issue sold 1,600 copies at one penny each, with sales rising in the following months.[57] *Freedom* saw greater sales of its successful pamphlets, leaflets, and booklets, often selling many thousands of copies.[58] The journal held successful discussion meetings and lectures in various halls and pubs and, before it was closed down by the authorities, at the community center called Marsh House. Like *Free Society* and *Mother Earth*, *Freedom* aimed to be "an independent voice in the wider movement" rather than an expression of a particular group or line.[59]

Like Goldman's *Mother Earth*, *Freedom* was sometimes accused of abandoning the working class for the intellectuals. The famous London journal was sometimes lampooned as stuffy and divorced from the streets: at a meeting of the West London Anarchists group in 1898, *Freedom* was colorfully described as "a philosophical middle-class organ, not intelligible to the working classes, not up-to-date in late information … edited and managed by an inaccessible group of arrogant persons, worse than the Pope and his seventy cardinals, and written by fossilized old quilldrivers, etc."[60] This cutting description was faithfully reported and plaintively contested by the respected historian Max Nettlau (identified as N.) in *Freedom*'s pages. Yet *Freedom* addressed itself to the working class as well as the larger society:

We, Socialist Anarchists, have a definite idea of what social relations might be. We have a decided opinion as to which moral, intellectual, economic and political tendencies now working in humanity make for a satisfactory state of society, and which do not. Therefore, as was unanimously decided by the English Anarchists at the recent London conference, our work is educational. We believe that revenge is sterile. Revenge is for the despairing and the weak; for the strong men of heart and hope there is Revolution. And, if the workers would only lift up their crushed heads and see it, they are strong. Strong in numbers, strong in justice of their cause, strong in the fact that, whatever weapons government may hold in its grasp, the food supplies are in the hands of the producers. A general strike, merely a strike of the great organized labor societies even, and the people would be masters of the situation, and, if they knew how to use their opportunities, would lay the foundation of a free and equal society.

To aid in waking the workers to a realisation of their tremendous strength; to develop into active, conscious convictions those vague yearnings for a social life on a new moral, economic, and political basis which are now so obviously forming themselves in men's minds; to root out the idea that authority and private property are necessarily factors in social union—this is the work of the Communist Anarchist.[61]

"Waking the workers"; developing "active, conscious convictions" out of "vague yearnings"; "root[ing] out" acceptance of capitalism and the state and offering a vision of "social union" grounded in mutual aid—this has been *Freedom's* purpose for a century and a half.

The years during and after World War I were turbulent and often unproductive. The divisions in the *Freedom* group, and the larger movement, over World War I were ferocious and weakened the movement considerably but did not destroy it altogether. In 1936 two young anarchists of Italian descent, Marie Louise Berneri and Vernon Richards, started the journal *Spain and the World* in London to support the Spanish anarchists during their revolution and civil war. The journal became a Freedom Press publication; it was subsequently renamed *Revolt!*, then, during World War II, became *War Commentary*, later reverting to the older name *Freedom*. Historian Susan Hinely sums up *Freedom's* work as a potent node in a global network: "*Freedom* served as the English-language clearing house for anarchist news, theory, and organization. Articles from *Freedom* were translated in the foreign left-wing press, and foreign-language copy from all over the world came into the London office of *Freedom*, to be translated and published in English. In this early stage of modern mass communications, the articles and lengthy correspondence columns of journals like *Freedom* were the media through which a global conversation could take place among an increasingly mobile and cosmopolitan radical network."[62]

In sum, each of these journals is a vigorous actant in anarchist assemblages. The flows among them of writers, readers, correspondents, and distributors; of ink, paper, and forms of printedness; of texts, arguments, and styles, which are, anarchist literary critic Paul Goodman insists, hypotheses about how the world works—all these flows are relations that enable more relations.[63] They produce the sorts of linkages that Manuel DeLanda tells us to look for in a robust assemblage: strong, dense, and reciprocal.[64] By following the advice that Jussi Parikka gives about assemblages—to look *"under the hood"* and track the layers and the flows of relationships—we can get a closer look at the textual contours of the anarchist undercommons.[65]

Texts and Genres

Anarchist journals labored to modify what was thinkable by welcoming ideas that were unthinkable. In previous chapters, I have looked at the journal's page as a technology and an artifact; here I am interested in the patterns of thinking, envisioning, and feeling that are available on the pages. What "perceptions, affects, names and ideas," in Rancière's words, are speaking to anarchist readers whose willingness to receive them is part of what makes them thinkable?[66] Writers, printers, and editors are putting concepts, percepts, and affects to work; relating them to old and new objects they care about; and building patterns to carry anarchism forward. The editors of *Mother Earth* sought to "create a medium for the free expression of our ideas, a medium bold, defiant, and unafraid."[67] *Freedom's* editors tasked their journal with developing "into active, conscious convictions those vague yearnings for a social life on a new moral, economic, and political basis."[68] *Free Society's* editors invited readers to "attack the contents of our publications. In doing so, do not shrink at a word or phrase—investigate, rather, the meaning underlying them."[69] What are these ideas, convictions, and yearnings, and what is the meaning underlying them?

Building on earlier chapters' exploration of the material and epistolary dimensions of anarchist print culture, here I am after a serviceable portrait of the journals' content. I'm dividing the writings into three overlapping groups. First is a set of texts that are primarily aimed at spreading anarchism's message through direct argument. Clearly it would be difficult to mistake the observations and arguments in the texts as anything other than anarchist. But that alone is not enough: that would make the journals *about* anarchism but not themselves anarchistic. A second set of elements is largely about the readers and supporters of the journals, drawing them into the movement and orchestrating their contributions. The journals are sites of participatory action, public dialogue, and personal self-development through expression. Many of the elements are interactive, encouraging people to become involved in the movement's various circulations.

A third pair of elements creatively combines anarchist messages with participatory textual forms. These short pieces are often written in the conversational first- or second-person voice rather than the more distant third. They mix genres, blurring essays, short stories, correspondence, and poetry. They cultivate an intimacy of address, approaching anarchism not simply by making arguments or declaring allegiances but by telling stories or offering narrative personae with whom it becomes possible to converse. These humble mixed genres create characters, enact scenes, stage encounters, or engage personal problems requiring political response. These texts circulated widely within the anarchist movement, frequently reprinted in pamphlets or other journals, contributing to the creation of an anarchist world of letters. They host the sort of hapticality that Harney and Moten find in "the touch of the undercommons...the capacity to feel through others, for others to feel through you."[70] Anarchism is not a politics that happens elsewhere and is subsequently reported in the pages of its journals. The journals embody the politics. The makers and readers of the journals make their way into anarchism largely through the journals. Many readers prized what *Free Society* editor James Morton called the "opportunities for associative action" that such publications provided.[71]

Spreading the Word: Main Elements and Arguments

Poems. Most issues of *Free Society* and *Mother Earth* begin with a poem, while *Freedom* often includes a poem within its inside pages. Sometimes the poem is a reproduction of a previously published work by a well-known writer, such as William Morris, Maxim Gorky, Ralph Waldo Emerson, Walt Whitman, or Percy Shelley. More often the introductory poem was written by one of their own, including Voltairine de Cleyre, Lola Ridge, Louisa Bevington, John Henry Mackay, and many, many others. *Free Society* honored de Cleyre, who is widely regarded as one of anarchism's best poets, by reprinting her poem "The Gods and the People" as "a neat 8 page tract" for sale at two cents per copy.[72] These three journals were not unusual in this regard: Yiddish-language anarchist publications also included poetry, often by the famous "sweatshop poets," as did publications in other languages.[73]

As one might expect when substantial numbers of activists try their hands at poetry, the outcome was uneven. The journals record humorous exchanges between would-be poets and exasperated editors or reviewers. To J. M. in Reavley, Missouri, *Free Society*'s editors wrote, "Why not write prose, friend? Not everyone is given to write poetry."[74] An unidentified reviewer in *Mother Earth* urged readers to look past the "great faults of arrangement" in a collection of "rebel verses" to appreciate them as "splendid pieces of fire." In terms of musicality and composition, the writer commented, the poetry may be "execrable," but its outrages can be excused because "it bites and rings."[75]

Happily, many of the poems escape such confines to offer poignant images of struggle and hope. Some rehearse a familiar political agenda, while others make no didactic demands but portray complex and open-ended circumstances in which people come to terms with suffering or find a way to resist. The poem as repeating introductory trope suggests that the lighter touch of poetry was a valued entry point to the announcements, arguments, reflections, and calls to arms that come later. Whitman, who was beloved by many anarchists, suggested that "the profoundest service that poems or any other writings can do for their reader is … to give him *good heart* as a radical possession and habit."[76] For publications generally outraged over injustice and determined to overcome it, the cultivation of *good heart* could be a valued gesture toward nurturing a receptive disposition.

Republication of classics. Issues frequently carry an article written by one of the heavy hitters of the movement. In *Free Society*, Kropotkin's "Law and Authority" and "Anarchist Morality" were published in installments in 1897–98, as was Leo Tolstoy's *The Slavery of Our Times*. Both *Freedom* and *Free Society* ran Errico Malatesta's influential essay "Between Two Workers," while *Mother Earth* issued it as a pamphlet.[77] Kropotkin's "Modern Science and Anarchism" was serialized in the first year of *Mother Earth*'s appearance. *Freedom* published a section of Berkman's *Prison Memoirs of an Anarchist* in 1913. Louise Michel, Jean Grave, and C. L. James were frequently republished in these and other anarchist journals. A local writer sometimes reviewed a classic text, as did Kate Austin in her review of Kropotkin's autobiography.[78]

These highly regarded texts offered access to the intellectual center of anarchism and let readers sample books that many could not otherwise afford. Readers could explore or reaffirm central anarchist ideas of mutual aid, revolution, freedom, self-organization, and other key concepts. Letting the classic authors speak, rather than only hearing others speak about them or apply their ideas, created a presence for these respected thinkers. When they came to town on the lecture circuit, their intellectual presence already had a foothold. They were brought into the ongoing conversations as voices with whom readers could converse. Additionally, serial publication creates an ongoing-ness of materials, inviting readers to stay tuned for the next installment, bringing readers back again and again. In the "intensely bookish culture" that Bantman finds in anarchism, intimacy with respected authors and texts created personal bonds as well as intellectual relationships.[79]

Current events. All three of these journals covered local, national, and global current events. They castigated their respective governments, indeed all governments, for their imperial adventures; featured stories of human suffering caused by states, capitalists, and other authorities; and made use of contemporary news reports to advance anarchist analyses. Anarchist news was transnational in its reach. *Free Society*'s regular column "News from Everywhere" and "International Notes" in *Mother Earth* and *Freedom* brought word of radical politics from all over the world. In *Freedom*'s column "American Notes," de Cleyre and Kelly regularly updated readers on anarchist news from the United States, including reports on American lecturers touring Britain. Kelly's playful prose and de Cleyre's skillful, cutting irony made for good reading and created a pleasurable bond across the Atlantic. The international columns kept readers informed of strikes and rebellions around the world. Immigrants had regular opportunities to stay informed on politics in the old country, and readers could see themselves as participants in a global political movement.

Coverage of current issues and events was often a vehicle for caustic disputes with anarchists' ideological enemies, especially social democrats, suffragists, and moderate labor reformers. There was pretty much universal agreement among anarchists that legal reforms were tragic misdirections of activist time and energy. Occasionally some crisis would elicit a call for unity within the Left: in 1906, for example, in opposition to British counterrevolutionary interventions in Russia, *Freedom*'s editors John Turner, Alfred Marsh, and Thomas Keell urged all progressive English people to "sink our differences for once, and let all of us—socialists, Democrats, Trade Unions, Radicals—march in protest under one flag—the flag of Humanity."[80] But more frequently anarchists despaired of a united front because they saw the rest of the Left as too willing to capitulate to the state, or capital, or both.

Anarchists were relentless in criticizing colonialism and supporting rebellions against colonial authorities, regularly calling attention to capitalism's "little wars": "the old, old story we English know so well; explorers, missionaries, traders, land grabbing, exploitation, and then armies and artillery to enforce the submission of the 'barbarians' to the tyranny of the whites who rob and enslave them."[81] *Free Society* and *Mother Earth* castigated the United States for its destruction of Native Americans and its imperial expansion in Cuba, Puerto Rico, the Philippines, and Hawaiʻi. *Freedom* equally railed against British imperialism in Ireland, India, Palestine, and Africa, as well as other European imperial ventures.[82] Hinely notes that *Freedom* was a reliable source of information for English speakers about colonial violence: "The late Victorian anarchist press is one of the best archives for tracking imperial history as it regularly reported on coercion by the state all over the globe, from India to the Sudan, Puerto Rico to Dahomey, Algeria to Tahiti."[83]

Remembering anarchist events. Anarchist publication calendars were punctuated by annual revisits to key historical events, especially the Paris Commune every spring and the execution of the Haymarket anarchists every fall. A lengthy speech by Kropotkin in memory of the Paris Commune was a front-page story in *Freedom* in April 1887. Louise Michel's speeches and essays on the Commune were highly regarded, as she was a veteran of the Commune and of the subsequent exile of Communards to New Caledonia. De Cleyre's fiery essay "The Commune is Risen" appeared in *Mother Earth* in 1913. *Free Society* was particularly attentive to the legacy of Haymarket. Lizzie Holmes, who had been an activist in Chicago during the Haymarket period and knew the executed men, often wrote these memorial pieces. The strongest versions of these memorials, such as "Why We Tell the Story," are invitations to think about the contested legacy of past struggles.[84] Holmes's 1899 reflection on Haymarket, "Revolutionists," remembers them as men who "do not hope—[they] *will.*" She contrasts the Haymarket martyrs, who are like "a furious storm which clears and purifies the air," with those "cheery souls who can conserve the possibilities of happiness until all can enjoy them." She argues that anarchism needs both: the "terrible courage" of the "lofty souls" as well as the "quiet work, endurance, patience, hopefulness, the simple *living* of those principles we love."[85]

To the same issue, Lizzie and her husband, William Holmes, contributed "Reminiscences," remembering their Haymarket friends: August Spies, they recalled, was sarcastic; Samuel Felden, tenderhearted. Parsons was brilliant, genial, charismatic: "Albert Parsons could quell a mob with his voice and his presence, meet in mental combat a room full of college bred preachers, make plain the truth of Anarchism to a hall full of stolid workingmen, and turn to a social gathering of friends and become its life."[86] Lizzie and William Holmes's tender memories and thoughtful reflections on the emotional economies needed for radical politics lifted the annual marking of the Haymarket executions out of the simple embrace of martyrdom to a more thoughtful reflection on how memory works.

This framing was important: the Haymarket executions brought many new recruits into anarchism; it was a symbolic turning point for a whole generation of radicals, including Goldman. Haymarket memories were cherished in the movement, but the question remains, *how* are they memories?

Agnes Inglis was one of those who suspected that the adoration of martyrs was unhealthy for a political movement.[87] It was probably de Cleyre who wrote in the column "American Notes" in *Freedom* in 1899 that the speeches of the Haymarket men had not traveled well: "*They read old.*"[88] Boston anarchist Helena Born's turn-of-the-century essay in *Free Society*, "The Commemoration in Boston," called on anarchists to use memorials to learn, to hold on to "the beautiful ideal of non-invasive self-sovereignty" while continuing to change.[89] Contestation over the meaning of Haymarket helped to shape discussions over the role of violence and the politics of memory in the movement. "Haymarket's long afterlife," in American studies scholar Shelley Streeby's notable phrase, went beyond the recirculation of fixed allegiances to retell possible futures, to connect current injustice to past heroism, and to constitute memory practices showing how the past will have been transformed.[90]

Accounts of speaking tours. My focus on print culture should not detract from the significant role played by the spoken word in making the anarchist movement. Johann Most, Goldman, Rocker, Louise Michel, Lucy Parsons, and Luigi Galleani were powerful speakers who routinely addressed and moved audiences of thousands. Other speakers included Henry Addis, editor of *The Firebrand*; Morton of *Free Society*; Harry Weinberger, a radical lawyer who defended Goldman and Berkman at their deportation hearings; and John Turner, printer and editor of *Freedom*.[91] These speaking tours were an important part of the glue holding anarchism together, as many people mobilized to make them happen. Organizers of the tours regularly took to the journals to announce the talks, report problems in renting halls and dealing with authorities, and recruit assistance from readers to solve problems. The trail of cities in which anarchists spoke was, consequently, an implicit map of the geographic distribution of anarchist communities, since speakers were dependent on local groups for needed arrangements.

Free Society's coverage of speaking tours often included lengthy accounts of speeches in other cities, frequently from other newspapers such as the *Boston Herald* and the *New York Tribune*. Some stories were amusing— evidently Kropotkin got into the United States during a time of antianarchist scrutiny at the border by shaving off his beard—while other accounts were filled with outrage, as when (no similar ruse being available) Michel was subsequently not allowed into the country.[92] *Mother Earth* featured a regular column called "On the Road" recounting Goldman's adventures on tour. *Freedom* covered tours in Great Britain by Goldman, de Cleyre,

Lillian Harman (printer of *Lucifer, The Lightbearer* and president of the Legitimation League in London), and others, including an amusing account of de Cleyre's tour of Scotland, where she evidently had the nerve to criticize William Shakespeare.[93]

Anarchists prided themselves on public lectures that went beyond tub-thumping showmanship to delve into anarchism's big ideas, formative events, and current issues. Inglis recalled the excitement of handing out forbidden information on birth control at a Goldman lecture in Ann Arbor.[94] Artist Robert Henri and civil libertarian Roger Baldwin credited their involvement with anarchism to the impact of a Goldman lecture on them. The consistent reporting on lecture tours invited readers both to participate in them and to envision their hometowns as part of a larger network of traveling speakers linking local audiences in a transnational radical project.

Support for strikes and other rebellions. Anarchist journals kept readers apprised of strikes and other acts of resistance. Striking coal miners in Ludlow, Colorado; dockworkers in London; and the "brave and generous" London match girls who participated in the strike of 1897, to mention a few examples, received regular encouragement.[95] Less well-known labor actions were also encouraged: the London charwomen who secured improved wages and working conditions in 1912 were congratulated for successfully organizing a branch of the National Federation of Women Workers. "It's not liberty as we understand it, nor even justice," opined *Freedom*, but it was well worth having.[96] While anarchists were disappointed when unions eschewed a radical agenda to strike for bread-and-butter issues, they recognized such strikes were important for the improvement they could bring to workers' immediate lives. The journals regularly supported the Magon brothers' rebellion in Mexico and in general applauded any rebellions against states, capitalists, or colonial authorities anywhere.

Updates on arrests and imprisonments. All three journals cover the arrests, trials, and imprisonments of anarchists and supporters in considerable detail, providing frequent updates and exploring surrounding controversies. News from countries with overtly brutal regimes, such as Spain and Russia, includes story after story of anarchists imprisoned, tortured, beaten, and murdered. Over and over, readers learned of various governments' attacks on their movement, which entailed the debilitating loss of leaders and activists, seizure of libraries, and closure of journals and schools. Coalitions could be formed around the trials as organizers used them to rally support from more mainstream organizations that may or may not have had sympathy with anarchists but were willing to defend free speech.

One high-profile case began when Henry Addis, A. J. Pope, and Abe Isaak were arrested in Portland for mailing *The Firebrand* issue containing Whitman's "A Woman Waits for Me." The charges were eventually dropped, but not before a considerable number of organizations, including the American Secular Union and the Free Thought Federation, gave public support to the anarchists.[97] The elderly Pope spent some time in jail because he refused to sign the release papers, reasoning that it would implicitly endorse the right of the state to arrest him in the first place.[98] Another high-profile case was the arrest of George Bedborough, editor of the British Legitimation League's journal *The Adult*, for selling Havelock Ellis's book *The Psychology of Sex*.[99] Bedborough was defended vigorously by Moses Harman in *Lucifer*, but Kelly, then in England working with *Freedom*, wrote to *Free Society* accusing Bedborough of becoming "an *informer* and a police agent."[100]

After the assassination of President William McKinley in 1901 by Leon Czolgosz, anarchists were widely vilified. *Free Society* published Goldman's analysis of the attentat in "The Tragedy at Buffalo" and an article by Isaak entitled "Why We Considered Czolgosz a Spy" (and his subsequent apology).[101] Lillian Harman wrote in *Mother Earth* about the arrest of Goldman and the Chicago anarchists (including Isaak and his family) and their detention and ultimate release in the aftermath of the presidential assassination.[102] Anarchist publications widely reported the 1916 arrest, conviction, and imprisonment of Keell and Lilian Wolfe of *Freedom* for violating the Defense of the Realm Act by publishing ideas that were "prejudicial to recruiting and discipline."[103] And on, and on, and on. The journals regularly carried accounts of the arrests and imprisonments of Rocker, Malatesta, Berkman, Goldman, Francisco Ferrer (Spanish educator and founder of the Modern Schools), Maria Rygier (editor of *L'Agitatore* of Bologna), and many others. Arrests were a badge of honor within the movement: when a Communist Party supporter accused Rocker in the 1930s of implicitly supporting the Nazis by opposing the Bolsheviks, Rocker retorted, "I have been jailed more times for the cause of freedom than you have hairs on your foolish head."[104] Goldman recounted taking a book with her to her own talks so she would have something to read in jail.[105]

As these examples suggest, anarchists were arrested frequently, so coverage of arrests, trials, convictions, and imprisonments was a regular aspect of the journals. The anarchists did not forget their own: *Free Society* and *Mother Earth* continued to provide updates on Berkman's situation in prison, for example, and to raise money for his legal fund (or escape attempt). A

photographer took Berkman's picture in prison and his defense committee sold copies for twenty-five cents to raise money for him.[106] This oddly
intimate gesture of support, repeated for other respected anarchists, resulted
in many comrades decorating their homes with small reproductions of photos of their movement's heroes. The ubiquity of arrest and imprisonment
probably discouraged some potential affiliates, while the respect afforded
to those persecuted by the state probably motivated others to step forward.

Ongoing debates. There were recurrent internal debates within the pages
of these journals. While there were many disputes, especially throughout
the long life of *Freedom*, I am focusing here on three ongoing sites of
significant disagreement: anarchists continued to argue over the relation
of individualist to communist anarchism; they split disastrously among
themselves over World War I; and they entertained a variety of contending ideas about gender and sexuality. Eventually, these debates came to be
framed largely as differences *within* anarchism rather than as a bright line
between proper anarchists and their opponents. Recognition of serious differences of analysis and action within the anarchist movement could lead to
fragmentation of the movement, but it also allowed readers and creators of
anarchist journals to see themselves as members of a thoughtful, dynamic
movement, not adherents of a static ideology.

First, individualist-communist debates: All three journals engaged the
debates over individualist anarchism, which accepted private property, and
communist anarchism, which advocated communal ownership. While this
was a formative dispute early in anarchism's days, by the turn of the twentieth
century, the argument had gotten stale, and many anarchists were looking for an "anarchist synthesis" or "anarchism without adjectives."[107] New
Jersey anarchist J. William Lloyd's *Free Society* essay "Are They Anarchists?"
distinguished the individualist dimension of anarchism that advocates "no-
government, non-invasion, equal liberty, and only that" from the "school
of libertarian thought which, starting from the position of the single or
alone man, declares that nature knows no right but might."[108] Lloyd made
room within anarchism for debates over labor and property while drawing
a line between anarchism and the sort of libertarianism that naturalized
capitalism. Nettlau complained in his 1921 essay in *Freedom* that he had
tried to bring about "understanding between Individualist and Communist
Anarchists" earlier, but each had been "feeling perfectly comfortable in its
isolation and exclusive belief to be in the right."[109] Yet things had changed,
and luminaries of the movement, including Goldman, de Cleyre, Nettlau,
Malatesta, Tarrida del Mármol, and Max Baginski generally agreed with

the argument for mutual toleration. Printer Edward Fulton was probably representative of this ecumenical position: in a letter to editor John Basil Barnhill, he commented, "My anarchism includes all. Those who want communism can have it for themselves, and individualists can have individualism. Liberty is broad enough for all things that do not compel special economic force, and deny other forms to anyone."[110] The appeal for unity across differences pushed anarchists toward Cuban anarchist Tarrida del Mármol's plea, "to call ourselves simply anarchists" and to continue to debate economic questions of labor and property without allowing those issues "to become the cause of division between anarchists."[111]

Second, debates over World War I: No such quasi-agreeable compromise was available to mediate the movement's fierce disputes over World War I. While *Free Society* had ceased publication a decade earlier, World War I was a dark time for the other two journals. *Mother Earth* took a consistent antiwar position, rejecting the warring nations' "murderous patriotism" and the misguided comrades "whose philosophical internationalism somersaults into rankest chauvinism the moment it is put to the practical test."[112] *Mother Earth* was closed down in 1918 due to the arrest, conviction, imprisonment, and eventual deportation of Goldman and Berkman for opposing conscription. Despite valiant efforts by Stella Ballantine, Fitzi Fitzgerald, and others, the journal could not be revived.

Freedom survived, barely. The London journal published raging disputes on the war, primed by Kropotkin's "Letter on the Present War," in *Freedom* in the October 1914 issue, which called for "everyone who cherishes the ideals of human progress altogether, and especially those that were inscribed by the European proletarians on the banner of the International Working Men's Association[,] ... to do everything in one's power, according to one's capacities, to crush down the invasion of the Germans into Western Europe."[113] Kropotkin, French anarchist Jean Grave, and about a dozen others authored a manifesto calling on anarchists to support the Allies in the war. Goldman, Berkman, Malatesta, Keell, Wolfe, and about thirty others proclaimed a countermanifesto calling on the international working class and anarchist movement to stick with its antiwar position. Philosopher Ruth Kinna succinctly sums up the outcome: "It ripped the anarchist movement apart."[114] *Freedom* limped along, contested from within the anarchist ranks as well as attacked from the outside. Keell and Wolfe moved the journal temporarily to Whiteway Colony in the Cotswolds; for a time a second journal, also calling itself *Freedom*, spun off from the first. Keell corresponded regularly with British American anarchist writer and editor William Owen, and for a time Owen lived with Keell, Wolfe, and their young son Tom Junior. Keell agonized over the journal's need for money, workers, and realistic supporters who understood the needs of a publication run on a shoestring budget. Owen advised that the journal would need at least £200 to rent an office in London and carry on for a year, as well as "brains and some business training."[115] Without the needed infusion of people and money, Owen encouraged Keell and Wolfe to pay past debts to the printer and move on. In a letter of March 2, 1928, Owen commiserated with Keell about the dispiriting effects of attacks from other activists:

> I myself have now fully fifty years of propaganda-making behind me, and I have started a good many papers some of which did very well while others came to grief chiefly through the attacks of so-called comrades who thought they could do better than I was doing and in certain instances were hungry for a job. I cannot remember that I ever had any sentiment about the failures, my invariable tactic being if I had the money and thought action feasible to start another paper. I am inclined to think that this is the course those of us who care only about the propaganda will have to follow.[116]

Keell, Wolfe, and Owen were veterans of the movement who kept a version of *Freedom* in print during very hard times. Freedom Press later put out *Spain and the World* and other subsequent titles, eventually returning to *Freedom* again after World War II.

Third, debates over gender and sexuality: All three journals entertained a range of discussions about gender and sexuality. They reliably refused to engage in moralizing over prostitution, instead insisting on an economic analysis of gender and poverty to make sense of sexual labor. *Mother Earth* brought sexuality and gender to the fore in its April 1916 issue on birth control as well as in Goldman's essays on marriage, love, suffrage, prostitution, sex, and women's liberation. Rachel Hsu's thorough study of *Mother Earth* finds "a variety of opinions regarding women, sexuality and family, although its writers all sought female emancipation from the control of the state, man-made institutions, and men."[117]

Freedom, over its long life, managed to be both supportive of gender equality and condescending to those who located sex and gender at the heart of anarchism: an 1898 article characteristically suggested that *Freedom*, "while never afraid to discuss it [sex] fully, have not thought it wise to give undue space to it."[118] *Freedom* seems to have followed Kropotkin's view that sexuality and gender relations will work themselves out after capitalism and the state are overthrown: Kropotkin famously advised Mary and Abe Isaak and Goldman that *Free Society* "would do more if it would not waste so much space discussing sex."[119] A 1913 *Freedom* article encouraged better housing, "collective housekeeping[,] and collective cooking" (presumably by women, since no men are mentioned) to liberate the "domestic drudge" and encourage the "breaking of the chains of domestic servitude without antagonising the sexes."[120] This is a fascinating gesture of halfheartedness: women are encouraged to share their domestic labor, to cook and clean together, which is probably more interesting than cooking and cleaning in isolation but keeps household labor entirely the province of women. While antagonizing the ruling class was always applauded in *Freedom*'s pages, antagonizing the ruling gender was less so: friction between men and women over gender politics probably created fear of working-class disunity as well as anxiety about men's loss of access to women's unpaid labor. Lily Gair Wilkinson, who wrote four fine feminist essays for *Freedom*, wrote a letter to *The Anarchist* on December 27, 1912, expressing her support for anarchism in everyday life: "I believe that if we begin with immediate personal things, greater and greater opportunities are likely to occur.... I wish to express anarchism in my life."[121] Perhaps, as British researcher Judy Greenway suggests, Wilkinson was disappointed with the movement's failure to adequately address gender inequality in its own circles. Certainly many women were: Greenway concludes that, "while men were theorising, women were actually trying to live out their theories. They did so with varying degrees of success."[122]

Of these three journals, *Free Society* was the most consistently outspoken on women's liberation. This may seem surprising, given that *Mother Earth* is better known for Goldman's anarchist feminist essays, but there were a lot of women writing for *Free Society* and doing the organizational labor to make the journal happen. While contributions to anarchist publications are often unsigned, or signed only with the writer's initials or by a pseudonym, in *Free Society* authors' bylines were usually attached to their writings, so women's contributions were less obscured. Viroqua Daniels, Lizzie Holmes, Lois Waisbrooker, Voltairine de Cleyre, Nellie Jerauld, Kate Austin, Mabel Gifford, Albina Washburn, Susan Patton, and Myra Peppers contributed regularly. Occasional essays appeared by Celia Whitehead, Mary Hansen, and a few other women. Articles by Goldman were sometimes reproduced from other publications.[123]

Free Society's editors regularly chastised male readers who undervalued the journal's arguments for women's freedom.[124] Editors were exasperated but not surprised when male readers disagreed. To a fellow in Summerland, California, the editors wrote, "We really rejoiced when we read your lamentations that your wife would not 'obey any more' since she has been reading our 'terrible sheet.' If women and working men alike would cease to obey and did resist tyranny[,] conditions would soon improve. But, by the way, do you really imagine that 'your wife' will love you better since you would 'not allow her to read Free Society'? Poor creature!"[125] In contrast, a letter from a male reader in Lacon, Illinois, elicited this editorial praise:

> We were delighted to hear at least from one man who is anxious to practice freedom in his own house. Women have asked for the issue containing the article "My Neighbor's Wife" but the majority of the male correspondents tell us that such articles are only creating strife in the family, and that the women will sexually be free after we have reached the millennium. Fortunately there are women who desire to enjoy some freedom while they live, but, sad to relate, they have to combat their respective husbands just as vigorously as any other monopolist. An Anarchist told me recently that his wife was a free woman. "If she loves another man besides me," he said, "she is free to do so, but she must then take her children and leave my house." "That's the argument of the capitalist," I replied. "He too, tells us that we are free to do as we please: if we don't like this country we can go somewhere else." The fact is many Anarchists are yet in the mire of superstition regarding the sex question; they cannot realize that freedom is always conducive to happiness, be that in the relation to our children or to the woman we call "our wife."[126]

Anarchist debates over the most desirable sexual arrangements were often framed as disputes between monogamists and varietists; while few anarchists defended the institution of marriage, heated differences remained between those who counseled loyalty to a single partner and those who saw greater freedom in a variety of sexual encounters. Famously, Lucy Parsons disagreed with Goldman on this issue, with Goldman advocating "free love" while Parsons saw casual sex as a deceptive arrangement that was likely to exploit women.[127] The pages of *Liberty* and *Lucifer, The Lightbearer* were full of these debates. Women writing for *Free Society* sometimes got impatient with these arguments, which became repetitive and often seemed more for titillation than enlightenment. Jerauld encourages anarchists to "attend to weightier matters" and aims "to set some of the sisters to thinking" because "once get the women started on the right path, and they will sweep all before them."[128] Holmes also writes to broaden the discussion: "The real question of 'women's rights' is merely a demand to be considered as human beings, not as pets, queens, toys or slaves."[129] Waisbrooker published a speech that she had initially given at a San Francisco Spiritualist meeting, demanding an end to both racial and gender inequality. She was confident that, "with self-ownership[,] no woman will submit to unwelcome relations."[130]

These and other recurrent debates invited readers and creators to see their journals, and thus the anarchist movement more generally, as a space of contestation, not only affirmation. As *Free Society*'s editors said in their inaugural issue, readers were invited, "with good digestion attending, [to] attack the contents of our publications. In doing so, do not shrink at a word or phrase—investigate, rather, the meaning underlying them."[131] When anarchists referred to their work as propaganda, they did not mean feeding predigested thoughts to a passive audience but rather actively engaging their community of sense in the thinking that it required.

Building a Movement: Participation of Readers

A second set of textual elements delivers their anarchist message while enabling participation in the journals and the movement. Local reports; letters to the editors; accounts of exchanging, distributing, and financing the journals; and arrangements for public gatherings were all recurring, interlinked moments in the movement's assemblages. They conducted, so to speak, the lively social and material bookkeeping of the anarchist movement, revealing members' presence and inviting new participants in.

Local detail. Kropotkin was not wrong when he urged researchers "to take collections of papers and read them all through—the news as well as the leading articles—the former, perhaps, even more than the latter."[132] The local news, reliably printed on the back pages of most publications, offered notices and reports of social gatherings, dances, fundraisers, appeals for funds, obituaries, available publications, and requests for correspondence. Anarchism's "picnic culture" was often featured in these pages.[133] One remarkable gathering in Chicago on September 5, 1897, reportedly brought together fifteen thousand people to celebrate the twentieth anniversary of the German-language anarchist journal *Arbeiter Zeitung*, edited by August Spies (who was executed in 1897 as one of the falsely accused Haymarket men). Twenty-seven clubs and unions participated.[134] Another detailed account of a July 28, 1901, picnic near Milwaukee describes the beautiful grounds and recounts the crowd of adults and children enjoying swimming, games, songs, food, short speeches, and "lively discussion and merry-making."[135]

Meetings were sometimes disrupted by competing speakers or local rough-necks, providing more humor and color for their reports. A large outdoor meeting of the Aberdeen Revolutionary Socialist Federation in 1891 was joined by "an old lady who is very anxious about our souls," who "occasionally assists us in getting a crowd by coming into our midst and screeching 'Come to Jesus, He will save you'" but "she cannot stand and bear the sound of the 'Marseillaise,' so when we want to rid ourselves of her we sing and she turns her back on us."[136] The local group in Leeds once reported in *Freedom* that their picnic was rained out, they got lost on a hike, and they found themselves stranded with a Christian group with whom they entered into a singing competition, trying to "rival the harmony" of the religious chorus. The Leeds group's report gently mocked themselves for subsequently solving all the problems of the movement over lemonade.[137]

The back pages can also offer local services, announce meetings of clubs and debating societies, advertise independent communities, solicit help for comrades in need, and communicate opportunities for housing or employment. *Mother Earth* often carried advertisements for local businesses; announcements of sympathetic organizations, such as the Harlem Liberal Alliance or the Ladies Liberal League; and invitations to attend the annual Yom Kippur picnic, to visit Home Colony in Washington State, or in myriad other ways to enter into anarchism's social networks. Social gatherings, as explained by a member of the Midland Counties Anarchist Communists in *Freedom* who is identified only as "the Modest One," were energizing and healing: "I am sure we would assist the propaganda considerably if we made more of our opportunities to meet together and mutually enjoy ourselves. Picnics and socials tend to develope [*sic*] our enthusiasm, prevent us getting pessimistic, and tone down the little personal bitternesses that will crop up amongst us."[138]

Publication of local news in these venues allowed readers to connect their immediate activism with national and global activities, and it could inspire others to organize in their hometowns. Local accounts could surprise and move readers: *Freedom* reports in 1913 that the opera star Enrico Caruso sang at the Atlanta penitentiary to nine hundred convicts, "the spontaneous act of a great artist with a great heart." Caruso is quoted as saying, "I cannot help it, as I think of all these men whom the world shuts out and bars shut in. I would rather give them a few moments' pleasure than sing before kings!"[139] In local reports, workers can become a part of the literature they sell at their meetings. Someone identified as G. H. G. from the market town of Huddersfield, England, reporting on their successful meetings and sales of literature, noted, "And thus do we habitually break the monotony of workaday life."[140] Unnamed comrades share their experiences with the larger movement's reading public as they get together to do their anarchism. There is much "good heart" in these accounts, to use Whitman's phrase, sometimes poignant, often humorous, as rank-and-file activists determinedly break the traditional boundary that Rancière traces in Western political theory between those who think and write versus those who only labor.

Letters to the editor. All of the journals include some arrangements for communicating directly with readers. Under headings such as "The Other Side" or "The Letter Box," *Free Society* printed and responded to letters from readers. This section offered an opportunity for the exchange of ideas, desires, fears, and complaints. The editors frequently reassured readers that those who could not afford to pay would still receive the journal, while pleading with everyone else to renew their subscriptions. During the first four years of publication, the journal received 433 letters and devoted a substantial amount of space to them. If Kenyon Zimmer is correct in estimating *Free Society*'s circulation at about three thousand, that is a significant proportion of letter writers, even if the same individuals wrote more than once.[141] Letters came from all over the United States, with a few from England and Canada. Cities with concentrations of letter writers included Chicago, San Francisco, Philadelphia, New York, Boston, Brooklyn, Kansas City, Los Angeles, Montreal, Pittsburgh, Salt Lake City, San Jose, and Ventura.[142] Readers from more isolated geographic areas connected with one another. For example, M. L. K. from Lowell, Washington, writes, "I try to carry out my ideas as best I can," and asks to "hear from some of the women comrades and readers of *Free Society*."[143] The consistently feminist stance of *Free Society*'s editors was sometimes contested by male readers; the editors appeared to take satisfaction in scolding these men for their unwillingness to extend their anarchism to their personal relations with women.

Correspondence in *Mother Earth* is usually less extensive than in *Free Society*, but it still achieves the purpose of enabling conversations. The issue of April 1911 features a prickly exchange of letters between Goldman and Bolton Hall, a lawyer and single-tax reformer, over the role of violence in the movement. In the July 1911 issue, a letter from the Russian anarcho-syndicalist Alexander Shapiro discusses the creation of the International Bureau for coordinating communication among groups, and letters from Japanese anarchists report on the aftermath of their comrades' execution for their attempt to assassinate the emperor. Beyond letters to the editor, other sections also encouraged participation: the "Observations and Comments" section of *Mother Earth* offered chatty accounts of current news, shared memories, and updates on the activities of friends. Goldman's accounts of her lecture tours, entitled "Ups and Downs of an Anarchist Propagandist" or "On the Trail," were something of an anarchist travelogue, inviting readers to experience city-by-city detail of their movement's national presence. In the June 1916 issue, Goldman published "To My Friends, Old and New" to answer letters she received while in jail for distributing information on birth control.

In some issues of *Freedom*, reports from other countries were printed in the form of letters: columns about Russia, South Africa, Norway, and other places took the form of letters from correspondents in each country. The "Notes" section was often informal, inviting readers to experience the text as a relaxed conversation with a comrade. While *Freedom* and *Mother Earth* are a bit more formal than *Free Society*, all three journals open up what Maria Tamboukou aptly characterizes as a publication's "relational and dialogic spaces between and among its contributors and its readers."[144] The letters section offered a place to affirm shared political values and agendas as well as to express oneself and debate controversies within the movement.

Fund-raising. Anarchist publications engaged in ceaseless fund-raising. Anarchists usually made their living in textiles, mining, construction, shipping, agriculture, cigar-making, sales, or skilled trades, with a few professionals and moneyed individuals in the mix.[145] They often put out their publications at the end of a long workday, a long workweek, and were chronically short of funds. Henry Addis reported that, to keep *The Firebrand*, the predecessor of *Free Society*, afloat, "one of the women comrades took in washing and during the hop season all went into the hop field."[146] Editors published detailed financial reports on how much money was collected for particular causes, such as the fund to appeal Berkman's prison sentence.[147] *Free Society* reported in its first issue that Goldman was raising money to send to anarchists being persecuted in Spain; $5.87 was scrupulously reported and sent to the fund-raising committee in New York.[148] Goldman's lecture tours and literature sales raised money to keep *Mother Earth* afloat. Parties, balls, rummage sales, and similar events brought in modest sums. There were sometimes multiple fund raisers going on at the same time: the Mother Earth Sustaining Fund, a fund for Italian or Russian political prisoners and their families, a Free Speech Defense Fund, a fund to support efforts to secure Berkman's release from prison, a fund to publish a book of de

Cleyre's writings, and others, each one with donations and expenses clearly recorded and published.

The effort that went into demonstrating the responsible handling and reporting of funds suggests that sometimes there must have been problems. Heiner Becker reports that *Freedom* survived many crises because, "apart from one minor incident, the group was spared (or managed to keep out) members who eventually ran away with the (always meagre) cash-box."[149] Yet overcompensating for real or potential theft was not the only implication of such fastidious record keeping and reporting: careful readers could notice, week after week or month after month, which dedicated comrades donated from their meager resources to keep the journals going. Wolfe, for instance, was a regular financial contributor to *Freedom*; since most of her work was behind the scenes, readers were most likely to encounter her written name in the many fund-raising accounts. Similarly with Philadelphia physician Natasha Notkin, who gave to all three publications and probably more besides. *Freedom* recognized in 1903, "The Russian tea parties organized by Comrade N. Notkin have long been famous, in more ways than one; but this year she surpassed herself."[150] Like writing letters to the editor and distributing the publications, making financial contributions was a concrete and modestly visible way of participating in the movement.[151]

Public space. In addition to providing conceptual space for sharing ideas, journals made public space available in their physical premises or affiliated clubs. The second issue of *Free Society* invited readers to the office: "The publication office of *Free Society* is located at 13 Oak Grove Ave where comrades will be welcome."[152] *Free Society* operated a lending library and also advertised efforts in other cities to set up anarchist libraries, soliciting contributions of materials. Comrades in Chicago announced their plans to establish a reading room and invited individuals with spare books to donate them.[153] Comrades in Bucharest also appealed to *Free Society* readers for reading materials.[154] Free reading rooms were announced in New York City, Boston, Saint Louis, and Philadelphia.[155] In "A Reading Course for Anarchists," de Cleyre calls for anarchist communities to form reading groups and pursue a course of study "as quiet students, not as disputatious wranglers."[156] No doubt she urged this course of action because there was a lot of disputatious wrangling going on, yet she was herself a teacher and knew that more thoughtful studies could also be pursued.

In March 1915 *Freedom* announced the "opening of Marsh House," which was "a clubhouse and rendezvous for London comrades." A few people lived in the large building, including Wolfe and Keell, which also had a library, sitting room, and large hall for gatherings: "It is a splendid opportunity to give fresh impetus to the movement, and the knowledge that there exists a place where one can always be assured of meeting comrades, and taking part in discussions, should go a long way toward making our propaganda more effective, and our views of social problems more clear."[157] Anarchists clubs flourished in London during the movement's high points, including the largely Jewish radical club frequented by Rudolf and Milly Rocker, the Autonomie Club; the Berner's Street Club, linked to the International Workingmen's Educational Association; and the Rose Street Club, linked to the journal *Freiheit*.[158] Goldman's apartment at 210 East Thirteenth Street in Greenwich Village was similarly a meeting place for radicals and intellectuals, and in journalist Hutchins Hapgood's words, "a home for lost dogs."[159] Justus Schwab's Liberty Hall saloon on the Lower East Side of New York City was "decorated and conceptualized as a free, anti-capitalist space."[160] Anarchism's radical hangouts and meeting places invited comrades to socialize, to plan, and to experience ordinary events of daily life as anarchist pleasures.

Distribution networks. Each issue lists the name and location of each distribution agent for the journal. *Free Society* had agents in Chicago, New York City, Buffalo, Philadelphia, Allegheny, Baltimore, Providence, Saint Louis, London, and Glasgow and was sold at newsstands in San Francisco. Many distributors were stalwart, keeping at their tasks for years, as did Hattie Lang in Buffalo and Natasha Notkin in Philadelphia. The work of distribution was not a lesser task but a crucial node in the network: anarchists who printed, edited, or wrote for their own journals also distributed others. For example, Thomas Cantwell, a printer and editor of *Freedom*, distributed *Free Society* in London; William Duff, who wrote for the London journal *Alarm*, distributed *Free Society* in Glasgow; Hippolyte Havel, who was later on the editorial board of *Mother Earth* in New York City and coeditor of *Road to Freedom* at Stelton, distributed *Free Society* in Chicago; and Jay Fox, who edited and printed *The Agitator* in Home Colony, Washington, and later in Chicago, also distributed *Free Society*. Several members of the *Mother Earth* inner circle distributed *Freedom* in the 1920s, including Fitzi Fitzgerald, Harry Kelly, and Havel.[161] Like contributing money, writing to the editors, or sending reports of local activities, serving as a distribution agent was a repeating public form of participation in anarchist print culture.

Exchanges of journals. All three of these journals regularly exchanged issues with dozens or hundreds of other publications, and they periodically published the names of the incoming journals and books. In Keell's address book from the 1920s, over 350 exchanges were recorded.[162] It is tempting for readers today to just skim such lists or skip them altogether, and to imagine that readers at the time did so as well. Yet I suspect that may not have been the case. Chronically short of funds, why would editors regularly waste paper, ink, and labor on these lists if they were mere formalities? I speculate that these lists, repeated week after week and month after month, in dozens or hundreds of journals in multiple languages, had some political significance. The following is a sample of what readers encountered.

At the beginning of *Free Society*'s run, the exchange list included these titles:

* *Freedom* (London, monthly)
* *La Questione Sociale* (Paterson, New Jersey)
* *New Dispensation* (Corvallis, Oregon, monthly)
* *Armstrong's Autonomist* (Houston, monthly)
* *Delnicke Listy* (Bohemian, New York City, weekly)
* *Progressive Thought* (Olathe, Kansas)
* *Dawn of Equity* (Olathe, Kansas)
* *Little Freethinker* (Snowville, Virginia, a journal for children)
* *The Altruist* (Saint Louis, monthly)
* *Lucifer, The Lightbearer* (Valley Falls, Kansas, or Chicago, weekly)[163]

Over time the list changed as new publications were added. By May 1, 1898, *Free Society*'s list of exchanges had grown to include the following:

* *L'Agitazione* (Italian, weekly)
* *Libertaire* (French, weekly)
* *Der Sozialist* (German, weekly)
* *Freiheit* (German, Buffalo, weekly)
* *L'avvenire* (Italian, Buenos Aires)
* *Volne Listy* (Bohemian, New York City, monthly)
* *The Adult* (London, monthly)
* *Solidarity* (New York City, semimonthly)
* *Sturmvogel* (German, New York City, semimonthly)
* *Der Arme Teufel* (German, Detroit, weekly)
* *Le Temp Nouveaux* (French, weekly)

* *Le Pere Peinard* (French, weekly)
* *La Tribune Libre* (French, Pennsylvania, weekly)
* *Germinal* (Spanish, Buenos Aires, weekly)
* *Miscarea Sociala* (Romanian, Bucharest, weekly)
* *Socailistische Monatscheft* (German, Berlin, monthly)
* *Del Niche Listy* (Bohemian, New York City, weekly)
* *The Altruist* (Saint Louis, monthly)
* *Lucifer, The Lightbearer* (weekly)[164]

Early in *Freedom*'s run, its exchange list included these publications, organized by country of origin:

* England: *Autonomie, Commonweal, Christian Socialist, Church Reformer, Free Russia, Herald of Anarchy, Justice, Land and Labour, Londoner Freie Presse, Personal Rights Journal, Seed-Time, Worker's Friend*
* North America: *Anarchist, Altruist, Coast Seamen's Journal, Fair Play, Freedom, Freie Arbeiter Stimme, Freiheit, Journal of the Knights of Labour, Journal of United Labour, Liberty, Licco Cubano, Lucifer, Parole, Reasoner, Reveil des Masses, Revista de Florida, South-West, Twentieth Century, Volné Listy, Vorbote*
* France: *La Révolte, Père Peinard*
* Spain: *Alarma, Jornalero, Productor, Revolucion Social, Socialismo, Tramontana, Vietima del Trabajo, Voz del Trabajo*
* Italy: *Avanti, Campana, Combattiano, Nuovo Cambattiamo*
* Belgium: *La Question Social*
* Holland: *Anarchist*
* Norway: *Fedraheimen*
* Austria: *Arbeiter Zeitung, Schlesischen Nachrichten*
* Portugal: *Revoluvgoo Sogial*
* Cuba: *El Productor*
* Buenos Aires: *El Persequido*
* Australia: *Australian Radical, Worker*[165]

Mother Earth sometimes advertised other journals, especially *Freedom, Freiheit,* and *The Agitator,* and often mentioned journals in the "International Notes." The August 1907 issue announced that *Mother Earth* received *La Demolizione* from France, *Humanidad Nueva* and *Salud y Fuerza* from Spain, *Universita Popolare* and *Il Grido della Folla* from Italy, *Revolucion* from Mexico, *Tierra* from Cuba, and a new (unnamed) journal from Japan. Even more than journals, *Mother Earth* gave considerable space to anarchist books for sale at their own or other radical bookstores. The following books were listed as available through *Mother Earth* in May 1906:

* Henry Thomas Buckle, *History of Civilisation in England*
* Edward Carpenter, *England's Ideal*; *Civilisation*; *Love's Coming of Age*; *Toward Democracy*
* *The Chicago Martyrs: The Famous Speeches*
* Ernest Crosby, *Garrison the Non-Resistant*; *Plain Talk in Psalm and Parable*; *Captain Jinks, Hero*; *Swords and Plowshares*; *Tolstoy and His Message*; *Tolstoy as a Schoolmaster*; *Broad-Cast*; *Edward Carpenter, Poet and Prophet*
* Joseph Elkins, *The Doukhobors*
* Jean Grave, *Moribund Society and Anarchism*
* J. M. Guyau, *Education and Heredity*; *A Sketch of Morality*
* Bolton Hall, *Free America*; *The Game of Life*; *Even as You and I*
* W. A. Hinds, *American Communities*
* C. L. James, *History of the French Revolution*; *Origin of Anarchism*
* Peter Kropotkin, *Fields, Factories and Workshops*; *Mutual Aid*; *Memoirs of a Revolutionist*; *Modern Science and Anarchism*; *Ideals of Russian Literature*; *The State*; *Anarchism*; *The Wage System*; *Anarchist Morality*
* Antonio Labriola, *Essays on the Materialistic Concept of History*
* H. D. Lloyd, *Wealth against Commonwealth*
* E. Malatesta and J. F. Morton, *Anarchism*
* O. Mason, *Woman's Share in Primitive Culture*
* Jean Meslier, *Superstition in All Ages*
* William Morris, *News from Nowhere*
* Friedrich Nietzsche, *Thus Spake Zarathustra*
* Thomas Paine, *Rights of Man*
* Winwood Reade, *The Martyrdom of Man*
* J. Sanborn, *Paris and the Social Revolution*
* W. Tcherkesoff, *Pages of Socialist History*
* J. Arthur Thomson, *The Science of Life*
* Leo Tolstoy, *The Slavery of Our Times*; *Bethink Yourself*; *Church and State*
* C. F. Volney, *Ruins of Empires*
* Edwin C. Walker, *Who Is the Enemy*
* Oscar Wilde, *The Ballad of Reading Gaol*; *The Soul of Man under Socialism*; *De Profundis*; *Intentions*; *Plays*
* J. Wilson, *Life without a Master*; *The New Dispensation*; *Living Thoughts*[166]

Anarchist publications invested considerable resources in exchanges, which linked each journal's scriptural community to the others and paved the way for other sorts of interactions. Publications regularly received through exchange relations joined each group's library, allowing visitors to have access to anarchist publications from around the world. Writers from one journal were invited to give speaking tours at the venues of other journals; local and global news was exchanged; campaigns were organized around shared issues. Established journals regularly welcomed new journals; on March 19, 1899, for example, *Free Society* welcomed *Modern Criminology*, edited by Italian anarchist Pietro Gori in Buenos Aires, and *The Radical*, a new monthly from Stockton, California.[167] *Freedom* notified readers in October 1897 that *Le Révolté* (The Rebel) was now gone because the leaders were imprisoned, and it was replaced by *La Révolte* (Rebellion); in the same issue, *Freedom* welcomed *L'Idée Ouvrière*, a new anarchist weekly in Le Hâvre.[168] *Free Society* only once severed its exchange agreement with another journal: in the May 13, 1900, issue, it ended its exchange with *The Altruist* because the latter publication "lie[d] about anarchists" and defended the US invasion of Cuba.[169]

I find myself drawn to these plain, repetitive lists. Their intellectual weight is palpable. I imagine readers encountering the lists: some would glance past the items, no doubt, but I imagine some readers looking to make sure the material they want to read has come in, maybe making plans to go and read the latest issues or purchase a recently arrived book. I imagine the impact of the weight and cadence of these lists, repeating over and over. The feel of that intellectual heft is part of the anarchist community of sense. These humble lists are an opening to understanding how assemblages work. Substantial time, energy, and resources went into these exchanges, which brought readers of one journal into the network of many journals. The exchanges meet DeLanda's criteria for assemblages: they are strong, dense, and reciprocal. They persist and adapt. The "bookish poor people" whom Christine Stansell characterizes as the rank and file of the anarchist movement, through lingering on the titles, the languages, the origins of each publication, could locate themselves as participants in a learned international community of sense.[170] When the journals reliably announce exchanges received or books for sale, they bring evidence of the commerce among the different nodes in the assemblages of anarchist print culture. The journals help to make the readers who help to make the journals, creating the subjectivities and opportunities needed for radical study.

Mixed Genres: Social Sketches and
Think Pieces

Anarchist literary critic Paul Goodman offers a powerful view of genres, or "styles" of language, as expressive ways of being in the world: "The intellectual power of a speaker operates primarily not on strings of sentences but *in* his global experience, in the situation in which he is cast, that includes the inherited code, the hearer, and the need to say his say."[171] In the interactive triangle created by the language practices we inherit, the reader-listener who hears us into speech, and "the need to say our say," genres emerge. Genres stage encounters between us and our worlds, both the ones we live in and the ones we struggle toward: "A style of speech," Goodman offers, "is an hypothesis about how the world is. A good style, colloquial or literary, is one that is adequate to cope with a wide and necessary range of experience. It proves itself as a way of being, it does not break down, it is believable."[172]

It is consistent with Goodman's evocation of "good style" as not necessarily novel but "genuine, coming from how the writer is, speaking his animal cries, squaring with what he sees, not avoiding the others, not censoring," to revisit Lisa Gitelman's powerful theorizing of genre as an assemblage of communicative elements that are recognizable to an audience.[173] Instead of a set of rules (regarding, for example, number of lines, cadence of syllables, or trajectory of plot), genre becomes a dynamic practice that achieves coherence through a relationship with those who express and receive it. Recall Gitelman's charming image: genres are "like words hidden in a random grid of letters." They make their appearance through their contrasts to the patterns and noise around them; they emerge "amid a jumble of discourse because of the ways they have been internalized by members of a shared culture."[174] Genre conventions, Liz Stanley notes, "provide a loose shape" rather than a determining structure. Like the correspondence that Stanley analyzes, anarchist writings are "performative and emergent and often play with 'other' genres or indeed shade into these."[175] Within the energy of radical study, anarchist writers could "mix and match" conventional genres, in the process of building on what they know, connecting with readers, and "saying their say."

Two further textual styles illustrate the dynamic possibilities that arise when the content of anarchist literature and the form of anarchist aesthetics are interwoven, giving rise to creatively mixed genres that can express ways of being in the world. Italian anarchist and printer Leda Rafanelli coined the term "social sketch" to describe one expressive mixed genre, a compressed short story containing elements of a poem. I am using the term "think piece" to describe another mixture of standard genres, a short essay drawing on elements of a letter.[176] Social sketches and think pieces contribute to anarchism's world of letters in ways that are both *about* anarchism and expressive *of* anarchism. Women typically created these mixed-genre writings, while editors, usually men, generally did not write them but nonetheless saw their value and included them in publications.[177] These writings are links to the anarchist version of what Harney and Moten called the "fugitive public."[178] The pages and the readers, the people and the things, are animated in relation to one another. Their vitality does not come out of them like a hidden kernel but sparks between them, enabled by their encounters.[179] When editor James Morton of *Free Society* included "general literary matter" as important in anarchist journals because it "will make our paper attractive to all readers, and thus vastly increase its influence in the movement," I imagine that it is social sketches and think pieces that he had in mind.[180]

Social sketches, according to Rafanelli, are "short, anonymous snapshots featuring everyday characters fighting against oppression from authoritative institutions."[181] They are fictive but are not quite short stories: they lack developed narrative but employ lyrical language to portray vivid characters and settings. In Rafanelli's words, they combine "wispy plots" with "a wealth of detail and many shades of color."[182] Rafanelli, like Rancière, is reaching for an authorial voice for the part that has no part:

> Whether wrapped in the fog of an icy, grey, cold evening; sunk in the somber darkness of the slums; lost within the modern-day chasm of a machine shop; or even strolling along the splendid seashore: there are creatures moving about everywhere, human beings who the novelist does not see, who the historian does not recognize, since there is nothing to differentiate them from the masses in which they flounder. They live in houses, in hovels, in the depths of the mines, in the cold solitude of the prisons, in the stillness of the convents, all victims of persecution and pain, all subjected to the orthodoxy of today's laws; even wounded and exasperated rebels, men, women, young adults: people who have been shipwrecked by life, who no one will ever throw a line to.[183]

Writing by encounter with those "who the novelist does not see, who the historian does not recognize" is a style that presumes, as Goodman remarks, some things about how the world is, about who can speak and what can be said.[184] Here I take a closer look at three examples of this mini-genre:

Lily Gair Wilkinson's compressed, lyrical stories of walking in *Freedom* in 1913; an unsigned story about suffering that is probably by Voltairine de Cleyre in *Mother Earth* in 1906; and, a year later, Sadakichi Hartmann's retrospective tale about a flower maker, also in *Mother Earth*.

In 1913 *Freedom* published four articles by Scottish anarchist Lily Gair Wilkinson that use the trope of walking to enlarge readers' ability to imagine and move through the space of streets, shops, and factories, through a rebellious past and into a fungible future, amenable to radical interventions.[185] Wilkinson's social sketches take her readers on a walk through London that is also a walk through history. Readers encounter narrative personae that are animated by vivid settings in their city and their history. Wilkinson enscripts *you*, the reader, into the walk: *you* encounter degraded workers and grim city streets; *you* long for respite in a park or garden; and *you* struggle to come to terms with the relentless requirements of capitalist workplaces.

Wilkinson's social sketches, like Rafanelli's, are "short, anonymous snapshots featuring everyday characters fighting against oppression from authoritative institutions."[186] Rafanelli, however, usually narrates her stories in the third person, while Wilkinson employs a more active grammar and variable voice, creating a cacophony of subject positions. In the first installment, "Women in Bondage," Wilkinson recommends that you "go out again and watch the women as they pass," encountering wealthy married ladies, women laborers, and prostitutes and inquiring about the specific intersection of sexuality and labor for each. Warning readers against "lumping together of the sexes, as if they formed two opposing camps," she insists that the result of the combined workings of patriarchy and capitalism is that "nearly all women are no better to slaves." First, you encounter a woman of the upper class: "her soft clothes, her smooth face, her confident manner," along with her "jewels of great price." These merely conceal married prostitution: "A rich man's wife is merely his most costly possession." Switching to the first-person plural, Wilkinson urges us, "Now turn to another type. Most of the women who pass us wherever we go are of this type—it is the type of woman who is poorly born, the working woman." Her father, brothers, and husband are "not free to work for themselves; they must spend their lives working for others," while she does the same work as they do for even lower wages and the housework for free. Since the average wage of women workers in Wilkinson's London was seven shillings per week, their struggles lead us to encounter the third type of woman in bondage, the prostitute. She is driven by poverty to a "bitter and cruel" bondage. All three types "enter bondage by selling their bodies; selling them for man's pleasure or selling them for the profit of an employer but always by selling that sacred thing, a woman's body."[187]

The second installment, "Women in Rebellion," walks the reader through women's radical history, introducing Emma Goldman, Louise Michel, Maria Rygier, and Marie Spiridonova, whose bold rebellions create a historical trajectory for the reader to continue. Their "splendid efforts to be free" inspire readers with possibilities.[188] While it is more conventional in grammar, voiced entirely in the third person, this essay uses the rhetorical strategies of a travelogue through time, where past events set the stage for current struggles and future victories. Wilkinson uses the rush of history and passion to awaken us so that, in the third serialized segment, we are ready to walk forth in freedom.

In the third installment, "Women's Freedom," Wilkinson takes the reader on a rebellious escape from dreary factory or office labor, moving through a series of working-class spaces in industrial London. The most delightfully written of the segments, this sketch opens with an announcement about freedom that she poses in order to subvert: "A free man or woman is one who can dispose of his or her person without let or hindrance, without reference to any master." Then she resumes the second-person voice, issuing this challenge: "If you, being a woman, resolved to be free in this social sense, to go out into the world as a woman in freedom, how would it fare with you?"[189] Wilkinson is transforming her reader, through direct address and an invitation to walk, into a woman who is capable of going out into the world in freedom. Wilkinson takes you on an urban thought experiment:

> For a time you might wander unhindered, elated by thoughts of liberty, but very soon you would find that you cannot dwell forever on the heights. Let us suppose that you feel tired, and that you enter a tea shop in default of a better place of rest. The shop looks sordid and dingy and you shudder slightly as a vision of true repose comes to mind— something with green fields and running water and the scent of grass and flowers in it. But, alas! You are not free to that extent; there being no Elysian fields—here in London with its dreary grey buildings and endless discomfort. So you enter the shop.[190]

Your determination "to go out into the world as a woman in freedom" is unsettled by your visit to the café: the nasty tea and stale bun, uncomfortable surrounds, and most of all, the "pale grim young woman who waits on you." Your encounter with the waitress undermines your ability to think of freedom merely as independence: "You realise in a flash that here again in the person of the shop-girl is a limitation of freedom—you are not free from *her*." Wilkinson continues, "You recognize the social nature of freedom: how none stands alone in life, but the life of each is dependent upon the lives of others, and affected by the life of others . . . and if your vision is clear enough, you realise that so long as one, even the least, of these human brothers and sisters is in bondage, there can be no true freedom for you."[191]

More epiphanies follow. You awake "glad and young and gay and *free*," but the clock insists you return to the office or the factory. You cannot leave: "The penalty of desertion is death." Wilkinson provokes you: "Turn back quickly to the city again and sell yourself once more into slavery before it is too late." Go back to "the monster army of modern industrial life," the production of "the few things needful and the many needless," where the air is polluted, the sunlight obscured, to be ruled by those who "know nothing of you, care nothing for you." The despair you feel at such impending defeat spurs you to honor old desires—for "green fields and running water and the scent of grass and flowers"—and to inspire new ones:[192]

> You have thus arrived at a great illumination through your vain striving after personal liberty. There can be no freedom for single individuals— one here and one there cannot be free in a social sense; but men and women, being socially interdependent, can only be free together—as a community, that is. And further, there can be no freedom while there is private property which prevents all men and women having free access to the means of life; not one here and one there must be possessors, but all must possess together—in common, that is.
>
> And this is Communism.[193]

In the final installment, also called "Women's Freedom," Wilkinson sketches an anarchist space in which a different set of encounters could emerge. Here she takes us to the future: "Women will have the same freedom as men, because they will be able to dispose of their lives as they choose." There will be no legally sanctioned marriage, no wage work; everyone will have access to the means of producing to meet their needs. We will "return to a simple and more wholesome kind of life, in which physical needs will be provided for by handicraft and agriculture rather than the complex industrial system of labour in crowded cities." Love will be free and joyous, and "for those who by nature may desire such a life," homes will be sites of "true companionship." While she imagines that women would "take the lead" in making free and loving home lives, *man's sphere is the home also*." Drawing heavily on William Morris's artisanal visions, Wilkinson leaves readers with an image of self-creating individuals in free, healthy, and loving communities. "Men and women will gain true emancipation when they strive together for freedom."[194]

Social sketches share with Rancière's prose a powerfully scenographic element: they design scenes—that is, place-orienting practices that house abbreviated struggles to develop characters' political engagements. They are, in Davide Panagia's words, "born of the particular." In *Rancière's Sentiments*, Panagia explores Rancière's "ecology of dispositions, sensibilities, and forms of participation by individuals, groups, objects, and histories who have been repeatedly judged as unentitled." Panagia explains, "Politics for Rancière happens when the extant norms of how things fit can neither sustain nor explain the existence of discrete parts that don't fit. Such fragments don't account for an exclusion so much as an inability to register a relation with an established sense of ordering. Thus what is required is the articulation of a new disposition, arrangement, or networks of sensibilities. Such acts of rearticulation are what Rancière calls *partager*, and they are acts that refer to moments of radical mediation where the inequalities of qualification that enable access to politics are rendered indistinct."[195] The specific, vivid settings in social sketches are best thought of not as foundations for settled conclusions but more as possibilities for further exploration. They seek to "register a relation" that has previously been disenabled. Social sketches do not just claim that the previously excluded can or should speak: they make places and people who do speak, who enter into a scene and engage its inhabitants in the service of articulating a disposition of hope or reflection or rage.

Political theorist Lori Marso points out that Wilkinson's governing trope has its own limits: "When we make walking the exemplary pose for feminist freedom, we sideline some things that are centrally important." Marso encourages us to "see freedom in other poses, registers, and spaces."[196] Her insight works well with the scenography of a different social sketch, a short piece of fiction entitled "Between the Living and the Dead," published in *Mother Earth* and probably authored by de Cleyre.[197] This street scene hosts the involuntary kinship of three suffering souls. A hospital patient in great pain, unable to sit or lie down, stares out her window at a man in the building across the street and a girl in the apartment below. The man is a consumptive who sits at his window and cradles the single geranium that shares his portal to the world. The disfigured girl suffers from congenital syphilis: the refrain of the story repeats, "The sins of the father shall be visited upon the children." The girl creeps out on her doorstep with her doll, which receives the caresses that her caregivers shun. A triangulated line of sight connects the three, "the unburied dead who from our coffin windows still looked out." No narrative is suggested, other than the "fatal narrowing circle" of mortality itself. Instead of a storyline, the three are linked by proximity and contrast: the woman heals; the man carefully sets aside the geranium in order to leave it unmolested as he jumps to his death on "the kind hard stone that was merciful to him"; the girl continues, "like an eye seen dull-blue under a lid that has never unclosed."[198]

De Cleyre's immobile souls may be in a better position than Wilkinson's walker to apprehend what Marso calls "the lessons of contingency, necessity, and unexpected possibilities available in every encounter."[199] De Cleyre's characters are both captive (in decaying bodies) and absent (from the life in the street on which they gaze). In some ways they are the opposite of Wilkinson's walker: they marvel at all the busy movement of those street creatures who "tramp so lustily" toward death. They looked on wearily, unmoving, "dead things with living eyes." In the relational space above the street, they may encounter one another's gazes and touch one another's pain. Unlike the biblical version of the story, there is no deliverance here, only a searing question: "Why was the dream of justice ever born in the human mind, if it must stand dumb before this terrible child?"[200] Anarchist editor Leonard Abbott aptly named de Cleyre "a priestess of pity and of vengeance."[201] Critic Crispin Sartwell similarly observes that, compared with orators who "breathed fire," de Cleyre "did a slow burn."[202] Compared with the resolutely hopeful walker in Wilkinson's story, de Cleyre often despaired, yet she always returned to the struggle. Her patient leaves the hospital, tormented by the memory of the lonely child but still attached to the dream of justice the child's suffering rebukes. As Abbott concludes about his friend de Cleyre, "I feel in her a tragic and tormented spirit. She fought without illusions, but she fought to the end."[203]

A third brief example of a social sketch is "The Flower-Maker" by German Japanese poet and critic Sadakichi Hartmann, one of the writers in the *Mother Earth* inner circle and one of the few men who wrote in this mixed genre in anarchist journals.[204] The text is spare and precise. Hartmann minimizes narrative to focus instead on close descriptions of settings, objects, and characters. The attenuated story goes like this: a young, lonely girl makes cloth flowers for a living in her sparse flat; she is seduced by a passing scoundrel, loses her fragile hold on respectability, and eventually becomes a prostitute. Hartmann refuses to take the woman's life as an object lesson or make her a figure in an allegorical tale about exploitation.

Instead, he focuses on the flowers, on her "expert hand," her tools, her raw materials: "the delicate little tool for crimping, the 'guffer' for making the dents in imitation of natural flower petals, and the creaser for making those almost-invisible cross lines that lend finish to the petals."[205]

In an unpublished essay on painting, Hartmann proclaims, "The old structures of pictorialism are tumbling down," and he urges artists to find inspiration in what he calls naked objects, "the object itself in all its nakedness, unadulterated by any sentimentalism." The flowers in his story could be the textual version of naked objects, carrying "an elusive vagueness of emotion or thought that connotes directly from the object represented and its significance in time and space."[206] In the making of the flowers, the repetition of the tools' use, the enduring feel and color of the fabric, the girl contends with things in her world and finds intimacy that Marso suggests is, in its quiet way, a worthy contender for what she calls "freedom in a minor key."[207] The artificial flowers speak to the reader, suggesting that imitations can be as real in their effects as the natural blooms the girl seldom sees.

Hartmann offers no pity to the girl, but there is respect in his close portrayal of her labor and her longing. He counsels her against regret: "You told me about riding through dark nights, with the sea wind in your faces, you and he so near. Would you exchange those madcap excursions into the Nirvana of the senses for a life of accidental purity? No, you wouldn't, Stella. Let's have another bottle! I paid the Madam. Take this for yourself, dear. No, I can't stay to-night. So long!"[208] Stella's customer gifts her with a bottle of wine and a night released from sexual labor. He also gifts her with respect. They both realize that she remembers an artificial love, like the flowers she deftly assembled, but the love and the flowers were still real in their effects and offer something dearer than remorse.

The writers of these social sketches individuate their characters with spare motions: a shy movement of the flower girl's knee, the embrace of a wax doll by a doomed child, a fatigued urban walker's confrontation with the expropriated labor behind her cup of bitter tea. These social sketches show, rather than tell of, worlds of pain and longing in which encounters emerge and unexpected connections are made. Calling on Rancière's scenography, Panagia suggests that "each scene of solidarity bespeaks a new experience of becoming-with."[209] The awful becoming-with of de Cleyre's suffering trio; the striving becoming-with of Wilkinson's determined walker in the class-ridden space of the city; the ambiguous becoming-with of Hartmann's prostitute with her silk flowers and her unreliable lovers: Panagia's take on Rancière works well for articulating the political aesthetic of these social sketches. Social sketches avoid the didactic tone that too often restricts anarchist writing: we are not asked to learn a lesson, but to extend ourselves into a situation. We are invited to be haunted by the wrecked worlds we glimpse. Probably all anarchist writers encourage readers to challenge social conventions of obedience and resignation, but these writers also rework genre conventions to invite fresh encounters between personal experience and political change.

I am using the term *think piece* to describe another kind of mixed genre, somewhere between an essay and a letter, also usually written by women. These reflective essays tend to be informal and often written in the first person. The author's voice and presence are strong. The writer addresses the reader personally, inviting a response. Think pieces are different from social sketches in that they lack vivid characters or settings. Yet the two styles are similar in that they cultivate intimacy with the reader and develop the political dimensions of personal feelings and experiences. They both exemplify *Freedom* editor Colin Ward's suggestion to develop anarchism by locating "the right growing points for the application of anarchist ideas to ordinary life."[210] Here I examine a few think pieces from the journals at hand: some short essays by Chicago labor leader and writer Lizzie Holmes in *Free Society*, inviting readers to bring emotion more fully into their political thinking in order to do more with their imaginations; a piece in *Free Society* in 1899 by writer and printer Lois Waisbrooker called "Why Is It So?" encouraging women to examine their investments in respectability; and an essay by the mathematician Mary Everest Boole, "Should Decorative Work Be a Drudgery?" in *Freedom* in 1895.

Think pieces address readers directly, pose practical questions, and invite us to connect our personal situations to larger political problems. Intertwining their analyses of capitalism, patriarchy, religion, and the state, these women were writing intersectionally and connecting the personal to the political many decades before second-wave feminism articulated those ideas. Think pieces generally focus on concrete problems of daily living that we can address by thinking together about them. Usually written in a first-person active voice, they engage readers in reflecting on a problem at hand and imagining a better way to handle it. They employ a conversational tone, addressing the reader as a reasonable person who is part of the "we" who want a better life.

Holmes is one of the most consistent writers of compelling think pieces in these three publications. In "Sentiment," she suggests that abstract writing is boring and calls for more consideration of "the sentiment, the feelings, the desires, the moral tone, if you will, of the people."²¹¹ Recognizing that anarchists tend to reiterate their main principles over and over, she asks for more: "Why not wonder a little of what we are going to think, when we are free to think whatever we wish?"²¹² In a gentle voice, Holmes criticizes anarchists for being averse to analyzing or encountering emotions. Calling on the image Max Stirner used in *The Ego and Its Own* to talk about fixed ideas, Holmes suggests that avoidance of thinking about emotion has become a "spook," a habit that haunts anarchism without being acknowledged. Holmes urges readers to bring feeling more fully into thinking:

> The very first inkling one has of a new truth comes in the form of a senti-ment. We *feel* a truth before we get it into our brains to work it up into a theory. The emotions, the feelings we experience are the greatest part of our lives, after all. Any form of society must depend to a greater or lesser extent on the sentiments felt by the people. But more than any other will the future welfare and order of a *free* society depend upon the sentiments of its members. The kind of sentiments cherished, the kind of emotions encouraged, the *feelings* of the community, will determine the kind of a society we have. The nearer we approach to a free, unruled condition, the more necessary it is, it seems to me, that the best, the warmest, the sweetest, the most poetic and beautiful sentiments should prevail.²¹³

Holmes wants anarchists to interconnect feeling and knowing, to eschew thinking as "closed logicians." Interlacing concepts, percepts, and affects invokes the sort of work that Rancière finds in optical machines, those "moving constellations" that generate, rather than merely represent, thoughts, images and feelings.²¹⁴ Holmes is calling on anarchists to create themselves. They should be anarchistic about anarchism: "I did believe that there would never be a stopping place for an anarchist, but I am afraid that for the materialistic, pumbline [*sic*] egoist—at whose side I have long marched, there are a few bars up yet, from which they steer their course very clear."²¹⁵ The demands of economic justice do not exhaust the challenges of radical change:

> It seems to me that about everything has been said for freedom that can be said: when we have reiterated again our principle of equal liberty; when we have pictured the present bad conditions in the most vivid colors; when we have shown the advantages of a self-controlled society, what more can we do? We have got to let the world come up to us before we can go any further, and in the meantime what shall we do? Why not wonder a little of what we are going to think, when we are free to think whatever

we wish? If we are nothing in the world *but* economic revolutionists, when free, economic conditions come, our occupation will be gone.[216]

The work of the anarchist undercommons is ongoing because its assemblages are unfinished. Harney and Moten's open-ended understanding of change resonates with Holmes's think piece called "Mental Barriers." Holmes reminds readers that building an anarchist future requires us to develop the capacity to be surprised. Change can be unexpected and its catalysts, unpredictable: "Every thought, every conception, every imagination, has its place in the world; it does not do to ignore one of them. Who knows which of them might prove the revolutionizer of the world?"[217] Halberstam puts it this way: "Revolution will come in a form we cannot yet imagine. Moten and Harney propose that we prepare now for what will come by entering into study. Study, a mode of thinking with others separate from the thinking that institutions requires of you, prepares us to be embedded in what Harney calls 'the with and for' and allows you to spend less time antagonized and antagonizing."[218] Holmes knows she can't fully imagine anarchy, can't predict it, can only stay open to imagining it with others. She has engaged in years of anarchist study, writing for *Free Society* and other journals, editing *The Alarm*, and working with Chicago anarchist Lucy Parsons organizing women garment workers. She would have brightened up considerably at Harney and Moten's argument that we "preserve by inhabiting" since that is what anarchists do: they make the change they seek through the process of calling for it.[219]

In an earlier think piece, Holmes analyzes "the war spirit" in US society. She is impatient with Americans for their blind national loyalties and their craving for empire: "Trust Americans for desperate, wholesale, reckless, abandoned patriotism every time. Trust them to let anything on earth be done to them while they are under its exciting spell....Anything goes that is American—robbery, oppression, invasion, corruption—just say it is 'American' and we will whoop it up for all it's worth." Her pronouns for marking patriotic Americans shift from "them" to "us" as she admits that she too is vulnerable to the stirring call of national flags, anthems, and campaigns: "Even I, with two hundred years of Americanism behind me, but with twenty years of cool economic, international study to tone it down, feel a rush of blood to the head and the fire of an idiotic frenzy possessing me when the war-whoop rings out, the drums beat, and the brass bands blare out for victory."[220] She positions Americans who crave empire not as simple dupes but as participants in a pervasive, seductive process of identity formation;

recognizing that she is not so different from them, she still insists that the war spirit can be challenged. Another think piece by Holmes on the public reception of soldiers returning from war in the Philippines gives a concrete suggestion as to how, exactly, the war spirit can be rethought. In "The Return," she describes the public events through which the government manufactures a glowing story of brave defenders returning from noble struggle. In contrast, Holmes observes that the soldiers appeared grim, generally glad to be home but embarrassed at the flowers, the parades, the extravagant public welcome. Soon, she notes, those soldiers will be looking for work and the money spent on the showy welcome ceremonies would have been useful to them. But "the face of the moment which welcomed them will be over and their need will not be remembered." She invites readers to enter into the experiences of returning soldiers, to feel disgust at the combination of showy patriotic enthusiasm with long-term public neglect, to help readers do the emotional and cognitive labor needed to resist the seductive calls to national loyalty ("support our troops") or the thrill of patriotic fervor. See through it, she says, see how it works. Scrutinize your own emotional investments and work on your visceral responses to state-orchestrated enthusiasms. Be ready to be surprised: "No one can prophecy in times like these. No one can tell what changes, what conditions may suddenly bring our cause to the front. Now is the time to be ever on the alert. Let no new phase of the situation pass unobserved. Something may grow out of it all that will show the common people of all countries that their cause is always the same."[221] We can create a different response, together.

Editor and printer Lois Waisbrooker wrote numerous think pieces in which, despite predictable ridicule from other anarchists, she shares the personal experiences that led her to combine anarchism, feminism, and spiritualism.[222] In "Why Is It So?," Waisbrooker pushes on a different sort of personal experience, that of women who value respectability and disdain prostitutes. Her think piece does not approach the question by asking respectable women to sympathize with sex workers, since pity could easily be offered without challenging the moral high ground of those in good repute. Instead, she invites ostensibly proper women to examine their own investments in patriarchy. Waisbrooker asks, "It has frequently been said that women are harder on their own sex for violating the sex code of morality than men are, and the question is asked, why is this so?"[223] She concurs with Moses Harman, editor of *Lucifer*, in using an analogy from capitalism to view sexual exchanges: "good" women cannot afford to become "bad," even by association, because they cannot risk being underbid in marriage markets. Husbands, in this analogy, are like employers; respectable women are labor; prostitutes are scabs. "Self-protection compels [the respectable woman] to be hard, unforgiving, unrelenting—to the woman in the case [of adultery], though she easily forgives the man, and why? Is it because man is the employer, the wage payer, and the woman the employed, the wage earner?"[224] Wives can legally claim their "wages" (women could sue for divorce for nonsupport), and husbands can legally claim wives' labor (men could sue for divorce for nonprovision of services). Harman and Weisbrooker argue, "What men want, what the employer class wants is not that all women should be virtuous and subscribe to the 'scale'—Oh, no! Their interests, their pleasure requires that there should be plenty of 'scabs' to take the places of the refractory Union women."[225] Weisbrooker invites respectable women to interrogate their own investment in women's sexual self-regulation, much as Holmes invites readers to scrutinize their participation in patriotism. Women whose sexuality is contained by patriarchal marriage have a great deal in common with those whose sexuality operates outside it: the availability of the "bad" women is essential to establishing the market value of the "good." The emotional economies of the patriarchal sexual system work on us at a visceral level, where shame and anxiety do their work, requiring our political responses to be calibrated at that level as well.

My final example of a think piece was published in *Freedom* in 1895, sent to them by mathematician and writer Mary Everest Boole. A friend of Boole's, upon hearing her ideas about needlework, told her they were "pure anarchism" and encouraged her to write them up for the journal. In "Should Decorative Work Be a Drudgery?" Boole suggests that we should respect both the "brain-and-nerve power" that creates the needlework and the craft's ability to *"refresh the eye"*:

> Mr. Ruskin sent the stone carvers who made the pillars for the Oxford Museum out into the fields, and each one chose the plant he thought he would best like to carve on the pillar entrusted to him. The colonnade so produced is far more interesting to look at than one in which all the capitals are alike; yet somehow the ordinary builder prefers to have his columns all alike. Why so? There is some jealousy, some fear, some feeling, I know not what, which tends to arrest a play of fancy in the individual worker. We hear of braiders going mad of the monotony of their patterns; of women sitting eight hours a day, working in one stitch and one shade of silk, to produce (on some article which so far

as *use* is concerned, could have been made in a loom) an effect which would have been much more *ornamental* had the stitch and shade been varied. What is the meaning of all this waste of eyesight and brain-and-nerve power? *Why is not the production of decoration made a recreation for the workers?*[226]

While Boole's think piece is uninformed about capitalism's investment in workers' deskilling or commodity fetishism, it is rich with the determination carried over from William Morris and John Ruskin that work should be art and objects should bring joy. Forty years later in the pages of *Freedom*, H. T. Burke pursues the same theme about anarchy and art: "What I would like to make clear is that anarchism is not really concerned with converting people who are violently opposed against us but rather it endeavours to make understandable the affinity between different human beings who compose society, how each individual act can satisfy the one who performs it, and at the same time mutually help others. Briefly, then, it attempts a difficult task: to make us profoundly conscious of our social interdependence."[227] Needlework could be a filament for developing our consciousness of our interdependence, connecting Boole's creative braider, weaver, or stitcher with the appreciative, newly clothed wearer, each of them touched by the other. This tactile mutual refreshment could be an example of what Harney and Moten call "hapticality, the touch of the undercommons"; it is "a way of feeling through others, a feel for feeling others feeling you." The "insurgent feel" of social interdependence refreshes the artist and the recipient.[228] The work of our eyes, brains, and hands can re-create us.[229]

Think pieces engage readers in reflecting on a problem at hand and imagining a better way to handle it. Some texts analyze patriarchal and capitalist arrangements and discuss the work needed to resist them. Others take on the limitations of anarchist ideas and look for ways to do better thinking. Social sketches and think pieces are examples of what Janet Altman calls "narrative instruments" that anarchist journals create and adapt: they provide "models and perspectives for interpretation."[230] They invite readers into the intellectual and political work that literature scholar Jesse Cohn imagines as anarchist literary theory, where we "enter a dialogue with the text, not only to critique it from an external perspective seen as superior but to reconstruct our perspective with the aid of the text itself."[231] As an intervention in the distribution of the sensible, these texts can nudge some ideas, images, and feelings from the unsayable to the sayable, by invitation and suggestion.

These short conversational texts use voice, tone, and pace to bring readers into the inquiry. They engage readers around pressing problems that bedevil people in their daily lives as they try to live with freedom and dignity under hostile circumstances. At their best, think pieces and social sketches invite readers to think together about the workings of power, both subtle and gross, in daily life. They are invitations to *study* in the sense that Harney and Moten use the term:

> Study is what you do with other people. It's talking and walking around with other people, working, dancing, suffering, some irreducible convergence of all three, held under the name of speculative practice. The notion of a rehearsal—being in a kind of workshop, playing in a band, in a jam session, or old men sitting on a porch, or people working together in a factory—there are these various modes of activity. The point of calling it "study" is to mark that the incessant and irreversible intellectuality of these activities is already present. These activities aren't ennobled by the fact that we now say, "oh, if you did these things in a certain way, you could be said to be have been studying." To do these things is to be involved in a kind of common intellectual practice. What's important is to recognize that that has been the case—because that recognition allows you to access a whole, varied, alternative history of thought.[232]

To study, as I am adapting Harney and Moten's idea, is not just to learn about anarchism but to learn with it and through it. Study acknowledges that "intellectual life is already at work around us."[233] Earlier chapters have argued that the printing, making, distributing, and archiving of anarchist journals are forms of study. They are both means to an end and valuable anarchist activities in and of themselves. This chapter has explored the content of selected journals, both *what* they say about the world and *how* they think the world into being. Anarchist radical study invites readers both to think about anarchism and to think the world anarchistically.

4

INTERSECTIONALITY
AND THING POWER

Agnes Inglis wrote to Joseph Ishill nearly a century ago about uncovering
the constitutive layers of anarchist print culture in the Joseph A. Labadie
Collection over the years:

> In such work as I do, here, your education comes with the work, new in-
> terests keep arising. I never, in the first place, took notice of the printing.
> The subject, the author was all. Then I found that the publisher was in-
> teresting. Then it dawned upon me that the donor was as interesting a
> personality as the writer! The one who thought so much of something
> that he or she put it in a trunk and kept it for years and years! And then
> I began to see such names as [printer] Percy Ballou's, and to notice the
> "embellishments," the small ones. And not only the cartoons that make
> a big show. And all this I card-catalogue and make data—for the scholar
> that will be coming.[1]

Work on behalf of "the scholar that will be coming" is something like a letter sent to the future, confident of a reply, ready for the recipient to become
the writer. With each additional angle on her material, Inglis reported, "the
Collection seems to become more and more alive."[2] With each filament we
can reconstruct today, each thread that blooms or fades, our radical history
becomes more accessible. Because assemblages are open-ended, new linkages are always possible. Assemblages reach to the future.

The anarchist librarian was a remarkable early example of what Cait McKinney, studying a later movement of women archivists, calls an information activist, an "unrelenting amateur" who played a major role in building anarchism's information infrastructure, defined as "technical systems in which resources operate in complex combination to make communication or knowledge work possible." Information infrastructures are neither static containers nor controlling structures: they are active fields of relationships in which diverse "management and pathfinding techniques" are entangled.[3]

Lisa Gitelman uses the phrase "interface effect" to talk about the interactions of platforms, operating systems, and applications within the information infrastructures of digital media. Older media also enact interfaces, understood as "an architecture of processes that works to generate the textual event."[4] Inglis worked at the interface of writing, printing, publishing, and archiving of anarchist materials. The semiotic and material practices of creating and circulating anarchist ideas so they can become thinkable by others become conjoined in the intimate dispositions of presses and journals, printers and readers, archivists and writers, creating, in Davide Panagia's lovely phrase, a "techne of collective participation" that made a global political movement.[5]

Not unlike Inglis, I work at the interface among organic, social, semiotic, and technical arrangements because that is where I find a promising political energy. Each type of letter—the graphemes that are assembled to produce text, the correspondence connecting the participants, and the manner of learnedness produced and circulated on the page—emerges through mutually constitutive relations with the others. Combined, they sketch the contours of what we can call, with Gitelman, anarchism's "scriptural economy," meaning "the totality of writers, writings and writing techniques."[6] All three kinds of anarchist letters combine the materiality of presses and publications with the organic, social energies of people and the semiotic practices of representation. Their interfaces, as media theorist Alexander Galloway explains, are "those mysterious zones of interaction that mediate between different realities." Galloway continues, "Interfaces are not simply objects or boundary points. They are autonomous zones of activity. Interfaces are not things, but rather processes that effect a result of whatever kind." Interfaces are not fixed points; they are dynamic effects of other things, and they "bring about transformations in material states."[7]

Looking to digital media for examples, Galloway names "windows, screens, key boards, kiosks, channels, sockets, and holes" as interfaces.[8] The idea of the interface works for older media as well: the contact zone between the printers' nimble fingers and the sorts with their nicks on one side to help establish orientation; the rhythm of the printers' bodies as they reach, turn, lift, and bend; the balance of the composing stick; the intervals needed to properly press the inked plate against the paper; the tightness and fit of the chase; the sharp interventions of the bodkin. The contact zones between documents and artifacts, and the inquiring minds and laboring bodies of archivists, are also interfaces; they are spaces where archival labor meets actual or potential memories and records, where a path through information is charted. Exchanges of correspondence enable interfaces where paper and ink meet hands and eyes, where memories and intentions circulate. These are interfaces where words and flesh engage wood, metal, paper, and ink, where, in Galloway's words, "information moves from one entity to another, from one node to another within the system." The interface is more than a doorway; it is a "fertile nexus" that enables a "reprocessing of some other medium that came before."[9] The compositor reads the handwritten or typed text of writer or editor, organizing those thoughts so that they hit the composing stick upside down and backward, in order to make their appearance on the inked paper in readable form. On rare occasions, a highly skilled printer composes the text while setting the type, skipping an intermediate visual step in order to conjure the needed arrangement of sorts while simultaneously giving birth to the ideas. The printer-press relation is not just a person, over here, plus a machine, over there. The space between is part of the printer-press intermedial space. My goal has been to bring the machinic and organic worlds of presses and printers into mutually interactive relations with the epistolary and literary worlds of printers, writers, archivists, and readers in order to shed light on the political world of anarchism. In this final chapter, I turn to the implications of my study of anarchism's "scriptural economy" for further developing anarchist theory.[10] I fancy myself to be a bit like Agnes, working on behalf of the scholars and activists who will be coming, building on existing successes and inviting new directions.

Developing Anarchist Theory

Anarchism has served as the needed foil for a host of containments, from Karl Marx's long, sarcastic denunciation of Max Stirner in *The German Ideology* to the alarm over "global anarchy" that provided the rationale for building an international police network and for inventing the discipline of international relations.[11] Anarchy has typically been recruited to represent violence, madness, and chaos. A more benign if condescending version of these demonizations is the backhanded compliment that anarchism is a nice idea in theory but would never work in practice. Yet I have suggested the opposite: the theory needs some work, but anarchism has been remarkably successful in practice. Putting aside for a moment the integral connections between theory and practice—since theory is a form of practice, it is something we *do*, and practice takes shape as theorized action—here I want to distinguish them temporarily in order to suggest some ways anarchist practice can be extended while anarchist theory can be strengthened.

Anarchist practice turns out to be both more successful and more ubiquitous than is usually imagined. Like feminists, anarchists have often been identified by whether they claim the identity for themselves, but a more useful approach may be to look instead at what they do together.[12] Individuals and groups who do their work by opposing unjust hierarchies of power, making their means consistent with the ends they seek, and building on practices of egalitarianism, self-organization, and mutual aid: these individuals and groups are, for practical purposes, doing anarchism. This chapter concludes with three examples of recent or current movements that do their work anarchistically: Food Not Bombs, Protect Maunakea 'Ohana, and the feminist bookstore movement. They have in common an inclusion of "thing power" in their daily operating procedures: they include material participants that are not human, often not organic, but that have the capacity to affect and be affected by the political relations around them. They create interfaces adjoining or disposing, in Panagia's words, "relational dynamics between entities."[13] These three movements, like the anarchists before them, embody our continuing need for shared material practice, for making things together, as part of doing radical politics.

Before venturing further into contemporary examples of thing power, the other side of the relationship between theory and practice requires attention: How can we build constructively on the theories we've inherited from the classical anarchists? I've suggested that, contrary to popular stereotypes, the practical accomplishments were remarkable though the theories need some work. What does anarchist theory need?

For starters, theories need constant attention; they are never finished, so any suggestions are partial and take their meaning from a larger process of engagement. Anarchists often stress that they value thinking as a fluid, open-ended process, not a fixed structure. Rudolf Rocker declared, "I am an anarchist not because I believe anarchism is the final goal, but because

I believe there is no such thing as a final goal. Freedom will lead us to continually wider and expanding understanding and to new social forms of life. To think that we have reached the end of our progress is to enchain ourselves in dogmas, and that always leads to tyranny."[14] Emma Goldman agreed: "'What I believe' is a process, not a finality. Finalities are for gods and governments, not for the human intellect."[15] The Russian anarchist Voline similarly argued, "The anarchist outlook could not and should not ever become rigid, immutable or stagnant. It must remain supple, lively, rich in terms of ideas."[16]

My directions for strengthening anarchist theory are twofold. First, to push anarchism toward greater intersectionality by engaging Black theory and history. Intersectional understandings of power and resistance, particularly the analysis of the Black undercommons by Stefano Harney and Fred Moten, have stimulated my understanding of anarchist journals as a form of radical study.[17] Harney and Moten's visionary essays, with Jack Halberstam's discerning introduction, travel well to anarchism, suggesting a heightened responsibility for anarchism to travel back, to enjoy as well as reciprocate the debt. Here, I turn to the resources of Black history, theory, and politics to understand what has been missing from classical anarchist theory and thus contribute to better theorizing as we go forward. Second, to bring the insights of new materialism more fully into anarchism's orbit. New materialism's prehension of matter as lively has provided tools to theorize presses and printers as constitutive elements of the anarchist movement. Going "under the hood" into the specificity of anarchism's three different kinds of letters—sorts, epistles, and learning—is one example of the kind of thing-inflected history from which theory can grow.[18]

Intersectionality and thing power come together fruitfully within anarchism. Intersectional thinkers, building on the matrices of gender, race, class, disability, age, sexuality, and what Judith Butler calls "the embarrassed etc." of the perpetually unfinished list, could readily weave thingness into the mix.[19] The interface of intersectionality and new materialism expands anarchism's dynamic processes and contact zones. The specific workings of mutually constitutive vectors of power are enhanced by the inclusion of nonhuman, nonorganic actants. The liveliness of things intertwines with intersectionality's more common participants, so that theorizable flows of matter and energy inform and complicate the rest. Thing power and intersectionality, then, can open each other up to new sorts of creative collaborations.

Becoming More Intersectional

The bare bones of intersectionality, so to speak, are baked into anarchism: there is no single substructure that determines anarchism's arrangements, no one foundation grounding a vertical order. Instead, each vector of power takes its shape in relation to others, reciprocally, horizontally: economies, states, religions, families, schools, and other organizations of power are processes that flow in their own ways while taking shape in relation to the flows of power around them. Philosopher David Wieck characterizes anarchism as "the *generic* social and political idea that expresses negation of all power, sovereignty, domination, and hierarchical division, and a will to their dissolution."[20] Saidiya Hartman succinctly remarks, "Anarchism is an open and incomplete word, and in this resides its potential."[21] Anarchism's anchor in a fluid, relational understanding of power works well with intersectional theories of power, as characterized by feminist theorist Patricia Hill Collins, "not as unitary, mutually exclusive entities, but as reciprocally constructing phenomena which in turn shape complex social inequalities."[22] Another scholar of intersectionality, Vivian May, contrasts the robust plurality of intersectional "matrix thinking" with the limitations of "single-axis thinking."[23] Matrix thinking eschews either/or logic and cultivates a disposition receptive to both/and analysis. *Theory*, May insists, is a verb; intersectional theory does its work by attending to simultaneous, intermeshed processes and hidden collusions.[24] While some feminists worry that finding intersectionality in classical anarchism does a disservice to intersectionality's grounding in the specific power relations experienced by Black women, others welcome the encounter in order, as sociologist Hillary Lazar suggests, to "better account for the diverse instantiations of oppression, while still recognizing the interdependence of systems of domination."[25] Cultivating a more vigorous interface between anarchism and intersectionality, I suggest, builds on anarchism's prior receptivity to multiple, unfinished understandings of power.

Yet numerous critics have observed that classical anarchism is weak in its analysis of Blackness. To consult just a few: in his new book *Anarcho-Blackness*, literary scholar Marquis Bey urges anarchists to "reckon full force with Blackness as Blackness serves as the distinct angle of vision for encountering the effects of State-sanctioned enslavement and oppression."[26] Political theorist Annie Menzel, whose reflections on Lily Gair Wilkinson are considered further below, points out that there is an "implicit anti-Blackness" in accepting an account of freedom that "relies heavily on a metaphor of enslavement abstracted from its actual human experience."[27] In *The Nation on No Map*, William Anderson argues that, "within the United States and Europe[,] they [anarchists] have failed to properly appeal to and struggle with masses of people who are not white."[28] In her master's thesis in history at Portland State University, Alecia Giombolini's close study of *The Firebrand*, the precursor of *Free Society*, leads her to conclude, "Instead of engaging with the true horrors of American slavery or examining its ongoing legacy, contributors to the newspaper instead chose to use slavery as a catchall comparison to the many modern evils against which the anarchists were struggling."[29] How could a political movement emerging in a time steeped in empire and the aftermath of slavery be so thoroughly radical in many ways yet fail to analyze Blackness as a significant element of power and resistance? I am curious about what produced this silence: What was it about anarchists' way of comprehending the world that left them unequipped to deal with Blackness?

Assemblages are sites of disconnection as well as connection—interfaces can wither or mutate or fail to develop. Assemblages bring order to heterogeneous, mobile elements but do not pin them down once and for all. Philosopher Thomas Nail succinctly explains, "Every assemblage is always simultaneously crisscrossed with multiple types of processes....If we want to know how an assemblage works, we must ask, 'What types of change are at work?'"[30] I see four kinds of change (or lack of change) at work in anarchism in its classical period that confounded its relation to Blackness: first, anarchists discursively abrogated the vocabulary of slavery and bondage by recruiting those terms to represent all forms of exploitation; second, they refrained from exploring the specific histories of the slave trade, plantation economies, and continuing racial brutality; third, their love of print made them inattentive to other creative modes of rebellion; and fourth, their wholesale contempt for "mere reform" made them too quick to dismiss forms of politics judged inadequately revolutionary.[31] As Bey notes, for anarchism to encounter Blackness would be for it to change.[32] Reasoning backward from the absence of this encounter to the circumstances that produced the absence, these four problems can become opportunities for anarchism to develop its analysis of Blackness and thus to move toward fuller intersectionality.

Jacques Rancière's influence, such as I have cultivated in this book, moves in more than one direction: it brings in the part that has no part, so that a fresh arrangement of the sensible emerges; but it also prods us to be aware of how our cherished redistributions of the sensible could implicitly disqualify unnamed parts from coming into view. Panagia succinctly explains how Rancière's understanding of politics requires continuing "acts of rearticulation": "Politics for Rancière happens when the extant norms of how things fit can neither sustain nor explain the existence of discrete parts that don't fit. Such fragments don't account for an exclusion so much as an inability to register a relation with an established sense of ordering. Thus what is required is the articulation of a new disposition, arrangement, or networks of sensibilities. Such acts of rearticulation are what Rancière calls *partager*, and they are acts that refer to moments of radical mediation where the inequalities of qualification that enable access to politics are rendered indistinct."[33] Taking Rancière seriously cannot help but raise the question of how anarchism itself manifests its own "inability to register a relation" with elements left unsayable. Italian anarchist Leda Rafanelli anticipates Rancière's questions when she challenges the prevailing distribution of the sensible by inviting in those "who the novelist does not see, the historian does not recognize." What possible distributions of the sensible do anarchists fail to recognize? What "wounded and exasperated rebels," in Rafanelli's words, fall outside the reach of anarchism's assemblages?[34]

Slaves and Slavery

There is no robust language to talk about slavery in classical anarchism. *Slave* came to mean something else—it became a word for everybody's exploitation. Except for those few who do not have to sell their labor for wages, we are all wage slaves. Nearly all women are sex slaves. Bondage is the general circumstance of being oppressed. *Chattel slavery* is anarchists' term for the old kind of slavery, the kind that allegedly ended. Wage slavery and sex slavery continue, but they have nothing to do with Blackness and Whiteness. Nowhere in the language of the classical anarchist movement is there a word for an owned person that names the legacy of that ownership continuing into the present. Nowhere is there a way to distinguish between those who have little property and those who are themselves property or are marked with the legacy of that appropriation.

Menzel's thoughtful analysis of Wilkinson's social sketch "Women's Freedom" shows how Wilkinson participates in "a broader legacy in European and North American white left thought ... that has tended to erase the fact that 'industrial capitalism' is racial capitalism all the way down to the core fact of the commodified Black human being."[35] Wilkinson is participating in a discursive strategy that was very familiar to her readers: "Nearly all women are no better than slaves," she declares; a rich married lady is "a willing slave."[36] Most men are slaves already, so women wanting the vote is just another way to seek bondage—that is, to become oppressed by the electoral pretensions of the state.[37] Lois Waisbrooker similarly drew on the ubiquitous metaphor in her think piece "Why Is It So?": "How true it is," Waisbrooker argues, "that one part of this slave system fits with every other part and when will the sex slave and the wage slave learn this one great truth? There is no way out of this muddle except by the total abolition of both."[38] Wilkinson's lovely tales of walking into freedom and Waisbrooker's personable reflections on sexual moralities are not enhanced by the vague language of slavery, which brings little intellectual heft to the table. Instead, what the two women gain is implicit membership in what humanities scholar Sabine Broeck calls the enslavement regime.

Broeck notes that enslavement has become an abstract discursive regime and also an ordinary one. Her target is the problematic deployment of race and gender metaphors in White feminism, but her point works for anarchism too. Unhinging slavery from its modern material referent "provided a springboard for white women [and men] to begin theorizing a catalog of their own demands for an acknowledgement of modern, free subjectivity as antagonistic to enslavement."[39] The enslavement regime produces a corrosive silence about actual slaves. The Left's long-running reliance on this bloated metaphor gives rise to what we can call, following Rancière, an anti-Black aesthetic. Belgian critic Paul de Man is not wrong to characterize metaphors as "smugglers of stolen goods."[40] Of course, the concept of slavery also inherits baggage from other sources, including ancient republics and empires, but the African slave regime was the most immediate referent for the anarchists. Universalizing "the slave" damages our understanding of actual slavery while assembling the meaning-making system to produce, legitimize, and at the same time hide the damage. Yet this universalizing gesture can undermine itself: once the discourse shifts enough that the metaphor comes to trouble readers or listeners, it stands out *as a metaphor* and we see that it is casually, cruelly ubiquitous. Menzel is not exaggerating when she attributes the slave-as-metaphor to the "broader legacy of European and North American white left thought."[41] Really, they all do it: Marx, Friedrich Engels, Mikhail Bakunin, Peter Kropotkin, Pierre-Joseph Proudhon, Stirner, Leo Tolstoy, Errico Malatesta, Gustav Landauer, Rudolf Rocker, Goldman, Alexander Berkman, Lucy Parsons, Voltairine de Cleyre. Wilkinson and Waisbrooker are just going with the flow: they are dipping into the available reservoir of meaning in which most anarchists implicitly participated. This is neither an apology nor an excuse: it is an observation about the cultural weight of this erasure of slaves from the old Left's distribution of the sensible. Of course, words can have more than one meaning and change their meaning over time. Yet the relentless drumbeat of the enslavement regime compromises access to what Hartman calls "the afterlife of slavery": "If slavery persists as an issue in the political life of black America, it is not because of an antiquarian obsession with bygone days or the burden of a too-long memory, but because black lives are still imperiled and devalued by a racial calculus and a political arithmetic that were entrenched centuries ago."[42] The Left needs to retain access to the older meaning of slavery in order to calibrate this afterlife. Announcing the transformation of chattel slavery to wage slavery and sex slavery eliminates the need to examine the former or to imagine it continuing to do its work after its alleged demise. Of course, they could have done both: used slavery as a metaphor for oppression and at the same time analyzed the actual institution of slavery and the experiences of slaves and the descendants of slaves. However, that would require attention to slavery's history, which leads us to the second problem.

History

Hand in hand with the emptying out of *slave* and *bondage* is the lack of historical analysis that anarchists brought to Blackness. They generally failed to analyze the specific historical trajectories of the slave trade, the plantation economies, and their aftermath. Nearly every anarchist I have read decries racism, understood as a prejudice held by White people against non-White people. Racism was seen as an individual psychological failure, not a collective structure and process emergent over time; anarchists may scold their comrades for expressing degrading attitudes toward fellow workers of a different skin color, as did Jo Labadie, Goldman, and Waisbrooker, but they do not offer structural analyses of the working of the color line in communities ordered by the "afterlife of slavery."[43] This lack of historical curiosity about the institution of slavery shows up in its absence from the pages of anarchist journals, which otherwise offer readers ample opportunities to learn about the history of capitalism and the state in, for example, Wisconsin writer C. L. James's oft-reproduced essays about the French Revolution, Kropotkin's famous analyses of evolution and social history, or Louise Michel's accounts of the Paris Commune.

Like the US domestic color line, Britain's colonial color line was largely unthought by anarchists. Humanities scholar Hazel Carby analyzes the racialized encounters and "imperial intimacies" linking Britain and Jamaica, interpreting school, military, church, and state documents as well as family histories to find the arrangements constituting and reconstituting Britain's racial histories. Carby traces "the bottomless depths of unacknowledged violence and brutality embodied in British character and values across the colonial and imperial landscape."[44] Stephen Best and Hartman listen to the words of slaves and ex-slaves in England and the United States and discern that same bottomlessness: abolition is incomplete because slavery's lingering violence is irreparable. Analyzing the writing of Ottobah Cugoana, an ex-slave who had been kidnapped in Ghana and forced to labor on the plantations in Granada, they write, "A life lived in loss—this perhaps is the great gift of Cugoano's harsh words and laments, the recognition that abolition could not redress the crime of slavery but could only commute its death sentence."[45] Black resistance to slavery and its aftermath, Best and Hartman conclude, was just noise to the Establishment: "Black noise represents the kinds of political aspirations that are inaudible and illegible within the prevailing formulas of political rationality; these yearnings are illegible because they are so wildly utopian and derelict to capitalism (for example, 'forty acres and a mule,' the end of commodity production and restoration of the commons, the realization of 'the sublime ideal of freedom,' the resuscitation of the socially dead). Black noise is always already barred from the court."[46] But it should not have been just noise to anarchists.

The default position of anarchism was to assume that anarchists were obviously against racism because it is a form of hierarchy: anarchists are against all hierarchies; ergo, they are against racism. As with sexism, anarchists generally thought, "We've got it covered," because, as Goldman said, anarchism "stand[s] for the spirit of revolt, in whatever form, against everything that hinders human growth."[47] Yet feminism came into anarchism largely through women's insistence that it wasn't good enough to wait until "after the revolution" to deal with patriarchy. It was not enough to be "on the list," slated for attention later. Nor is it enough for anarchists to be generically against inequality: vectors of power each need their specific histories, and their stories need to be told in the voices of those who have the situated knowledges to which the structures of power give rise.[48] There was a Black radical press available to anarchists in the early twentieth century, as historian Kerri Greenidge demonstrates, including Black writers and editors who condemned capitalism and criticized the conservative impact of Black churches.[49] These writers could have been engaged as fellow travelers unwinding a specific and valuable thread in what Lazar calls the "tangled knot" of intersectional power relations.[50] Their insights could have nudged classical anarchism away from what Lazar identifies as its "humanitarian concern with universal freedom" toward "addressing the simultaneity of various oppressions...to encourage deeper, multi-directional intersections across them."[51] We cannot substitute a formal critique of power relations for a history of domination and struggle. It is difficult to imagine that power relations could be otherwise if we cannot understand how they came to be as they are.

Writing

Anarchists' devotion to the written word has been a source of joy for me. I love their noble labor as "bookish poor people" writing, printing, distributing, and preserving the publications that made their movement.[52] Yet perhaps the primacy anarchists gave to writing led them to overlook other media, other groundings of radical communities, and other possible forms of political expression.

Hartman documents a rich landscape of sexual, economic, and cultural resistance in early twentieth-century New York and Philadelphia that I do not glimpse in anarchist accounts of that place and time. In the cities Hartman recovers, "young black women were in open rebellion," but, as she notes, Kropotkin paid no attention to their mutual aid societies and Goldman failed to recognize them in the streets.[53] The insurgencies of young Blacks in New York and Philadelphia could have been visible in dance halls, in jazz clubs, on the streets, in the jails, in a manner of walking, or dancing, or loving, but those inscriptions were not legible within anarchist print economies. "The radical imagination and everyday anarchy of ordinary colored girls," Hartman shows, were not interpretable as expressions of sexual modernism, free love, bohemian experiments, or a "refusal to be governed."[54] As I argued in the preceding chapter, anarchists were reliably outraged at colonialism, seeing it as a gigantic theft of land, labor, and culture, but they seem to have lacked the resources to flip the anticolonial gaze around and look for, in Menzel's words, "enslaved people's own vast repertoires of resistance, refusal, relation, endurance, and other practices of freedom."[55] Anarchists looked worldwide for the sorts of resistance they hoped for and respected, such as the armed peasant rebellion led by the Magon brothers in Mexico, the

Ukrainian guerrilla war led by Nester Mahkno, or John Brown's famous raid on Harpers Ferry, but other expressions of the "vast repertoire" Menzel flags do not achieve this visibility.[56] Classical anarchists' limited idea of what counted as properly revolutionary led to the final lacuna I see as limiting their encounter with Blackness: their too-rigid opposition between radical and reformist politics.

Reform

A final aspect of anarchism's prevailing distribution of the sensible that likely had consequences for its incapacity to apprehend Blackness was its dismissal of any politics that seemed too reformist, too accepting of established institutions. While many anarchists were involved in the abolition movements, once chattel slavery was officially ended, anarchists expected, or at least desired, the next step to be the end of the state itself, not petitioning the state to recognize more people as citizens, to make fairer policies, or to enforce laws without prejudice. The range of politics they welcomed included armed rebellions; general strikes, in which the workers seize control of the means of production and run it themselves; Modern Schools, the radical schools founded on the philosophy of Spanish anarchist Francisco Ferrer; militant opposition to conscription and war; the creation of independent, self-governing communities to prefigure the desired form of life by acting as though it were already here; and of course publications, speeches, and theatrical productions advocating their ideas. No matter how obdurately White authorities suppressed Black efforts at change, for anarchists, Black politics seeking equal citizenship and equality before the law, often grounded in Christian churches or doctrine, was not sufficiently revolutionary.

Pulling the history of Blackness into anarchism could clarify the devasting consequences not only of lacking rights but of lacking the right to have rights in the first place. Ironically, as we have seen in chapter 3, many anarchists reluctantly accepted reformist union strategies: they were not enthusiastic about bread-and-butter unions and strikes for better wages and working conditions, but they by and large accepted workers' need for these practical improvements in their lives. A more robust analysis of life structured by the color line could have suggested a similar openness to "mere reform" with regard to race-based struggles for civil liberties. An unnamed writer in *Freedom* wrote in 1906, "We are not slaves but rebels, and when we struggle for our own freedom we know we are striving for the freedom of all without distinction."[57] This sentiment would have to be rethought once it was recognized that slaves could also be rebels, and striving for the freedom of all would require making distinctions regarding how people are situated and how they came to be there.

Bey implicitly pushes anarchism toward stronger intersectionality, defining his work as "a reconfigurative project, to express what anarchism might be, what it might look like, when encountering a sustained engagement with Blackness in general, and Black queer and trans feminisms in particular." Like Rancière, Rocker, Goldman, and Voline, Bey embraces thinking as an ongoing, open-ended process: "There is no 'end' because to *know* the end is to think one knows the totality of the landscape, a line of thinking that cannot account for what falls outside the dictates of legibility." Like Lizzie Holmes a century ago, Bey anticipates "those who might queerly emerge" when hierarchy and domination cease.[58] A more vigorous engagement with Blackness, including understanding why the classical anarchists largely eschewed that engagement, enhances the terrain of the anarchist undercommons.

Bringing in New Materialism

My second direction for strengthening anarchist theory is greater inclusion of the rich conceptual world of new materialism, in productive conversation with the old.[59] Studying printers and presses invites a confluence between the "old" materialism needed to analyze class and gender relations in the printing trades and the new materialism needed to theorize presses and pages themselves as lively. By *old materialism* I mean Marxist and Marxist-inspired analyses of the structural conditions of class and gender relations, a literature to which anarchists are fully indebted. Marxist-feminist histories of the print trades illustrate their essential contributions. Sociologists Ava Baron and Cynthia Cockburn and historian Christina Burr knit together Marxist and feminist perspectives to analyze the class, gender, and age divisions among print shop workers in order to track the relation of labor deskilling to expectations for proper masculinity and adulthood.[60] These inquiries tell us a great deal about the structure of work, the politics of union organizing, and the relation between production and reproduction in working-class families, but they shed less light on the productive sensory power of presses and printing. For these insights, I turn to new materialism's attention to the liveliness of things, and the mutually constitutive relations between human and nonhuman entities; these theoretical energies can usefully work with prior materialisms to expand our ways of understanding radical politics. New materialism does not replace the old, but it leaves room for it while directing attention to a different register of relations between humans and the other-than-human world. Recall Jane Bennett's concept of "thing power"—"the strange ability of ordinary, man-made items to exceed their status as objects and to manifest traces of independence or aliveness, constituting the outside of our own experience." This is not the same as finding spirit in matter but rather is tracing the affect of materiality itself. Assemblages include the nonhuman and the nonsentient in their capacities to affect and be affected. Complex feedback loops and vigorous semiotic and material grounding generate both predictable patterns and the capacity to surprise participants. Assemblages emerge in the in-between, "through events in which both the subject and the objects are formed" and "bodies are continuously articulated with their outsides."[61]

The exciting insights of new materialism enable me to see the print shops' physical objects, pungent smells, clattering sounds, and laboring bodies as actants that mutually constitute each other. Printers' swift hands, strong backs, and sharp eyes work with the presses to knit together chains of events in which each element acts on and is acted on by others. Using language that maps beautifully onto the world of letterpress printing, since typesetters are also known as compositors, Bruno Latour directs us toward compositionism of the human and the nonhuman in mutually constituting one another.[62] John Protevi addresses the capacity of material systems to self-organize, a particularly apt concept to bring to anarchism, which relies for its success on the self-organizing potential of humans and materials. Through "a direct linkage of the social and the somatic," Protevi argues, material flows, affective relations, and sense-making practices inform and reinform one another in complex feedback loops.[63] With Latour and Protevi, Bennett theorizes things as actants; an actant, she tells us, "has sufficient coherence to make a difference, produce effects, alter the course of events." Actants are efficacious; they do things. Bennett explains this liveliness as "the capacity of things—edibles, commodities, storms, metals—not only to impede or block the will and designs of humans but also to act as quasi agents or forces with trajectories, propensities, or tendencies of their own."[64] An actant is not an agent in the traditional sense that people have been seen as "causing" things to happen or being "in charge." Actants participate in human and nonhuman assemblages, they resonate with other actants and with human agents in complex ways, and they express their influence in congregation.

Anarchist print culture offers an excellent site for theorizing the relation of old and new materialisms. Anarchism itself, as a project to liberate working people from the tyranny of bosses, states, churches, families, and empires, would make no sense at all absent the framing logic of (some version of) old materialism. Yet the constitutive relations of printers and presses come into focus more forcefully through the theoretical energy of new materialism. The relation between them hinges on the question one seeks to answer. To adequately understand *why* anarchists did what they did, we need the resources of old materialism, which highlights struggles for human dignity and equality and accounts for the structural conditions that deny those values to the masses of people. Yet to generate a stronger understanding of *how* anarchists did what they did, we need new materialism, which helps us grasp how anarchists produced themselves in struggle. The interface of the two materialisms is a "fertile nexus," in Galloway's words: anarchism can help the new and old materialisms to more fully find their working relationship with each other.[65] By putting them both to work in the world of anarchist print culture, they can generate a version of McKinney's "pathfinding techniques" for charting routes for thinking through anarchism's active fields of relations.[66]

What Does Anarchist Practice Offer?

The anarchism of the three movements I will briefly examine here—Food Not Bombs, Protect Maunakea ʻOhana, and the feminist bookstore movement—is not only or primarily in their ideas or their organizations, but in their practices of doing and making things together.[67] Food Not Bombs is self-consciously anarchist; as political theorist Sean Parson remarks, it is "one of the most recognized anarchist groups in the world."[68] The Protect Maunakea ʻOhana and the feminist bookstore movement use a different political vocabulary but are engaging in a compatible politics of mutual aid and radical self-governance. Each movement, I speculate, owes its power and its success in part to the "thing power" enfolded into it. Struggles to enact political change, as Bennett succinctly remarks, require "aesthetic-affective energy to spark or fuel them."[69] I have argued in this book that assemblages of printers, presses, publications, and reading publics helped to spark and fuel anarchism. The shape and function of the resonance among the assemblage's operators and connectors can, in Bennett's words, "call us up short and reveal our profound implication in nonhumanity."[70]

By looking briefly at the practices and effects of three current or recent expressions of radical politics, we can further glimpse the productive power of the things we touch as they touch us.

Food Not Bombs

Food Not Bombs is a global movement that combines the provision of free vegetarian (usually vegan) food with efforts to reclaim public space and critique militarism, capitalism, and the state. Unhoused people are offered food and information about the system that creates homelessness and poverty. They are also offered opportunities to participate in the consensus decision-making process and prefigurative politics that guide the group's actions. They are treated with dignity, as comrades. Food is not a commodity or a service but a filament connecting activists and participants in a network of mutual aid.

Founded in 1980, Food Not Bombs emerged out of the antinuclear movement of that time. There are about a thousand chapters in sixty countries that are "experimenting with democracy and collectively sharing vegan food with the poor and hungry, while fighting against the forces of gentrification, militarism, and capitalism." Food Not Bombs operates by direct democracy, nonviolently, in solidarity with people who need food; its groups "foreshadow the world we want to see."[71] It also expresses solidarity with other radical groups by providing food at protests, including the Occupy Wall Street actions, and responds to crises by delivering food to disaster zones, including in the immediate aftermath of Hurricane Katrina. Its capacity to emerge with food when needed leads Parson to quip that it is "the catering wing of the U.S. radical left."[72] Its recognizable logo—a purple fist clenched around a leafy orange carrot—accompanies its members at their "foodshares," which political scientist David Spataro characterizes as "a mixture of street demonstration, political theater, grassroots organizing, and community meal all in one ritual use of public space."[73]

Food, of course, has many levels of meaning for organic beings. It sustains bodies, creates relationships, organizes economies and cultures. In one sense, Food Not Bombs is giving away food—as the activists say, "We just wanna warm some bellies"—in the same way that the anarchists were circulating ideas: "We just want to get the word out." Yet their way of alleviating hunger, like the anarchists' way of publishing journals, is grounded in a larger world-building process. As anthropologist Sarah Fessenden explains in her excellent dissertation,

In another sense, they are not "just" providing food. This food is the site and symbol of a protest, a protest that started in 1980 in Cambridge, MA. The vision then as well as now is to assert "food, not bombs," a project to end hunger in the long term. But this group does not just hold up a sign in protest. This group does not just dumpster dive for their own subsistence. This group does not just eat vegetarian food. This group does not just put up posters. This group does not just serve food without a permit. Instead, it is a direct action project that recovers wasted (vegetarian and vegan) food, prepares it in collective kitchens using anarchistic (dis)organization, and serves it for free to anyone in want or need of it in public spaces. Together, these constructive practices constitute the protest of Food Not Bombs. "We just wanna warm some bellies" not just in the moment but in such a way as to prefigure a world where people could freely feed themselves and help their neighbors do the same.[74]

Prefiguring a just world by acting as though it has already arrived sets a challenging standard of political action. The People of Color Caucus within Food Not Bombs has called its White comrades to account for perpetuating racism.[75] While I have encountered no reports of sexism, it seems likely that a movement based on food would tap traditional gender roles to some degree. My argument is not that Food Not Bombs is an unflawed movement, but that it is energized by the actancy of food. Food Not Bombs' thing power is food, and the spaces of food: gathering the food (from retail or wholesale donations or from dumpsters), preparing the food (in anarchist kitchens), and sharing the food (usually in public parks or streets). The food becomes anticapitalist: volunteers transform it from commodity to useful, accessible item, from unvalued waste or excess to a freely shared element in a food community. As cofounder of Food Not Bombs Jo Swanson observes, "The simple act of sharing is a powerful force. It is the opposite of greed."[76] The food becomes antiviolent: as Fessenden says, "This food not only avoids harming animals, it avoids violent food systems." The food becomes antihierarchical, organized through egalitarian processes of shared labor. "Their style of food acquisition, preparation, and distribution," Fessenden concludes, "imbue[s] the food with revolutionary flavor, making it into this direct action protest object."[77] Food Not Bombs' foodshares exemplify Bennett's argument that "the locus of agency is always a human-nonhuman collective."[78]

Food Not Bombs' decentralized organization makes every local group autonomous, so differences emerge in their spatial arrangements. The San

Francisco group famously distributed food in highly visible public parks and in front of government buildings, welcoming the subsequent confrontation with authorities. Just as the authorities a century ago often confiscated the anarchists' presses, the police today often treat the food itself, not just the people, as dangerous: Swanson reports that "buckets of soup and bags of bread [were] hurled onto the sidewalk and smashed under officers' boots."[79] A San Francisco activist saved himself and his food "when he jumped into a fountain in front of City Hall with a pot of soup, to avoid being arrested by the police."[80] The Vancouver group, as Fessenden recounts, distributed food in a poor neighborhood, in front of a friendly establishment, because that's where they found hungry people. The Harrisonburg group, anarchist writer and activist Peter Gelderloos reports, served indoors and included nonvegetarian food, judging those adjustments to the usual project to best serve their participants.[81] No doubt other local groups make their own revisions to the basic process. But in each case, the space where the groups set up their tables, food, banners, and literature is transformed, and it acts back on them. The Food Not Bombs' sensorium is rich: tactile, kinesthetic, visual, auditory, olfactory, and gustatory sensory pathways are all recruited. "Symbolically," Fessenden notes, "volunteers imbue the food with new meaning."[82] And the food imbues the volunteers as well. Hands stained orange or purple from chopping raw vegetables, noses provoked by the stench of dumpsters, backs and arms strengthened from hauling boxes of donated foodstuffs, mouths and stomachs satisfied by food shared, eyes and ears enriched by art, music, and ideas moving around them: Food Not Bombs enables human bodies and spirits to transition from handling potential waste to creating edible food that is also a protest object. Fessenden summarizes, "In this dinner party, the food itself takes center stage, its personality being partly beneficent and partly mischievous: food for protest, for building community, and for sustenance. It is food of memory, anticipation, and hope that both suggests the possibility of a better world and makes that world in the present."[83] Intense learning and teaching is going on, via the strong, dense, and reciprocal relations that create assemblages and enable radical study. Every foodshare is at the same time a blow against the establishment. As activist Cindy Lu emphasizes:

> Don't get it twisted that Food Not Bombs is just some sweet little group that provides food for events and feeds people once a week. We are interested in smashing the state—a state that sees food as a commodity, in terms of salable, over-priced "units"—not as a source of nourishment

for hungry people. Sourcing and giving away free food is a revolutionary, anti-capitalistic act...and Food Justice ties in with Racial Justice and ties in with Earth Justice and ties in with Class Warfare....Food insecurity is yet another means of terrorism and violence that the system perpetrates. Food is a Human Right, not a privilege to be earned, and free food is yet another building block of the Revolution![84]

Protect Maunakea

In July 2019 the state of Hawai'i declared its intention to begin building the Thirty-Meter Telescope on the mountain of Maunakea on the island of Hawai'i. The telescope would have been the fourteenth telescope complex built on the summit by the University of Hawai'i, along with a consortium of other universities and organizations, as part of its program in astronomy. Past promises by the state to remove obsolete equipment have not been honored.

Measuring thirty-two thousand feet from the ocean floor to the summit, Maunakea is the tallest mountain in the world. In Native Hawaiian spiritual traditions, it is sacred; yet, as Kanaka Maoli (Native Hawaiian) scholars often note with regard to translations from Hawaiian to English, simple translations of such words as *sacred* are often insufficient.[85] Maunakea is alive and meaningful within webs of relationships with people, land, water, ocean, sky, and ancestors. As scholars Bryan Kamaoli Kuwada and No'u Revilla explain, "What the 2019 iteration of the struggle has shown us is that one of the battles at its root is actually a clash of ontologies. Life narrative versus life narrative. In a worldview where land is commodity and real estate, unliving and unconnected to humanity, those standing against the construction of something that will bring knowledge to the masses can only be anti-progress or anti-science. Yet in our worldview, where the mountain is alive, is our relation, is the umbilicus of our world, those standing against that same construction can only be kia'i, only protectors."[86] A place-based philosophy such as Native Hawaiian ontology is strongly oriented to exploring and valuing relations of people to the entities around them. As scholar Noelani Goodyear-Ka'ōpua indicates, the protectors of Maunakea are unmaking settler colonialism by "protecting Indigenous relationships between human and nonhumans."[87] Another contemporary scholar, Jamaica Heolimeleikalani Osorio, imagines those relations not just as the outcome of her people's identity but as its source: "What if protecting 'āina is what makes us Kanaka in the first place?"[88]

Native Hawaiians' efforts to protect the mountain from desecration have been ongoing for decades and have entailed legal challenges, petitions, policy arguments, educational and cultural initiatives, and face-to-face confrontations. As scholar J. Kēhaulani Kauanui has stated, the struggle "goes beyond—and much deeper than—any statist solutions. Kanaka Maoli [Native Hawaiians] are engaged in projects of land renewal and stewardship that center decolonial and nonproprietary relationships between and among people and all living entities, what we might call self-determination, but that do not hinge on state recognition."[89] The actions of the protectors at Maunakea embody creative resonance between human affects and actions, the material and cultural objects people make together, and the physical space of the mountain and its environment.

In 2018 the Hawai'i Supreme Court gave approval for construction of the Thirty-Meter Telescope to proceed, reasoning that the summit had been so damaged by the previous installations of astronomical equipment, additional construction would not do much further harm. When construction was scheduled to begin in 2019, Native Hawaiians and their allies came to take action: at first dozens, later thousands, they created a traditional place of refuge, or sanctuary, known as pu'uhonua at the place called Pu'uhuluhulu, across the main road from the Mauna Kea Access Road leading to the summit. On the access road itself, the protectors created a space called Ala Hulu Kūpuna, a space of gathering and daily protocols that also became the site of intense confrontations between protectors of the mauna and heavily armed law enforcement. A group of eight protectors chained themselves to the cattle guard to stop the transport of construction equipment up the mountain, an action that issued in a twelve-hour standoff with police. Two days later, thirty-eight kūpuna (elders) were arrested for peacefully blocking the road, and they were immediately replaced by scores of other protectors. Participation at the site grew at times to several thousand people, tents stretching a mile in either direction from the central camp.

The protectors turned the sanctuary and access road into a space of collective political expression, run by volunteer leaders who emerged from the community and were responsible for its needs. The space was complex and self-organizing. As scholar Māhealani Ahia observes, "Pu'uhonua o Pu'uhuluhulu has been referred to as an autonomous zone, a social justice experiment in community empowerment, a kauhale village, an 'ohana [family]. What I witnessed was the continual spontaneous eruption of need and fulfillment. Grounded in ancestral understandings of pu'uhonua as places of refuge, protection from punishment by governing authorities, and spaces of healing and restitution, the puʻuhonua established in 2019 has evolved uniquely. Kuleana can be defined as responsibility, accountability, rights, and privileges, but perhaps also as an ability to respond."[90] The camp included a check-in tent where the guiding principles of kapu aloha (the ethical and behavioral guide for participants to show respect and care to all) were explained and donations were received, a busy food tent that fed three meals a day to all who came, a splendid university that offered many dozens of classes, a library, an art tent, child care, medical care, caregiving for the elderly, safe spaces for women and māhū [mixed gender], a sanitation system, a security system, a trash-collection system, an arrangement for regulating traffic, a media team, and an ethos of welcoming care. As with Food Not Bombs, my argument is not that the movement to protect Maunakea is flawless: protectors organized safe spaces and needed protocols for women and māhū because they sometimes experienced sexist insults and assaults.[91] Rather, my argument is that protectors created an encampment that is comparable to spaces formed by anarchist organizations while uniquely Native Hawaiian in its philosophy and ethics. Kauanui observes, "If we consider anarchist praxis as a form of political practice that is horizontal and grounded in mutual aid and free association (consent-based relationships), we can see the direct action and mobilization of people on the front lines at Mauna Kea moving in unity within that tradition, while deeply grounded in Kanaka Maoli ethics of care and responsibility."[92] Goodyear-Kaʻōpua and Yvonne Mahelona similarly note, "A noncapitalist community grounded in living Hawaiian cultural practice is rising, like the kupukupu ferns that grow from cracks in the black lava rock and unfurl toward the sun."[93]

The protectors invited everyone to join the encampment to eat, talk story, and learn. The mouth of the access road was transformed by careful preparation and maintenance into a place for the kūpuna to reside, for visitors to be received, and for protocols of music, dancing, chanting, and singing to take place three times a day. The camp was edged by dozens of flags sent by other political movements to express their support. The camp itself enacted what it sought, prefiguring the self-governing society the protectors aimed to create. Scholar Emalani Case saw a community creating itself:

> When I returned to the Mauna in 2019, I returned to a sanctuary built by acts of radical sovereignty, or radical acts that did not need the permission of the colonial state, acts that were directed toward the better futures we dream of, the futures we create the conditions for every day.

While at Mauna Kea, I witnessed people come together, sharing, giving, and supporting each other, guided by the value of kapu aloha (a commitment to act with aloha). At the Mauna we had the freedom to breathe, and the air tasted sweet. We had the freedom to act, to chant, sing, and dance, to gather, to find strength in each other and the ʻāina (land). Being at the puʻuhonua, and being at the Mauna, taught me that we all deserve to be free, that we all deserve the freedom to grow, and further, that I must be active in ensuring that freedom extends to everyone.[94]

The confrontation with law enforcement at the puʻuhonua was matched by a struggle for control of the public message. At one point, Governor David Ige announced at a press conference that the puʻuhonua was unsafe, riddled with drug and alcohol abuse, peopled by jobless slackers camping illegally. Kuwada and Revilla recall their response to this malicious account: "It was a surreal experience to be sitting in the puʻuhonua, surrounded by aunties and uncles, moms and dads, classmates and colleagues, friends and their children all working in the kitchen or cleaning the portable toilets, or leading people on hikes, and hearing the governor describe a completely alternate reality to what was taking place around us." Yet the puʻuhonua continued to prove the authorities wrong, sustaining a self-governing community for nearly nine months, until curtailed by the public health requirements of the global pandemic. Kuwada and Revilla write, "Kiaʻi [protectors] rejected the binary and racist vision of extractive capitalism, which represented Hawaiians as either vanishing Natives unloved by science or hypervisible savages, too drunk and jobless to protect what is rightfully theirs. ʻŌiwi [Native Hawaiians] are more than our historical trauma—we are lovers, makers, protectors."[95] The acts of loving, making, and protecting that Kuwada and Revilla find at the center of Puʻuhonua o Puʻuhuluhulu have transformed the space, in the words of scholar Kamakaokaʻilima Long, into "much more than a staging ground to defend a mountain. It has become a place where Hawaiians are gathering by the thousands, gathering in mass reverence for our kupuna and with a deep sense of our power and commitment to justice. This space has transformed from one of resistance to one of resurgence. With the kūpuna tent at the head, the access road has transformed into a ceremonial space and the call to the people has been to come to the mountain."[96]

Making things together—material things like food and the camp itself, as well as cultural things like songs, stories, poems, dances, films, plays, pictures, and conversations—is an essential part of Puʻuhonua o Puʻuhuluhulu. Indeed, Kuwada and Revilla ask in their introduction to their edited collection of interviews with and writings of protectors, "What do we need? What can we make together?"[97] Osorio notes that much is being made: the actions on the mauna have given birth to "the greatest creative outpouring of our collective lifetime. Song writers, poets, kumu hula, filmmakers, and playwrights are all taking part in telling and protecting this mo'olelo [story]."[98]

Certainly more than one kind of production has been important at the pu'uhonua. The massive task of organizing and maintaining the pu'uhonua needed electronic communication. As media activist Kawena Kapahua points out, the protectors' sophisticated digital media presence enabled them to effectively challenge the state's tired old narrative "of Hawaiians doing drugs and making trouble." Digital technologies also enable the continuing expression of support for the struggle, the creative storytelling of the protectors for their future. Kapahua notes, "Mo'olelo cannot be passed without breath. One cannot speak without breathing. Just as we exchange breath when we greet each other, breath is exchanged when we exchange stories—even online."[99] Recognizing the importance of digital media to the struggle, I nonetheless suggest that there is something irreplaceable about physical presence, face-to-face relations, and shared material encounters. The richness of the immediate sensory experience and the creative collaboration of making things together pack their own punch.

Native Hawaiian ontology sees a living force expressed in nonorganic things; the ontology of new materialism, in contrast, sees things themselves as lively. These two theories of being emerge from different histories and give rise to different worlds. Yet I imagine that these ontologies could be comrades in the struggle for mutual aid, self-governance, and freedom. The protesters at Food Not Bombs and the protectors at Maunakea would, I suspect, recognize some shared ideas: that abundance is possible, that scarcity is created by capitalism and colonialism, that mutual aid promotes collective thriving, that people can govern themselves. They might also recognize a family resemblance in their constitutive relation to the things they do and make together.

The Feminist Bookstore Movement

During the 1970s, 1980s, and 1990s, a vigorous network of feminist bookstores arose in North America and across the world. By 1978 there were ninety-six feminist bookstores in the United States.[100] Mostly run by lesbian feminists, they were committed to antiracism and opposed to capitalism. They understood themselves to be revolutionaries. Usually running the stores collectively, the bookwomen developed cooperative labor practices, learned to listen actively to one another, and shared their successes and failures through their newsletter with other bookwomen running other stores. Feminist bookstores cultivated relations with feminist presses, which also strove for nonhierarchical structures and valued political engagement over profit.[101] In her remarkable account of the movement, feminist scholar Kristen Hogan succinctly concludes that they "were training each other as feminists and literary activists...they were learning to be allies." The bookstores were not just *about* feminism, they were expressions *of* feminism, and "the process was as important as the result."[102]

Most feminist bookstores have gone out of business, but they have left an enduring legacy by influencing mainstream book vendors to carry feminist literature and by leaving footprints, including strategy, vocabulary, and a philosophy of spatial design, that can contribute to radical politics today. Most were forced out of the market by the big chain bookstores, which in turn were driven out of business by online competition. A few feminist bookstores survived; after 2009, there was a minor resurgence of feminist and other independent bookstores, which have often revised their business models by creating not-for-profit arms, marketing more lucrative merchandise in addition to books, expanding to include a coffee shop or performance space, or renting out their stores for events.[103]

The movement created a publication, the *Feminist Bookstore News*, expressing the requirements of feminist literary activism. Issued five or six times a year, it began as a stapled, folded bundle of legal-size pages and in ten years grew into a forty-eight-page journal, professionally printed.[104] It circulated "a collection of booklists, skill sharings, information about publishers, news of the book industry, notices of new feminist bookstores, and conversations about feminist practice." The newsletter was formative for the movement: Hogan calls it "the groundbreaking engine of the feminist bookstore movement and its transformation of individual bookstores into a transnational feminist literary activist force."[105] Focused on developing feminist media, publications, and accountability across racial difference within their movement, the bookwomen used their newsletter "to build a vocabulary, to document and share important changes in publishing, and to wield influence in numbers to shape and sustain feminist information."[106] The newsletter enabled transparency of operation by providing a vehicle to share financial reports, staffing, and other store news. The interactive network of feminist bookstores provided meeting places, information exchanges, educational spaces, and links to publishers for their customers and allies.[107] Hogan argues that feminist books changed the lives even of people who didn't read them, because they changed lives in the surrounding communities.[108]

While Food Not Bombs can be contemptuous of any suggestion it develop "business sense," radical bookstores have a more agonized relation to markets.[109] "Activist entrepreneurship" or "retail activism," as urban planning professor Kimberly Kinder explains, develops small businesses as expressions of movements for social change, producing a wrenching clash between the requirements of success as a business and success as a radical movement.[110] Hogan, who spent time working in feminist bookstores in Austin and Toronto, makes a compelling argument for the latter: "Feminists must continue to prioritize antiracist alliances over traditional economic survival. I read a legacy of grappling with accountability and alliance building, rather than the continued life of a few feminist bookstores, as the success of the feminist bookstore movement." While they developed an inefficient business model by capitalist standards, they created spaces that were "astoundingly productive for feminist movement building."[111]

Beyond the newsletter and the books themselves, two specific manifestations of what Bennett calls "the complex interinvolvement of humans and multiple nonhuman actants" were tangible in the feminist bookstores: the booklists they created and the physical arrangements of the books in the store.[112] All bookstores have "display strategies," Kinder explains, but in radical stores they "do more than put books on shelves." They construct the store so that the "visual vocabulary" makes visitors welcome, provides a safe environment, empowers marginalized people, and claims space for cherished ideas and movements.[113] The bookwomen filled their newsletter and their bookstores with books they wanted women to read (as opposed to books they thought would sell). Feminist writer Randie Farmelant notes that books "earn their keep" by their inherent value to feminist readers rather than their ability to turn a profit.[114] Organizing the booklists required extensive knowledge of the literature and the capacity to imagine the space not as a container for publications but more like a spatial anthology of the feminist movement, with each section needing to be defined and understood in relation to all the others. They brought noncommercial, political order to a motley congregation of feminist publications. Hogan explains, "Feminist bookwomen gathered books together into lists as though they were writing manifestos, poetry, and theory—and they were. Feminist bookwomen created bibliographies for mailing lists, for newsletters, for orders, and for classes. Lists were one forum through which feminist bookwomen taught readers, including each other, to become literary activists. With these lists, which often reflected changing shelf section titles, feminist bookwomen put books in conversation with each other, demonstrated the existence of a field of knowledge, and mapped new vocabularies for understanding feminist literature."The booklists, created and shared through the newsletter, had an effect on how books could appear and what they could mean. The lists shared news of publications, put "texts in conversation with others," improved distribution, supported small presses, and sustained publishers with orders from the stores. The circulation of booklists put pressure on the mainstream book industry to publish feminist work. Hogan concludes, "Bookwomen had become the feminist watchdogs of the industry."[115]

A second and related manifestation of thing power was the creative approach the bookwomen took to the physical display of books. For all bookstores, as Kinder remarks, "curation is a governing tool."[116] In the feminist bookstores, the physical shelving of books was a moment in a process of making conversations possible among the bookwomen, among the customers, within the movement. Hogan explains,

> I create the term "feminist shelf" to describe bookwomen's complex practice of using spatial organization, programming, and reflection to map shelf sections as ways of relating to each other, as feminist love; to change reading and relational practices by creating new contexts for each text and for ourselves through the books on the shelf or the list; to build a collective accountability to new vocabularies for lesbian antiracist feminism through events, narrative signs, and newsletters; to enact a feminist ethics of dialogue, speaking with each other rather than for each other, as sections and programming required accountability for our own identities in relationship; and, throughout, to revise this knowledge building in conversation as bookwomen discussed, contested, and re-defined these contexts in collective meetings, transnational gatherings, and through the *Feminist Bookstore News*.[117]

The physical arrangements of the shelves and books were changed as the bookwomen worked together through difficult conversations to understand the needs and desires of different communities; they pursued an "ethics of dialogue and accountability." Organizing their store was part of organizing their movement, an emergent process that is never done once and for all but requires continued reframing: "The feminist shelf offered a cyclical process of bookwomen shaping books into fields of knowledge that changed reading practices, then talking together and revising their understandings of their own and each other's identities—particularly across racialized and class differences, and then rearranging and revising the shelf, and thus, reading practices."[118]

By "making space for dialogue rather than speaking for others," the bookwomen could encounter the histories and struggles of different communities within the stores and render them intelligible to one another. The seemingly banal question of where to put a book turned out to be a theory-making enterprise: Are Canadian indigenous women part of Canadian studies? Can memoir be theory? There were many possible avenues for passage across the literary terrain. The bookwomen created feminist shelf assemblages by putting the same book in several different sections and changing the arrangement over time as a result of their conversations: "They imagined and reimagined what these texts meant to each other, how they redefined each other." Dionne Brand's collection of poetry *No Language Is Neutral* could be located with "black Canadian Women, Caribbean women, Lesbian Non-Fiction, and Poetry." Zora Neale Hurston's *Dust Tracks on a Road* could, depending on what intertextual conversations came to the fore, be literary fiction, Harlem Renaissance fiction, life narrative, and a guide to finding love.[119] Sharon Fernandez of the Toronto Women's Bookstore recalls, with understatement, "It was a little complex. We weren't creating little ghettos of you go here if you want this, no, we're part of the whole community."[120] The physical impact of the feminist shelves on readers even gave rise to a map drawn by feminist geographer Joni Seager, a floor plan that was also "a cognitive map in which to place their own reading."[121] Feminist shoppers, accustomed to the feminist shelf, often felt a sense of loss when encountering beloved publications as mere commodities. Farmelant writes that when her local feminist bookstore closed and she was forced to seek the feminist magazine *Bust* at Borders, she was disgusted to finally locate it on a shelf between *Glamour* and *Allure*, "grouped with the enemy."[122] Feminist booklists and shelves operated as another version of Rancière's little optical machines: they hosted creative processes calling assemblages into being and enabling collective projects via shared material practices.

The feminist bookstore movement was made and remade on the shelves, both expressing and creating the parameters of feminist literary activism and of feminists' relationships with one another. Again, as with Food Not Bombs and Protect Maunakea 'Ohana, the feminist bookstores were not flawless; their strength came in part from their determination to create an antiracist praxis to change themselves as well as the larger society. "The books on the shelf made possible conversations across racial difference within the collective," which in turn made possible the rearrangement of the books on the shelves. The process of organizing and reorganizing books, constructing and reconstructing reading practices, could "transform readers into activists." They "honed a practice of feminist accountability that could inform and sustain today's feminisms," a dialogue to express their politics and ethics and figure out how to live by them.[123]

Because feminist books were not treated as separate objects but as voices in relation, a book located in a feminist bookstore was not precisely the "same" as the identical publication located in a chain outlet or an online store. Each book was more than itself. "Feminist bookstores were never just bookstores," just as Food Not Bombs is never just a food line and Protect Maunakea was not just a camp.[124] The land, the access road, the park, the food, the booklists, the shelves—these are material components of politics. They are sites or opportunities for people to do and make things together. Like the presses, correspondence, and publications of the classical anarchist movement, they are actants; they are not just background for political action but rather participants in the politics they enable.

Concluding Thoughts

So what do scrappy young anarchists feeding people and overthrowing capitalism, an indigenous nation rising to overthrow colonialism and become self-governing, and women organizing to buy and sell feminist literature have in common? They are all radical movements for social transformation based on mutual aid, self-organization, and direct democratic participation. Women play significant roles at all levels of leadership and organization. Many similarities as well as differences could be found in their philosophies, in the ontologies of being that provide the context for their politics. I am drawing attention to their thing power: they are strong in part because they make things together, they enter into the sensoriums of things, they touch and are touched in a creative resonance of political practice. The making of things leads to being able to make more things, and the makers are also made by reciprocal touch.

Because relationality is constitutive of things and their people, useful objects like sorts, missives, publications, food, lists, and books and constitutive spaces like parks, camps, land, shelves, and retail establishments are not just prostheses for bodies and minds that already are but in fact world extenders making people and worlds that can be. Interior and exterior are fruitfully confused. Their entanglements and interfaces resonate and facilitate creative collaborations. As was the case with Emma Goldman's famous suitcase, which accompanied her on her decades of cross-country lecture tours, it becomes hard to separate the container from the contained. Meaning is made in the convergence of material, social, and semiotic practices. In the ontological continuity and confusion across categories, each person and thing is bigger than itself.

In their media practices, anarchists may have implicitly identified a constitutive condition of possibility for the flourishing of radical political communities in our time as well as theirs. Material practices can embody ideas. Spaces for enabling this productive process have to be discovered and created. If letterpress printing, epistolary relations, and radical scholarship played the role I am suggesting in creating and sustaining the anarchist movement, then contemporary activists may need comparably lively sites in which material, organic, social, and semiotic practices come together to generate worlds. Attending patiently to multidirectional relations among loosely bounded actants can be a way to nurture liveliness in both our theories and our things.

Without thing power, there is a missing interface in radical assemblages. More accurately, there is always some kind of thing power—the microbes in our guts, the ground under our feet, the electricity flowing through the grid, and so on—but radical politics, I speculate, requires or at least benefits from vigorous, cultivated thing power. People have to make things together, be made by things together, to fuel what Fessenden calls their "direct action projects."[125] The absence of material actants weakens the circuits of radical study. Perhaps there are virtual substitutes for thing power, but I doubt it.[126] In his reflections on Black anarchism, William Anderson succinctly comments, "Wherever we go, we have to build."[127] Radical groups may utilize digital media for organizing and communicating, but I suspect their strongest political work builds face-to-face, hand-to-hand, in conjunction with other agents and actants. Their entanglements are part of their creative process, in resonance with other elements, collaborating to give birth to unrealized possibilities.

Like the anarchists of old, we live in a time that *needs* effective resistance. Present radicalisms look different when they have an affirmative history of their own. Political activism looks different when it is enhanced by an abiding sensory intimacy with the things we use and make. Scholarship looks different when it turns toward the practices needed to open up our histories and reframe our struggles. By understanding how anarchists' print culture worked during their lives, we can cultivate its best elements in ours.

APPENDIX A

Compositors, Pressmen, and Bookbinders

Note: These individuals were identified as printers, including both credentialed professionals and amateurs who participated in printing, in documents, correspondence, secondary literature, or other printed sources. Most were directly involved in printing anarchist material, while a few issued publications that had significant overlap with anarchism. Some are only mentioned in passing in correspondence or memoirs, so it is difficult to know much about their training or experience, but I have included them so that future researchers might pick up the trail.

1 Abate, Erasmo (a.k.a. Hugo Rolland)—Italian housepainter who wrote and set type for *La Comune* (Philadelphia)[1]

2 Aldred, Guy—Set up the Bakunin Press in London (1907) and the Strickland Press in Glasgow (1939–68); editor and printer for *Herald of Revolt* and *The Word* (Glasgow)[2]

3 Anderson, Margaret—Coeditor of the *Little Magazine* (New York)[3]

4 Angiollilo, Michel—Italian-born typographer, lived in London, assassinated the Spanish prime minister[4]

5 Apolo, Antonio—Spanish typographer working at the Imprenta de Antonio Marzo, which published *La Revista Blanca* and its *Suplemento*, and wrote for *El Progreso*[5]

6 Atabekian, Alexandre—Armenian physician and printer; cofounded a cooperative print shop in Moscow in 1918 and set type for their journal *Pocin*[6]

7 Baldazzi, Giovanni (a.k.a. John Baldazzi; Baldazza)—Italian-born printer, wrote for several anarchist publications[7]

8 Ballou, Percy—Printer of *Free Comrade*, owner of Mangus Press; married Bertha Johnson's sister Perry in 1906 (United States)[8]

9 Balzano, Ugo—Italian-born typographer, member of Circolo Studi Sociali di Cleveland[9]

10 Baracchi, Giovanni—Milanese bookbinder, moved to Paterson, New Jersey[10]

11 Baraldi, Ciro—Milanese typographer, contributed to the Modern Schools and several journals[11]

12 Bek-Fran, Robert—Munich-born, printed and wrote for *Why?* and *Resistance* (New York)[12]

13 Berkman, Alexander—Russian-born, trained as a printer in New Haven, Connecticut, printed Most's *Freiheit* (New York)[13]

14 Berman, Nahum H.—Russian Jewish pressman and compositor for *The Rebel* (Boston)[14]

15 Bertoni, Luigi—Swiss typographer for *Il Risveglio / Le Réveil* (Geneva)[15]

16 Bianki, Peter—Russian-born printer, active in the Union of Russian Workers[16]

17 Blundell, William—Compositor for the English journal *Commonweal* (London)[17]

18 Bogin, Sigor—Russian-born printer, lived at Mohegan Colony (New York)[18]

19 Born, Helena—Immigrated to the United States from England in 1890, trained as a typographer (Boston)[19]

20 Borrás, Antonia Fontanillas—Spanish typographer, helped put out *Solidaridad Obrera*[20]

21 Boscolo, Felice—Milanese typographer, arrested during protests of Francisco Ferrer's execution in October 1909[21]

22 Bowman, Guy—English printer and editor of *The Syndicalist* (Walthamstow, England)[22]

23 Brady, Ed—Austrian-born compositor, worked with Emma Goldman (United States)[23]

24 Bruciati, Ermanno—Milanese typographer, arrested in antianarchist police action in March 1890[24]

25 Cagnola, Pietro—Milanese typographer, arrested in antianarchist police action in March 1890[25]

26 Caldwell, John Taylor—Scottish seaman, helped set up *The Word*, assisted Guy Aldred at Strickland Press (Glasgow)[26]

27 Caminita, Ludovico—Sicilian-born typesetter, printer for *Cronaca Sovversiva*, editor for *La Questione Sociale* (Paterson, New Jersey)[27]

28 Campos, José C.—Cuban-born printer, helped produce *El Depertar* and *The Rebel* (Brooklyn)[28]

29 Cantine, Holley—New York–born printer and coeditor for *Retort* (Woodstock, New York)[29]

30 Cantwell, Thomas—English printer and manager of *Freedom* (London)[30]

31 Cerri, Attilio—Milanese typographer, arrested during antianarchist sweep in March 1890[31]

32 Chatterton, Dan—Blind printer, created *Chatterton's Commune, The Atheistic Communistic Scorcher* (London)[32]

33 Ciancabilla, Giuseppe—Italian-born printer, coeditor of *La Protesta Umana* and *L'Aurora* (United States)[33]

34 Cooney, Blanche—Printer and coeditor, *The Phoenix* (Woodstock, New York)[34]

35 Cooney, James P.—Printer and coeditor, *The Phoenix* (Woodstock, New York)[35]

36 Cores, George—Leicester shoemaker, set type for *Freedom* (London)[36]

37 Crocker, Donald—Contributed to *The Clarion* and *Road to Freedom* (United States)[37]

38 Deanin, Sonya—Helped print and distribute *Frayhayt* (New York)[38]

39 Derkach, Alexander—Russian-born printer, active in the Union of Russian Workers[39]

40 Derzanski, Barnett—Helped Keell and Lilian Wolfe put out *Freedom* (London and Whiteway)[40]

41 Drobner, Gustav—Compositor in Leipzig, distributed anarchist materials[41]

42 Elia, Roberto—Italian-born typesetter for *La Plebe* and *Cronica Sovversiva* (Vermont and Massachusetts)[42]

43 Ellington, Richard—US-born, helped print the Libertarian League's journal, *Views and Comments* (New York)[43]

44 Epstein, Marc—Printer for *Mother Earth*, *Vanguard*, and the Free Theatre programs (New York)[44]

45 Eramo, Giovanni—Printer for *Cronaca Sovversiva* (Vermont and Massachusetts)[45]

46 Estevé, Pedro—Catalan-born printer and editor for *La Questione Sociale* (Paterson, New Jersey) and *Cultura Obrera* (New York City)[46]

47 Exall, George—Compositor for *The Anarchist* (London)[47]

48 Felicani, Aldino—Boston-based printer for *La Notizia* and *Controcorrente*[48]

49 Finch, Bob—Helped print *Freedom* with his uncle John Humphrey (London)[49]

50 Fischer, Adolf—German-born, set type for *Arbeiter-Zeitung*, coedited *Der Anarchist* (Chicago)[50]

51 Fontanillas Borrás, Antonia (a.k.a. Tona)—Spanish-born, helped print *Solidaridad Obrero* (Barcelona)[51]

52 Fox, Jay—Irish-born printer and editor for *The Demonstrator*, *The Agitator*, and *The Syndicalist* (Home Colony, Washington; and Chicago)[52]

53 Fulton, Edward—Printer and editor for *Age of Thought*, *New Order*, *The Mutualist*, and *The Egoist* (United States)[53]

54 Gans, Joseph—Printer arrested in a demonstration of the movement for the unemployed (New York)[54]

55 Govan, Charles—Edited and printed *Discontent* (Home Colony, Washington)[55]

56 Grave, Jean—French typesetter and editor[56]

57 Greenberg, Bronka—Printed forbidden material in the anarchist resistance in Warsaw in the 1930s[57]

58 Guabello, Adelegisa—Worked in a print shop with her husband, Alberto (Paterson, New Jersey)[58]

59 Guabello, Alberto—Husband of Adelegisa (Paterson, New Jersey)[59]

60 Harman, Lillian—Compositor for *Lucifer* (Valley Falls, Kansas)[60]

61 Harman, Moses—Editor and sometimes compositor for *Lucifer* (Valley Falls, Kansas; and Chicago)[61]

62 Hirschauge, Eliezer—Polish-born printer, printed *Deyes* and pamphlet on Peter Kropotkin (Tel Aviv)[62]

63 Holmes, Sarah Elizabeth—Set type for *Liberty* and *Science of Society* (Boston)[63]

64 Humphrey, John J.—Set type for *Freedom* (London)[64]

65 Isaak, Abe, Jr.—Son of Abe Isaak Sr.; set type for *Free Society* (Chicago, San Francisco, New York)[65]

66 Isaak, Abe, Sr.—Born in Odessa, set type for *The Firebrand* (Portland, Oregon) and *Free Society* (San Francisco, Chicago, New York)[66]

67 Ishill, Anatole—Son of Joseph; printed under his own imprint at Freeman Press[67]

68 Ishill, Joseph—Romanian-born compositor, set type for the *Modern School Magazine* and the *Path of Joy* (Stelton, New Jersey); ran Oriole Press (Berkeley Heights, New Jersey)[68]

69 Jeger, Moritz—Polish Jewish immigrant to England, had a print shop in Liverpool and worked with Rudolf Rocker on *Dos Freie Vort*[69]

70 Katzes [Katz], Arthur—Russian-born printer, member of the editorial board of *Khleb I Volia* (paper of the Union of Russian Workers)[70]

71 Keell, Thomas—English printer, manager, and editor of *Freedom* (London and Whiteway)[71]

72 Kelly, Harry—Born in Missouri, trained as a pressman, worked on *The Rebel* (Boston) and *Freedom* (London)[72]

73 Kropotkin, Peter—Set type for *Le Révolté* (Berne); also learned bookbinding[73]

74 Labadie, Joseph—Michigan-born printer, set type for his own poems and essays (Detroit)[74]

75 Labadie, Laurance—A reluctant printer, son of Jo Labadie; edited *Discussion: A Journal for Free Spirits*[75]

76 Lachowsky, Hyman—Printer for *Frayhayt* (New York)[76]

77 Lane, Joseph—Published "An Anti-Statist, Communist Manifesto"; published William Morris's *Commonweal* until he resigned due to ill health in 1889[77]

78 Langdon, Emma—Linotype operator at the *Cripple Creek Daily Record*, Colorado[78]

79 Latorre, Paulino Pallás—Spanish typesetter, tried to kill General Martínez Campos in Barcelona[79]

80 Leech, Frank—Lancashire-born, operated a printing press and ran a refuge for Spanish and German refugees[80]

81 Lenoble (first name unknown)—Romanian-born compositor for *Arbeiterfreund*, arrested for defying the Defense of the Realm Act in 1916 (London)[81]

82 Leuenroth, Edgard—Brazilian typesetter, founder of Printworkers' Union and numerous journals[82]

83 Leval, Gaston—French anarchist, historian of the Spanish Revolution, printer and editor for *Cahiers de l'Humanisme Libertaire* (Paris)[83]

84 Livshis, Peter—Son of Anna and Jake Livshis in Chicago; became a printer[84]

85 London, Ephraim—Printed *Der Morgenshtern* (New York)[85]

86 López, Alfredo—Cuban printer, anarcho-syndicalist[86]

87 Lorenzo, Anselmo—Spanish printer, edited *La Huelga General* with Francisco Ferrer[87]

88 Lum, Dyer—Writer and editor, as well as a bookbinder[88]

89 MacDonald, Ethel—Scottish printer and editor, worked on *The Word* (Glasgow)[89]

90 Mancer, A.—Helped print *Freedom* and *Voice of Labor* while Keell was in prison (London)[90]

91 Marchese, Giuseppe—Typographer for *L'Era Nuova* (Paterson, New Jersey)[91]

92 Mazzotta, Beniamino—Italian-born printer, coeditor of *La Scopa* (Paterson, New Jersey)[92]

93 Meacham, P. S.—Worked with Sellars and Mancer to bring out *Freedom* and *Voice of Labor* while Keell was in prison (London)[93]

94 Meelis, Tom—Dutch-born printer, member of Emma Goldman's Libertarian Group in Canada[94]

95 Metzkow, Max—German-born compositor for Lum's *Alarm* and Most's *Freiheit*; helped Seymour print *The Anarchist* (London and United States)[95]

96 Michaels, Emmanuel—With Derzanski, helped Keell and Lilian Wolfe put out *Freedom* (London and Whiteway)[96]

97 Monanni, Giuseppe—Self-taught typographer; Leda Rafanelli's partner in Italy[97]

98 Moroni, Alberto—Born in Milan, son of Antonio; printed anarchist material and participated in the antifascist resistance[98]

99 Moroni, Antonio—Milan-born printer, father of Alberto; printed anarchist material and participated in the antifascist resistance; father and son were imprisoned for five years for printing antifascist lyrics to a popular song[99]

100 Morris, J. H.—Printer for *The Firebrand* (Portland, Oregon)[100]

101 Morris, William—Artist, writer, printer, founded Kelmscott Press (London)[101]

102 Morton, Charles—Compositor for *Freedom* (London)[102]

103 Most, Johann—Bookbinder, editor, and writer for *Freiheit*[103]

104 Mratchny, Mark—Printer for Nester Makhno's guerrilla army in Russia[104]

105 Naroditsky, Papa—Printer for *Germinal*, taught Rudolf Rocker to print[105]

106 Nicholl, David—Printed and published *The Commonweal* (London)[106]

107 Nimes, Floyd E.—Industrial Workers of the World printer, worked on *Solidarity* (New Castle, Pennsylvania)[107]

108 Novik, Peter—Russian-born printer, joined the Union of Russian Workers in the United States[108]

109 Novikov, Ivan—Russian-born printer, set linotype for *Novy Mir*[109]

110 Orodovsky [Oradovsky], Markus—"First-class printer" whom Emma Goldman met in Odessa[110]

111 Paraire, Antoni Pellicer—Spanish typographer, active in La Academia, a typographic workshop printing material for the labor movement[111]

112 Parsons, Albert—Chicago typographer, editor, and orator[112]

113 Patrick, Jenny—Scottish printer, worked on *The Word* (Glasgow)[113]

114 Pearson, W.—Compositor for *Freedom* (London)[114]

115 Penichet, Antonio—Cuban printer and writer[115]

116 Perrazzini, Giuseppe—Milanese typographer, arrested during antianarchist police sweeps in March 1890[116]

117 Pissarro, Esther Bensusan—Printer and wood engraver for Eragny Press in England[117]

118 Pissarro, Lucien—Printer and wood engraver for Eragny Press in England[118]

119 Pope, Kenneth—Brother of Macie; set type for the *New Era* (Home Colony, Washington)[119]

120 Pope, Macie—Set type for the *New Era* and *Discontent* (Home Colony, Washington)[120]

121 Proudhon, Pierre-Joseph—French typesetter, author[121]

122 Rafanelli, Leda—Italian typesetter, author, publisher[122]

123 Rainer, Dachine—Printed and coedited *Retort* with Holley Cantine (Woodstock, New York)[123]

124 Reinsdorf, August—German compositor; friend of Johann Most[124]

125 Replogle, Georgia—Compositor and coeditor for *Egoism* (San Francisco)[125]

126 Rinke, Otto—German anarchist, printed *Der Rebell* out of his living room (London)[126]

127 Robins, Bob—Traveled with his partner, Lucy, in a horse-drawn camper with a handpress; worked on the Mooney campaign with Berkman and Fitzi Fitzgerald[127]

128 Rocker, Fermin—Lithographer and artist; son of Rudolf and Milly Rocker (England and New York)[128]

129 Rocker, Milly—Set type for *Germinal*; partner of Rudolf Rocker (London)[129]

130 Rocker, Rudolf—Bookbinder; partner of Milly Rocker; set type for *Germinal* (London)[130]

131 Rogers, Dorothy—Helped write and print *Why?* (New York City)[131]

132 Romero Rosa, Ramón—Puerto Rican typesetter and labor organizer, cofounder of *Ensayo Obrero*[132]

133 Roodenko, Igal—Typographer for *Views and Comments*, journal of the Libertarian League (New York)[133]

134 Rossetti, Olivia and Helen—Printed and edited *The Torch* (London)[134]

135 Ruiz, Francisco—Spanish typographer for *La Anarquía*[135]

136 Ryde (first name unknown)—Printer for *Arbeiterfreund*; arrested under the Defense of the Realm Act in 1916 (England)[136]

137 Salsedo, Andrea—Sicilian-born typographer, affiliated with *Cronoca Sovversiva*[137]

138 Sartin, Max—Bookbinder; associated with *L'Adunata dei Refrattari*[138]

139 Schatz, Harry—Russian-born printer; on the editorial board of *Khleb I Volia* (paper of the Union of Russian Workers)[139]

140 Schultze, Moritz—Prussian-born compositor, helped Rinke print *Der Rebell* in his flat in London[140]

141 Schumm, George—Typographer for *Liberty* (Boston)[141]

142 Schwab, Michael—Bookbinder (Chicago)[142]

143 Schwartz, Clarence Lee—Typographer for *Lucifer* when Moses Harman was in prison; compositor for *Liberty* (United States)[143]

144 Scott, Paul—Taught children to print at the Stelton Modern School (New Jersey)[144]

145 Sellars, F.—Compositor for *Freedom* and *Voice of Labor* while Keell and Lilian Wolfe were in prison (London)[145]

146 Serge, Victor—Learned to print in the Belgian colony in Stockel[146]

147 Seymour, Henry—Printed *The Anarchist* (London)[147]

148 Shahn, Ben—Outstanding lithographer and graphic artist, active in the movement to save Nicola Sacco and Bartolomeo Vanzetti (United States)[148]

149 Shatoff, William—Russian-born printer and laborer, printed Margaret Sanger's birth control pamphlet and *Golos Truda* (Voice of Labor) (United States and Soviet Union)[149]

150 Simkin (first name unknown)—Canadian printer, made Nicola Sacco and Bartolomeo Vanzetti pamphlet (Toronto)[150]

151 Sola—A "Somali fireman" who became a bookbinder at Whiteway Colony (England)[151]

152 Stroud, Fred—Compositor and machine operator for *Freedom* (London)[152]

153 Thorn, Martin—Printed and edited *News of No Importance* (United States)[153]

154 Thorne, Ahrne—Born in Poland, printer for Yiddish publications in New York City, later edited *Fraye Arbeter Shtime*[154]

155 Timmerman, Claus—German typesetter, wrote, set up, and printed *Der Sturmvogel* (United States)[155]

156 Tochatti, James—Scottish-born tailor, printed and published the London journal *Liberty*[156]

157 Travaglio, Eugene—Italian-born compositor, set type for *Free Society* (Chicago), edited several journals including *La Protesta Umana* and *The Petrel* (San Francisco)[157]

158 Tucker, Benjamin—Editor of *Liberty* (Boston)[158]

159 Turner, John—English printer and publisher of *Freedom* (London)[159]

160 Waisbrooker, Lois—US anarchist, spiritualist, and feminist; set type and operated the handpress to print *Foundation Principles*[160]

161 Ward, Colin—English writer and architect, learned to print as a child, helped print *Freedom* (London)[161]

162 Warren, Josiah—A professional musician; built his own press, cast type, wrote, set, and printed the articles in the *Peaceful Revolutionist*[162]

163 Weider, Albert—Printer for *Der Arme Teufel*, edited by Erich Mühsam in Germany, 1902–4; wrote while he set type[163]

164 Werner, Emil-August—German-born composer, active in the Jura Federation in Switzerland[164]

165 Wess, William "Woolf"—Born in Lithuania, active in the Jewish labor movement in London, set type for *Freedom* (London)[165]

166 Widmar, Franz—Slovenian printer, editor of *La Questione Sociale* (Paterson, New Jersey)[166]

167 Winn, Ross—Tennessee printer, printed *Winn's Firebrand* and *The Advance*[167]

168 Woodcock, George—Learned to print on *Freedom* (London)[168]

169 Worden, Frank H.—Set type for *Discontent* and *The Demonstrator* (United States)[169]

170 Yarros, Victor—Set type with Holmes for *Liberty* (Boston)[170]

171 Yvetôt, George Louis François—French anarchist typesetter[171]

172 Zamboni, Mammolo—Italian printer, father of Anteo, who was executed for trying to kill Benito Mussolini[172]

173 Zerboni, Enrico—Typesetter in Milan, arrested in antifascist resistance[173]

APPENDIX B

Brief Biographies

Carlo Abate (1860–1941) was a sculptor, printmaker, and engraver for Luigi Galleani's insurrectionary anarchist paper *Cronaca Sovversiva* (Subversive Chronicle) from 1903 to 1918. The paper was printed in a shop organized by the Industrial Workers of the World. While making his living as an artist and a teacher in an art school in Barre, Vermont, he created a striking visual repertoire of revolutionary icons for the journal.

Holley Cantine (1916–77) was a US writer and printer who, with his companion Dachine Rainer, put out the journal *Retort* from their home in Woodstock, New York. He also translated Voline's *The Unknown Revolution* from Russian to English. Imprisoned as a conscientious objector during World War II, he and Rainer wrote about resistance behind bars in *Prison Etiquette: The Convict's Compendium of Useful Information*. Cantine is remembered as a spirited man with a great fondness for German band music. An extant photograph shows a substantial bearded man with a workman's cap, playing the tuba.

Dan Chatterton (1820–95) was born into a poor working-class family from an artisan neighborhood in Clerkenwell, London. Chatterton apprenticed as a bootmaker and was active in the Chartist movement and other radical groups, becoming a well-known character on the London radical scene. Fiercely atheistic and pro–birth control, he printed a number of pamphlets, championing the needs of the poor and decrying the elites of church and state who lived heedless of others' suffering. He published his journal *Chatterton's Commune: The Atheistic Communistic Scorcher* from 1884 until his death in 1895. Lacking a press, Chatterton "printed" by pressing the sorts on the page with his hands. A portrait from 1891 shows a small, tattered man wearing a long coat and a wide-brimmed hat.

Pedro Esteve (1866–1925) was born in Barcelona, Spain, and emigrated to Paterson, New Jersey, in 1892 via Paris and Cuba, later moving to Tampa, Florida, and other cities. Apprenticed at fourteen to a professional press shop, he became a typesetter, editor, writer, public speaker, and labor organizer. A photograph of Esteve later in life shows a bespectacled figure with a high forehead, bushy mustache, and narrow beard. Esteve and his partner, Maria Roda, also an anarchist activist, had ten children. Esteve edited *La Questione Sociale*, *El Despertar*, and *Cultura Obrera*.

Jay Fox (1870–1961) was raised in Chicago and was a member of the Knights of Labor; he participated in the Haymarket events and the Seattle general strike. For a time he lived at the anarchist colony in Home, Washington, where he printed and edited *The Agitator*. He later returned to Chicago and renamed his paper *The Syndicalist*. A photograph of Fox as a young man shows dark, unruly hair, prominent features, and a serious countenance.

Edward H. Fulton (birth and death dates unknown) was a trained compositor living in the midwestern United States who edited and printed *Age of Thought*, *The Mutualist*, *New Order*, and *The Egoist*, among others. He subscribed to *Freedom*, which he praised as "by far the best paper of our kind that I have found anywhere."[1] Fulton was deaf but still played the violin: "I get the tone through the vibration of collar bone, and from it to back-bone and spinal column, which reaches the brain."[2] He describes standing with his daughter in the window and playing a duet. A photograph of Fulton on the cover of his July 4, 1896, issue of *Age of Thought* shows an earnest-looking young man with pale skin, round cheeks, and curly hair.

Lillian Harman (1869–1929) was the daughter of anarchist Moses Harman, editor of the journal *Lucifer, The Lightbearer*, based primarily in Valley Falls, Kansas. Lillian learned to print from her father and by age thirteen was setting type for *Lucifer*. The family farmed during the day and wrote, printed, and assembled the journal in the evenings. Later Lillian served a jail term for "living in sin" with coeditor Edwin Walker. She became president of the Legitimation League in England and wrote for its journal *The Adult*, which advocated sexual freedom. Lillian had a daughter with Walker and two more children with her second companion, Chicago union activist George O'Brien. A photograph from Lillian's youth shows the profile of a light-skinned, strong-featured woman with a mass of curly hair piled on top of her head.

Eliezer Hirschauge (1911–54) was born in Poland and apprenticed as a compositor at age sixteen. After surviving brutal incarceration in work camps in the USSR after World War II, Eliezer and his companion, Dina Huzarski, arrived in a refugee camp, where he organized schools and printed and edited a newspaper. In 1947 Eliezer and Dina emigrated to Israel. They had two children, who proudly posed for a photo in which they were holding between them a copy of a book by Rudolf Rocker. Photos show a dark-haired, clean-shaven man. Dina describes Eliezer as "a master compositor by trade and a great idealist."[3] Joseph Ishill and Rudolf Rocker corresponded with Eliezer, and Joseph wrote to Rudolf when Eliezer died suddenly of a heart attack at age forty-three: "Our affinities that brought us together was [*sic*] not only typographical, but idealistically as well. He was a man whom I admired and now I deeply regret his premature departure."[4]

Agnes Inglis (1879–1952) was born in Michigan and raised by a middle-class Presbyterian family with whom she largely maintained positive relations while becoming radicalized. A slender and modest young woman, she organized talks and Industrial Workers of the World events and tried to save the men being threatened with deportation during the Red Scare after World War I. Concerned that Joseph Labadie's extensive donation of anarchist materials was being neglected by the University of Michigan library, she took on the task of organizing the collection as well as expanding it to be one of the best collections of anarchist material in the world.

Joseph Ishill (1888–1966) was born in Romania, apprenticed to a print shop at age fourteen, and in 1909 emigrated to the United States. Like William Morris, he was recognized both within the radical movement and within the printing and design trades, where he became known as "the anarchist printer." A shy and earnest man, he founded the Oriole Press in Berkeley Heights, New Jersey, and published over two hundred books and pamphlets by anarchists and fellow travelers. His wife, Rose Freeman Ishill, with whom he had three children, was an accomplished poet and translator, partnering with Joseph on many of his publications. Joseph was particularly known for collaborating with engravers to produce elegantly illustrated books with classic ornamentation.

Bertha F. Johnson (1880–1958) was the younger sister of Pearl Johnson Tucker. More robust and easygoing than Pearl, Bertha received her degree in medicine from the New York Medical Hospital and College for Women in 1905 and worked in the field of children's health. Unable to find work as a physician after moving to rural Pennsylvania with her husband, Emery Andrews, she took up the work of a farm wife and also became the custodian and archivist of anarchist materials and records left to her by family and friends. The sisters were devoted to each other.

Thomas Keell (1866–1938) was an English anarchist and printer who lived with his companion, Lilian Wolfe, and their son Tom Jr. in South London, and later at the anarchist community Whiteway Colony near Stroud, Gloucestershire. Tall, bearded, and generally quiet, Keell was compositor for *Freedom* and *Voice of Labor* as well as business manager and editor. When the anarchist movement split over World War I, Keell would not give *Freedom* over to those he called prowar anarchists. He retired to Whiteway in 1927, taking the journal with him, and lived on his pension from the London Society of Compositors. The countryside suited him, as he was an active walker and cyclist. He issued periodic *Freedom Bulletins* from Whiteway and was the publisher of *Spain and the World* until his death.

Jo Labadie (1850–1933) was born in Paw Paw, Michigan. His family was descended from French settlers and Ojibway Indians. After his years as a tramp printer, Labadie settled in Detroit and was an organizer for the Knights of Labor and a writer and printer for several labor publications. Labadie credited his wife, Sophie, for patiently saving and maintaining the mountains of anarchist materials that he subsequently donated to the University of Michigan in 1912, forming the foundation of the collection named after him, which he understood to be his primary legacy. Ebullient and charming, he was known locally as "the gentle anarchist" and was a cherished figure in the Detroit area.

Max Metzkow (1854–1945) was a German-born compositor who became active in antiwar work there. After serving a prison term for encouraging soldiers to resist, he moved to London in 1883 and set type for Johan Most's journal *Freiheit*. In 1888 he moved to the United States and set type on Dyer Lum's journal *The Alarm*. Metzkow was an unassuming man who met nearly all of the illustrious figures in the anarchist movement, including William Morris, Charlotte Wilson, Peter Kropotkin, Louise Michel, Rudolf Rocker, Joseph and Rose Ishill, Alexander Berkman, Harry Kelly, Max Baginski, Thomas Keell, and many others. In his elegant handwriting, he corresponded with Agnes Inglis for many years. He was one of the rank-and-file anarchists whose accomplishments Inglis was determined to record for future scholars.

Louis Moreau (1883–1958) was a French artist who apprenticed to be a lithographer and later became a painter and wood engraver. He contributed to several anarchist journals and was Ishill's partner in their understanding of anarchism, their aesthetic goals, and their publishing ventures. Moreau created the striking woodcuts populating the pages of Élie Reclus's 1931 book *Plant Physiognomies*, translated by Rose Freeman Ishill and printed by Joseph Ishill.

William Morris (1834–96) is best remembered as an English poet, designer, and socialist, but he was also a letterpress printer who inspired many anarchists. In 1891 he learned to print from his neighbor Emery Walker and established Kelmscott Press in London, which gave energy to letterpress as an art, craft, and politics. He married the talented embroiderer Jane Burden and they had two children. A robust and temperamental man, he was known for cultivating a European medieval aesthetic in printing and for founding the Arts and Crafts movement.

Georgia Replogle (?–1904) was the typesetter and coeditor of the journal *Egoism* with her partner, Henry Replogle, in San Francisco. Her close friend Lillian Harman described her as sympathetic and supportive. Her writings show her sly sense of humor as well as her bitter protest against women's subordination to violent, vicious men.

Rudolf Rocker (1873–1958) was a German-born bookbinder, labor leader, and outstanding writer and intellectual. Known as "the anarchist rabbi" (although he was not Jewish), Rocker lived for many years in the Jewish neighborhoods of London's East End. He learned Yiddish and edited as well as set type for several publications. After being interned in England during World War I as an enemy alien, he subsequently fled the Nazis in 1933, escaping Germany with the manuscript of *Nationalism and Culture*. A short, round man with a gentle presence, Rocker and his companion Milly Witcop, also an anarchist, had one son, Fermin, who became a lithographer and noted painter. They moved to the United States and lived for many years at the anarchist colony Mohegan in upstate New York.

Pearl Johnson Tucker (1879–1948) came from a radical family of Spiritualists and labor activists. She worked at Benjamin Tucker's Unique Book Shop in New York City from 1906 to 1908 and became Benjamin's partner. After a fire destroyed the warehouse in 1908, Pearl and Benjamin moved to France, where she homeschooled their daughter Oriole. A small, dainty, and very determined woman, Pearl became the custodian and archivist of Benjamin's remaining materials and records.

Lilian Wolfe (1875–1974) was active in the Freedom collective for most of her life. Raised in a middle-class English family, she became radicalized during her years working at the telegraph office. A pacifist, feminist, and vegetarian as well as an anarchist, Wolfe ran the bookstore and library, managed the finances, answered the phones, sold literature, greeted visitors, and generally made the place work. A 1945 photo shows a slender, serious, dark-haired woman selling *War Commentary* on the London streets.

APPENDIX C

Printers Interviewed

* Bagdonas, Eric, Stumptown Printers Worker Cooperative, Portland, Oregon, https://www.subtonworks.com/

* Coughlin, Michael, printer and bookmaker, Minneapolis, https://www.letterpressbookpublishing.com/author/mike/

* Faye, Jules Remedios, Stern and Faye, Letterpress Printers, Mount Vernon, Washington, http://www.sternandfaye.com/

* Good, Peter, *The Cunningham Amendment*, Bawdeswell, England

* Green, Joseph, Jeff Shay, and Connie Blauwkamp, C. C. Stern Type Foundry, Museum of Metal Typography, Portland, Oregon, https://www.culturaltrust.org/get-involved/nonprofits/c-c-stern-type-foundry/

* Leeds, Ali Cat, Entangled Roots Press, Portland, Oregon, https://entangledroots.com/about/

* Loring, Nick, The Print Project, Shipley, England, https://theprintproject.co.uk/

* Overbeck, Charles, Eberhardt Press, Portland, Oregon, https://www.eberhardtpress.org

* Shadburne, Ruby, Ruby Press, Portland, Oregon, https://www.rubypress.com/

NOTES

Preface

Some portions of the introduction, chapter 1, and chapter 4 appeared in "Anarchist Printers and Presses: Material Circuits of Power," *Political Theory* 42, no. 4 (2014): 391–414, © 2014 SAGE Publications.

Some portions of the introduction and chapter 3 appeared in "Anarchist Women and the Politics of Walking," *Political Research Quarterly* 70, no. 4 (2017): 708–19, © 2017 University of Utah; and in "Assemblages of Anarchists: Political Aesthetics in *Mother Earth*," *Journal of Modern Periodical Studies* 4, no. 2 (2013): 171–94, copyright © 2014 The Pennsylvania State University, University Park, PA.

1 Cornell, *Unruly Equality*, 26.

2 Zimmer, *Immigrants against the State*, 11.

3 Flores, "Socialist Newspapers and Periodicals."

4 For data on Socialist Party members and voters in the United States, see "Socialist Party of America." For data on anarchist publications, see Zimmer, "American Anarchist Periodical Circulation Data."

5 Goodway, "'Freedom' 1886–2014."

6 Patten, "Islands of Anarchy."

7 Leighten, *Re-ordering the Universe*, 50.

8 Gitelman, *Scripts, Grooves*, 216.

9 Parikka, *What Is Media Archaeology?*, 39, 70.

10 Parikka, *What Is Media Archaeology?*, 73.

11 Hogan, *Feminist Bookstore Movement*, 178.

Acknowledgments

1 Quail, *Slow Burning Fuse*, xiv, xv.

Introduction

1 Ishill to Inglis, January 14, 1945, 1, Agnes Inglis Papers, Box 10, Joseph A. Labadie Collection (emphasis in original).

2 In *Kropotkin: Reviewing the Classical Anarchist Tradition*, Ruth Kinna points out the problems of using the familiar categories of classical or first-wave anarchism, followed by second-wave anarchism in the 1960s and third-wave anarchism since the 1990s. I share her concern about the self-fulfilling prophecies built into progress narratives: If a movement "develops" from simpler to more complex or weaker to stronger ideas, then why bother to read the earlier figures? You already know they have been superseded. Yet I need recognizable language to mark the historical era stretching from around 1870 to around 1940, so in that sense I am calling this era "classical."

3 Zimmer, *Immigrants against the State*, 1. Barry Pateman from the Kate Sharpley Library points out that these statistics may be unreliable because governments often exaggerate radical threats in order to justify police budgets and legitimize repression (personal communication, June 23, 2021). Zimmer's estimate may be a bit high, but there is good reason to think that anarchism was more widespread and influential than established histories usually recognize.

4 Thompson, *William Morris*, 589.

5 Benedict Anderson, *Under Three Flags*; James Scott, *Two Cheers for Anarchism*; Swain et al., *Unchaining Solidarity*.

6 Deleuze and Guattari, *What Is Philosophy?*, 16.

7 Fox, "Propaganda Again," 7.

8 In his analysis of Italian-language periodicals in the United States, historian of anarchism Davide Turcato states, "An anarchist periodical was never an end in itself, but was always instrumental to a larger project of dissemination of political ideas" ("Other Nation," 44). I respectfully suggest that there was more to it than that. A number of other scholars have developed larger accounts of anarchist print culture. Jennifer Guglielmo suggests, in her detailed historical ethnography of Italian American anarchist communities in *Living the Revolution*, that the journals were elements in a

network of community relationships, not just a means to an end but also an end in themselves. In *Immigrants against the State*, Zimmer similarly includes creating transnational communities and sustaining collective identities along with transmitting anarchism's message as part of the functional importance of the journals. Christopher Castañeda and Montse Feu argue, with regard to Spanish-language anarchist communities, that "Spanish-speaking people widely dispersed over time and space found solidarity and maintained their radical culture through print communication and organizing" ("Introduction," 26). James Yeoman summarizes the early publications of Spanish anarchists: "Not simply a repository of information, but the symbolic and material site where numerous, dynamic elements of anarchism converged" (*Print Culture*, 40). Reflecting on the impact of the paratextual notes in most journals, including letters, announcements, and subscriptions, Constance Bantman comments, "These notes delineate a social history of anarchist politics, and show the periodicals' organizing role as platforms for information exchange, publicizing activist undertakings, and building unity" ("Jean Grave," 472).

9 I located letterpress printers to interview by searching the internet, by attending letterpress conferences, and by word of mouth. I am also indebted to Chris Fritton's charming book *The Itinerant Printer: Modern Adventures in Tramping* (N.P.: Chris Fritton, 2018).

10 Deleuze and Guattari, *Thousand Plateaus*, 7.

11 Bennett, *Influx and Efflux*, x.

12 Bennett, *Influx and Efflux*, xiii.

13 DeLanda, *New Philosophy of Society*, 4.

14 DeLanda, *New Philosophy of Society*, 56 (italics in original).

15 DeLanda, *New Philosophy of Society*, 56–57.

16 DeLanda, *New Philosophy of Society*, 32.

17 Anderson, *Under Three Flags*, 4.

18 Bantman, *French Anarchists in London*, 159.

19 Johnson to Inglis, July 5, 1935, 1, Agnes Inglis Papers, Box 11, Labadie Collection.

20 Ferretti et al., introduction to *Historical Geographies*, 1–2.

21 Levy, "Anarchists and the City," 8.

22 Hoyt, "Uncovering and Understanding," 29.

23 Shaffer, *Anarchists of the Caribbean*, 23.

24 DeLanda, *New Philosophy of Society*, 56, 31 (italics in original).

25 Kropotkin, *Memoirs of a Revolutionist*, 216.

26 Goldman, "Letter from Emma Goldman," 4. Goldman is speaking of Agnes Davies, a London activist who helped put out *Freedom*, and Harry Kelly, a printer from Missouri who was part of the Mother Earth group, the Freedom group, and the Modern School movement.

27 Cores, *Personal Recollections*, 6.

28 William Morris, *Collected Works*, 185.

29 Zimmer, "American Anarchist Periodical Circulation Data, 1880–1940."

30 Hoyt, "Inky Protest," 36. Numbers vary for several reasons: publications often changed names, were suppressed and subsequently reestablished, or have been lost.

31 Brodie, "Rebel Youths," 5.

32 US Department of Justice, *Investigation Activities*, 12.

33 Shpayer-Makov, "Anarchism."

34 Bekken, "First Anarchist Daily Newspaper," 10.

35 Bekken, "First Anarchist Daily Newspaper," 11.

36 Harney and Moten, *Undercommons*, 67.

37 Benedict Anderson, *Imagined Communities*, 6.

38 Benedict Anderson, *Imagined Communities*, 35.

39 *Online Etymology Dictionary*, s.v. "letter"; Lexico, s.v. "letter."

40 Bennett, *Vibrant Matter*, 9.

41 Hughes, "Library of Jacques Derrida," 403 (italics in original).

42 Tsing, *Mushroom*, 52.

43 Moran, "To Spread the Revolution."

44 Enckell, "School and the Barricade," 14.

45 Harney and Moten, *Undercommons*, 61.

46 Pakieser, *I Belong Only to Myself*, 10–11.

47 Bey, *Anarcho-Blackness*, 11.

48 Bennett, *Vibrant Matter*, 2–6.

49 Connolly, *Fragility of Things*, 75 (italics in original).

50 Connolly, *Fragility of Things*, 76.

51 Ishill to Rocker, [month illegible], 1944, 1–2, Rudolf Rocker Papers, File 123, International Institute of Social History (emphasis in original).

52 Holmes, "Mental Barriers," 1.

53 Halberstam, "Wild Beyond," 6.

54 Connolly, *Fragility of Things*, 205–6n9.

55 Connolly, *Fragility of Things*, 205–6n9 (italics in original).

56 Halberstam, "Wild Beyond," 11.

57 Bennett, *Vibrant Matter*, 20–24.

58 Keell to Ishill, March 21, 1934, 2, Joseph Ishill Papers, Box 4, Houghton Library.

59 Wolfe to Ishill, August 3, 1938, 1, Joseph Ishill Papers, Box 4, Houghton Library.

60 Bennett, *Influx and Efflux*, 8.

61 Senta, *Luigi Galleani*, 145

62 Nelson, *Arbeiterpresse und Arbeiterbewegung,* 87. See also Laura Green-wood, "Book-Anarchists."

63 See Barton, "Global War on Anarchism."

64 Barry Pateman, then associate director of the Emma Goldman Papers Project, shared this anecdote with me on March 8, 2008.

65 Bennett, *Vibrant Matter,* 23.

66 Connolly, *Fragility of Things,* 74 (italics in original).

67 Connolly, *Fragility of Things,* 79 (italics in original).

68 Goyens, *Beer and Revolution.*

69 Brodie, "Rebel Youths," 10–11. See also Avrich, *Anarchist Voices,* 452.

70 Havel, *Proletarian Days,* 357.

71 Keell to Ishill, January 17, 1928, 1, Joseph Ishill Papers, Box 4, Houghton Library.

72 Keell to Ishill, January 17, 1928, 2, Joseph Ishill Papers, Box 4, Houghton Library.

73 Bennett, *Vibrant Matter,* 23.

74 Thompson, *Making,* 589.

75 Chesterton, *Man Who Was Thursday.*

76 Goldman, *Living My Life,* vol. 2, 550–52.

77 Bantman, *French Anarchists in London,* 192.

78 Ishill, *Free Vistas,* no. 2, 1–2.

1. Printers and Presses

1 Ishill, *Havelock Ellis,* 14–15.

2 Rancière, *Aisthesis,* 194–95.

3 I borrow this phrase from John L. Walters's introduction to Kitching, *A–Z of Letterpress,* 7.

4 Rancière, *Aisthesis,* 138.

5 Deleuze and Guattari, *What Is Philosophy?,* 51.

6 Rancière, *Aisthesis,* xvi.

7 See appendix A for a list of anarchist printers I have assembled to date. My hunch is that there were many more anarchist printers active in the United States and Britain (not to mention the rest of the world) from 1870 to 1940, but many of them are commonly referred to in publications and correspondence as editors or publishers rather than as printers. Editor and printer Jay Fox said of his work that "a fellow has to be everything from the 'printer's devil' to the editor-in-chief." Fox to Labadie, May 4, 1911, 1, Joseph A. Labadie Papers, Box 3, Joseph A. Labadie Collection. It takes a lot of archival digging to identify the printers.

8   Tuchman, *This Proud Tower*, 99.

9   Kittler, *Gramophone, Film, Typewriter*, xii.

10 Brown, ed., *Modern School Magazine* 3, no. 8 (January 1917), quoted in Ishill, *Oriole Press*, 394 (italics in original).

11 Personal conversation with Barry Pateman, Emma Goldman Papers Project, May 14, 2012, Berkeley, CA.

12 Kropotkin, "Appeal to the Young."

13 Interview with Jules Remedios Faye, June 18, 2015, Mount Vernon, WA.

14 Overbeck, *Tramp Printers*, 141. See also Essente, "Revival of Letterpress Printing."

15 Gitelman, *Paper Knowledge*, x.

16 Gitelman, *Paper Knowledge*, 9.

17 Henry Replogle, "New Papers," 3.

18 Kelly, "Thomas Cantwell," 28–29.

19 Hayles, *Writing Machines*, 3.

20 Parikka, *What Is Media Archaeology?*, 83 (italics in original).

21 Rancière, *Aisthesis*, xi.

22 Duffy, *Skilled Compositor*, 1.

23 Gitelman, *Paper Knowledge*, 158n9.

24 Gitelman, *Paper Knowledge*, 25, 26.

25 Gitelman, *Paper Knowledge*, 40.

26 Carlotta Anderson, *All-American Anarchist*, 188, 156.

27 Carlotta Anderson, *All-American Anarchist*, 36–37.

28 Rumble, "From the Shop Floor," 90.

29 Hicks, *Tramp Printer*, 16.

30 Gitelman, *Paper Knowledge*, 11.

31 Carlotta Anderson, *All-American Anarchist*, 38.

32 Hicks, *Tramp Printer*, 13, 161, 36.

33 Gitelman, *Paper Knowledge*, 51.

34 Hicks, *Tramp Printer*, 13.

35 Hicks, *Tramp Printer*, 49.

36 Hicks, *Tramp Printer*, 104.

37 Greeley, quoted in Hicks, *Tramp Printer*, 270.

38 Howells, quoted in Lawson, *Compositor as Artist*, 20.

39 Folsom, "Whitman Making Books" (italics in original).

40 Other engravers who worked with Ishill include Lucienne Bloch, Maurice Duvalet, Ivy Ellis, Frans Masereel, Bernard Sleigh, and John Buckland Wright.

41 Sander, *Wood Engraving*, 20, quoted in Hoyt, "Carlo Abate," 4n4.

42 Hoyt, "Carlo Abate," 13.

43 Hoyt, "Carlo Abate," 15.

44 Hoyt, "Inky Protest," 38.

45 Davaldès, "Louis Moreau," 317.

46 Davaldès, "Louis Moreau," 318.

47 Kooistra, "Fundamental Sympathy," 20.

48 Freeman to Ishill, December 21, 1931, 1, in Ishill, *Oriole Press*, 290.

49 Ishill to Inglis, April 12, 1938, 1, Agnes Inglis Papers, Box 10, Labadie Collection.

50 Fulton to Labadie, January 15, 1920, 1, Joseph Ishill Papers, Box 10, Houghton Library.

51 Cornell, "New Wind," 127.

52 Avrich, *Anarchist Voices*, 234. Other former Stelton students interviewed by Avrich in *Anarchist Voices* also, late in life, fondly remembered learning how to set type: Abe Bluestein (439), Rina Garst (252), Emma Gilbert (227), Beatrice Markowitz (309), and Magda Schoenwetter (230).

53 Rudolf Rocker, "Pages from an Autobiography," xx.

54 Hoyt, "They Called Them 'Galleanisti,'" 102–20.

55 Wright to Ishill, June 22, 1933, 1, in Ishill, *Oriole Press*, 387.

56 Banks, *True to Type*, n.p. (italics in original).

57 Cockburn, *Brothers*, 49.

58 Cockburn, *Brothers*, 116.

59 Interview with Peter Good, November 4, 2012, Bawdeswell, England. Good's collected papers and publications are held in the John Rylands Research Institute and Library, University of Manchester; see Smith, "Papers of Peter Good."

60 Colin Ward, "Self-Employed Society."

61 Moran, "*Firebrand.*"

62 Daniels, "To Those," 3.

63 Nettlau, "Tom Keell," 2.

64 Malatesta, "Personal Issue." My thanks to Andrew Hoyt for pointing out this scuffle over the role of the printer.

65 Hicks, *Tramp Printer*, 14.

66 Interview with Eric Bagdonas, Stumptown Printers, August 19, 2013, Portland, OR.

67 Interview with Ali Cat Leeds, Entangled Roots Press, August 14, 2013, Portland, OR.

68 Hicks, *Tramp Printer*, 13.

69 Rumble, "Showdown of 'Swifts,'" 621.

70 Banks, *True to Type*, n.p.

71 Hicks, *Tramp Printer*, 110.

72 *Typographical Journal* (Washington, DC: Communications Workers of America, July 15, 1889), 6, quoted in Carlotta Anderson, *All-American Anarchist*, 38.

73 Carlotta Anderson, *All-American Anarchist*, 38.

74 Hicks, *Tramp Printer*, 279.

75 Hicks, *Tramp Printer*, 108. See also Finkelstein, *Moveable Types*, 23.

76 Bekken, "First Anarchist Daily Newspaper," 5–9.

77 The earliest evidence of women working as printers in the West comes from Florence in 1476, where the nuns of the Convent of San Jacopo di Ripoli printed "the first complete edition of the works of Plato" (Davidson, *Unseen Hands*, 6). However, I have not come across any anarchist women printers who had a background in a religious order. It may be that the tradition of printing nuns spurred Joseph and Rose Ishill to bequeath Joseph's press to the Dominican Monastery of Our Lady of the Rosary in Summit, New Jersey. Their colophon was a nun in full habit standing at the type case, setting type.

78 Cockburn, *Brothers*, 24.

79 Cockburn, *Brothers*, 16.

80 Cockburn, *Brothers*, 3.

81 Tusan, "Performing Work," 115.

82 Davidson, *Unseen Hands*, 11–13.

83 Baron, "Women and the Making," 32.

84 Cockburn, *Brothers*, 153.

85 Cockburn, *Brothers*, 191.

86 Rumble, "Showdown of 'Swifts,'" 626.

87 Moses Harman, "Lucifer's Coming of Age," 266.

88 Guglielmo, *Living the Revolution*, 153.

89 Boyer and Morais, *Labor's Untold Story*, 152–53.

90 Acrata and Sharkey, "Antonia Fontanillas Borrás."

91 Rowbotham, *Rebel Crossings*, 95. See also Marsh, *Anarchist Women*, 27.

92 Pakieser, *I Belong Only to Myself*, 20.

93 Pakieser, *I Belong Only to Myself*, 5.

94 Stansell, *American Moderns*, 266.

95 Avrich, *Anarchist Voices*, 336, 465.

96 Goldman, *Living My Life*, vol 1, 165.

97 Slaughter, "First American Egoist Journal."

98 Passet, "Power through Print," 237.

99 Hodgart, *Ethel MacDonald*, 16.

100 See Offen, *Woman Question in France*, esp. chap. 6, "Sexual Conflict in the Printing Industry." My thanks to Gizem Sozen at the University of Victoria for pointing me toward this material.

101 Tucker, "On Picket Duty" (1888), 1.

102 Relatively little is written about Tucker's printing experience, but he mentions it in a letter to his friend and investor Henry Bool. After their failed

financial venture in creating Tucker Publishing Co., Tucker promised to "take off my coat, go to the case myself in our little printing office, get out Liberty once a month and as much pamphlet work as possible, and do all that I can for our cause with both hands and head." Tucker to Bool, May 20, 1900, 3–4, Joseph Ishill Papers, Box 12, Houghton Library.

103   Tucker, "On Picket Duty" (1891), 1.

104   Georgia Replogle, "Pointers," 1. MacDonald, *Fifty Years of Freethought*, notes that Georgia was a faster compositor than her partner, Henry, so she worked as a printer at a daily newspaper in Oakland, California, while he did the housework. Quoted in Slaughter, "First American Egoist Journal," 6.

105   Perhaps he was being ironic and the whole exchange was a tongue-in-cheek performance of anarchist feminism. I have, however, found no evidence to that effect. My impression of Tucker is that he was exhaustingly earnest and not the least bit ironic.

106   Slaughter, "First American Egoist Journal," 6; McElroy, *Debates of Liberty*, 133–34.

107   Nettlau, "Early Days of Freedom," 2.

108   Becker, "Thomas Keell," 20.

109   Fulton to Labadie, May 31, 1897, 1, Joseph A. Labadie Papers, Box 3, Labadie Collection.

110   W. H. Parsons, "Interview."

111   Codina, "Pedro Esteve," 58, 72.

112   Hirschauge, "Tenth Anniversary." My thanks to Eliezer's son Menachem Hirschauge on Kibbutz Ruhama and his grandson Orr Hirschauge of Tel Aviv for sharing their memories of Eliezer and Dina.

113   Inglis to Metzkow, November 10, 1930, 1, Agnes Inglis Papers, Box 14, Labadie Collection. See also Avrich and Avrich, *Sasha and Emma*, 63–64.

114   Hicks, *Tramp Printer*, 19.

115   Tygiel, "Tramping Artisans," 92.

116   Overbeck, *Tramp Printers*, 50.

117   Overbeck, *Tramp Printers*, 45.

118   Finkelstein, *Moveable Types*, 6.

119   Emma Greenwood, "Work, Identity," 192; Finklestein, *Moveable Types*, 6.

120   Hicks, *Tramp Printer*, 21.

121   Hicks, *Tramp Printer*, 30, 116. See also Howells and Dearman's chapter on the Missouri River Pirates in *Tramp Printers*.

122   Hicks, *Tramp Printer*, 12.

123   Hicks, *Tramp Printer*, 28.

124   Hicks, *Tramp Printer*, 107.

125   Hicks, *Tramp Printer*, 172.

126 Hicks, *Tramp Printer*, 175.

127 Fisher, *Uncommon Gentry*, xv.

128 Gitelman, *Paper Knowledge*, 40.

129 Hirschauge, "Tenth Anniversary."

130 Derzanski to Keell, September 9, 1928, Freedom Archives, File 397, International Institute of Social History.

131 Slaughter, "First American Egoist Journal," 6.

132 James Cooney to Schroeder, February 28, 1939, 1, Joseph Ishill Additional Papers, Supplementary Box 5, Joseph Ishill Collection, Houghton Library.

133 Fulton to Labadie, November 15, 1897, 1, and Fulton to Labadie, November 22, 1923, 1–2, Joseph A. Labadie Papers, Box 3, Labadie Collection.

134 Carlotta Anderson, *All-American Anarchist*, 51.

135 Kelly, "Roll Back the Years," chap. 18, p. 4.

136 Avrich, *Anarchist Voices*, 164.

137 Hicks, *Tramp Printer*, 25.

138 Moran, "Firebrand."

139 Zimmer, *Immigrants against the State*, 92.

140 Woodcock, *Letter to the Past*, 270.

141 Cores, *Personal Recollections*, 10.

142 Ishill, foreword to *Peter Kropotkin*, iv.

143 Dumartheray, "Letter from an Old Comrade," 129.

144 Papa Naroditsky and his three sons later printed *Freedom* at their shop Narod Press. See Richards, "Printers We Have Known," 28.

145 Rudolf Rocker, *London Years*, 74.

146 Kelly, "Roll Back the Years," chap. 9, p. 2.

147 Kelly, "Roll Back the Years," chap 9, pp. 2–2A, 3. "Made ready the forms" means to assemble the components of the page and lock them into the chase. A. D. was Agnes A. Davies.

148 Kelly, "Nicholas Tchaikovsky," 44.

149 Kelly, "Roll Back the Years," chap. 9, p. 3.

150 Kelly, "Nicholas Tchaikovsky," 44.

151 Cores, *Personal Recollections*, 12.

152 Colin Ward and Goodway, *Talking Anarchy*, Kindle loc. 665–66.

153 Addis, "Look at Our Postoffice [*sic*] System!!," 1.

154 Addis, "History of the Firebrand," 4.

155 Tochatti, "Between Ourselves," 4.

156 Rogers to Inglis, May 14, 1946, 1, Agnes Inglis Papers, Box 22, Labadie Collection.

157 Caldwell, *With Fate Conspire*, 142.

158 Fox to Labadie, February 12, 1911, 1, Joseph A. Labadie Papers, Box 3, Labadie Collection.

159 Gussie Winn to Goldman, quoted in Slifer and Greenhead, *Ross Winn*, 12.

160 Goldman, quoted in Slifer and Greenhead, *Ross Winn*, 16.

161 W. H., "News at Home," 20.

162 Kavanagh, "Some Little Known Anarchists," 4.

163 Andrew Whitehead, "Dan Chatterton."

164 Berkman et al., *Prison Blossoms*, xvi.

165 Berkman et al., *Prison Blossoms*, ix.

166 Berkman et al., *Prison Blossoms*, xii.

167 Protevi, *Political Affect*, 12.

168 Hayles, *Writing Machines*, 75.

169 Ishill to Rocker, [month illegible], 1944, 1–2, Rudolf Rocker Papers, File 123, International Institute of Social History.

170 Interview with Peter Good, November 14, 2012, Bawdeswell, England.

171 Interview with Jules Remedios Faye, June 18, 2015, Mount Vernon, WA.

172 Bennett, *Vibrant Matter*, 32.

173 Avrich and Avrich, *Sasha and Emma*, 158.

174 Caldwell, *With Fate Conspire*, 142.

175 Walker, "Kansas Liberty and Justice," 2.

176 Becker and Walter, "Freedom: People and Places," 7.

177 Quail, *Slow Burning Fuse,* 293.

178 Becker, "Notes on *Freedom*," 20–22.

179 Beauchamp, "Fight for a Free Press," 63–64. See also Peace Pledge Union, "Joan Beauchamp."

180 "Copy of Telegram from the Printers," *Adult* 1, no. 6 (January 1898): 175.

181 *Ideas and Figures*, no. 34 (October 1, 1910), quoted in Suriano, *Paradoxes of Utopia*, 225. See also "Anarchist Newspaper Offices Destroyed," 49.

182 Attacking printing equipment is a form of assault with a long history: famously, the abolitionist Elijah Lovejoy lost three presses as well as his life in 1837 to proslavery mobs (Neumann, "Elijah Lovejoy"). The Mormon church is still trying to live down Joseph Smith's order to burn the printing press of an opposition newspaper in 1844 (Church of Jesus Christ of Latter-Day Saints, "Navoo Expositor"). In variations on the theme, proslavery mobs threw an offending press into the river in Lawrence, Kansas, in 1856 and broke up a press in the street in Keokuk, Iowa, in 1863 (U.S. History, "Sack of Lawrence"; Manber and Dahlstrom, "Printing Press," 236).

In recent years, printing presses have been burned and operators attacked, sometimes killed—for example, in Sri Lanka in 2007, Côte d'Ivoire in 2011, and Hong Kong in 2019 (International Federation of Journalists,

"Arsonists Destroy Printing House"; Media Foundation for West Africa, "Arsonists Destroy Pro-Gbagbo"; Gorrie, "Arson!"). The popular computer game *Assassin's Creed* even includes a mission that entails destroying a printing press.

183 Gitelman, *Paper Knowledge*, x.

184 Gitelman, *Paper Knowledge*, 28.

185 Kittler, *Gramophone, Film, Typewriter*, xii.

186 Parikka, *What Is Media Archaeology?*, 36.

187 Rancière, quoted in Shapiro, *Punctuations*, 27; Harney and Moten, *Undercommons*, 67, 68.

188 Shapiro, *Punctuations*, 19.

189 Lawson, *Compositor as Artist*, 9; Rumble, "From the Shop Floor," 100.

190 Rumble, "From the Shop Floor," 100.

191 Hicks, *Tramp Printer*, 110.

192 Howells and Dearman, *Tramp Printers*, para. 5.

193 Fritz1, "Linotype vs. Handset 1D?" See also Hicks, *Tramp Printer*, 125.

194 Richards, "Printers We Have Known," 29.

195 Fox, "Propaganda Again," 7.

196 Fox, "Propaganda Again," 7.

197 Tucker to Ishill, January 3, 1935, in Ishill, *Oriole Press*, 382–83 (italics in original). Anthony Bliss, in "William Morris and Book Design," indicates that it was a talk Morris attended by his neighbor and expert printer Emory Walker, using lantern slides that enlarged and enhanced pictures of old letter designs, that spurred Morris to establish his own press.

198 Colebrook, *William Morris, Master-Printer*, 5.

199 Peterson, introduction to *William Morris, Master-Printer*, vii.

200 Peterson, introduction to *William Morris, Master-Printer*, vii.

201 Goudy, "Printing as an Art," 34.

202 Jackson, "Aesthetics of Printing," 55. See also Stansky, *Redesigning the World*, 6, 46.

203 Nettlau, "Early Days of Freedom," 2.

204 Antliff, "Agitating Beauty," 254–57.

205 I was privileged to attend a printing workshop at the Morris Society in spring 2020 and to print (awkwardly) on Morris's nearly two-hundred-year-old press. My thanks to the staff of the William Morris Society.

206 Ishill to Goldman, July 16, 1930, 2, Joseph Ishill Papers, Box 10, Houghton Library.

207 Carlotta Anderson, *All-American Anarchist*, 243.

208 Fulton to Labadie, December 19, 1936, 1, Joseph A. Labadie Papers, Box 3, Labadie Collection.

209 Fulton to Labadie, September 14, 1924, 1, Joseph Ishill Papers, Box 10, Houghton Library.

210 Slifer and Greenhead, *Ross Winn*, 10.

211 Slifer and Greenhead, *Ross Winn*, 31.

212 Becker and Walter, "Freedom," 6.

213 Moran, "*Firebrand.*"

214 S. D., "Peppery Pot," 1.

215 My thanks to the Woodstock Historical Society for showing me the site of Holley Cantine's printery and for sharing their collection of *Revolt*. Thanks also to Mary Baldridge for sharing her memories of Cantine and other radicals in Woodstock.

216 Jackson to Ishill, March 14, 1933, in Ishill, *Oriole Press*, 314.

217 Nettlau, "Albert Libertad," 90.

218 Avrich, *Modern School Movement*, 233.

219 Dolgoff, *Fragments*, 8.

220 Cooney, *My Own Sweet Time*, 95.

221 Caldwell, *With Fate Conspire*, 144. Perhaps she feared the sort of helter-skelter chaos that Helena and Olivia Rossetti lampooned in their fictionalized portrayal of *The Torch*'s office. See Meredith, *Girl among the Anarchists*.

222 Kelly, "Thomas Cantwell," 29.

223 Overbeck, *Tramp Printers*, 15.

224 See Fiona Otway, *Kiss the Paper*.

225 Rose Freeman Ishill to Coates, April 18, 1926, 1, Joseph Ishill Papers, Box 5, Houghton Library.

226 Personal conversation with Sister Mary Catherine Perry, Dominican Monastery of Our Lady of the Rosary, March 6, 2018, Summit, New Jersey. My thanks to Sister Mary Catherine for sharing her memories of Ishill's press.

227 Caldwell, *With Fate Conspire*, 122–23. Many printers talk about the hours or days they spend cleaning and maintaining their presses. It is unclear why the Glasgow group instead worked with a machine that was "un-oiled, and defective" (Caldwell, *With Fate Conspire*, 123).

228 Interview with Ruby Shadburne, Ruby Press, August 16, 2013, Portland, OR.

229 Interview with Eric Bagdonas, Stumptown Printers Workers Cooperative, August 19, 2013, Portland, OR.

230 Personal conversation with Sister Mary Catherine Perry, Dominican Monastery of Our Lady of the Rosary, March 6, 2018, Summit, New Jersey.

231 Cockburn, "Material of Male Power," 44. Cockburn learned typesetting early in her studies in 1978, noting, "It is impossible to understand the claims and counter-claims about skill without understanding the labour process on which they are founded" (Cockburn, *Brothers*, 46).

232 Interview with Peter Good, November 4, 2012, Baldeswell, England.

233 Interview with Ruby Shadburne, Ruby Press, August 16, 2013, Portland, OR.

234 Reid, "Gerald Manley Hopkins."

235 Interview with Peter Good, November 4, 2012, Bawdeswell, England.

236 Overbeck, *Tramp Printers*, 64.

237 Cockburn, *Brothers*, 47.

238 Inglis to Ishill, October 28, 1935, 1, Joseph Ishill Papers, Box 4, Houghton Library.

239 Interview with Jules Remedios Faye, June 18, 2015, Mount Vernon, WA.

240 Le Warne, *Utopias on Puget Sound*, 208. The precise dates of publication of *The Word* were 1872–90 and 1892–93; publication was interrupted by the two years Ezra Haywood spent in prison after his conviction for sending obscene material (discussions of love, sexuality, and marriage) through the mail.

241 Antliff, "Agitating Beauty," 263–64.

242 Rob Ray, *Beautiful Idea*, 25, 29, 53.

243 Becker and Walter, "Freedom," 6.

244 Caldwell, *With Fate Conspire*, 142.

245 Dolgoff, *Fragments*, 79. See also Marqusee, *Wicked Messenger*, 45.

246 Interview with Nick Loring, the Print Project, May 28, 2014, Shipley, England.

247 Interview with Ali Cat Leeds, Entangled Roots Press, August 14, 2013, Portland, OR.

248 Interview with Jules Remedios Faye, June 18, 2015, Mount Vernon, WA.

249 Rumble, *Swifts*, 8. Old, abandoned letterpress equipment again became available in the 1970s when computerized printing took over. Roger Mason bought up much of the equipment available in England to sell to letterpress printers who were determined to carry on. He tells sad and hilarious stories about finding old presses in barns, basements, and chicken coops, covered with chicken poop. See Mason, *Print and Be Damaged*.

250 Carlotta Anderson, *All-American Anarchist*, 212.

251 Caldwell, *With Fate Conspire*, 142. See also Bridgeland and Jones, "John Taylor Caldwell."

252 Rainer, "Holley Cantine," 182.

253 Llewellyn Jones, "Editorial," 8. See also Wingert, "Gems of Printing," 4.

254 Ishill, *Peter Kropotkin*, iv.

255 Paul Scott, "Some Personal Reflections," 13.

256 Paul Scott, "Some Personal Reflections," 14.

257 "Our Printing Office," 44.

258 Moses Harman, "Lucifer's Coming of Age."

259 "The Propaganda," *Freedom* 12, no. 130 (September 1898): 64.

260 "International Anarchist Federation of the English Provinces," *Freedom* 22, no. 225 (January 1908): 8.

261 "Press Maintenance Fund," *Commune* 1, no. 3 (July–August 1923): 28.

262 Banks, *True to Type*, n.p.

263 Hostettler, *Printer's Terms*.

264 Tetenbaum, "10 Steps to Perfect Typesetting."

265 Drucker, "Letterpress Language," 8.

266 Interview with Joseph Green, Jeff Shay, and Connie Blauwkamp, C. C. Stern Type Foundry, Museum of Metal Typography, August 17, 2013, Portland, OR.

267 Folsom, "Whitman Making Books," n161.

268 Interview with Jules Remedios Faye, June 18, 2015, Mount Vernon, WA.

269 Ritchie, *Of Bookmen and Printers*, 128.

270 Graphic Design Supplies, "What Is Cockling?"

271 Formax Printing Solutions, "Printing Lingo."

272 Thorn to Ishill, November 25, 1943, 1, Joseph Ishill Papers, Box 4, Houghton Library.

273 Bill Brown, "Thing Theory," 4.

274 Standard to Ishill, February 21, 1945, in Ishill, *Oriole Press*, 374.

275 Interview with Jules Remedios Faye, June 18, 2015, Mount Vernon, WA.

276 My thanks to Nicole Grove for helping me think through this aspect of printing.

277 Bonnie Mak, *How the Page Matters*, 5.

278 Bonnie Mak, *How the Page Matters*, 5.

279 Bonnie Mak, *How the Page Matters*, 8.

280 Drucker, "Letterpress Language," 10. See also Bonnie Mak, *How the Page Matters*, 17.

281 Bonnie Mak, *How the Page Matters*, 34.

282 Shahn, "Love and Joy," 145–46.

283 Shahn, "Love and Joy," 145.

284 Bonnie Mak, *How the Page Matters*, 18.

285 Gitelman, *Paper Knowledge*, x.

286 Shapiro, *Punctuations*, 6.

287 Johnson to Inglis, May 23, 1935, 1, Agnes Inglis Papers, Box 11, Labadie Collection (emphasis in original).

288 This masthead was used for most of 1902 and perhaps longer; other years saw a plainer design.

289 Serif typefaces are classical styles that have short lines protruding at an angle from the top or bottom of the vertical stroke.

290 Shapiro, *Punctuations*, 4.

291 Shapiro, *Punctuations*, 17.

292 Interview with Charles Overbeck, Eberhardt Press, August 15, 2013, Portland, OR.

293 Interview with Charles Overbeck, Eberhardt Press, August 15, 2013, Portland, OR.

294 Llewellyn Jones, "Editorial," 7.

295 Hayles, *Writing Machines*, 131.

296 Stansky, *Redesigning the World*, 235.

297 William Morris, "Note by William Morris."

298 Morris, quoted in Colebrook, *William Morris, Master-Printer*, 26.

299 Skoblow, quoted in Boos, "Introduction."

300 Abbott to Ishill, October 1, 1917, 1, Joseph Ishill Papers, Box 1, Houghton Library.

301 Lupton, *Thinking with Type*, 14.

302 Morris, quoted in Boos, "Introduction." My thanks to Anne Bush, Department of Art and Art History, University of Hawai'i, for sharing her knowledge of Morris's printing. She emphasized that Morris was often inconsistent in these matters, so my comparison of the two men's font preferences is tentative. Personal conversation, December 17, 2020, Honolulu, HI.

303 De Cleyre to Labadie, September 11, 1905, 1, Joseph Ishill Papers, Box 10, Houghton Library.

304 Carlotta Anderson, *All-American Anarchist*, 33.

305 Fulton to Labadie, January 15, 1920, 3, Joseph A. Labadie Papers, Box 3, Labadie Collection.

306 Keell to Inglis, December 11, 1931, 2, Agnes Inglis Papers, Box 12, Labadie Collection.

307 Keell to Labadie, October 19, 1922, 1, Joseph A. Labadie Papers, Box 4, Labadie Collection.

308 Traubel, "Walt Whitman in Camden," cited in Bennett, *Influx and Efflux*, 26.

309 Ironically, Morris rejected small books, exactly the thing that Labadie cherished. In Morris's characteristically cheeky tone, he opined, "I wish to make a protest against the superstition that only small books are comfortable to read.... A small book seldom does lie quiet, and you have either to cramp your hand by holding it, or else to put it on the table with a paraphernalia of matters to keep it down, a tablespoon on one side, a knife on another, which things always tumble off at a critical moment" (Morris, quoted in Boos, "Introduction").

310 Janssen, *Technique*, 13.

311 Drucker, "Letterpress Language," 10.

312 Rancière, *Aisthesis*, x.

313 Gitelman, *Paper Knowledge*, 36.

314 Abbott to Ishill, July 2, 1951, 1, and January 6, 1934, 1, Joseph Ishill Papers, Box 1, Houghton Library.

315 Calvert to Ishill, December 29, 1939, 1, Joseph Ishill Papers, Box 1, Houghton Library.

316 Duff to Ishill, November 1, 1933, 1, Joseph Ishill Papers, Box 2, Houghton Library.

317 Frank to Ishill, January 19, 1930, 1, Joseph Ishill Papers, Box 3, Houghton Library.

318 Ridge to Rose Ishill, January 6, 1931, 1, Joseph Ishill Papers, Box 6, Houghton Library.

319 Rocker to Ishill, November 21, 1951, 1, Joseph Ishill Papers, Box 6, Houghton Library.

320 Starrett [Valkenberg] to Ishill, December 22, 1934, 1, Joseph Ishill Papers, Box 9, Houghton Library.

321 Avrich and Avrich, *Sasha and Emma*, 192.

322 Berkman to Ishill, September 30, 1932, 1, Joseph Ishill Papers, Box 1, Houghton Library.

323 Cherkerzov/Tcherkesoff to Ishill, December 2, 1923, 1–2, Joseph Ishill Papers, Supplementary Box 2, Houghton Library.

324 Sartin to Ishill, July 6, 1933, 1, and June 28, 1933, 1, Joseph Ishill Papers, Box 7, Houghton Library.

325 Rabe to Ishill, n.d., 1, Joseph Ishill Papers, Supplementary Box 4, Houghton Library.

326 Goldman to Ishill, November 29, 1934, 1, Joseph Ishill Papers, Box 3, Houghton Library.

327 Tucker to Ishill, March 15, 1930, 2, Joseph Ishill Papers, Box 8, Houghton Library. Pearl Johnson Tucker, Benjamin's partner, never forgave Ishill for tolerating errors in his texts. As Ishill's English improved (or perhaps as Rose proofread more often), errors declined. See the next chapter for a discussion of Pearl's relation to Joseph.

328 *Free Society*, no. 19 (March 20, 1898): 4.

329 Nettlau, "Tom Keell," 2.

330 "Apology," 2.

331 Quail, *Slow Burning Fuse*, 169.

332 Hong, "Constructing the Anarchist Beast," 113.

333 Bradford, "Fizzboomski."

334 Rancière, *Aisthesis*, x.

335 Goldman to Ishill, July 23, 1928, in Ishill, *Oriole Press*, 301.

1   Ishill to Rocker, October 15, 1953, 2, Rudolf Rocker Papers, File 123, International Institute of Social History (IISH).

2   Ishill succeeded in his first goal the following year: Ellis, *Unpublished Letters*. He subsequently published a book on Emma Goldman, but it was not a collection of letters: Ishill, *Emma Goldman*.

3   Ishill to Rocker, October 15, 1953, 1, Rudolf Rocker Papers, File 123, IISH.

4   Jolly, *In Love and Struggle*, 2. Liz Stanley ("Epistolarium," 204), editor of Olive Schreiner's letters, estimates that Schreiner wrote twelve thousand to fifteen thousand letters, about two-thirds of which Schreiner herself destroyed. Stanley comments that Lewis Carroll wrote over ninety-eight thousand letters, and she characterizes this as "out of the ordinary" (226n21). Compared with many anarchists, these folks were pikers.

5   Drinnon and Drinnon, *Nowhere at Home*, xiv.

6   Drinnon and Drinnon, *Nowhere at Home*; Porter, *Vision on Fire*; Falk, Pateman, and Moran, *Emma Goldman*, vols. 1 and 2; Falk and Pateman, *Emma Goldman*, vol. 3; Falk, *Emma Goldman*, vol. 4; Emma Goldman Papers Project, "Scanned Documents."

7   Gitelman, *Paper Knowledge*, 17.

8   Rancière, *Politics of Aesthetics*, 12.

9   Stanley, "Epistolarium," 217.

10 Stanley, "Epistolarium," 217 (italics in original).

11 Wingrove, "Agony of Address," 24.

12 Wingrove, "Agony of Address," 24.

13 Wingrove, "Agony of Address," 23.

14 Stanley, "Epistolarium," 218. Stanley sketches two other ways to define *epistolarium*. One is "'a collection' of the entirety of the surviving correspondences that a particular letter writer was involved in" (218). Anarchists' surviving letters are scattered in multiple sites, few of which claim to possess "the entirety," especially of those writers who are not well known. The other definition provided by Stanley is "the 'ur-letters' produced in transcribing, editing and publishing actual letters (or rather versions of them)" (218), to which I aim to contribute in this chapter.

15 Rancière, *Politics of Aesthetics*, 12.

16 Tamboukou, *Sewing, Fighting and Writing*, 25.

17 Tamboukou, "Interfaces in Narrative Research," 628–29.

18 DeLanda, *New Philosophy of Society*, 9.

19 The fact of the exchange is significant, independent of the words on the page. Writing back is an affective act. Writing back promptly and regularly in itself creates a bond, independent of the content of the letter.

20 Pearl Tucker to Inglis, February 27, 1942, 1, Agnes Inglis Papers, Box 19, Joseph A. Labadie Collection.

21 Tamboukou, *Sewing, Fighting and Writing*, 146 (italics in original).

22 Wingrove, "Agony of Address," 19.

23 MacArthur, *Extravagant Narratives*, 25.

24 Tamboukou, "Epistolary Lives," 159.

25 Mesnil, *Joseph Ishill*, n.p.

26 Johnson to Inglis, July 5, 1935, 1, Agnes Inglis Papers, Box 11, Labadie Collection.

27 Vallance, "Rudolf Rocker."

28 Brian Morris, "Guest Editorial."

29 Fermin Rocker, *East End Years*, 23.

30 Rudolf Rocker, "Behind Barbed Wire," 604–5.

31 Rocker to Ishill, May 8, 1938, 1, Joseph Ishill Papers, Box 6, Houghton Library.

32 Rocker to Ishill, April 24, 1943, 1, Joseph Ishill Papers, Box 6, Houghton Library; Ishill to Rocker, August 12, 1945, 1, Rudolf Rocker Papers, File 123, IISH.

33 See Emma Gilbert and Ray Shedlovsky in Avrich, *Anarchist Voices*, 227, 234.

34 Rudolf Rocker, "Lifework of Joseph Ishill," 6.

35 Ishill to Rocker, April 24, 1953, 2, Rudolf Rocker Papers, File 123, IISH.

36 Wexler, "Interview," 9.

37 Wingert, "Gems of Printing," 4.

38 Rose Ishill, "To Joseph Ishill," 23.

39 Wexler, "Interview," 10.

40 Rudolf Rocker, "Lifework of Joseph Ishill," 1.

41 Ishill to Rocker, April 24, 1953, 1, Rudolf Rocker Papers, File 123, IISH.

42 Rocker to Ishill, February 3, 1950, 1, Joseph Ishill Papers, Box 6, Houghton Library.

43 Rocker to Ishill, December 26, 1954, 2, Joseph Ishill Papers, Box 6, Houghton Library.

44 Rocker to Ishill, January 22, 1951, 1, Joseph Ishill Papers, Box 6, Houghton Library.

45 Rocker to Ishill, January 22, 1951, 1, Joseph Ishill Papers, Box 6, Houghton Library.

46 Rocker to Ishill, May 6, 1949, 2, Joseph Ishill Papers, Box 6, Houghton Library.

47 Rocker to Ishill, November [no day], 1955, 1, Joseph Ishill Papers, Box 6, Houghton Library.

48 Inglis to Ralph and Edith Chaplin, June 20, 1942, 1, Joseph Inglis Papers, Box 4, Labadie Collection.

49 Inglis, "Reflections Part I," 41.

50 Inglis, "Reflections Part I," 91. Pitchfork (James) Henderson got his nickname after the Hoover Steel Ball Corporation strike of December 1916 in Ann Arbor. Ernest Schleiffer was a leader of the machinists' strike in New Haven, Connecticut. Gordon Cascaden was a writer for the Detroit publication *Auto Workers' News* and an Industrial Workers of the World activist.

51 Herrada, "Agnes Inglis," 152.

52 Agnes wrote Pearl about her brother Jim, the capitalist. "It seems ironical that back of all my work in the Collection is Jim. I sometimes wonder if he realizes it. He admires my sticking to it and is delighted that the work is an accomplished fact and recognized now. It makes him happy." Inglis to Pearl Tucker, August 3, 1946, 1, Agnes Inglis Papers, Box 19, Labadie Collection.

53 Bertha Johnson's papers, dealing primarily with her medical career, are held in the Sophia Smith Collection at Smith College. The Benjamin R. Tucker Papers, containing some correspondence with Pearl and Bertha, are held at the New York Public Library. I have not consulted those archives.

54 Inglis to Clevans, April 15, 1937, 1, Agnes Inglis Papers, Box 4, Labadie Collection; Johnson to Inglis, February 27, 1949, 1, Agnes Inglis Papers, Box 11, Labadie Collection.

55 Johnson to Inglis, September 7, 1933, 3, Agnes Inglis Papers, Box 11, Labadie Collection.

56 Johnson to Inglis, December 29, 1945, 1, Agnes Inglis Papers, Box 11, Labadie Collection.

57 Pearl Tucker to Inglis, May 27, 1942, 1, Agnes Inglis Papers, Box 11, Labadie Collection (emphasis in original).

58 Johnson to Inglis, April 16, 1934, 1, Agnes Inglis Papers, Box 11, Labadie Collection.

59 Johnson to Inglis, April 1, 1934, 1, Agnes Inglis Papers, Box 11, Labadie Collection.

60 Johnson to Inglis, January 20, 1943, 3, Agnes Inglis Papers, Box 11, Labadie Collection.

61 Inglis to Pearl Tucker, March 7, 1943, 3, Agnes Inglis Papers, Box 19, Labadie Collection.

62 Avrich, "Interview with Oriole Tucker."

63 Benjamin Tucker to Ishill, May 1, 1934, in Ishill, *Oriole Press*, 381.

64 Johnson to Inglis, February 15, 1934, 1, Agnes Inglis Papers, Box 11, Labadie Collection.

65 Pearl Tucker to Inglis, November 28, 1943, 3–4, Agnes Inglis Papers, Box 11, Labadie Collection. See also Johnson to Inglis, March 4, 1941, 1, Agnes Inglis Papers, Box 11, Labadie Collection.

66 Johnson to Inglis, March 14, 1934, 1, Agnes Inglis Papers, Box 11, Labadie Collection (emphasis in original).

67 Johnson to Inglis, March 22, 1934, 1, Agnes Inglis Papers, Box 11, Labadie Collection.

68 Johnson to Inglis, March 22, 1934, 2, Agnes Inglis Papers, Box 11, Labadie Collection.

69 Inglis to Armand, June 8, 1948, 1, Agnes Inglis Papers, Box 1, Labadie Collection.

70 Johnson to Inglis, July 5, 1935, 1, Agnes Inglis Papers, Box 11, Labadie Collection. Alice Baker Greystone Furst collected a great deal of literature for the Labadie Collection. She was an antique dealer who lived in Greenwich Village and also was active in the Neighborhood Playhouse.

71 McKinney, *Information Activism*, 22.

72 Johnson to Inglis, November 22, 1950, 1, Agnes Inglis Papers, Box 11, Labadie Collection.

73 Tamboukou, "Interfaces in Narrative Research," 627.

74 Plummer, *Documents of Life 2*, 55.

75 Stanley, "Epistolarium," 201, 203.

76 Tamboukou, "Epistolary Lives," 161.

77 MacArthur, *Extravagant Narratives*, 119.

78 McKinney, *Information Activism*, 78. McKinney is drawing on Thrift, "Feminist Eventfulness."

79 Inglis to Wolfe, June 22, 1947, 1, Agnes Inglis Papers, Box 20, Labadie Collection.

80 Wolfe to Inglis, September 2, 1947, 4, Agnes Inglis Papers, Box 20, Labadie Collection.

81 Johnson to Inglis, November 27, 1938, 1, Agnes Inglis Papers, Box 11, Labadie Collection.

82 Johnson to Inglis, November 27, 1938, 2, Agnes Inglis Papers, Box 11, Labadie Collection.

83 Wolfe to Inglis, December 14, 1946, 2, Agnes Inglis Papers, Box 20, Labadie Collection; Wolfe to Inglis, September 10, 1947, 1, Agnes Inglis Papers, Box 20, Labadie Collection.

84 Roy, "Goody Two-Shoes," 98.

85 Altman, *Epistolarity*, 4.

86 Altman, *Epistolarity*, 187.

87 Altman, *Epistolarity*, 146; Rocker to Ishill, August 9, 1952, 1, Joseph Ishill Papers, Box 6, Houghton Library; Ishill to Rocker, March 22, 1943, 1, Rudolf Rocker Papers, File 123, IISH.

88 Altman, *Epistolarity*, 144.

89 Altman, *Epistolarity*, 144–45.

90 Altman, *Epistolarity*, 119.

91 Altman, *Epistolarity*, 89.

92 Inglis to Johnson, January 18, 1946, 1, Agnes Inglis Papers, Box 11, Labadie Collection.

93 Altman, *Epistolarity*, 117.

94 Altman, *Epistolarity*, 121 (italics in original).

95 Tamboukou, *Sewing, Fighting and Writing*, 93.

96 Keell to Inglis, March 22, 1930, 4, Agnes Inglis Papers, Box 12, Labadie Collection (emphasis in original).

97 Wolfe to Inglis, March 26, 1939, 1, Agnes Inglis Papers, Box 20, Labadie Collection.

98 Stanley, "Epistolarium," 209.

99 Inglis to Baldwin, July 3, 1932, 1, 2, Agnes Inglis Papers, Box 1, Labadie Collection.

100 Inglis to Metzkow, June 26, 1940, 1, Agnes Inglis Papers, Box 14, Labadie Collection.

101 Metzkow to Inglis, May 26, 1945, 1, Agnes Inglis Papers, Box 14, Labadie Collection.

102 Metzkow to Inglis, October 10, 1940, 4, Agnes Inglis Papers, Box 14, Labadie Collection.

103 Johnson to Inglis, March 22, 1934, 1, Agnes Inglis Papers, Box 11, Labadie Collection.

104 Johnson to Inglis, April 16, 1934, 1, Agnes Inglis Papers, Box 11, Labadie Collection.

105 Johnson to Inglis, October 11, 1934, 3, Agnes Inglis Papers, Box 11, Labadie Collection.

106 Inglis to Baldwin, October 3, 1934, 1, Agnes Inglis Papers, Box 1, Labadie Collection.

107 Agostinelli to Inglis, [probably 1947], 2, Agnes Inglis Papers, Box 1, Labadie Collection.

108 Altman, *Epistolarity*, 189, 13, 43, 185.

109 Inglis to Baldwin, October 3, 1934, 1, Agnes Inglis Papers, Box 1, Labadie Collection.

110 Stanley, "Epistolarium," 213.

111 Stanley, "Epistolarium," 214.

112 Tamboukou, "Epistolary Lives," 160.

113 Altman, *Epistolarity*, 120.

114 Altman, *Epistolarity*, 120. This is an accident of the archives: I went to Harvard before I went to Amsterdam, so I read Rocker's letters to Ishill a year before I read Ishill's letters to Rocker.

115 Altman, *Epistolarity*, 112n1.

116 Stanley, "Epistolarium," 218.

117 Altman, *Epistolarity*, 112.

118 Tamboukou, *Sewing, Fighting and Writing*, 40.

119 Tamboukou, *Sewing, Fighting and Writing*, 34, 36, 41, 42.

120 Eichhorn, *Archival Turn*, 30.

121 Tamboukou, *Sewing, Fighting and Writing*, 40.

122 Wolfe to Inglis, December 14, 1946, 2, Agnes Inglis Papers, Box 20, Labadie Collection.

123 Roy, "Good Two-Shoes," 98.

124 Tamboukou, "Interfaces in Narrative Research," 628–29.

125 Johnson to Inglis, August 15, 1933, 1, Agnes Inglis Papers, Box 11, Labadie Collection.

126 Josephine Tilton's estate was administered by Carrie Denton. See "Estate of Josephine Tilton (Executor—Carrie Denton)," in Carrie D. Denton Papers; Legal Papers, 1868–1958, Box 6, Wellesley Historical Society, Wellesley, MA, https://wellesleyhistoricalsociety.org/. My thanks to Benjamin Laird, "The Code of Things," https://thecodeofthings.com/, for sharing his knowledge of the relation between Josephine Tilton and Carrie Denton.

127 Johnson to Inglis, March 16, 1933, 2, Agnes Inglis Papers, Box 11, Labadie Collection.

128 Johnson to Inglis, March 7, 1934, 1, Agnes Inglis Papers, Box 11, Labadie Collection.

129 Inglis to Armand, June 8, 1948, 1, Agnes Inglis Papers, Box 1, Labadie Collection.

130 Pearl Tucker to Inglis, December 4, 1946, 4, Agnes Inglis Papers, Box 19, Labadie Collection. Pearl is referring to American anarchist and abolitionist Lysander Spooner.

131 Pearl Tucker to Inglis, December 24, 1942, 2, Agnes Inglis Papers, Box 19, Labadie Collection.

132 Inglis to Chaapel, November 22, 1942, 2, Agnes Inglis Papers, Box 4, Labadie Collection.

133 Wolfe to Inglis, December 14, 1946, 3, Agnes Inglis Papers, Box 20, Labadie Collection.

134 I say "allegedly" because I've not heard the side of the stories that might have come from Ishill, Aldred, or Swede. My point is not that these incidents did or did not happen as reported. It is that the reports stirred such strong responses, suggesting an intervention in the circulation of the currencies of the movement.

135 Tamboukou, "Epistolary Lives," 159.

136 Alfred Whitehead, *Essays in Science*, 26, quoted in Tamboukou, "Epistolary Lives," 163. See Tamboukou, *Sewing, Fighting and Writing*, for a more extensive consideration of Whitehead's importance for epistolary work.

137 The Bolsheviks dismantled the Kropotkin Museum soon after Kropotkin's death in 1921.

138 Goldman to Inglis, February 22, 1931, 1–2, Agnes Inglis Papers, Box 8, Labadie Collection.

139 McKinney, *Information Activism*, 173.

140 Herrada and Hyry, "Agnes Inglis," 10.

141 Inglis to Keell, January 30, 1935, 1, Agnes Inglis Papers, Box 12, Labadie Collection.

142 Johnson to Inglis, May 15, 1945, 3, Agnes Inglis Papers, Box 11, Labadie Collection.

143 I am speculating, perhaps wildly. Adeline Champney's partner was Fred Schulder, who had been Bertha's boyfriend before she married Emery. Fred was a distributor of Benjamin Tucker's journal *Liberty*. Adeline died in 1945, the year she sent Bertha the typewriter. See Avrich, *Anarchist Voices*, 9.

144 O'Hagan, *Our Fathers*, 89.

145 Rocker's notes on his copy of Nettlau, "Tom Keell," 2, Rudolf Rocker Papers, File 513, IISH.

146 Tamboukou, *Sewing, Fighting and Writing*, 40–41.

147 Ishill to Rocker, July 21, 1957, 4, Rudolf Rocker Papers, File 123, IISH (emphasis in original).

148 Ishill to Rocker, April 24, 1953, 4, Rudolf Rocker Papers, File 123, IISH.

149 Ishill to Rocker, October 8, 1953, 2, Rudolf Rocker Papers, File 123, IISH.

150 Ishill to Rocker, July 21, 1957, 1, Rudolf Rocker Papers, File 123, IISH.

151 Hughes, "Library of Jacques Derrida," 413.

152 Ishill to Rocker, July 18, 1950, 1–2, Rudolf Rocker Papers, File 123, IISH (emphasis in original).

153 A small book about Ishill's publications locates holdings of his books in these libraries in 1960: Berkeley Heights, New York Public Library, Library of Congress, University of Michigan, University of North Carolina at Chapel Hill, University of California at Berkeley, Rutgers, Princeton, Brown, Ohio State, Illinois State, Yale, Dartmouth, and Harvard. See Marian Brown, *Joseph Ishill*.

154 IISH, "Detailed History."

155 Inglis to Beal, August 26, 1938, 1, Agnes Inglis Papers, Box 2, Labadie Collection.

156 Rocker to Ishill, November 21, 1951, 1, Joseph Ishill Papers, Box 6, Houghton Library.

157 Rocker to Ishill, October 12, 1953, 1, Joseph Ishill Papers, Box 6, Houghton Library.

158 Ishill to Rocker, October 2, 1956, 1, Rudolf Rocker Papers, File 123, IISH.

159 Ishill to Rocker, February 14, 1949, 1, Rudolf Rocker Papers, File 123, IISH.

160 Ishill to Rocker, August 15, 1950, 1, Rudolf Rocker Papers, File 123, IISH.

161 Ishill to Rocker, June 18, 1953, 1, Rudolf Rocker Papers, File 123, IISH.

162 Ishill to Rocker, February 5, 1951, 3, 4, Rudolf Rocker Papers, File 123, IISH.

163 Ishill to Rocker, January 12, 1956, 1, Rudolf Rocker Papers, File 123, IISH.

164 Ida Pilat Isca translated the text from German to English. Valerio and Ida Isca to Rocker, January 12, 1955, 1, Rudolf Rocker Papers, File 123, IISH.

165 Ishill to Rocker, January 12, 1956, 2, Rudolf Rocker Papers, File 123, IISH.

166 Ishill to Rocker, April 21, 1956, 3, Rudolf Rocker Papers, File 123, IISH.

167 Altman, *Epistolarity*, 133.

168 Gitelman, *Paper Knowledge*, x.

169 New York Academy of Medicine Library, "Bertha Johnson Collection."

170 Johnson to Inglis, March 16, 1933, 1, Agnes Inglis Papers, Box 11, Labadie Collection.

171 Johnson to Inglis, February 15, 1934, 1, Agnes Inglis Papers, Box 11, Labadie Collection.

172 Johnson to Inglis, December 12, 1945, 1, Agnes Inglis Papers, Box 11, Labadie Collection.

173 Johnson to Inglis, January 28, 1934, 1, Agnes Inglis Papers, Box 11, Labadie Collection.

174 Johnson to Inglis, August 9, 1935, 3, Agnes Inglis Papers, Box 11, Labadie Collection.

175 Johnson to Inglis, October 11, 1934, 2, Agnes Inglis Papers, Box 11, Labadie Collection.

176 Johnson to Inglis, March 16, 1933, 2, Agnes Inglis Papers, Box 11, Labadie Collection.

177 Johnson to Inglis, March 25, 1941, 1, Agnes Inglis Papers, Box 11, Labadie Collection.

178 Johnson to Inglis, January 14, 1936, 2, Agnes Inglis Papers, Box 11, Labadie Collection.

179 Johnson to Inglis, August 21, 1933, 2, Agnes Inglis Papers, Box 11, Labadie Collection.

180 Johnson to Inglis, December 5, 1941, 4, Agnes Inglis Papers, Box 11, Labadie Collection.

181 See Johnson to Inglis, December 12, 1935; December 21, 1933; December 14, 1934; and March 4, 1941, Agnes Inglis Papers, Box 11, Labadie Collection.

182 Johnson to Inglis, November 28, 1941, 5, Agnes Inglis Papers, Box 11, Labadie Collection.

183 Johnson to Inglis, September 6, 1942, 1, Agnes Inglis Papers, Box 11, Labadie Collection.

184 Johnson to Inglis, March 16, 1933, 1, Agnes Inglis Papers, Box 11, Labadie Collection.

185 Johnson to Inglis, July 7, 1947, 1, Agnes Inglis Papers, Box 11, Labadie Collection.

186 Johnson to Inglis, June 1, 1950, 3, Agnes Inglis Papers, Box 11, Labadie Collection.

187 Johnson to Inglis, September 28, 1948, and February 27, 1949, Agnes Inglis Papers, Box 11, Labadie Collection.

188 Find a Grave, "Dr Bertha Florence Johnson." See also "Dr. Bertha Johnson of Granville Ctr. Dies at Ossining," *The Daily Review*, Towanda, PA (February 3, 1958): 2. My thanks to Matt Hicks, Editor-in-Chief, the *Daily and Sunday Review*, Towanda, PA, for digging Bertha's obituary out of the morgue and sending it to me.

189 Hughes, "Library of Jacques Derrida," 419.

190 Dinshaw, *How Soon Is Now?*, 4.

191 Hughes, "Library of Jacques Derrida," 419.

192 Inglis, "My Garden," in "Reflections, Part II," 2.

193 Bertha mentioned to Agnes that she had read Rocker's *The Six* and was reading his magnum opus, *Nationalism and Culture*. Johnson to Inglis, September 7, 1943, Agnes Inglis Papers, Box 11, Labadie Collection.

194 Johnson to Inglis, February 28, 1950, 1, Agnes Inglis Papers, Box 11, Labadie Collection.

195 Inglis to Maisel, May 3, 1937, 1, Agnes Inglis Papers, Box 13, Labadie Collection.

196 Inglis, "Sunday April 28th 1928," in Reflections, Part II, n.p., Agnes Inglis Papers, Box 25, Labadie Collection.

197 Rocker to Dick, April 1, 1956, 1, Paul Avrich Collection, Box 3, Folder 6, Library of Congress.

198 Ishill to Rocker, June 18, 1953, 1, Rudolf Rocker Papers, File 123, IISH.

199 Nettlau, "Tom Keell," 2, Rudolf Rocker Papers, File 513, IISH. In his obituary, Nettlau is quoting a letter he received from Keell on June 2, a few days before Keell's death.

200 Goldman, "W. Starrett"; Nettlau, "Tom Keell," 2.

201 Wolfe to Inglis, May 23, 1946, 1, Agnes Inglis Papers, Box 20, Labadie Collection.

202 Wolfe to Inglis, September 2, 1947, 2, Agnes Inglis Papers, Box 20, Labadie Collection.

203 Inglis to Pearl Tucker, March 7, 1943, 2, Agnes Inglis Papers, Box 19, Labadie Collection.

204 Walter, *Anarchist Past*, 205, 206–7.

205 Frances Solokov, a.k.a. Vi Subversa, later became the lead singer for the punk band Poison Girls. My thanks to Kitty Cooper and Sue Cooper for introducing me to Frances and to Frances for two delightful afternoons discussing her participation in *Freedom*.

206 See Rob Ray, *Beautiful Idea*; Cornell, "New Anarchism Emerges"; Avrich, *Anarchist Voices*; and Goodway, *Anarchist Seeds*.

207　See McMillian, *Smoking Typewriters*; Aubert, *Detroit Printing Co-op*; and Slifer, *So Much*.

208　See Beins, *Liberation in Print*.

209　Cantarow, O'Malley, and Strom, *Moving the Mountain*, 93.

210　De Cleyre to Berkman, August 7, 1906, 1, Paul Avrich Collection, Box 3, Folder 1, Library of Congress. This is a sassy jibe at Emma Goldman, whom de Cleyre found hard to take.

211　Inglis to Metzkow, November 10, 1930, 1, Agnes Inglis Papers, Box 14, Labadie Collection.

212　Inglis to Wolfe, October 27, 1946, 1, Agnes Inglis Papers, Box 20, Labadie Collection.

213　Inglis to Pearl Tucker, October 21, 1944, 2, Agnes Inglis Papers, Box 19, Labadie Collection. See Anarchist FAQ Editorial Collective, "Anarchist FAQ," for a discussion of Yarros and Tucker.

214　Inglis, "To the Labadie Collection."

215　Dinshaw, *How Soon Is Now?*, 4.

216　Hughes, "Library of Jacques Derrida," 421.

3. Radical Study

1　"Publications of Joseph Ishill," 115–16.

2　Kropotkin, *Memoirs of a Revolutionist*, 275.

3　Brodie, "Rebel Youths," 1.

4　Colin Ward, "Notes of an Anarchist," 19.

5　Rancière, *Flesh of Words*, 3.

6　For comments on anarchism's neglect of race, see Black Rose Anarchist Federation, *Black Anarchism*; Bey, *Anarcho-Blackness*; Menzel, "Minor Perambulations, Political Horizons"; and Evren, "There Ain't No Black!" For gender, see Greenway, "Gender Politics"; and Jeppesen and Nazar, "Genders and Sexualities."

7　A Chicago anarchist who is now widely regarded as Black, Lucy Parsons, edited and wrote for several anarchist and Industrial Workers of the World publications but avoided talking about race. See Jacqueline Jones, *Goddess of Anarchy*. Black Industrial Workers of the World activist Ben Fletcher provided a searing indictment of racism within capitalism and the labor movement, but I have not seen his work published outside Industrial Workers of the World venues. See Cole, *Ben Fletcher*. In *Under Three Flags*, Benedict Anderson shows that an anarchist imaginary was emerging within networks of Cuban, Filipino, Chinese, and other anticolonial struggles. Evren points to a rich range of non-European anarchisms in "There Ain't No Black!"

8   Colin Ward, "Notes of an Anarchist," 19.

9   Rancière, *Flesh of Words*, 3.

10 Stansell, *American Moderns*, 96.

11 Ray and Stob, introduction to *Thinking Together*, 3.

12 Ray and Stob, introduction to *Thinking Together*, 4.

13 Dinshaw, *How Soon Is Now?*, 6.

14 Dinshaw, *How Soon Is Now?*, 29.

15 Dinshaw, *How Soon Is Now?*, 5.

16 McKinney, *Information Activism*, 30.

17 Dinshaw, *How Soon Is Now?*, 22.

18 Harney and Moten, *Undercommons*, 114.

19 Rancière, *Philosopher and His Poor*, 219.

20 Rancière, *Dissensus*, 37, 36.

21 Halberstam, "Wild Beyond," 6.

22 Halberstam, "Wild Beyond," 9.

23 Harney and Moten, *Undercommons*, 82.

24 Harney and Moten, *Undercommons*, 61–62.

25 Harney and Moten, *Undercommons*, 57, 18.

26 Harney and Moten, *Undercommons*, 62.

27 Harney and Moten, *Undercommons*, 65, 78.

28 Gitelman, *Paper Knowledge*, 2.

29 The platform culture of the lecture series was also an important ingredient in anarchist counterpublics. I have investigated that aspect of the movement in *Emma Goldman: Political Thinking in the Streets*. Orating and writing were intertwined in ways that I do not have space to investigate fully here.

30 Pakieser, *I Belong Only to Myself*, 50.

31 Keell, quoted in Colin Ward, "Notes of an Anarchist," 20.

32 Bantman, *French Anarchists*, 20.

33 "Use for Anthropometry," 66.

34 *Freedom* 8, no. 84 (January/February 1894): 4.

35 For example, Holmes's "Red Indians" appeared in *Freedom*; her essays "World's Beautiful Failures" and "Twenty-Five Years After" appeared in *Mother Earth*.

36 Kelly to Keell, April 9, 1911, 1, Freedom Archives, File 403, International Institute of Social History (IISH).

37 Zimmer, "American Anarchist Periodical Circulation."

38 Avrich, *American Anarchist*, 79–80.

39 Longa, *Anarchist Periodicals*, 91–92.

40 Moran, "*Firebrand*."

41 Other subtitles include "Liberty, Not Bread, Will Free Mankind" (February 3, 1901); "Formerly The Firebrand" (February 17, 1901); "A Periodical of Anarchist Work, Thought and Literature" (January 5, 1902–February 21, 1904); and the long-winded version, "An Exponent of Anarchist-Communism: Holding That Equality of Opportunity Alone Constitutes Liberty; That in the Absence of Monopoly Price and Competition Cannot Exist and That Communism Is an Inevitable Consequence" (February 20, 1898–December 29, 1901).

42 "Salutary," *Free Society*, no. 1 (November 14, 1897): 4.

43 Rancière, in Panagia, *Rancière's Sentiments*, 109n17.

44 Morton, "Shall We Have?," 2.

45 Morton, "Do for Free Society?," 2.

46 Morton, "Do for the Propaganda?," 2.

47 Longa, *Anarchist Periodicals*, 86, 231–32, 29, 174–78.

48 Hsu, *Emma Goldman*, 1.

49 Falk, "Into the Spotlight," 61.

50 Glassgold, "Introduction," xxxvi, xxii.

51 Falk, "Raising Her Voices," 42.

52 Goldman and Baginski, "Mother Earth," 4 (capitalization in original).

53 Goldman and Berkman, "Our Sixth Birthday," 3.

54 Monk, "Emma Goldman," 117.

55 Drinnon, *Rebel in Paradise*, 99.

56 "Freedom," *Freedom* 1, no. 1 (October 1886): 1.

57 Becker, "Notes on *Freedom*," 10. There are no credits given for many of the photos and graphics in *The Raven*. However, several issues include dramatic illustrations by Clifford Harper of Kenneth Rexroth's poems in "A Bestiary" (written for his daughters Mary and Katherine and published in his collection *In Defense of the Earth* [1956]).

58 Becker, "Notes on *Freedom*," 19.

59 "History of Freedom Press."

60 Nettlau, "Anarchist Communist Conference," 85.

61 "Outlook," 1–2.

62 Hinely, "Charlotte Wilson," 26.

63 Goodman, *Speaking and Language*, 171.

64 DeLanda, *New Philosophy of Society*, 56–57.

65 Parikka, *What Is Media Archaeology?*, 83 (italics in original).

66 Rancière, *Aisthesis*, xi.

67 Goldman and Berkman, "Our Sixth Birthday," 3.

68 "Outlook," 1–2.

69 "Salutary," *Free Society*, no. 1 (November 14, 1897): 4.

70 Harney and Moten, *Undercommons*, 98.

71 Morton, "Do for the Propaganda?," 2.

72 *Free Society* 5, no. 6 (December 18, 1898): 4.

73 See Torres, *Horizons Blossom, Borders Vanish*.

74 *Free Society* 5, no. 43 (September 9, 1899): 4.

75 "Blood of the Prophets," 41–43.

76 Whitman, quoted in Bennett, *Influx and Efflux*, 71 (italics in original).

77 Hsu, *Emma Goldman*, 316.

78 Austin, "Kropotkin's Autobiography," 2.

79 Bantman, *French Anarchists*, 20.

80 Turner, Marsh, and Keell, "Call for Action," 1.

81 "Another Little War," 21. There were a few exceptions to these generalizations. Historian Christopher Castañeda shows that support for anticolonial struggles in Cuba at the turn of the twentieth century was complicated among Spanish-speaking anarchists in the United States in that some saw the struggle for Cuban independence as just another state trying to establish itself. See Castañeda, "Times of Propaganda," 87–88.

82 *Free Society* opposed the annexation of the Hawaiian Islands. See A. G., "Annexation," 5.

83 Hinely, "Charlotte Wilson," 31.

84 Holmes, "Why We Tell the Story," 1.

85 Holmes, "Revolutionists," 1 (italics in original).

86 Holmes and Holmes, "Reminiscences," 2.

87 In her rough draft of her unpublished autobiography, Inglis writes, "Why suffer for a people that extol suffering and that inflict suffering? The idea of martyrdom will some day pass out. It's a ridiculous psychology. A people who believe in martyrs aren't worth being a martyr for." Inglis, "Reflections, Part II," 121.

88 There is no author listed for this column of "American Notes," but it was probably either Harry Kelly or Voltairine de Cleyre, and the tone sounds more like de Cleyre. *Freedom* 13, no. 137 (April 1899): 26 (italics in original).

89 Born, "Commemoration in Boston," 3.

90 Streeby, *Radical Sensations*, 42. I'm grateful to my colleague Michael Shapiro for his provocations to think about the politics of the future perfect tense.

91 See, for example, "Anarchist Lecturers," *Free Society* no. 28 (May 22, 1898): 8. In his analysis of print culture in Caribbean anarchism, Shaffer refers to these as "celebrity anarchists," whose visits "were covered and editorialized in the local anarchist press in the same way that mainstream newspapers would cover a visiting foreign dignitary" (*Anarchists of the Caribbean*, 26, 25).

92 "News from Everywhere," 7; *Free Society*, no. 4 (December 5, 1897): 3.

93 Duff, "Voltairine de Cleyre's Tour," 69.

94 Inglis, "Reflections, Part I."

95 "Match Girls Strike," 89.

96 "Solidarity an Aid," 97.

97 "Press Censorship," 8.

98 Addis, "Look at our Postoffice [*sic*] System!!," 2.

99 Seymour, "Battle for Freedom," 1–2.

100 Kelly, "Letter from England," 4 (italics in original).

101 Goldman, "The Tragedy at Buffalo," 1; Isaak, "Why We Considered," 4.

102 Lillian Harman, "Unconditionally Released," 8.

103 Walter, "Lilian Wolfe," 24.

104 Dolgoff, *Fragments*, 64.

105 Goldman, *Living My Life*, 191.

106 *Free Society* 5, no. 6 (December 18, 1898): 4.

107 Voline, "Anarchist Synthesis"; Tarrida del Mármol, "Anarchism without Adjectives."

108 Lloyd, "Are They Anarchists?," 6.

109 Nettlau, "Mutual Toleration versus Dictatorship," 43.

110 Fulton to Barnhill, March 11, 1925, 1, Joseph Ishill Papers, Box 10, Houghton Library.

111 Tarrida del Mármol, "Anarchism without Adjectives."

112 "Observations and Comments," 246.

113 Kropotkin, "On the Present War," 76–77.

114 Kinna, *Government of No One*, 129.

115 Owen to Keell, March 2, 1928, 2, William Charles Owen Papers, 4327.5 1–4, File 2, IISH.

116 Owen to Keell, March 2, 1928, 3, William Charles Owen Papers, 4327.5 1–4, File 2, IISH.

117 Hsu, *Emma Goldman*, 166. I've analyzed Goldman's views on gender and sexuality in more detail in *Emma Goldman: Political Thinking in the Streets*, 249–76.

118 "Discussion of the Sex Question," 43.

119 Goldman, *Living My Life*, 253. See also Avrich, "Kropotkin in America," 17–18.

120 "Women's Burden," 45.

121 Wilkinson, cited in Greenway, "Gender Politics," 3.

122 Greenway, "Sex, Politics and Housework."

123 Men who were regular writers for *Free Society* included Abe Isaak, James Morton, Ross Winn, William Holmes, Jay Fox, Con Lynch, C. L. James, A. L. Ballou, Steven Byington, M. A. Cohen, Wat Tyler, Jacob Wilson, and Henry Addis.

124 Not all comrades were supportive. A few issues after Lizzie Holmes's splendid think piece "Mental Barriers," L. S. Oliver condescingly char-

acterized Holmes as "our ever interesting little comrade" ("Sentiments," 3). A year later *Freedom* acknowledged "the Chicago group," "among whom were a number of intelligent, able women workers" including Holmes, Lucy Parsons, and Sarah Ames. "The Rise of the Movement in America," *Freedom* 15, no. 155 (February 1901): 10. Male writers were seldom characterized in print as intelligent, interesting, or little.

125 "Letterbox," *Free Society* 6, no. 1 (November 19, 1899): 4.

126 "Letterbox," *Free Society* 5, no. 12 (January 29, 1899): 4.

127 Parsons, "Case of Sex Slavery," 3; Goldman, "Marriage and Love."

128 Jerauld, "God and Grundy," 3.

129 Holmes, "Love of Authority," 2–3.

130 Waisbrooker, "Standard of Judgment," 3.

131 "Salutary," *Free Society*, no. 1 (November 14, 1897): 4.

132 Kropotkin, *Memoirs of a Revolutionist*, 275.

133 See Goyens, *Beer and Revolution*, 168–82.

134 "News from Nowhere," 7.

135 C. Pluetzner, "A Summer Outing," *Free Society* 7, no. 28 (August 11, 1901): 3.

136 "Notes," *Freedom* 5, no. 55 (June 1891): 46.

137 Mac, "Tale of a Wet Trip," 43–44.

138 "Propaganda," 63–64.

139 "Caruso and the Convicts," 33.

140 G.H.G., "Propaganda Notes," 91.

141 Zimmer, "American Anarchist Periodical Circulation."

142 While a list of letter writers' home cities is less informative than a list of subscribers, I have been unable to locate the latter for *Free Society*.

143 "The Other Side," *Free Society*, no. 8 (January 2, 1898): 2.

144 Tamboukou, *Sewing, Fighting and Writing*, 92.

145 For a discussion of anarchist debates about proper work for members of their movement, see McKinley, "'Quagmires of Necessity.'"

146 Addis, "Look at Our Postoffice [*sic*] System!!," 1.

147 "News and Notes," *Free Society*, no. 3 (November 28, 1897): 8.

148 "News from Nowhere," *Free Society*, no. 1 (November 14, 1897): 7.

149 Becker, "Notes on *Freedom*," 14.

150 *Freedom* 17, no. 176 (May 1903): 25. The writer gives Notkin a lot of credit for raising two hundred dollars to support "the propaganda," including *Freedom*; then, in the inimitably snarky way anarchists had of mocking those with lifestyles considered too bourgeois, the writer observes "a certain amount of prosperity lingering round the movement there" (25).

151 The financial records of the Spanish-language journal *Cultura Obrera* 4, no. 187 (December 9, 1916): 4, report a twenty-five-cent donation from

Charlie Chaplin. While anarchists often employ playful pseudonyms, it could well be that the real Chaplin supported the journal.

152 *Free Society*, no. 2 (November 21, 1897): 8.

153 *Free Society*, no. 31 (June 12, 1898): 2.

154 Horvitz, "An Appeal for Literature," 4.

155 *Free Society* 6, no. 14 (February 18, 1900): 4.

156 De Cleyre, "Reading Course," 1.

157 "Opening of Marsh House," 17.

158 Moses, "Texture of Politics."

159 Hapgood, quoted in Goldman, *Living My Life*, 517.

160 Goyens, introduction to *Radical Gotham*, 9.

161 Freedom Archives, File 32, IISH.

162 Freedom Archives, File 30: Freedom Exchanges Home and Foreign, January 1920, IISH. No wonder Keell complained to Ishill that he was too busy with correspondence to print beautiful texts. Even though the date of this address book is 1920, it was clearly in use through the whole decade. The last entry date is in 1930. Some journals are marked as "ceased" or "moved"; some titles are struck through, with no notation other than the last date sent. It looks as though Keell did not know what happened to some of them.

163 *Free Society*, no. 2 (November 21, 1897): 8.

164 *Free Society*, no. 25 (May 1, 1898): 8.

165 "Our Exchange List," *Freedom* 5, no. 52 (March 1891): 8.

166 "Books to Be Had through Mother Earth," 62–63.

167 "Notes and Comments," 2.

168 *Freedom* 2, no. 13 (October 1887): 4.

169 "Letterbox," *Free Society* 6, no. 26 (May 13, 1900): 4.

170 Stansell, *American Moderns*, 96.

171 Goodman, *Speaking and Language*, 54 (italics in original).

172 Goodman, *Speaking and Language*, 171–72.

173 Goodman, *Speaking and Language*, 195.

174 Gitelman, *Paper Knowledge*, 17.

175 Stanley, "Epistolarium," 217.

176 My teacher Michael Weinstein introduced me to the idea of a think piece when I was his undergraduate student at Purdue University. I am indebted to all that he taught me, and I miss him.

177 So far I have only found one man who wrote in these mixed genres in the journals at hand, and that was the German Japanese poet Sadakichi Hartmann. Perhaps being a poet, actor, and bohemian literary figure gave him "permission" to write in ways that are otherwise associated with women.

178 Harney and Moten, *Undercommons*, 61.

179 For this discussion I selected a few of the most intriguing examples from the three journals at hand. Other social sketches deserving attention include these in *Mother Earth*: de Cleyre, "Where the White Rose Died"; Hartmann, "Ride into the Desert"; Hartmann, "Dispossessed"; and Hartmann, "Searchlight Vista." Other think pieces deserving attention include these in *Free Society*: Jerauld, "What Shall We Teach?"; Daniels, "Few Significant Facts"; Daniels, "Government"; Holmes, "Return"; and Holmes, "Work in the Future." And they include these in *Freedom*: Bessie Ward, "Daisy Lord and Others"; Holmes, "Red Indians"; and Holmes, "Keynote of Success."

180 Morton, "Shall We Have?," 2.

181 Pakieser, *I Belong Only to Myself*, 50. Rafanelli drew the concept of social sketches from Italian socialist writer Edmondo De Amicis, who wrote short accounts of soldiers' lives, drawing on his own military experience. Rafanelli's extensive work was unpublished and unknown for forty years after her death, except for her brief (alleged) affair with Benito Mussolini when he was a socialist. Upon publication of some of her stories and memoirs by Nerosubianco Edizioni, an Italian publisher, in 2010, this began to change. Pakieser's edition is the first English translation of Rafanelli. However, her work was known to Italian speakers in the United States through the "woman's page" of *Lotta di Classe* (Class Struggle), the official journal of the New York City Italian-language section of the Cloak and Skirt Makers' Union. See Guglielmo, *Living the Revolution*, 190.

182 Pakieser, *I Belong Only to Myself*, 10.

183 Pakieser, *I Belong Only to Myself*, 10.

184 Goodman, *Speaking and Language*, 171.

185 For more extensive analysis of Wilkinson's social sketches, see the *Political Research Quarterly*'s 2017 symposium: Ferguson, "Anarchist Women"; Marso, "Freedom's Poses"; and Menzel, "Minor Perambulations, Political Horizons." Steve Johnson, Lori Marso, and Annie Menzel made the 2016 Maxwell Lecture at the University of Utah, which gave birth to the symposium, a great pleasure. Thanks also to Mary Rhodes, Matt Rose, and others at the Halsway Manor National Centre for Folk Art, near Taunton, England, for sharing their knowledge about Wilkinson. This art center was founded by Lily and Arthur Gair Wilkinson's daughter Frances and contains paintings by both of Frances's parents.

186 Pakieser, *I Belong Only to Myself*, 50.

187 Wilkinson, "Women in Bondage," 26–27.

188 Wilkinson, "Women in Rebellion," 34.

189 Wilkinson, "Women's Freedom," 46.

190 Wilkinson, "Women's Freedom," 46.

191 Wilkinson, "Women's Freedom," 46 (italics in original).

192 Wilkinson, "Women's Freedom," 46 (italics in original).

193 Wilkinson, "Women's Freedom," 46.

194 Wilkinson, "Women's Freedom (Con)," 55 (italics in original).

195 Panagia, *Rancière's Sentiments*, 4, x, 5.

196 Marso, "Freedom's Poses," 721.

197 De Cleyre, "Between the Living," 58, 61. While no author is given for this story, Robert Helms and I are confident that it was de Cleyre. Helms is a Philadelphia researcher and editor of the website Dead Anarchists. The main reason for our conviction that de Cleyre is the author is the familiar tone of the piece: the unremitting pain, the lack of redemption, the outrage at an unjust god, and the imagery of life in a coffin sound like her work. The title is from the book of Numbers 16:48, which she could have learned during her early education in a convent school. Anarchist literary critic Leonard Abbott, who was a friend of de Cleyre's, remarked that she "hesitates between life and death," an apt account of this triangle of desperate characters as well as a likely reference to the title of this piece. Abbott, "Voltairine de Cleyre's Posthumous Book," 269.

One year earlier, according to Helms, de Cleyre was in the hospital for treatment for syphilis, a disease considered so shameful that only a few of her friends knew she had it. As does the woman in the story, de Cleyre considered suicide. Helms noticed that the suggestive printer's ornament at the end of the story appears to be a stylized version of de Cleyre's initials: a capital *V* lying on its side, a fancy lower-case *d*, and a capital *C* tilting to the right (Helms, personal correspondence, June 20, 2013). The printer may have been in on the secret arrangement and acknowledged de Cleyre's authorship in code. In his discussion of *Mother Earth*, Goldman's biographer Richard Drinnon criticizes the journal for failing to showcase any up-and-coming new writers, but I suspect that de Cleyre, never known outside the anarchist movement, was one of theirs. Drinnon, *Rebel in Paradise*, 100.

198 De Cleyre, "Between the Living," 58, 61.

199 Marso, "Freedom's Poses," 721.

200 De Cleyre, "Between the Living," 59, 60. I analyze this story more extensively in my essay "Assemblages of Anarchists."

201 Abbott, "Priestess of Pity."

202 Sartwell, "Priestess of Pity," 5.

203 Abbott, "Priestess of Pity," 232.

204 Hartmann, "Flower-Maker." Hartmann was a prolific, eccentric poet, artist, actor, and writer. He was well known outside anarchist circles and was one of the lively connectors between the anarchist and bohemian worlds of New York City.

205 Hartmann, "Flower-Maker," 464–65.

206 Hartmann, "On Pictorial Projection," 229.

207 Marso, "Freedom's Poses," 726.

208 Hartmann, "Flower-Maker," 467.

209 Panagia, *Rancière's Sentiments*, 4.

210 Colin Ward, "Notes of an Anarchist," 20.

211 Holmes, "Sentiment," 2.

212 Holmes, "Mental Barriers," 1.

213 Holmes, "Mental Barriers," 1 (italics in original).

214 Rancière, *Aisthesis*, xi.

215 Holmes, "Mental Barriers," 1. I imagine she means "plumbline," which is a phrase from Benjamin Tucker, the editor of the long-running anarchist journal *Liberty*. Tucker definitely has "a few bars up" to considering feeling as a form of knowing. Laura Greenwood points out that this discussion continued in *Free Society*, with articles by Jay Fox in 1902 arguing that the best way to "arouse men to think and reason" was not found in the "work of denunciation" but in the "work of love." Someone named S. Mints argued back, contending that people who are invested in anarchism primarily through their emotions are more likely to leave the movement than are those invested more through their intellect. See Laura Greenwood, "Book-Anarchists," 25.

216 Holmes, "Mental Barriers," 1 (italics in original).

217 Holmes, "Mental Barriers," 1.

218 Halberstam, "Wild Beyond," 11.

219 Harney and Moten, *Undercommons*, 82.

220 Holmes, "War Spirit," 1.

221 Holmes, "Return," 2.

222 Waisbrooker edited and sometimes printed several anarchist journals, including *Clothed with the Sun*, when she lived at Home Colony in Washington. Given how widespread the Spiritualist movement was at the time, there were probably many more individuals and groups who connected it with anarchism and feminism. Waisbrooker persisted in interlinking the movements in the pages of *Free Society*, even though few other writers expressed much tolerance for her views. In response to provocation by a writer identified only as S. D., Waisbrooker writes that she is a Spiritualist based on her personal experience and knows that other workers are as well: "I do not sneer at those of you who do not believe, at those of you who have not had that evidence, and why should you sneer at me?" ("Just a Question," 3). While Waisbrooker is not well known now, she was a presence in anarchism at the turn of the last century. Writing in "American Notes" in *Freedom* in 1897, de Cleyre recognizes Waisbrooker for keeping *Lucifer* going during the trial and incarceration of its editor Moses Harman (69).

223 Waisbrooker, "Why Is It So?," 1.

224 Waisbrooker, "Why Is It So?," 1.

225 Waisbrooker, "Why Is It So?," 1. It is unclear in this passage whether Waisbrooker is quoting Harman, paraphrasing him, or simply agreeing with him.

226 Boole, "Should Decorative Work," 20–21 (italics in original).

227 Burke, "Anarchism and Art," 2.

228 Harney and Moten, *Undercommons*, 98.

229 In the next issue of *Freedom*, Mary Boole reported in a sweet letter to the editor on a science lecture she attended by the anarchist geographer Élisée Reclus. People attended who would not have gone to hear about anarchism, yet afterward they told her they would have to rethink their uninformed views of the movement. She concludes, sensibly, "If you wish to destroy prejudices in your opponents, do not fling at them either bombs or hard arguments *about Anarchism*; but send some Anarchist, whose conduct they will be forced to respect, to teach them some art or science which they themselves desire to learn, and let him make his own impression" ("Correspondence," 43 [italics in original]). Unfortunately, the editors responded with a snarky remark to the effect that it wasn't their fault if people didn't get them, and the correspondence ceased.

230 Altman, *Epistolarity*, 9.

231 Cohn, "What Is Anarchist?," 117.

232 Harney and Moten, *Undercommons*, 110.

233 Harney and Moten, *Undercommons*, 112.

4. Intersectionality and Thing Power

1 Inglis to Ishill, June 3, 1934, 1, Agnes Inglis Papers, Box 10, Joseph A. Labadie Collection.

2 Inglis to Ishill, June 3, 1934, 4, Joseph Ishill Papers, Box 4, Houghton Library.

3 McKinney, *Information Activism*, ix, 7.

4 Gitelman, *Paper Knowledge*, 18.

5 Panagia, "Political Ontology," 716.

6 Gitelman, *Paper Knowledge*, x.

7 Galloway, *Interface Effect*, vii.

8 Galloway, *Interface Effect*, vii.

9 Galloway, *Interface Effect*, 31, 33, 44.

10 Gitelman, *Paper Knowledge*, x.

11 See Barton, "Global War on Anarchism"; and Krishna, "Anarchy, Security, Hierarchy."

12 For a discussion of feminism as doing with others, see Rentschler and Thrift, "Doing Feminism," 246.

13 Panagia, "Political Ontology," 716.

14 Rudolf Rocker, *London Years*, 111.

15 Goldman, "What I Believe," 35.

16 Voline, "Anarchist Synthesis," 432.

17 There are many other elements of intersectionality that are good candidates for further encounters with anarchism, including indigenous politics, feminist theory, queer theory, disability studies, and radical ecology. For a few examples of indigenous anarchism, see Kauanui, "Politics of Indigeneity"; and Johnson and Ferguson, "Anarchism and Indigeneity." For feminist and queer anarchism, see Bottici, *Anarchafeminism*; Heckert and Cleminson, *Anarchism and Sexuality*; and Daring et al., *Queering Anarchism*. For anarchism and disability, see Ben-Moshe, Nocelle, and Withers, "Queer-Cripping Anarchism." For ecological anarchism, see Ryley, *Making Another World Possible*; and Springer et al., *Undoing Human Supremacy*.

18 Parikka, *What Is Media Archaeology?*, 83.

19 Butler, *Gender Trouble*, 143.

20 Wieck, "Negativity of Anarchism," 6 (italics in original).

21 Hartman, "Black in Anarchy," xv–xvi.

22 Collins, "Intersectionality's Definitional Dilemmas," 2.

23 Vivian May, *Pursuing Intersectionality*, 33.

24 Vivian May, *Pursuing Intersectionality*, 20, 29.

25 Lazar, "Intersectionality," 158. For reservations about this move, see Hemmings, *Considering Emma Goldman*, 104–5.

26 Bey, *Anarcho-Blackness*, 15.

27 Menzel, "Minor Perambulations, Political Horizons," 731.

28 William Anderson, *Nation on No Map*, 81.

29 Giombolini, "Anarchism on the Williamette," 89.

30 Nail, "What Is an Assemblage?," 34.

31 I began my efforts to understand classical anarchists' thinking on race with my study of Emma Goldman, where I could see the problems with her lack of historical analysis and her contempt for all reform, but I had not discerned the significance of different arts (visual, literary, performative, graphic, etc.) or the collapse of the vocabulary of slavery. As I expanded my study to a larger range of anarchist writers and texts, a bigger picture became available. For the earlier discussion, see Ferguson, *Emma Goldman*, 211–48.

32 Bey, *Anarcho-Blackness*, 2.

33 Panagia, *Rancière's Sentiments*, 5.

34 Pakieser, *I Belong Only to Myself*, 10.

35 Menzel, "Minor Perambulations, Political Horizons," 732.

36 Wilkinson, "Women in Bondage," 26, 27.

37 Wilkinson, "Women in Rebellion," 34.

38 Waisbrooker, "Why Is It So?" 1.

39 Broeck, "Enslavement as Regime," 12.

40 De Man, "Epistemology of Metaphor," 19.

41 Menzel, "Minor Perambulations, Political Horizons," 732.

42 Hartman, *Lose Your Mother,* 6.

43 Hartman, *Lose Your Mother,* 6.

44 Carby, *Imperial Intimacies,* 231.

45 Best and Hartman, "Fugitive Justice," 2–3. Cugoana published *Thoughts and Sentiments on the Evil Wicked Traffic of the Slavery and Commerce of the Human Species* in London in 1787.

46 Best and Hartman, "Fugitive Justice," 9. They are quoting "the sublime ideal of freedom" from a petition to the Massachusetts legislature by the Boston Committee of Slaves in 1773. See Dorothy Porter, *Early Negro Writing.*

47 Goldman, *Anarchism and Other Essays,* 63.

48 For the classic analysis of situated knowledge, to which my thinking is always indebted, see Haraway, "Situated Knowledges."

49 Greenidge, "Holding a Mirror," 107–27.

50 Lazar, "Until All Are Free," 48.

51 Lazar, "Intersectionality," 160, 170.

52 Stansell, *American Moderns,* 96.

53 Hartman, *Wayward Lives, Beautiful Experiments,* xv, 229–31.

54 Hartman, *Wayward Lives, Beautiful Experiments,* xv.

55 Menzel, "Minor Perambulations, Political Horizons," 732.

56 An exception to this critique was Louise Michel, whose imprisonment in New Caledonia by the French government after the destruction of the Paris Commune led her to interact with the Kanak community and support their 1878 uprising. She was the only imprisoned Communard to do so. See Eichner, "Language of Imperialism."

57 "Who Is Guilty?," 1.

58 Bey, *Anarcho-Blackness,* 2, 26, 17.

59 "Old" and "new" are somewhat misleading qualifiers here. "New" materialism has old roots in, for example, the work of Lucretius and Spinoza, while "old" materialism is continually refreshed. These terms will do for now to make the distinctions I need.

60 See Baron, "Contested Terrain Revisited"; Baron, "Women and the Making"; Burr, "Defending 'The Art Preservative'"; and Cockburn, *Brothers.*

61 Bennett, *Vibrant Matter,* xxii, xxiv.

62 Latour, "'Compositionist Manifesto,'" 484.

63 Protevi, *Political Affect,* xi.

64 Bennett, *Vibrant Matter*, viii.

65 Galloway, *Interface Effect*, 33.

66 McKinney, *Information Activism*, 7.

67 I am inviting these movements into my discussion of anarchist "thing power" because they each illustrate the significant ability of nonhuman actants to make their mark in political struggle. Other movements could also serve, including Occupy Wall Street, the Zapatistas, the protectors at Standing Rock, feminist and anarchist zine makers, info shops, Kurdish resistance in Rojava, and others. I selected these three because they are quite different in their self-understanding and their practical objectives and yet they share robust engagements with worlds of things.

68 Parson, *Cooking Up a Revolution*, 25.

69 Bennett, "Vital Materiality," 100.

70 Bennett, "Vital Materiality," 100.

71 Parson, *Cooking Up a Revolution*, 5.

72 Parson, *Cooking Up a Revolution*, 24.

73 Spataro, "Against a De-politicized," 192.

74 Fessenden, "'We Just Wanna Warm,'" 3.

75 Food Not Bombs, "People of Color Caucus."

76 Swanson, preface to *Hungry for Peace*, 11.

77 Fessenden, "'We Just Wanna Warm,'" 148, 146.

78 Bennett, "Vital Materiality," 101.

79 Swanson, preface to *Hungry for Peace*, 8.

80 Parson, *Cooking Up a Revolution*, 15.

81 Gelderloos, "Critical History."

82 Fessenden, "'We Just Wanna Warm,'" 135.

83 Fessenden, "'We Just Wanna Warm,'" 193.

84 Lu, quoted in Fessenden, "'We Just Wanna Warm,'" 151.

85 Kuwada and Revilla, "Introduction," 517. My thanks to my colleague Noenoe Silva for her research into the many layers and nuances in Hawaiian language.

86 Kuwada and Revilla, "Introduction," 518–19.

87 Goodyear-Kaʻōpua, "Protectors of the Future," 185.

88 Osorio, *Rise Like a Mighty Wave*, 148.

89 Kauanui, quoted in Cornum, "Fight for the Future."

90 Ahia, "Mālama Mauna," 609.

91 Ahia, "Mālama Mauna," 610–11. For thoughtful reflections on the meaning of māhū, see Teves, *Defiant Indigeneity*, 83–88.

92 Kauanui, quoted in Cornum, "Fight for the Future."

93 Goodyear-Kaʻōpua and Mahelona, "Protecting Maunakea."

94 Case, "Ea," 572.

95 Kuwada and Revilla, "Introduction," 519, 521.

96 Long, "Fight of the Indigenous."

97 Kuwada and Revilla, "Introduction," 521.

98 Osorio, "Front Lines of Mauna Kea."

99 Kapahua, "Stories from the Mauna," 580, 581.

100 Hogan, *Feminist Bookstore Movement*, 2.

101 Murray, *Mixed Media*, 127.

102 Hogan, *Feminist Bookstore Movement*, 45.

103 Kinder, *Radical Bookstore*, 91.

104 See Travis, "Women in Print Movement," for a more detailed history of the *Feminist Bookstore News*.

105 Hogan, *Feminist Bookstore Movement*, 35.

106 Hogan, *Feminist Bookstore Movement*, 35.

107 Liddle, "More Than a Bookstore," 157.

108 Hogan, *Feminist Bookstore Movement*, 2.

109 Fessenden reports that the online suggestion to the Vancouver Food Not Bombs group that they develop some business sense was greeted by "a refrain of 'FUCK BUSINESS SENSE SO HARD'" (all caps in original) and another response that "Food not Bombs is strictly non profit. Zero interest in money. We just wanna warm some bellies, man." Fessenden, "'We Just Wanna Warm,'" 2.

110 Kinder, *Radical Bookstore*, 4.

111 Hogan, *Feminist Bookstore Movement*, xxv, 45.

112 Bennett, "Vital Materiality," 102.

113 Kinder, *Radical Bookstore*, 144, 147.

114 Farmelant, "End of an Era," 20.

115 Hogan, *Feminist Bookstore Movement*, 111, 38, 65–66.

116 Kinder, *Radical Bookstore*, 195.

117 Hogan, *Feminist Bookstore Movement*, 109.

118 Hogan, *Feminist Bookstore Movement*, 109.

119 Hogan, *Feminist Bookstore Movement*, 131, 112, 135, 111–12.

120 Quoted in Hogan, *Feminist Bookstore Movement*, 135.

121 Hogan, *Feminist Bookstore Movement*, 113.

122 Farmelant, "End of an Era," 18.

123 Hogan, *Feminist Bookstore Movement*, 12, 108, 71.

124 Hogan, *Feminist Bookstore Movement*, 167.

125 Fessenden, "'We Just Wanna Warm,'" 205.

126 Maybe I am wrong. For thoughtful reflections on virtual movement building, see Cayden Mak, "Building Online Power."

127 William Anderson, *Nation on No Map*, 114.

1   Avrich, *Anarchist Voices*, 159.

2   Hodgart, *Ethel MacDonald*, 20.

3   Stansell, *American Moderns*, 246.

4   Yeoman, *Print Culture*, 88–89.

5   Yeoman, *Print Culture*, 165–66.

6   Selbuz, "Biography of Armenian Anarchist."

7   Zimmer, "First Red Scare."

8   Johnson to Inglis (March 22, 1934): 1, Agnes Inglis Box 11 Labadie.

9   Zimmer, "First Red Scare."

10 Zimmer, *Immigrants against the State*, 54.

11 Buttá, "Anarchist Theories and Practices," 203.

12 Avrich, *Anarchist Voices*, 488n104.

13 Avrich and Avrich, *Sasha and Emma*, 41, 43.

14 Longa, *Anarchist Periodicals*, 210n3; Avrich, *Modern School Movement*, 192.

15 "International Notes," *Freedom* 16, no. 167 (April–May 1902): 14.

16 Zimmer, "First Red Scare."

17 Cores, *Personal Recollections*, 7.

18 Avrich, *Anarchist Voices*, 256.

19 Rowbotham, *Rebel Crossings*, 95.

20 Acrata and Sharkey, "Antonia Fontanillas Borrás."

21 Buttá, "Anarchist Theories and Practices," 195.

22 Cores, *Personal Recollections*, 10.

23 Avrich and Avrich, *Sasha and Emma*, 111.

24 Buttá, "Anarchist Theories and Practices," 118.

25 Buttá, "Anarchist Theories and Practices," 118.

26 Caldwell, *With Fate Conspire*, 142.

27 Zimmer, *Immigrants against the State*, 80–83; Guglielmo, *Living the Revolution*, 147.

28 Castañeda, "Anarchism and the End."

29 Avrich, *Anarchist Voices*, 469; Rainer, "Holley Cantine."

30 Kelly, "Thomas Cantwell."

31 Buttá, "Anarchist Theories and Practices," 118.

32 Andrew Whitehead, "Dan Chatterton."

33 Avrich, *Anarchist Voices*, 164; Zimmer, *Immigrants against the State*, 92–93.

34 Basin, "From the Ashes"; Blanche Cooney, *My Own Sweet Time*.

35 James Cooney to Schroeder, February 28, 1939, Joseph Ishill Additional Papers, Supplementary Box 5, Houghton Library.

36 Cores, *Personal Recollections*, 12.

37 Avrich, *Anarchist Voices*, 420; Longa, *Anarchist Periodicals*, 38, 231.

38 Avrich, *Anarchist Voices*, 336.

39 Zimmer, "First Red Scare."

40 Derzanski to Keell, September 9, 1928, Freedom Archives, File 397, International Institute of Social History.

41 Carlson, *Anarchism in Germany*, 365.

42 Avrich, *Anarchist Voices*, 498n238; Zimmer, "First Red Scare."

43 Avrich, *Anarchist Voices*, 472–73.

44 Avrich, *Modern School Movement*, 152.

45 Avrich, *Anarchist Voices*, 113.

46 Codina, "Pedro Esteve," 58, 72.

47 "Sudden Death of G.H. Exall," *Freedom* 26, no. 279 (July 1912): 56.

48 Avrich, *Anarchist Voices*, 118, 140.

49 Cores, *Personal Recollections*, 12.

50 Avrich, *Haymarket Tragedy*, 86–87.

51 Acrata and Sharkey, "Antonia Fontanillas Borrás."

52 Avrich, *Anarchist Voices*, 293, 333.

53 Fulton to Labadie, December 19, 1936, Joseph A. Labadie Papers, Box 3, Joseph A. Labadie Collection.

54 Avrich and Avrich, *Sasha and Emma*, 222.

55 Avrich, *Anarchist Voices*, 291.

56 Bantman, "Jean Grave and French Anarchism," 452.

57 Avrich, *Anarchist Voices*, 465.

58 Guglielmo, *Living the Revolution*, 153.

59 Guglielmo, *Living the Revolution*, 153.

60 Moses Harman, "Lucifer's Coming of Age," 266.

61 Moses Harman, "Lucifer's Coming of Age," 266.

62 Hirschauge, "Tenth Anniversary."

63 Inglis to Fetz, October 8, 1944, Agnes Inglis Papers, Box 7, Labadie Collection.

64 Cores, *Personal Recollections*, 12.

65 Avrich, *Anarchist Voices*, 28.

66 Avrich, *Anarchist Voices*, 28.

67 Ishill to Inglis, April 12, 1938, Agnes Inglis Papers, Box 10, Labadie Collection.

68 Ishill, *Oriole Press*.

69 Rudolf Rocker, *London Years*, 46–49.

70 Zimmer, "First Red Scare."

71 Becker, "Thomas Keell."

72 Avrich, *Modern School Movement*, 190–96.

73 Dumartheray, "Letter from an Old Comrade," 129; Tcherkesoff, "Friend and Comrade," 24.

74 Carlotta Anderson, *All-American Anarchist.*

75 Carlotta Anderson, *All-American Anarchist.*

76 Avrich, "Anarchist Lives," 5.

77 Walter, *Anarchist Past*, 218.

78 Boyer and Morais, *Labor's Untold Story*, 152–53.

79 Yeoman, *Print Culture*, 78.

80 Colin Ward and Goodway, *Talking Anarchy*, 23.

81 Rudolf Rocker, "Behind Barbed Wire," 447.

82 Rodrigues, "Edgard Leuenroth."

83 Dolgoff, *Anarchist Collectives*, 178.

84 Inglis to Schulder, August 6, 1950, 1, Agnes Inglis Papers, Box 16, Labadie Collection.

85 Zimmer, *Immigrants against the State*, 23.

86 Shaffer, *Anarchist Cuba*, 9.

87 "Death of Anselmo Lorenzo," 2.

88 Carlotta Anderson, *All American Anarchist*, 154; Avrich and Avrich, *Sasha and Emma*, 85.

89 Caldwell, *With Fate Conspire*, 144.

90 Quail, *Slow Burning Fuse*, 293.

91 Zimmer, *Immigrants against the State*, 138.

92 Zimmer, *Immigrants against the State*, 177.

93 Quail, *Slow Burning Fuse*, 293.

94 Avrich, *Anarchist Voices*, 82; Avrich and Avrich, *Sasha and Emma*, 373.

95 Avrich and Avrich, *Sasha and Emma*, 63–64; Inglis to Barnard, April 21, 1941, 1, Agnes Inglis Papers, Box 1, Labadie Collection; Metzkow to Inglis, July 25, 1940, 1, Agnes Inglis Papers, Box 14, Labadie Collection.

96 Rob Ray, *Beautiful Idea*, 53.

97 Pakieser, *I Belong Only to Myself*, 52.

98 Taddei, "Alberto Moroni."

99 De Agostini, "Milan's Anarchists"; Buttá, "Anarchist Theories and Practices in Milan," 232.

100 Moran, "*Firebrand.*"

101 William Morris, "Note by William Morris."

102 Cores, *Personal Recollections*, 7.

103 Goldman, *Living My Life*, vol 1, 64.

104 Avrich, *Anarchist Voices*, 381.

105 Fishman, *East End Jewish Radicals*, 243; Rudolf Rocker, *London Years*, 72.

106 *Commonweal, Grand Jubiliee Number* 1, no. 1 (June 20, 1897): 4.

107 Inglis to Ishill, October 28, 1935, 2, Agnes Inglis Papers, Box 10, Labadie Collection.

108 Zimmer, "First Red Scare."

109 Zimmer, "First Red Scare."

110 Goldman, *Living My Life*, vol. 2, 838–39; Zimmer, "First Red Scare."

111 "Antoni Pellicer Paraire."

112 Avrich, *Haymarket Tragedy*, 86–87.

113 Caldwell, *With Fate Conspire*, 123.

114 Cores, *Personal Recollections*, 7.

115 Shaffer, *Anarchist Cuba*, 16–17.

116 Buttá, "Anarchist Theories and Practices," 118.

117 Genz, *History of the Eragny Press*, 35–38.

118 Genz, *History of the Eragny Press*, 35.

119 Avrich, *Anarchist Voices*, 291.

120 Avrich, *Anarchist Voices*, 291.

121 Dana Ward, "Proudhon: A Biography."

122 Pakieser, *I Belong Only to Myself*, 20.

123 Rainer, "Holley Cantine," 182.

124 Carlson, *Anarchism in Germany*, 79.

125 Marsh, *Anarchist Women*, 55.

126 Carlson, *Anarchism in Germany*, 323–24.

127 Lang, *Tomorrow Is Beautiful*, 112; Goldman, *Living My Life*, vol 2, 648.

128 Avrich, *Anarchist Voices*, 37.

129 Rudolf Rocker, *London Years*, 74

130 Rudolf Rocker, *London Years*, 74.

131 Rogers to Inglis, May 14, 1946, 1, Agnes Inglis Papers, Box 22, Labadie Collection.

132 Encyclopedia.com, "Romero Rosa, Ramón."

133 Avrich, *Anarchist Voices*, 472.

134 Goldman, *Living My Life*, vol 1, 165.

135 Yeoman, *Print Culture*, 77.

136 Rudolf Rocker, "Behind Barbed Wire," 447.

137 Avrich, *Anarchist Voices*, 498n238.

138 Sartin to Ishill, September 26, 1945, 1, Joseph Ishill Papers, Box 4, Houghton Library.

139 Zimmer, "First Red Scare."

140 Carlson, *Anarchism in Germany*, 268.

141 Avrich, *Anarchist Voices*, 11, 37.

142 Avrich, *Haymarket Tragedy*, 86–87.

143 Schwartz to Ishill, n.d., Joseph Ishill Papers, Box 17, Houghton Library.

144 Avrich, *Anarchist Voices*, 243; Avrich, *Modern School Movement*, 302.

145 Quail, *Slow Burning Fuse*, 293.

146 Parry, *Bonnot Gang*, 33.

147 Metzkow to Inglis, October 18, 1940, 1, Agnes Inglis Papers, Box 14, Labadie Collection.

148 Shahn, "Love and Joy."

149 Avrich and Avrich, *Sasha and Emma*, 239; Avrich, *Modern School Movement*, 130, 177n72.

150 Avrich, *Anarchist Voices*, 185.

151 Shaw, *Whiteway*, 209.

152 Cores, *Personal Recollections*, 12.

153 Thorn to Ishill, November 25, 1943, 1, Joseph Ishill Papers, Box 4, Houghton Library.

154 Avrich, *Anarchist Voices*, 80.

155 Goldman, *Living My Live*, vol 1, 156; Avrich and Avrich, *Sasha and Emma*, 45.

156 Cores, *Personal Recollections*, 13.

157 Travaglio to Labadie, October 22, 1912, 2, Joseph A. Labadie Papers, Box 7, Labadie Collection; Avrich, *Anarchist Voices*, 160–62.

158 Tucker to Ishill, March 15, 1930, 1, Joseph Ishill Papers, Box 8, Houghton Library.

159 Becker, "John Turner," 12–13.

160 Passet, *Sex Radicals*, 117.

161 Colin Ward and Goodway, *Talking Anarchy*, 21.

162 Baile, *Josiah Warren*, 20.

163 Inglis to Bab, March 31, 1946, 1, Agnes Inglis Papers, Box 1, Labadie Collection.

164 Carlson, *Anarchism in Germany*, 78.

165 Rob Ray, *Beautiful Idea*, 19, 29; Cores, "William (Woolf) Wess Obituary."

166 Avrich, *Anarchist Voices*, 155; Zimmer, *Immigrants against the State*, 55.

167 Slifer and Greenhead, *Ross Winn*, 12.

168 Woodcock, *Letter to the Past*, 270.

169 Inglis to Fetz, August 2, 1942, 1, Agnes Inglis Papers, Box 7, Labadie Collection; Worden to Inglis, July 5, 1942, 1, Agnes Inglis Papers, Box 20, Labadie Collection.

170 Inglis to Fetz, October 8, 1944, 1, Agnes Inglis Papers, Box 7, Labadie Collection.

171 Goldman, "International Anarchist Congress," 244n33.

172 Sartin to Ishill, January 15, 1952, 2, and Zamboni to Ishill, April 10, 1952, 1, both in Joseph Ishill Additional Papers, Supplementary Box 4, Houghton Library.

173 De Agostini, "Milan's Anarchists." A printer named Zerboni, probably the same person, was also mentioned by Armando Borghi as owning a print shop called Guerra di Classe in Berlin; he was arrested with Virgilia D'Andrea and Armando Borghi. Rudolf Rocker Papers, File 410, International Institute of Social History.

Appendix B

1 Fulton, "Another View," 38.
2 Fulton to Labadie, January 15, 1920, Joseph Ishill Papers, Box 10, Houghton Library.
3 Hirschauge, "Tenth Anniversary."
4 Ishill to Rocker, October 15, 1956, 3, Rudolf Rocker Papers, File 123, International Institute of Social History.

LETTERS REFERENCED

Houghton Library, Harvard University

Abbott, Leonard, to Joseph Ishill. October 1, 1917. Joseph Ishill Papers, Box 1 [MS Am 1614].

Abbott, Leonard, to Joseph Ishill. January 6, 1934. Joseph Ishill Papers, Box 1 [MS Am 1614].

Abbott, Leonard, to Joseph Ishill. July 2, 1951. Joseph Ishill Papers, Box 1 [MS Am 1614].

Berkman, Alexander, to Joseph Ishill. September 30, 1932. Joseph Ishill Papers, Box 1 [MS Am 1614].

Calvert, Bruce, to Joseph Ishill. December 29, 1939. Joseph Ishill Papers, Box 1 [MS Am 1614].

Cherkerzov/Tcherkesoff, Varlam, to Joseph Ishill. December 2, 1923. Joseph Ishill Papers, Supplementary Box 2 [MS Am 1614.2].

Cooney, James P., to Theodore Schroeder. February 28, 1939. Joseph Ishill Additional Papers, Supplementary Box 5 [MS Am 1614.1].

de Cleyre, Voltairine, to Jo Labadie. September 11, 1905. Joseph Ishill Papers, Box 10 [MS Am 1614].

Duff, William, to Joseph Ishill. November 1, 1933. Joseph Ishill Papers, Box 2 [MS Am 1614].

Frank, Herman, to Joseph Ishill. January 19, 1930. Joseph Ishill Papers, Box 3 [MS Am 1614].

Fulton, Edward H., to John Basil Barnhill. March 11, 1925. Joseph Ishill Papers, Box 10 [MS Am 1614].

Fulton, Edward H., to Jo Labadie. January 15, 1920. Joseph Ishill Papers, Box 10 [ms Am 1614].

Fulton, Edward H., to Jo Labadie. September 14, 1924. Joseph Ishill Papers, Box 10 [ms Am 1614].

Goldman, Emma, to Joseph Ishill. November 29, 1934. Joseph Ishill Papers, Box 3 [ms Am 1614].

Inglis, Agnes, to Joseph Ishill. June 3, 1934. Joseph Ishill Papers, Box 4 [ms Am 1614].

Inglis, Agnes, to Joseph Ishill. October 28, 1935. Joseph Ishill Papers, Box 4 [ms Am 1614].

Ishill, Joseph, to Emma Goldman. July 16, 1930. Joseph Ishill Papers, Box 10 [ms Am 1614].

Ishill, Rose Freeman, to Grace Stone Coates. April 18, 1926. Joseph Ishill Papers, Box 5 [ms Am 1614].

Keell, Thomas, to Joseph Ishill. January 17, 1928. Joseph Ishill Papers, Box 4 [ms Am 1614].

Keell, Thomas, to Joseph Ishill. March 21, 1934. Joseph Ishill Papers, Box 4 [ms Am 1614].

Rabe, Henry, to Joseph Ishill. N.d. Joseph Ishill Papers, Supplementary Box 4 [ms Am 1614.1].

Ridge, Lola, to Rose Freeman Ishill. January 6, 1931. Joseph Ishill Papers, Box 6 [ms Am 1614].

Rocker, Rudolf, to Joseph Ishill. May 8, 1938. Joseph Ishill Papers, Box 6 [ms Am 1614].

Rocker, Rudolf, to Joseph Ishill. April 24, 1943. Joseph Ishill Papers, Box 6 [ms Am 1614].

Rocker, Rudolf to Joseph Ishill. May 6, 1949. Joseph Ishill Papers, Box 6 [ms Am 1614].

Rocker, Rudolf, to Joseph Ishill. February 3, 1950. Joseph Ishill Papers, Box 6 [ms Am 1614].

Rocker, Rudolf, to Joseph Ishill. January 22, 1951. Joseph Ishill Papers, Box 6 [ms Am 1614].

Rocker, Rudolf, to Joseph Ishill. November 21, 1951. Joseph Ishill Papers, Box 6 [ms Am 1614].

Rocker, Rudolf, to Joseph Ishill. August 9, 1952. Joseph Ishill Papers, Box 6 [ms Am 1614].

Rocker, Rudolf, to Joseph Ishill. October 12, 1953. Joseph Ishill Papers, Box 6 [ms Am 1614].

Rocker, Rudolf, to Joseph Ishill. December 26, 1954. Joseph Ishill Papers, Box 6 [ms Am 1614].

Rocker, Rudolf, to Joseph Ishill. November [no day], 1955. Joseph Ishill Papers, Box 6 [ms Am 1614].

Sartin, Max, to Joseph Ishill. June 28, 1933. Joseph Ishill Papers, Box 7 [ms Am 1614].

Sartin, Max, to Joseph Ishill. July 6, 1933. Joseph Ishill Papers, Box 7 [MS Am 1614].

Sartin, Max, to Joseph Ishill. September 26, 1945. Joseph Ishill Papers, Box 4 [MS Am 1614].

Sartin, Max, to Joseph Ishill. January 15, 1952. Joseph Ishill Additional Papers, Supplementary Box 4 [MS Am 1614.1].

Schwartz, Clarence Lee, to Joseph Ishill. n.d. Joseph Ishill Papers, Box 17 [MS Am 1614].

Starrett, Walter [Van Valkenberg], to Joseph Ishill. December 22, 1934. Joseph Ishill Papers, Box 9 [MS Am 1614].

Thorn, Martin, to Joseph Ishill. November 25, 1943. Joseph Ishill Papers, Box 4 [MS Am 1614].

Tucker, Benjamin, to Harry Bool. May 20, 1900. Joseph Ishill Papers, Box 12 [MS Am 1614].

Tucker, Benjamin, to Joseph Ishill. March 15, 1930. Joseph Ishill Papers, Box 8 [MS Am 1614].

Wolfe, Lilian, to Joseph Ishill, August 3, 1938. Joseph Ishill Papers, Box 4 [MS Am 1614].

Zamboni, Mammolo, to Joseph Ishill. April 10, 1952. Joseph Ishill Additional Papers, Supplementary Box 4 [MS Am 1614.1].

Joseph A. Labadie Collection, Special Collections Research Center, University of Michigan Library

Agostinelli, Diva, to Agnes Inglis. [Probably 1947]. Agnes Inglis Papers, Box 1.

Fox, Jay, to Jo Labadie. February 12, 1911. Joseph A. Labadie Papers, Box 3.

Fox, Jay, to Jo Labadie. May 4, 1911. Joseph A. Labadie Papers, Box 3.

Fulton, Edward H., to Jo Labadie. May 31, 1897. Joseph A. Labadie Papers, Box 3.

Fulton, Edward H., to Jo Labadie. November 15, 1897. Joseph A. Labadie Papers, Box 3.

Fulton, Edward H., to Jo Labadie. January 15, 1920. Joseph A. Labadie Papers, Box 3.

Fulton, Edward H., to Jo Labadie. November 22, 1923. Joseph A. Labadie Papers, Box 3.

Fulton, Edward H., to Jo Labadie. December 19, 1936. Joseph A. Labadie Papers, Box 3.

Goldman, Emma, to Agnes Inglis. February 22, 1931. Agnes Inglis Papers, Box 8.

Inglis, Agnes, to E. Armand. June 8, 1948. Agnes Inglis Papers, Box 1.

Inglis, Agnes, to Julius Bab. March 31, 1946. Agnes Inglis Papers, Box 1.

Inglis, Agnes, to Roger Baldwin. July 3, 1932. Agnes Inglis Papers, Box 1.

Inglis, Agnes, to Roger Baldwin. October 3, 1934. Agnes Inglis Papers, Box 1.

Inglis, Agnes, to Harry Barnard. April 21, 1941. Agnes Inglis Papers, Box 1.

Inglis, Agnes, to Fred Beal. August 26, 1938. Agnes Inglis Papers, Box 2.

Inglis, Agnes, to Belle Chaapel. November 22, 1942. Agnes Inglis Papers, Box 4.

Inglis, Agnes, to Ralph and Edith Chaplin. June 20, 1942. Agnes Inglis Papers, Box 4.

Inglis, Agnes, to Joanna Clevans. April 15, 1937. Agnes Inglis Papers, Box 4.

Inglis, Agnes, to Beatrice Fetz. August 2, 1942. Agnes Inglis Papers, Box 7.

Inglis, Agnes, to Beatrice Fetz. October 8, 1944. Agnes Inglis Papers, Box 7.

Inglis, Agnes, to Emma Goldman. March 19, 1925. Agnes Inglis Papers, Box 8.

Inglis, Agnes, to Joseph Ishill. June 3, 1934. Agnes Inglis Papers, Box 10.

Inglis, Agnes, to Joseph Ishill. October 28, 1935. Agnes Inglis Papers, Box 10.

Inglis, Agnes, to Bertha Johnson. January 18, 1946. Agnes Inglis Papers, Box 11.

Inglis, Agnes, to Thomas Keell. January 30, 1935. Agnes Inglis Papers, Box 12.

Inglis, Agnes, to Belle Maisel. May 3, 1937. Agnes Inglis Papers, Box 13.

Inglis, Agnes, to Max Metzkow. November 10, 1930. Agnes Inglis Papers, Box 14.

Inglis, Agnes, to Max Metzkow. June 26, 1940. Agnes Inglis Papers, Box 14.

Inglis, Agnes, to Fred Schulder. August 6, 1950. Agnes Inglis Papers, Box 16.

Inglis, Agnes, to Pearl Johnson Tucker. March 7, 1943. Agnes Inglis Papers, Box 19.

Inglis, Agnes, to Pearl Johnson Tucker. October 21, 1944. Agnes Inglis Papers, Box 19.

Inglis, Agnes, to Pearl Johnson Tucker. August 3, 1946. Agnes Inglis Papers, Box 19.

Inglis, Agnes, to Lilian Wolfe. October 27, 1946. Agnes Inglis Papers, Box 20.

Inglis, Agnes, to Lilian Wolfe. June 22, 1947. Agnes Inglis Papers, Box 20.

Inglis, Agnes, to Frank Worden. July 20, 1942. Agnes Inglis Papers, Box 20.

Ishill, Joseph, to Agnes Inglis, April 12, 1938. Agnes Inglis Papers, Box 10.

Ishill, Joseph, to Agnes Inglis. January 14, 1945. Agnes Inglis Papers, Box 10.

Johnson, Bertha, to Agnes Inglis. March 16, 1933. Agnes Inglis Papers, Box 11.

Johnson, Bertha, to Agnes Inglis. August 15, 1933. Agnes Inglis Papers, Box 11.

Johnson, Bertha to Agnes Inglis. August 21, 1933. Agnes Inglis Papers, Box 11.

Johnson, Bertha, to Agnes Inglis. September 7, 1933. Agnes Inglis Papers, Box 11.

Johnson, Bertha, to Agnes Inglis. November 8, 1933. Agnes Inglis Papers, Box 11.

Johnson, Bertha, to Agnes Inglis. December 21, 1933. Agnes Inglis Papers, Box 11.

Johnson, Bertha, to Agnes Inglis. January 28, 1934. Agnes Inglis Papers, Box 11.

Johnson, Bertha, to Agnes Inglis. February 15, 1934. Agnes Inglis Papers, Box 11.

Johnson, Bertha, to Agnes Inglis. March 7, 1934. Agnes Inglis Papers, Box 11.

Johnson, Bertha, to Agnes Inglis. March 14, 1934. Agnes Inglis Papers, Box 11.

Johnson, Bertha, to Agnes Inglis. March 22, 1934. Agnes Inglis Papers, Box 11.

Johnson, Bertha, to Agnes Inglis. April 1, 1934. Agnes Inglis Papers, Box 11.

Johnson, Bertha, to Agnes Inglis. April 16, 1934. Agnes Inglis Papers, Box 11.

Johnson, Bertha, to Agnes Inglis. October 11, 1934. Agnes Inglis Papers, Box 11.

Johnson, Bertha, to Agnes Inglis. December 14, 1934. Agnes Inglis Papers, Box 11.

Johnson, Bertha, to Agnes Inglis. May 23, 1935. Agnes Inglis Papers, Box 11.

Johnson, Bertha, to Agnes Inglis. July 5, 1935. Agnes Inglis Papers, Box 11.

Johnson, Bertha, to Agnes Inglis. August 9, 1935. Agnes Inglis Papers, Box 11.

Johnson, Bertha, to Agnes Inglis. December 12, 1935. Agnes Inglis Papers, Box 11.

Johnson, Bertha, to Agnes Inglis. January 14, 1936. Agnes Inglis Papers, Box 11.

Johnson, Bertha, to Agnes Inglis. November 27, 1938. Agnes Inglis Papers, Box 11.

Johnson, Bertha, to Agnes Inglis. March 4, 1941. Agnes Inglis Papers, Box 11.

Johnson, Bertha, to Agnes Inglis. March 25, 1941. Agnes Inglis Papers, Box 11.

Johnson, Bertha, to Agnes Inglis. November 28, 1941. Agnes Inglis Papers, Box 11.

Johnson, Bertha, to Agnes Inglis. December 5, 1941. Agnes Inglis Papers, Box 11.

Johnson, Bertha, to Agnes Inglis. September 6, 1942. Agnes Inglis Papers, Box 11.

Johnson, Bertha, to Agnes Inglis. January 20, 1943. Agnes Inglis Papers, Box 11.

Johnson, Bertha, to Agnes Inglis. September 7, 1943. Agnes Inglis Papers, Box 11.

Johnson, Bertha, to Agnes Inglis. May 15, 1945. Agnes Inglis Papers, Box 11.

Johnson, Bertha, to Agnes Inglis. December 12, 1945. Agnes Inglis Papers, Box 11.

Johnson, Bertha, to Agnes Inglis. December 29, 1945. Agnes Inglis Papers, Box 11.

Johnson, Bertha, to Agnes Inglis. July 7, 1947. Agnes Inglis Papers, Box 11.

Johnson, Bertha, to Agnes Inglis. September 28, 1948. Agnes Inglis Papers, Box 11.

Johnson, Bertha, to Agnes Inglis. February 27, 1949. Agnes Inglis Papers, Box 11.

Johnson, Bertha, to Agnes Inglis. February 28, 1950. Agnes Inglis, Papers Box 11.

Johnson, Bertha, to Agnes Inglis. June 1, 1950. Agnes Inglis Papers, Box 11.

Johnson, Bertha, to Agnes Inglis. November 22, 1950. Agnes Inglis Papers, Box 11.

Keell, Thomas, to Agnes Inglis. March 22, 1930. Agnes Inglis Papers, Box 12.

Keell, Thomas, to Agnes Inglis. December 11, 1931. Agnes Inglis Papers, Box 12.

Keell, Thomas, to Jo Labadie. October 19, 1922. Joseph A. Labadie Papers, Box 4.

Metzkow, Max, to Agnes Inglis. July 25, 1940. Agnes Inglis Papers, Box 14.

Metzkow, Max, to Agnes Inglis. October 10, 1940. Agnes Inglis Papers, Box 14.

Metzkow, Max, to Agnes Inglis. October 18, 1940. Agnes Inglis Papers, Box 14.

Metzkow, Max, to Agnes Inglis. May 26, 1945. Agnes Inglis Papers, Box 14.

Rogers, Dorothy, to Agnes Inglis. May 14, 1946. Agnes Inglis Papers, Box 22.

Scheltema, Anna, to Agnes Inglis. November 18, 1950. Agnes Inglis Papers, Box 16.

Schwartz, Anna, to Agnes Inglis. August 24, 1951. Agnes Inglis Papers, Box 16.

Travaglio, Eugene, to Jo Labadie. October 22, 1912. Joseph A. Labadie Papers, Box 7.

Tucker, Pearl Johnson, to Agnes Inglis. February 27, 1942. Agnes Inglis Papers, Box 19.

Tucker, Pearl Johnson, to Agnes Inglis. May 27, 1942. Agnes Inglis Papers, Box 11.

Tucker, Pearl Johnson, to Agnes Inglis. December 24, 1942. Agnes Inglis Papers, Box 19.

Tucker, Pearl Johnson, to Agnes Inglis. November 28, 1943. Agnes Inglis Papers, Box 11.

Tucker, Pearl Johnson, to Agnes Inglis. December 4, 1946. Agnes Inglis Papers, Box 19.

Wolfe, Lilian, to Agnes Inglis. March 26, 1939. Agnes Inglis Papers, Box 20.

Wolfe, Lilian, to Agnes Inglis. May 23, 1946. Agnes Inglis Papers, Box 20.

Wolfe, Lilian, to Agnes Inglis. August 22, 1946. Agnes Inglis Papers, Box 20.

Wolfe, Lilian, to Agnes Inglis. December 14, 1946. Agnes Inglis Papers, Box 20.

Wolfe, Lilian, to Agnes Inglis. September 2, 1947. Agnes Inglis Papers, Box 20.

Wolfe, Lilian, to Agnes Inglis. September 10, 1947. Agnes Inglis Papers, Box 20.

Worden, Frank, to Agnes Inglis. July 5, 1942. Agnes Inglis Papers, Box 20.

Derzanski, Barnett, to Thomas Keell. September 9, 1928. Freedom Archives, File 397.
Isca, Valerio and Ida, to Rudolf Rocker. January 12, 1955. Rudolf Rocker Papers, File 123.
Ishill, Joseph, to Rudolf Rocker. December 24, 1937. Rudolf Rocker Papers, File 123.
Ishill, Joseph, to Rudolf Rocker. March 22, 1943. Rudolf Rocker Papers, File 123.
Ishill, Joseph, to Rudolf Rocker. [Month illegible], 1944. Rudolf Rocker Papers, File 123.
Ishill, Joseph, to Rudolf Rocker. August 12, 1945. Rudolf Rocker Papers, File 123.
Ishill, Joseph, to Rudolf Rocker. February 14, 1949. Rudolf Rocker Papers, File 123.
Ishill, Joseph, to Rudolf Rocker. July 18, 1950. Rudolf Rocker Papers, File 123.
Ishill, Joseph, to Rudolf Rocker. August 15, 1950. Rudolf Rocker Papers, File 123.
Ishill, Joseph, to Rudolf Rocker. February 5, 1951. Rudolf Rocker Papers, File 123.
Ishill, Joseph, to Rudolf Rocker. April 24, 1953. Rudolf Rocker Papers, File 123.
Ishill, Joseph, to Rudolf Rocker. June 18, 1953. Rudolf Rocker Papers, File 123.
Ishill, Joseph, to Rudolf Rocker. October 8, 1953. Rudolf Rocker Papers, File 123.
Ishill, Joseph, to Rudolf Rocker. October 15, 1953. Rudolf Rocker Papers, File 123.
Ishill, Joseph, to Rudolf Rocker. January 12, 1956. Rudolf Rocker Papers, File 123.
Ishill, Joseph, to Rudolf Rocker. April 21, 1956. Rudolf Rocker Papers, File 123.
Ishill, Joseph, to Rudolf Rocker. October 2, 1956. Rudolf Rocker Papers, File 123.
Ishill, Joseph, to Rudolf Rocker. October 15, 1956. Rudolf Rocker Papers, File 123.
Ishill, Joseph, to Rudolf Rocker. July 21, 1957. Rudolf Rocker Papers, File 123.
Kelly, Harry, to Thomas Keell. April 9, 1911. Freedom Archives, File 403.
Owen, William, to Thomas Keell. March 2, 1928. William Charles Owen Papers, 4327.5, File 2.

Paul Avrich Collection, Rare Book and Special Collections Division, Library of Congress, Washington, DC

de Cleyre, Voltairine, to Alexander Berkman. August 7, 1906. Avrich Collection, Box 3, Folder 1.
Rocker, Rudolf, to James Dick, Mohegan Colony. April 1, 1956. Avrich Collection, Box 3, Folder 6.

BIBLIOGRAPHY

Abbott, Leonard D. "A Priestess of Pity and of Vengeance." *Mother Earth* 7, no. 7 (September 1912): 230–32.

Abbott, Leonard D. "Voltairine de Cleyre's Posthumous Book." *Mother Earth* 9, no. 8 (October 1914): 269.

Acklesberg, Martha. *Free Women of Spain: Anarchism and the Struggle for the Emancipation of Women.* Oakland, CA: AK Press, 1991.

Acrata, Liprepensador, and Paul Sharkey. "Antonia Fontanillas Borrás (1917–2014)." *KSL: Bulletin of the Kate Sharpley Library*, no. 80 (October 2014). https://www.katesharpleylibrary.net/547f75.

Addis, Henry. "The History of the Firebrand." *The Firebrand* 2, no. 5 (March 8, 1896): 3–4.

Addis, Henry. "Look at Our Postoffice [*sic*] System!!" *Free Society*, no. 2 (November 21, 1897): 1–2.

A. G. "The Annexation of the Hawaiian Islands and Contract Slavery." *Free Society*, no. 36 (July 17, 1898): 5.

Ahia, Māhealani. "Mālama Mauna: An Ethics of Care Culture and Kuleana." *Biography* 43, no. 3 (2020): 607–12.

Ahmed, Sara. "Orientations Matter." In *New Materialisms: Ontology, Agency, and Politics*, edited by Diane Coole and Samantha Frost, 234–57. Durham, NC: Duke University Press, 2010.

Altman, Janet Gurkin. *Epistolarity: Approaches to a Form.* Columbus: Ohio State University Press, 1982.

American Amateur Press Association. "Resources for Letterpress Printers." Accessed April 29, 2022. http://www.aapainfo.org/lpress.html.

"American Notes." *Freedom* 13, no. 137 (April 1899): 26–27.

Anarchist FAQ Editorial Collective. "The Anarchist FAQ Version 15.4 (17-Mar-2020)." Anarchist Library, March 17, 2020. https://theanarchistlibrary.org /library/the-anarchist-faq-editorial-collective-an-anarchist-faq-full.

"Anarchist Lecturers." *Free Society*, no. 28 (May 22, 1898): 8.

"Anarchist Newspaper Offices Destroyed." *Freedom* 24, no. 255 (July 1910): 49.

Anderson, Benedict. *Imagined Communities: Reflections on the Origin and Spread of Nationalism*. London: Verso, 1983.

Anderson, Benedict. *Under Three Flags: Anarchism and the Anti-colonial Imagination*. London: Verso, 2007.

Anderson, Carlotta. *All-American Anarchist: Joseph A. Labadie and the Labor Movement*. Detroit: Wayne State University Press, 1998.

Anderson, William C. *The Nation on No Map*. Chico, CA: AK Press, 2021.

"Another Little War." *Freedom* 1, no. 6 (March 1887): 20–21.

Antliff, Allan. "Agitating Beauty: The Anarchist Politics of the Book." In *Mutual Aid: An Illuminated Factor of Evolution*, by Peter Kropotkin, 254–69. Oakland, CA: PM Press, 2021.

"Antoni Pellicer Pariare." Real Academia de la Historia. Accessed June 26, 2022. https://dbe.rah.es/biografias/31683/antoni-pellicer-paraire.

"An Apology." *Spain and the World* 2, no. 37 (July 15, 1938): 2.

Aubert, Danielle. *The Detroit Printing Co-op: The Politics of the Joy of Printing*. Los Angeles: Inventory Press, 2019.

Austin, Kate. "Kropotkin's Autobiography." *Free Society* 6, no. 1 (November 19, 1899): 2.

Avrich, Paul. *An American Anarchist: The Life of Voltairine de Cleyre*. Oakland, CA: AK Press, 2018.

Avrich, Paul. "Anarchist Lives." In *Fighters for Anarchism: Mollie Steimer and Senya Fleshin*, edited by Abe Bluestein, 4–20. London: Libertarian Publications, 1983.

Avrich, Paul. *Anarchist Voices: An Oral History of Anarchism in America*. Oakland, CA: AK Press, 2005.

Avrich, Paul. *The Haymarket Tragedy*. Princeton, NJ: Princeton University Press, 1984.

Avrich, Paul. "An Interview with Oriole Tucker." In *Benjamin R. Tucker and the Champions of Liberty*, edited by Michael E. Coughlin, Charles H. Hamilton, and Mark A. Sullivan. Saint Paul: Coughlin and Sullivan, 1987. https://uncletaz .com/liberty/oriole.html.

Avrich, Paul. "Kropotkin in America." *International Review of Social History* 25, no. 1 (April 1980): 1–34.

Avrich, Paul. *The Modern School Movement: Anarchism and Education*. Princeton, NJ: Princeton University Press, 1980.

Avrich, Paul, and Karen Avrich. *Sasha and Emma: The Anarchist Odyssey of Alexander Berkman and Emma Goldman*. Cambridge, MA: Harvard University Press, 2012.

Baile, William. *Josiah Warren: The First American Anarchist*. Boston: Small, Maynard, 1906.

Banks, Colin. *True to Type: Introducing Letterpress Printing and the Works of Small Presses*. London: Crafts Council Gallery, 1994.

Bantman, Constance. *The French Anarchists in London, 1880–1914: Exile and Transnationalism in the First Globalisation.* Liverpool: Liverpool University Press, 2013.

Bantman, Constance. "Jean Grave and French Anarchism: A Relational Approach (1870s–1914)." *International Research on Social History* 62 (2017): 451–77.

Baron, Ava. "Contested Terrain Revisited: Technology and Gender Definitions of Work in the Printing Industry, 1850–1920." In *Women, Work and Technology: Transformations*, edited by Barbara D. Wright, Myra Marx Feree, Gail O. Mellow, Linda H. Lewis, Maria-Luz Daza Sampler, Robert Asher, and Kathleen Claspell, 58–83. Ann Arbor: University of Michigan Press, 1987.

Baron, Ava. "Questions of Gender: Deskilling and Demasculinization in the U.S. Printing Industry, 1830–1915." *Gender and History* 1, no. 2 (Summer 1989): 178–99.

Baron, Ava. "Women and the Making of the American Working Class: A Study of the Proletarianization of Printers." *Review of Radical Political Economics* 14, no. 3 (Fall 1982): 23–42.

Barton, Mary S. "The Global War on Anarchism: The United States and International Anarchist Terrorism, 1898–1904." *Diplomatic History* 39, no. 22 (April 2015): 303–30.

Basin, Lyuba. "From the Ashes: The Phoenix Quarterly." J. Willard Marriott Library blog, University of Utah. Accessed April 29, 2022. https://blog.lib.utah.edu/from-the-ashes-the-phoenix-quarterly/.

Beauchamp, Joan. "Fight for a Free Press." *Freedom* 32, no. 354 (November 1918): 63–64.

Becker, Heiner. "John Turner." In *Freedom: A Hundred Years, October 1886 to October 1986*, edited by the editors of *Freedom*, 12–13. London: Freedom Press, 1986.

Becker, Heiner. "Notes on *Freedom* and the Freedom Press, 1886–1928." *The Raven* 1 (1986): 4–24.

Becker, Heiner. "Thomas Keell 1866–1938." In *Freedom: A Hundred Years, October 1886 to October 1986*, edited by the editors of *Freedom*, 20–23. London: Freedom Press, 1986.

Becker, Heiner, and Nicolas Walter. "Freedom: People and Places." In *Freedom: A Hundred Years, October 1886 to October 1986*, edited by the editors of *Freedom*, 4–7. London: Freedom Press, 1986.

Beins, Agatha. *Liberation in Print: Feminist Periodicals and Social Movement Identity.* Athens: University of Georgia Press, 2017.

Bekken, Jon. "The First Anarchist Daily Newspaper: *The Chicagoer Arbeiter-Zeitung*." *Anarchist Studies* 3, no. 1 (1995): 3–23.

Ben-Moshe, Liat, Anthony J. Nocelle, and A. J. Withers. "Queer-Cripping Anarchism: Intersections and Reflections on Anarchism, Queerness, and Disability." In *Queering Anarchism: Addressing and Undressing Power and Desire*, edited by C. B. Daring, J. Rogue, Deric Shannon, and Abbey Volcano, 207–20. Oakland, CA: AK Press, 2012.

Bennett, Jane. *Influx and Efflux: Writing Up with Walt Whitman.* Durham, NC: Duke University Press, 2020.

Bennett, Jane. *Vibrant Matter: A Political Ecology of Things*. Durham, NC: Duke University Press, 2010.

Bennett, Jane. "Vital Materiality and Non-human Agency: An Interview with Jane Bennett." By Gulshan Khan. *Contemporary Political Theory* 8 (December 2008): 90–105.

Berkman, Alexander, Henry Bauer, Carl Nold, Miriam Brody, and Bonnie Buettner. *Prison Blossoms: Anarchist Voices from the American Past*. Cambridge, MA: Belknap Press of Harvard University Press, 2011.

Best, Stephen, and Saidiya Hartman. "Fugitive Justice." *Representations* 92 (Fall 2005): 1–15.

Bey, Marquis. *Anarcho-Blackness: Notes toward a Black Anarchism*. Chico, CA: AK Press, 2020.

Black Rose Anarchist Federation. *Black Anarchism: A Reader*. Accessed October 16, 2021. https://www.blackrosefed.org/wp-content/uploads/2016/02/Black-Anarchism-A-Reader-4.pdf.

Bliss, Anthony. "William Morris and Book Design." In *William Morris: The Sanford and Helen Berger Collection*, edited by Anthony Bliss and Margaretta M. Lovell, 32–47. Berkeley, CA: Bancroft Library and University Art Museum, 1984.

"The Blood of the Prophets." *Mother Earth* 1, no. 12 (February 1907): 41–43.

Bolt, Christine. *The Women's Movement in the United States and Britain from the 1790s to the 1920s*. Amherst: University of Massachusetts Press, 1993.

Bookfair 2020. "Statement to Announce London Bookfair 2020." Accessed October 16, 2021. https://freedomnews.org.uk/statement-to-announce-london-bookfair-2020/.

"Books to Be Had through Mother Earth." *Mother Earth* 1, no. 5 (May 1906): 62–63.

Boole, Mary Everest. "Correspondence." *Freedom* 9, no. 97 (September 1895): 43.

Boole, Mary Everest. "Should Decorative Work Be a Drudgery?" *Freedom* 9, no. 96 (August 1895): 20–21.

Boos, Florence S. "Introduction to the Kelmscott Press." William Morris Archive. Accessed October 16, 2021. https://morrisarchive.lib.uiowa.edu/exhibits/show/bookarts/kelmscottpress/bookarts-kp-introduction.

Born, Helena. "The Commemoration in Boston." *Free Society* 6, no. 55 (December 2, 1900): 3.

Bottici, Chiara. *Anarchafeminism*. London: Bloomsbury Academic, 2022.

Bottici, Chiara. "Anarchafeminism: Towards an Ontology of the Transindividual." Paper presented at UNESCO Night of Philosophy, Paris, November 16, 2018. Public Seminar, December 2, 2019. https://publicseminar.org/2019/12/anarchafeminism/.

Boyer, Richard O., and Hebert M. Morais. *Labor's Untold Story*. New York: Cameron and Associations, 1955.

Bradford, Walter. "Fizzboomski the Anarchist." Comics 1.0, Barnacle Press. Accessed April 29, 2022. https://www.barnaclepress.com/comic/Fizzboomski%20the%20Anarchist/.

Bridgeland, Gina, and Bob Jones. "John Taylor Caldwell 1911–2007." *KSL: Bulletin of the Kate Sharpley Library*, no. 49 (January 2007). https://www.katesharpleylibrary.net/66t20c.

Brodie, Morris. "Rebel Youths: English-Language Anarchist Periodicals of the Great Depression, 1932–1939." *Radical Periodicals* 3, no. 1 (2018): 1–18.

Broeck, Sabine. "Enslavement as Regime of Western Modernity: Re-reading Gender Studies Epistemology through Black Feminist Critique." *Gender Forum* 22 (2008): 3–18.

Brown, Bill. "Thing Theory." *Critical Inquiry* 28 (August 2001): 1–23.

Brown, Marian C. *Joseph Ishill and the Oriole Press*. Berkeley Heights, NJ: Oriole, 1960.

Brown, William Thurston, ed. *The Modern School Magazine* 3, no. 8 (January 1917).

Burke, H. T. "Anarchism and Art." *Freedom*, no. 68 (January 1936): 2–3.

Burr, Christina. "Defending 'The Art Preservative': Class and Gender Relations in the Printing Trades Unions, 1850–1914." *Labor / Le Travail* 31 (Spring 1993): 47–73.

Butler, Judith. *Gender Trouble: Feminism and the Subversion of Identity*. New York: Routledge, 1990.

Buttá, Fausto. "Anarchist Theories and Practices in Milan: A History of the Milanese Anarchist Movement, 1870–1926." PhD diss., University of Western Australia, 2011. https://api.research-repository.uwa.edu.au/ws/portalfiles/portal/3330576/Butta_Fausto_2011.pdf.

Caldwell, John. *With Fate Conspire: Memoirs of a Glasgow Seafarer and Anarchist*. West Yorkshire, UK: Northern Herald Books, 1999.

Cantarow, Ellen, Susan G. O'Malley, and Sharon Strom. *Moving the Mountain: Women Working for Social Change*. New York: Feminist Press, 1980.

Cantine, Holley, and Dachine Rainer, eds. *Prison Etiquette: The Convict's Compendium of Useful Information*. Carbondale: Southern Illinois University Press, 2001.

Carby, Hazel V. *Imperial Intimacies: A Tale of Two Islands*. London: Verso, 2019.

Carlson, Andrew R. *Anarchism in Germany*. Vol. 1, *The Early Years*. Metuchen, NJ: Scarecrow, 1972.

"Caruso and the Convicts." *Freedom* 26, no. 289 (May 1913): 33.

Case, Emalani. "Ea: Lessons in Breath, Life and Sovereignty from Mauna Kea." *Biography* 43, no. 3 (2020): 568–74.

Castañeda, Christopher. "Anarchism and the End of Empire: José Cayetano Campos, Labor, and Cuba Libre." In *Writing Revolution: Hispanic Anarchism in the United States*, edited by Christopher Castañeda and Montse Feu, 81–98. Urbana: University of Illinois Press, 2019.

Castañeda, Christopher. "Times of Propaganda and Struggle: *El Despertar* and Brooklyn's Spanish Anarchists, 1890–1905." In *Radical Gotham: Anarchism in New York City from Schwab's Saloon to Occupy Wall Street*, edited by Tom Goyens, 75–99. Urbana: University of Illinois Press, 2017.

Castañeda, Christopher, and Montse Feu. "Introduction: Hispanic Anarchist Print Culture: Writing from Below." In *Writing Revolution: Hispanic Anarchism in the United States*, edited by Christopher Castañeda and Montse Feu, 14–32. Urbana: University of Illinois Press, 2019.

Chesterton, G. K. *The Man Who Was Thursday*. London: Modern Library, 2001.

Church of Jesus Christ of Latter-Day Saints. "Navoo Expositor." Accessed October 18, 2021. https://www.churchofjesuschrist.org/study/history/topics/nauvoo -expositor?lang=eng.

Cockburn, Cynthia. *Brothers: Male Dominance and Technological Change*. London: Pluto, 1984.

Cockburn, Cynthia. "The Material of Male Power." *Feminist Review* 9 (October 1981): 41–58.

Codina, Joan Casanovas L. "Pedro Esteve (Barcelona 1865–Weehauken, N.J. 1925): A Catalan Anarchist in the United States." *Catalan Review* 5, no. 1 (July 1991): 57–77.

Cohn, Jesse. "What Is Anarchist Literary Theory?" *Anarchist Studies* 15, no. 2 (2007): 115–31.

Cole, Peter. *Ben Fletcher: The Life and Times of a Black Wobbly*. Oakland, CA: PM Press, 2021.

Colebrook, Frank. *William Morris, Master-Printer*. Lecture, November 27, 1886, Printing School, St. Bride Foundation, Institute of London. Edited with a new introduction by William S. Peterson. Wood engraving by John De Pol. Council Bluffs, IA: Yellow Barn, 1989.

Collins, Patricia Hill. "Intersectionality's Definitional Dilemmas." *Annual Review of Sociology* 41 (2015): 1–20.

Composing Room Memories: Letters from Eminent Americans concerning the Advantages and Satisfactions Gained from an Acquaintance with Type. San Francisco: Red Tower, 1938.

Connolly, William. *The Fragility of Things: Self-Organizing Processes, Neoliberal Fantasies, and Democratic Activism*. Durham, NC: Duke University Press, 2013.

Coole, Diana, and Samantha Frost. "Introducing the New Materialisms." In *New Materialisms: Ontology, Agency, and Politics*, edited by Diane Coole and Samantha Frost, 1–43. Durham, NC: Duke University Press, 2010.

Cooney, Blanche. *In My Own Sweet Time: An Autobiography*. Athens, OH: Swallow, 1993.

"Copy of Telegram from the Printers." *The Adult* 1, no. 6 (January 1898): 175.

Cores, George. *Personal Recollections of the Anarchist Past*. London: Kate Sharpley Library, 1992. Originally written 1947.

Cores, George. "William (Woolf) Wess Obituary." *Direct Action* 1, no. 10 (August 1946). https://theanarchistlibrary.org/library/george-cores-william-woolf -wess-obituary-en.

Cornell, Andrew. "A New Anarchism Emerges, 1940–1954." *Journal for the Study of Radicalism* 5, no. 1 (Spring 2011): 105–31.

Cornell, Andrew. "New Wind: The Why? Resistance Group and the Roots of Contemporary Anarchism, 1942–1954." In *Radical Gotham: Anarchism in New*

York City from Schwab's Saloon to Occupy Wall Street, edited by Tom Goyens, 122–41. Urbana: University of Illinois Press, 2017.

Cornell, Andrew. *Unruly Equality: U.S. Anarchism in the Twentieth Century.* Oakland: University of California Press, 2016.

Cornum, Lou. "Fight for the Future." *New Inquiry*, August 2, 2019. https://thenewinquiry.com/fight-for-the-future/?fbclid=IwAR1t5lgdDGfYdo-PMqVkgKE7G380WyfLqmC_fE1PCgEc5RSJU82vsu5fGE.

Cott, Nancy. *The Grounding of Modern Feminism.* New Haven, CT: Yale University Press, 1987.

Daniels, Viroqua. "A Few Significant Facts." *Free Society*, no. 1 (November 14, 1897): 1–2.

Daniels, Viroqua. "Government." *Free Society* 6, no. 31 (June 17, 1900): 1.

Daniels, Viroqua. "To Those." *The Firebrand*, April 5, 1896, 3.

Daring, C. B., J. Rogue, Deric Shannon, and Abbey Volcano, eds. *Queering Anarchism: Addressing and Undressing Power and Desire.* Oakland, CA: AK Press, 2012.

Davaldès, Manuel. "Louis Moreau." In *The Oriole Press: A Bibliography*, edited by Joseph Ishill, 311–23. Berkeley Heights, NJ: Oriole, 1953.

Davidson, Rebecca Warren. *Unseen Hands: Women Printers, Binders, and Book Designers.* Princeton, NJ: Princeton University Press, 2005.

de Agostini, Mauro. "Milan's Anarchists in the Fight for Liberation." Translated by Paul Sharkey. *Lettera ai Compagni* 17, no. 7 (July 1985) and no. 8 (August 1985). https://www.katesharpleylibrary.net/jq2cw6.

"Death of Anselmo Lorenzo." *Freedom* 29, no. 309 (January 1915): 2–3.

de Cleyre, Voltairine. "American Notes." *Freedom* 11, no. 120 (November 1897): 69.

de Cleyre, Voltairine. "Between the Living and the Dead." *Mother Earth* 1, no. 8 (October 1906): 58–61.

de Cleyre, Voltairine. "A Reading Course for Anarchists." *Free Society* 6, no. 46 (September 20, 1900): 1.

de Cleyre, Voltairine. "Where the White Rose Died." *Mother Earth* 3, no. 1 (March 1908): 44–48.

DeLanda, Manuel. *A New Philosophy of Society: Assemblage Theory and Social Complexity.* London: Continuum, 2006.

Deleuze, Gilles, and Félix Guattari. *A Thousand Plateaus: Capitalism and Schizophrenia.* Translated by Brian Massumi. Minneapolis: University of Minnesota Press, 1987.

Deleuze, Gilles, and Félix Guattari. *What Is Philosophy?* Translated by Hugh Tomlinson and Graham Burchell. New York: Columbia University Press, 1994.

de Man, Paul. "The Epistemology of Metaphor." *Critical Inquiry* 5, no. 1 (Autumn 1978): 13–30.

Dinshaw, Carolyn. *How Soon Is Now? Medieval Texts, Amateur Readers, and the Queerness of Time.* Durham, NC: Duke University Press, 2012.

"The Discussion of the Sex Question." *Freedom* 12, no. 128 (July 1898): 43.

Dolce Press. "Letterpress Printing Vocational Film (1947)." YouTube, June 2, 2008. Video, 10:40. https://www.youtube.com/watch?v=bPCiWiLu-W4.

Dolgoff, Sam, ed. *The Anarchist Collectives: Workers Self-Management in the Spanish Revolution.* New York: Free Life Editions, 1974.

Dolgoff, Sam. *Fragments: A Memoir.* Cambridge, UK: Refract, 1986.

"Dr. Bertha Johnson of Granville Ctr. Dies at Ossining." *The Daily Review,* Towanda, PA (February 3, 1958): 2.

Drinnon, Richard. *Rebel in Paradise: A Biography of Emma Goldman.* Boston: Beacon, 1970.

Drinnon, Richard, and Anna Marie Drinnon, eds. *Nowhere at Home: Letters from Exile of Emma Goldman and Alexander Berkman.* New York: Schocken Books, 1975.

Drucker, Johanna. "Letterpress Language: Typography as a Medium for the Visual Representation of Language." *Leonardo* 17, no. 1 (1984): 8–16.

Duff, William. "Voltairine de Cleyre's Tour in Scotland." *Freedom* 11, no. 120 (November 1897): 69.

Duffy, Patrick. *The Skilled Compositor, 1850–1914: An Aristocrat among Working Men.* Aldershot, UK: Ashgate, 2000.

Dumartheray, Francis. "A Letter from an Old Comrade." In *Peter Kropotkin: The Rebel, Thinker and Humanitarian,* edited by Joseph Ishill, 129. Berkeley Heights, NJ: Free Spirit, 1923.

Dumont Press Graphix. 50th Anniversary Website. Accessed October 16, 2021. https://dumontpressgraphix.ca/home.

Ehrlich, Carol. "Socialism, Anarchism and Feminism." In *Quiet Rumors: An Anarcha-feminist Reader,* edited by the Dark Star Collective, 41–50. San Francisco: AK Press, 2002.

Eichhorn, Kate. *The Archival Turn in Feminism: Outrage in Order.* Philadelphia: Temple University Press, 2013.

Eichner, Carolyn. "Language of Imperialism, Language of Liberation: Louise Michel and the Kanak-French Colonial Encounter." *Feminist Studies* 45, no. 2 (2019): 377–408.

Ellis, Havelock. *The Unpublished Letters of Havelock Ellis to Joseph Ishill.* Berkeley Heights, NJ: Oriole, 1954.

Emma Goldman Papers Project. "Scanned Documents." Emma Goldman Papers. Accessed April 29, 2022. https://www.lib.berkeley.edu/goldman /PrimarySources/scanneddocuments.html.

Enckell, Marianne. "The School and the Barricade." Translated by Douglas Cook. *Progressive Librarian,* special supplement to no. 16 (Fall 1999): 11–17.

Encyclopedia.com. "Romero Rosa, Ramón 1863–1907." Accessed October 18, 2021. https://www.encyclopedia.com/humanities/encyclopedias-almanacs -transcripts-and-maps/romero-rosa-ramon-1863-1907.

Ernst, Wolfgang. "Media Archaeology: Method and Machine versus History and Narrative of Media." In *Media Archaeology: Approaches, Applications, and Implications,* edited by Erkki Huhtamo and Jussi Parikka, 239–55. Berkeley: University of California Press, 2011.

Essente, Hali. "The Revival of Letterpress Printing." Slow Living, April 22, 2020. http://www.slowlivingtoday.com/2015/home-garden/revival-letterpress-printing/.

"Estate of Josephine Tilton (Executor—Carrie Denton)," in Carrie D. Denton Papers; Legal Papers, 1868–1958, Box 6, Wellesley Historical Society, Wellesley, MA. Accessed June 27, 2022. https://wellesleyhistoricalsociety.org/.

Evren, Süreyyya. "There Ain't No Black in the Anarchist Flag! Race, Ethnicity and Anarchism." In *The Continuum Companion to Anarchism*, edited by Ruth Kinna, 299–314. London: Continuum Books, 2012.

Falk, Candace, ed. *Emma Goldman: A Documentary History of the American Years*. Vol 4, *Democracy Disarmed, 1917–1919*. Stanford, CA: Stanford University Press, forthcoming.

Falk, Candace. "Into the Spotlight." In *Emma Goldman: A Documentary History of the American Years*, vol. 3, *Light and Shadows, 1910–1916*, edited by Candace Falk and Barry Pateman, 1–171. Stanford, CA: Stanford University Press, 2012.

Falk, Candace. "Raising Her Voices." In *Emma Goldman: A Documentary History of the American Years*, vol. 2, *Making Speech Free, 1902–1909*, edited by Candace Falk, Barry Pateman, and Jessica Moran, 1–80. Berkeley: University of California Press, 2005.

Falk, Candace, and Barry Pateman, eds. *Emma Goldman: A Documentary History of the American Years*, vol. 3, *Light and Shadows, 1910–1916*. Stanford, CA: Stanford University Press, 2012.

Falk, Candace, Barry Pateman, and Jessica Moran, eds. *Emma Goldman: A Documentary History of the American Years*, vol. 1, *Made for America, 1890–1901*. Berkeley: University of California Press, 2003.

Falk, Candace, Barry Pateman, and Jessica Moran, eds. *Emma Goldman: A Documentary History of the American Years*, vol. 2, *Making Speech Free, 1902–1909*. Berkeley: University of California Press, 2005.

Farmelant, Randie. "End of an Era: Will the Feminist Bookstore Soon Be a Thing of the Past?" *Off Our Backs* 33, no. 5/6 (May–June 2003): 18–22.

Farrow, Lynn. "Feminism as Anarchism." In *Quiet Rumors: An Anarcha-feminist Reader*, edited by the Dark Star Collective, 15–20. San Francisco: AK Press, 2002.

Ferguson, Kathy E. "Anarchist Printers and Presses: Material Circuits of Power." *Political Theory* 42, no. 4 (August 2014): 391–414.

Ferguson, Kathy E. "Anarchist Women and the Politics of Walking." *Political Research Quarterly* 70, no. 4 (2017): 708–19.

Ferguson, Kathy E. "Assemblages of Anarchists: Political Aesthetics in *Mother Earth*." *Journal of Modern Periodical Studies* 4, no. 2 (2014): 171–94.

Ferguson, Kathy E. *Emma Goldman: Political Thinking in the Streets*. Lanham, MD: Rowman and Littlefield, 2011.

Ferretti, Federico, Gerónimo Barrera de la Torre, Anthony Ince, and Francisco Toro. Introduction to *Historical Geographies of Anarchism: Early Critical Geographers and Present-Day Scientific Challenges*, edited by Federico Ferretti,

Gerónimo Barrera de la Torre, Anthony Ince, and Francisco Toro, 1–4. London: Routledge, 2018.

Fessenden, Sarah. "'We Just Wanna Warm Some Bellies': Food Not Bombs, Anarchism, and Recycling Wasted Food for Protest." PhD diss., University of British Columbia, 2017. https://open.library.ubc.ca/cIRcle/collections/ubctheses/24 /items/1.0343605.

Find a Grave. "Dr Bertha Florence Johnson." March 10, 2012. https://www .findagrave.com/memorial/86533341/bertha-florence-johnson.

Finkelstein, David. *Moveable Types: Roving Creative Printers of the Victorian World*. Oxford: Oxford University Press, 2018.

Fisher, Paul. *An Uncommon Gentry*. Columbia: Linotype School, School of Journalism, University of Missouri, 1952.

Fishman, William. *East End Jewish Radicals, 1875–1914*. London: Duckworth, 1975.

Flores, Rebecca. "Socialist Newspapers and Periodicals 1900–1920." Mapping American Social Movements through the Twentieth Century. Accessed August 2, 2021. https://depts.washington.edu/moves/SP_map-newspapers.shtml.

Flynn, Elizabeth G. *The Rebel Girl: An Autobiography*. New York: International Publishing, 1973.

Folsom, Ed. "Whitman Making Book/Books Making Whitman: A Catalog and Commentary." Walt Whitman Archive, Obermann Center for Advanced Studies, University of Iowa, 2005. https://whitmanarchive.org/criticism/current /anc.00150.html.

Food Not Bombs. "People of Color Caucus." March 28, 2008. http://www .foodnotbombs.net/people_of_color.html.

Formax Printing Solutions. "Printing Lingo: What Does Registration Mean?" Accessed October 18, 2021. https://www.formaxprinting.com/blog/2010/04 /printing-lingo-what-does-registration-mean/.

Foucault, Michel. "Nietzsche, Genealogy, History." In *Language, Counter-memory and Practice*, edited by Donald F. Bouchard, 139–64. Ithaca, NY: Cornell University Press, 1977.

Fox, Jay. "The Propaganda Again." *Free Society* 11, no. 1 (January 3, 1904): 7.

"Freedom." *Freedom* 1, no. 1 (October 1886): 1.

"Freedom Exchanges Home and Foreign." January 1920. File #30, Freedom Archive, International Institute of Social History, Amsterdam.

Freeman, R. Austin. R. Austin Freeman to Joseph Ishill, December 21, 1931. In *The Oriole Press: A Bibliography*, edited by Joseph Ishill, 289–90. Berkeley Heights, NJ: Oriole, 1953.

Fritton, Chris. *The Itinerant Printer: Modern Adventures in Tramping*. N.p.: Chris Fritton, 2018.

Fritzi. "Linotype vs. Handset 1D?" Briar Press. Accessed October 18, 2021. http:// www.briarpress.org/29099.

Fulton, Edward H. "Another View of 'Political Anarchism.'" *Freedom* 39, no. 428 (July–August 1925): 38.

Galloway, Alexander. *The Interface Effect*. Cambridge, UK: Polity, 2012.

Gelderloos, Peter. "A Critical History of Harrisonburg Food Not Bombs." *Social Anarchism* 39 (2006). http://theanarchistlibrary.org/library/peter-gelderloos-a -critical-history-of-harrisonburg-food-not-bombs.

Gemie, Sharif. "Anarchism and Feminism: A Historical Survey." *Women's History Review* 5, no. 3 (1996): 417–44.

Genz, Marcella D. *A History of the Eragny Press, 1894–1914*. London: British Library, 2004.

G. H. G. "Propaganda Notes, Huddersfield." *Freedom* 27, no. 295 (November 1913): 91.

Giombolini, Alecia Jay. "Anarchism on the Willamette: *The Firebrand* Newspaper and the Origins of a Culturally American Anarchist Movement, 1895–1898." MA thesis, Portland State University, Paper 4471, 2018. https://doi.org/10.15760 /etd.6355.

Gitelman, Lisa. *Paper Knowledge: Toward a Media History of Documents*. Durham, NC: Duke University Press, 2014.

Gitelman, Lisa. *Scripts, Grooves and Writing Machines: Representing Technology in the Edison Era*. Palo Alto, CA: Stanford University Press, 1999.

Glassgold, Peter. "Introduction: The Life and Death of *Mother Earth*." In *Anarchy! An Anthology of Emma Goldman's "Mother Earth,"* edited by Peter Glassgold, xv–xxxvi. Washington, DC: Counterpoint, 2001.

Goldman, Emma. *Anarchism and Other Essays*. New York: Dover, 1969.

Goldman, Emma. Emma Goldman to Joseph Ishill, July 23, 1928. In *The Oriole Press: A Bibliography*, edited by Joseph Ishill, 298–302. Berkeley Heights, NJ: Oriole, 1953.

Goldman, Emma. "The International Anarchist Congress." *Mother Earth*, October 1907. In *Emma Goldman: A Documentary History of the American Years*, vol. 2, *Making Speech Free, 1902–1909*, edited by Candace Falk, Barry Pateman, and Jessica Moran, 234–45. Berkeley: University of California Press, 2005.

Goldman, Emma. "A Letter from Emma Goldman." *Free Society* 6, no. 39 (August 12, 1900): 4.

Goldman, Emma. *Living My Life*. Vols. 1 and 2. New York: Dover, 1970. Originally published by Alfred A. Knopf, 1931.

Goldman, Emma. "Marriage and Love." In *Anarchism and Other Essays*, 227–39. New York: Dover, 1969.

Goldman, Emma. "Talk with Emma Goldman." *New York Sun*, January 6, 1901. In *Emma Goldman: A Documentary History of the American Years*, vol. 1, edited by Candace Falk, Barry Pateman, and Jessica Moran, 423–31. Berkeley: University of California Press.

Goldman, Emma. "The Tragedy at Buffalo." *Free Society* 7, no. 33 (October 6, 1901): 1.

Goldman, Emma. "W. Starrett." *Spain and the World* 2, no. 37 (July 15, 1938): 2.

Goldman, Emma. "What I Believe." In *Red Emma Speaks: Selected Writings and Speeches by Emma Goldman*, edited by Alex Kates Shulman, 34–46. New York: Vintage Books, 1972.

Goldman, Emma. "What Is There in Anarchy for Woman?" *St. Louis Post-Dispatch Sunday Magazine*, October 24, 1897, 9.

Goldman, Emma, and Max Baginski. "Mother Earth." *Mother Earth* 1, no. 1 (March 1906): 4.

Goldman, Emma, and Alexander Berkman. "Our Sixth Birthday." *Mother Earth* 6, no. 1 (March 1911): 2–4.

Goodman, Paul. *Speaking and Language: Defence of Poetry*. New York: Random House, 1971.

Goodway, David. *Anarchist Seeds Beneath the Snow: Left-Libertarian Thought and British Writers from William Morris to Colin Ward*. Liverpool: Liverpool University Press, 2006.

Goodway, David. "'Freedom' 1886–2014: An Obituary." History Workshop, April 12, 2014. https://www.historyworkshop.org.uk/freedom-1886-2014-an -obituary/.

Goodway, David. "The Kate Sharpley Library." *Anarchist Studies* 16, no. 1 (2008): 91–96.

Goodyear-Kaʻōpua, Noelani. "Kuleana Lāhui: Collective Responsibility for Hawaiian Nationhood in Activists' Practice." *Affinities: A Journal of Radical Theory, Culture and Action* 5 (2011): 130–63.

Goodyear-Kaʻōpua, Noelani. "Protectors of the Future, Not Protestors of the Past: Indigenous Pacific Activism and Mauna a Wākea." *South Atlantic Quarterly* 116, no. 1 (January 2017): 184–94.

Goodyear-Kaʻōpua, Noelani, and Yvonne Mahelona. "Protecting Maunakea Is a Mission Grounded in Tradition." *Zora*, September 5, 2019. https://zora .medium.com/protecting-maunakea-is-a-mission-grounded-in-tradition -38a62df57086.

Gorrie, James. "Arson! Thugs Hit Hong Kong Epoch Times Printing Press." *Epoch Times*, November 20, 2019. https://www.theepochtimes.com/arson-thugs-hit -hong-kong-epoch-times-printing-press_3152007.html.

Goudy, Frederick. "Printing as an Art." In *Ishill's Variorum*, edited by Joseph Ishill, 34. Berkeley Heights, NJ: Oriole, 1963.

Goyens, Tom. *Beer and Revolution: The German Anarchist Movement in New York City, 1880–1914*. Urbana: University of Illinois Press, 2007.

Goyens, Tom. Introduction to *Radical Gotham: Anarchism in New York City from Schwab's Saloon to Occupy Wall Street*, edited by Tom Goyens, 1–11. Urbana: University of Illinois Press, 2017.

Goyens, Tom. *Radical Gotham: Anarchism in New York City from Schwab's Saloon to Occupy Wall Street*. Urbana: University of Illinois Press, 2017.

Graeber, David. "On Playing by the Rules: The Strange Success of #OccupyWall Street." Accessed October 18, 2021. https://www.mauldineconomics.com /images/uploads/overmyshoulder/Occupy_Wall_Street.pdf.

Graphic Design Supplies. "What Is Cockling and What to Do about It?" Accessed October 18, 2021. https://graphicdesignsupplies.co.uk/what-is-cockling -and-what-to-do-about-it/.

Greenidge, Kerri K. "Holding a Mirror up to Nature: William Monroe Trotter, the *Boston Guardian*, and the Transnational Black Radical Press, 1901–19." *Radical History Review* 2021, no. 141 (2021): 107–27.

Greenway, Judy. "The Gender Politics of Anarchist History: Re/membering women, Re/minding men." Paper presented at the Annual Meeting of the Political Studies Association, Edinburgh, April 2010. http://www.judygreenway .org.uk/wp/the-gender-politics-of-anarchist-history-remembering-women -reminding-men/.

Greenway, Judy. "Sex, Politics and Housework." Accessed October 18, 2021. http:// www.judygreenway.org.uk/wp/sex-politics-and-housework/.

Greenwood, Emma L. "Work, Identity and Letterpress Printers in Britain, 1750–1850." PhD diss., University of Manchester, 2015.

Greenwood, Laura. "Book-Anarchists on Bomb-Anarchists: *Free Society*, Diversity of (Textual) Tactics, and Anarchist Counternarratives of the McKinley Assassination." *Journal for the Study of Radicalism* 15, no. 1 (2021): 1–36.

Guglielmo, Jennifer. *Living the Revolution: Italian Women's Resistance and Radicalism in New York City, 1880–1945*. Chapel Hill: University of North Carolina Press, 2011.

Halberstam, Jack. "The Wild Beyond: With and for the Undercommons." In *The Undercommons: Fugitive Planning and Black Study*, by Stefano Harney and Fred Moten, 2–13. Brooklyn: Autonomedia, 2013.

Haraway, Donna. "Situated Knowledges: The Science Question in Feminism and the Privilege of Partial Perspective." *Feminist Studies* 14, no. 3 (Autumn 1988): 575–99.

Harman, Lillian. "Unconditionally Released." *Mother Earth* 7, no. 33 (October 6, 1901): 8.

Harman, Moses. "Lucifer's Coming of Age." *Lucifer, The Lightbearer* 5, no. 33 (August 3, 1901): 264–67.

Harney, Stefano, and Fred Moten. *The Undercommons: Fugitive Planning and Black Study*. Brooklyn: Autonomedia, 2013.

Hartman, Saidiya. "Black in Anarchy." In *The Nation on No Map*, by William C. Anderson, xii–xvii. Chico, CA: AK Press, 2021.

Hartman, Saidiya. *Lose Your Mother: A Journey along the Atlantic Slave Route*. New York: Farrar, Straus and Giroux, 2007.

Hartman, Saidiya. *Wayward Lives, Beautiful Experiments: Intimate Histories of Social Upheaval*. New York: W. W. Norton, 2019.

Hartmann, Sadakichi. "Dispossessed." *Mother Earth* 7, no. 1 (March 1907): 56–58.

Hartmann, Sadakichi. "The Flower-Maker." *Mother Earth* 2, no. 10 (December 1907): 464–67.

Hartmann, Sadakichi. "On Pictorial Projection." In *Sadakichi Hartmann: Critical Modernist*, edited by Jane Calhoun Weaver, 227–30. Berkeley: University of California Press, 1991.

Hartmann, Sadakichi. "The Ride into the Desert." *Mother Earth* 2, no. 12 (February 1908): 586–89.

Hartmann, Sadakichi. "Searchlight Vista." *Mother Earth* 3, no. 3 (May 1908): 162–64.

Havel, Hippolyte. *Proletarian Days: A Hippolyte Havel Reader*. Edited by Nathan Jun. Oakland, CA: AK Press, 2018.

Hayles, N. Katherine. *Writing Machines*. Cambridge, MA: MIT Press, 2002.

Heckert, Jamie, and Richard Cleminson, eds. *Anarchism and Sexuality: Ethics, Relationship and Power*. New York: Routledge, 2011.

Helquist, Michael. *Marie Equi: Radical Politics and Outlaw Passions*. Corvallis: Oregon State University Press, 2015.

Hemmings, Clare. *Considering Emma Goldman: Feminist Political Ambivalence and the Imaginative Archive*. Durham, NC: Duke University Press, 2018.

Hemmings, Clare. "What Is a Feminist Theorist Responsible For?" *Feminist Theory* 8, no. 1 (2007): 69–76.

Hemmings, Clare. *Why Stories Matter: The Political Grammar of Feminist Theory*. Durham, NC: Duke University Press, 2011.

Herrada, Julie. "Agnes Inglis (1870–1952) and the Birth of a Radical Archive." In *Object Lessons and the Formation of Knowledge: The University of Michigan Museums, Libraries, and Collections, 1817–2017*, edited by Kerstin Barndt and Carla M. Sinopoli, 150–55. Ann Arbor: University of Michigan Press, 2017.

Herrada, Julie, and Tom Hyry. "Agnes Inglis: Anarchist Librarian." *Progressive Librarian*, special supplement to no. 16 (Fall 1999): 7–10.

Hicks, John Edward. *Adventures of a Tramp Printer, 1880–1890*. Kansas City, MO: Midamericana, 1950.

Hinely, Susan. "Charlotte Wilson, the 'Woman Question,' and the Meanings of Anarchist Socialism in Late Victorian Radicalism." *International Review of Social History* 57, no. 1 (April 2012): 3–36.

Hirschauge, Dina. "Tenth Anniversary of the Death of Eliezer Hirschauge, 1911–1954." Translated by Murray Glickman. *KSL: Bulletin of the Kate Sharpley Library*, no. 84 (October 2015). https://www.katesharpleylibrary.net/tb2szq.

"The History of Freedom Press." Spunk.org. Accessed October 18, 2021. http://www.spunk.org/library/pubs/freedom/sp000606.txt.

Hodgart, Rhona M. *Ethel MacDonald: Glasgow Woman Anarchist*. 2nd ed. London: Kate Sharpley Library, 2003.

Hogan, Kristen. *The Feminist Bookstore Movement: Lesbian Antiracism and Feminist Accountability*. Durham, NC: Duke University Press, 2016.

Holmes, Lizzie. "The Keynote of Success." *Freedom* 9, no. 93 (May 1895): 7.

Holmes, Lizzie. "Love of Authority." *Free Society* no. 50 (October 23, 1898): 2–3.

Holmes, Lizzie. "Mental Barriers." *Free Society* 6, no. 10 (January 21, 1900): 1.

Holmes, Lizzie. "The Red Indians and the American Government." *Freedom* 5, no. 52 (March 1891): 18.

Holmes, Lizzie. "The Return." *Free Society* 5, no. 46 (October 1, 1899): 2.

Holmes, Lizzie. "Revolutionists." *Free Society* 5, no. 51 (November 5, 1899): 1.

Holmes, Lizzie. "Sentiment." *Free Society*, no. 41 (August 21, 1898): 2–3.

Holmes, Lizzie. "Twenty-Five Years After." *Mother Earth* 7, no. 9 (November 1912): 300–305.

Holmes, Lizzie. "The War Spirit." *Free Society*, no. 29 (May 28, 1898): 1.

Holmes, Lizzie. "Why We Tell the Story." *Free Society* 5, no. 18 (March 12, 1899): 1.

Holmes, Lizzie. "Work in the Future." *Free Society* 5, no. 41 (August 20, 1899): 1.

Holmes, Lizzie. "The World's Beautiful Failures." *Mother Earth* 2, no. 4 (June 1907): 184–89.

Holmes, Lizzie, and William Holmes. "Reminiscences." *Free Society* 5, no. 51 (November 5, 1899): 2–3.

Hong, Nathaniel. "Constructing the Anarchist Beast in American Periodical Literature, 1880–1903." *Critical Studies in Mass Communication* 9, no. 1 (March 1992): 110–30.

Horvitz, J. "An Appeal for Literature." *Free Society* 6, no. 8 (January 7, 1900): 4.

Hostettler, Rudolf. *The Printer's Terms*. London: Alvin Redman Unlimited, 1949.

Howells, John, and Marion Dearman. *Tramp Printers*. Pacific Grove, CA: Discovery, 1996.

Hoyt, Andrew. "And They Called Them 'Galleanisti': The Rise of the *Cronaca Sovversiva* and the Formation of America's Most Infamous Anarchist Faction (1895–1912)." PhD diss., University of Minnesota, 2018.

Hoyt, Andrew. "Carlo Abate, Luigi Galleani, and the Art of the *Cronaca Sovversiva*." Unpublished paper, Department of American Studies, University of Minnesota, 2011.

Hoyt, Andrew. "The Inky Protest of an Anarchist Printmaker: Carlo Abate's Newspaper Illustrations and the Artist's Hand in the Age of Mechanical Reproduction." In *Protest on the Page: Essays on Print and the Culture of Dissent*, edited by James L. Baughman, Jennifer Ratner-Rosenhagen, and James P. Danky, 32–58. Madison: University of Wisconsin Press, 2015.

Hoyt, Andrew. "Uncovering and Understanding Hidden Bonds: Applying Social Field Theory to the Financial Records of Anarchist Newspapers." In *Historical Geographies of Anarchism: Early Critical Geographers and Present-Day Scientific Challenges*, edited by Federico Ferretti, Gerónimo Barrera de la Torre, Anthony Ince, and Francisco Toro, 25–39. London: Routledge, 2018.

Hsu, Rachel Hui-Chi. *Emma Goldman, "Mother Earth," and the Anarchist Awakening*. Notre Dame, IN: University of Notre Dame Press, 2021.

Hughes, Laura. "In the Library of Jacques Derrida: Manuscript Materiality after the Archival Turn." *New Literary History* 49, no. 3 (Summer 2018): 403–24.

Huhtamo, Erkki, and Jussi Parikka. "Introduction: An Archaeology of Media Archaeology." In *Media Archaeology: Approaches, Applications, and Implications*, edited by Erkki Huhtamo and Jussi Parikka, 1–24. Berkeley: University of California Press, 2011.

Inglis, Agnes. "Reflections Part I." n.d. Box 25, Agnes Inglis Papers, Joseph A. Labadie Collection, Special Collections Research Center, University of Michigan Library.

Inglis, Agnes. "Reflections, Part II." n.d. Box 25, Agnes Inglis Papers, Joseph A. Labadie Collection, Special Collections Research Center, University of Michigan Library.

Inglis, Agnes. "Sunday April 28th 1928." 1928. In "Reflections, Part II." Box 25, Agnes Inglis Papers, Joseph A. Labadie Collection, Special Collections Research Center, University of Michigan Library.

Inglis, Agnes. "To the Labadie Collection." 1932. In "Reflections, Part II." Box 25, Agnes Inglis Papers, Joseph A. Labadie Collection, Special Collections Research Center, University of Michigan Library.

"International Anarchist Federation of the English Provinces." *Freedom* 22, no. 225 (January 1908): 7–8.

International Federation of Journalists. "Arsonists Destroy Printing House in Sri Lanka." November 21, 2007. https://www.ifj.org/media-centre/news/detail /article/arsonists-destroy-printing-house-in-sri-lanka.html.

International Institute of Social History (IISH). "A Detailed History of the IISH." Accessed October 16, 2021. https://iisg.amsterdam/en/about/history/detailed -history-iish.

"International Notes." *Freedom* 16, no. 167 (April–May 1902): 14.

Isaak, Abe. "Why We Considered Czolgosz a Spy." *Free Society* 7, no. 34 (October 13, 1901): 4.

Isca, Valerio. "Ida Pilat Isca (1896–1980)." Translated by Paul Sharkey. Kate Sharpley Library. Accessed October 18, 2021. https://www.katesharpleylibrary.net/n2z47f.

Ishill, Joseph. *Emma Goldman: A Challenging Rebel*. Berkeley Heights, NJ: Oriole, 1957.

Ishill, Joseph. Foreword to *Peter Kropotkin: The Rebel, Thinker and Humanitarian*, edited by Joseph Ishill, i–v. Berkeley Heights, NJ: Free Spirit, 1923.

Ishill, Joseph, ed. *Free Vistas: An Anthology of Life and Letters*. Vol. 1. Berkeley Heights, NJ: Oriole, 1933.

Ishill, Joseph, ed. *Havelock Ellis: In Appreciation*. Berkeley Heights, NJ: Oriole, 1929.

Ishill, Joseph, ed. *Ishill's Variorum: A Compendium of Thoughts and Reflections, Culled from Goudy's "Ars typographica," and Other Literary Sources*. Berkeley Heights, NJ: Oriole, 1963.

Ishill, Joseph, ed. *The Oriole Press: A Bibliography*. Berkeley Heights, NJ: Oriole, 1953.

Ishill, Joseph, ed. *Peter Kropotkin: The Rebel, Thinker and Humanitarian*. Berkeley Heights, NJ: Free Spirit, 1923.

Ishill, Rose Freeman. "To Joseph Ishill." In *Petals Blown Adrift*, 23. Berkeley Heights, NJ: Oriole, 1918.

Jackson, Holbrook. "The Aesthetics of Printing." In *Ishill's Variorum: A Compendium of Thoughts and Reflections, Culled from Goudy's "Ars typographica," and Other Literary Sources*, edited by Joseph Ishill, 53–57. Berkeley Heights, NJ: Oriole, 1963.

Jackson, Holbrook. Holbrook Jackson to Joseph Ishill, March 14, 1933. In *The Oriole Press: A Bibliography*, edited by Joseph Ishill, 314–15. Berkeley Heights, NJ: Oriole, 1953.

Janssen, Frans A. *Technique and Design in the History of Printing*. Netherlands: Hes and De Graff, 2004.

Jeppesen, Sandra. "Toward an Anarchist-Feminist Analytics of Power." In *The Anarchist Imagination*, edited by Carl Levy and Saul Newman, 110–31. London: Routledge, 2019.

Jeppesen, Sandra, and Holly Nazar. "Genders and Sexualities in Anarchist Movements." In *The Continuum Companion of Anarchism*, edited by Ruth Kinna, 162–91. London: Continuum Books, 2012.

Jerauld, Nellie M. "God and Grundy." *Free Society*, no. 12 (January 30, 1898): 1–3.

Jerauld, Nellie M. "What Shall We Teach Our Children?" *Free Society*, no. 2 (November 21, 1897): 3.

Johnson, Kahala, and Kathy E. Ferguson. "Anarchism and Indigeneity." In *The Palgrave Handbook on Anarchism*, edited by Carl Levy and Matthew Adams, 697–714. London: Palgrave Macmillan, 2019.

Jolly, Margaretta. *In Love and Struggle: Letters in Contemporary Feminism*. New York: Columbia University Press, 2008.

Jones, Jacqueline. *Goddess of Anarchy: The Life and Times of Lucy Parsons, American Radical*. New York: Basic Books, 2017.

Jones, Llewellyn. "Editorial: A Birthday Tribute." *Chicago Evening Post Literary Review*, July 26, 1929. In *The Oriole Press: A Bibliography*, edited by Joseph Ishill, 6–11. Berkeley Heights, NJ: Oriole, 1953.

Jun, Nathan, ed. *Proletarian Days: A Hippolyte Havel Reader*. Chico, CA: AK Press, 2018.

Jun, Nathan. Review of *Emma Goldman: Political Thinking in the Streets*, by Kathy E. Ferguson. *Contemporary Political Theory* 12 (April 15, 2013): e-8–e-10.

Kapahua, Kawena. "Stories from the Mauna, Kuʻu One Hānau." *Biography* 43, no. 3 (2020): 575–81.

Kauanui, J. Kēhaulani. "The Politics of Indigeneity, Anarchist Praxis, and Decolonization." *Anarchist Developments in Cultural Studies* 2021, no. 1 (2021): 9–42.

Kavanagh, Mat. "Some Little Known Anarchists—Dan Chatterton." *Freedom*, no. 46 (February 1934): 4.

Kelly, Harry. "A Letter from England." *Free Society* 5, no. 12 (January 29, 1899): 4.

Kelly, Harry. "Nicholas Tchaikovsky." *Freedom* 33, no. 363 (August 1919): 44–45.

Kelly, Harry. "Roll Back the Years: Odyssey of a Libertarian." Edited by John Nicholas Beffel. Unpublished manuscript. N.d. Archives of Labor History and Urban Affairs, Wayne State University.

Kelly, Harry. "Thomas Cantwell." *Mother Earth* 1, no. 12 (February 1907): 28–31.

Kinder, Kimberly. *The Radical Bookstore: Counterspace for Social Movements*. Minneapolis: University of Minnesota Press, 2021.

Kinna, Ruth. "Anarchism and Feminism." In *Brill's Companion to Anarchism and Philosophy*, edited by Nathan Jun, 253–84. Leiden: Brill, 2018.

Kinna, Ruth. *The Government of No One: The Theory and Practice of Anarchism*. London: Pelican Books, 2019.

Kinna, Ruth. *Kropotkin: Reviewing the Classical Anarchist Tradition*. Edinburgh: Edinburgh University Press, 2016.

Kitching, Alan. *The A–Z of Letterpress: Founts from the Typography Workshop*. Introduction by John L. Walters. London: Lawrence King, 2015.

Kittler, Friedrich A. *Gramophone, Film, Typewriter*. Translated and introduced by Geoffrey Winthrop-Young and Michael Wutz. Stanford, CA: Stanford University Press, 1999.

Kooistra, Lorraine Janzen. "Fundamental Sympathy: The Gothic, the Fin-de-Siècle Printing Revival and the Digital." *Journal of the William Morris Society* 24, nos. 1–2 (2020–21): 7–23.

Kornegger, Peggy. "Anarchism: The Feminist Connection." In *Quiet Rumors*, edited by the Dark Star Collective, 21–31. San Francisco: AK Press, 2002.

Krishna, Sankaran. "Anarchy, Security, Hierarchy: Reading IR with Jasbir Puar." *The Disorder of Things* (blog), November 26, 2018. https://thedisorderofthings .com/2018/11/26/anarchy-security-hierarchy/.

Kropotkin, Peter. "An Appeal to the Young." First appeared in French as "Aux jeunes gens," *Le Révolté*, June 25, July 10, August 7, and August 21, 1880. Anarchist Library, February 16, 2009. https://theanarchistlibrary.org/library/petr -kropotkin-an-appeal-to-the-young.

Kropotkin, Peter. "A Letter on the Present War." *Freedom* 28, no. 306 (October 1914): 76–77.

Kropotkin, Peter. *Memoirs of a Revolutionist.* Boston: Houghton Mifflin, 1930.

Kuwada, Bryan Kamaoli, and No'u Revilla. "Introduction: Mana from the Mauna." *Biography* 43, no. 3 (2021): 515–26.

Lang, Lucy Robins. *Tomorrow Is Beautiful.* New York: Macmillan, 1938.

Latour, Bruno. "An Attempt at a 'Compositionist Manifesto.'" *New Literary History* 41, no. 3 (Summer 2010): 471–90.

Lawson, Alexander. *The Compositor as Artist, Craftsman, and Tradesman.* Athens, GA: Press of the Nightowl, 1990.

Lazar, Hillary. "Intersectionality." In *Anarchism: A Conceptual Approach*, edited by Benjamin Franks, Nathan Jun, and Leonard Williams, 157–74. New York: Routledge, 2018.

Lazar, Hillary. "Until All Are Free: Black Feminism, Anarchism and Interlocking Oppression." *Perspectives on Anarchist Theory* 29 (2016): 35–50.

League for Mutual Aid Collection. Papers, 1920–1972. Walter P. Reuther Library, Wayne State University. Accessed October 18, 2021. https://reuther.wayne.edu /files/LR000455.pdf.

Leighten, Patricia. *Re-ordering the Universe: Picasso and Anarchism, 1897–1914.* Princeton, NJ: Princeton University Press, 1989.

Leighten, Patricia. "The World Turned Upside Down: Modernism and Anarchist Strategies of Inversion in *L'assiette au Beurre*." *Journal of Modern Periodical Studies* 4, no. 2 (2014): 133–70.

"Letterbox." *Free Society* 5, no. 12 (January 29, 1899): 4.

"Letterbox." *Free Society* 6, no. 1 (November 19, 1899): 4.

"Letterbox." *Free Society* 6, no. 26 (May 13, 1900): 4.

Levy, Carl. "Anarchists and the City: Governance, Revolution, and the Imagination." In *Historical Geographies of Anarchism: Early Critical Geographers and Present-Day Scientific Challenges*, edited by Federico Ferretti, Gerónimo Barrera de la Torre, Anthony Ince, and Francisco Toro, 7–24. London: Routledge, 2018.

Le Warne, Charles Pierce. *Utopias on Puget Sound, 1885–1915.* Seattle: University of Washington Press, 1975.

Lexico. S.v. "letter." Accessed October 18, 2021. https://www.lexico.com/en /definition/letter.

Liddle, Kathleen. "More Than a Bookstore: The Continuing Relevance of Feminist Bookstores for the Lesbian Community." *Journal of Lesbian Studies* 9, no. ½ (2005): 145–59.

Lloyd, J. William. "Are They Anarchists?" *Free Society*, no. 1 (November 14, 1897): 6.

Long, K. Kamakaoka'ilima. "The Fight of the Indigenous Protectors of Mauna Kea." *Funambulist*, no. 25 (August 30, 2019). https://thefunambulist.net /magazine/25-self-defense/ the-fight-of-the-indigenous-protectors-of-mauna-kea-by-k-kamakaokailima-long.

Longa, Ernesto. *Anarchist Periodicals in English Published in the United States (1833–1955)*. Lanham, MD: Scarecrow, 2010.

Lupton, Ellen. *Thinking with Type: A Critical Guide for Designers, Writers, Editors, and Students*. New York: Princeton Architectural Press, 2004.

Mac. "Tale of a Wet Trip." *Freedom* 14, no. 151 (September–October 1900): 43–44.

MacArthur, Elizabeth. *Extravagant Narratives: Closure and Dynamics in the Epistolary Form*. Princeton, NJ: Princeton University Press, 2014.

MacDonald, George. *Fifty Years of Freethought: Story of the Truth Seeker from 1875*. New York: Truthseeking, 1931.

Mak, Bonnie. *How the Page Matters*. Toronto: University of Toronto Press, 2013.

Mak, Cayden. "Building Online Power." *Perspectives on Anarchist Theory* 32 (2021): 26–33.

Malatesta, Errico. "A Personal Issue." *La Questione Sociale*, 5, no. 16 (December 23, 1899). In *The Complete Works of Malatesta*, vol. 4, *Towards Anarchy, Malatesta in America, 1899–1900*, edited by Davide Turcato, 184–85. Chico, CA: AK Press, 2018.

Manber, Jeffrey, and Neil Dahlstrom. "The Printing Press on the Cover." *Annals of Iowa* 36 (1962): 236.

Mapping American Social Movements through the Twentieth Century. "Socialist Party of America History and Geography." Accessed August 2, 2021. https:// depts.washington.edu/moves/SP_intro.shtml.

Marino, Katherine. *Feminism for the Americas: The Making of an International Human Rights Movement*. Chapel Hill: University of North Carolina Press, 2019.

Marqusee, Mike. *Wicked Messenger: Bob Dylan and the 1960s*. New York: Seven Stories Press, 2003.

Marsh, Margaret S. "The Anarchist-Feminist Response to 'the Woman Question' in the Late Nineteenth Century." *American Quarterly* 30, no. 4 (Fall 1978): 533–47.

Marsh, Margaret S. *Anarchist Women, 1870–1920*. Philadelphia: Temple University Press, 1981.

Marso, Lori Jo. "Freedom's Poses." *Political Research Quarterly* 70, no. 4 (2017): 720–27.

Mason, Roger Burford. *Print and Be Damaged, or, How I Put My Back Out Saving Letterpress for My Grandchildren's Children*. Francistown, NH: Typographeum, 1994.

"The Match Girls Strike." *Freedom* 2, no. 13 (October 1887): 89.

May, Todd. "Anarchism from Foucault to Rancière." In *Contemporary Anarchist Studies: An Introductory Anthology of Anarchy in the Academy*, edited by Randall Amster, Abraham DeLeon, Luis A. Fernandez, Anthony J. Nocella II, and Deric Shannon, 11–17. London: Routledge, 2009.

May, Vivian. *Pursuing Intersectionality: Unsettling Dominant Imaginaries*. New York: Routledge, 2015.

McElroy, Wendy. *The Debates of Liberty: An Overview of Individualist Anarchism, 1881–1908*. Lanham, MD: Lexington Books, 2003.

McHenry, Keith. *Hungry for Peace: How You Can Help End Poverty and War with Food Not Bombs*. Tucson, AZ: See Sharp, 2012.

McKinley, Blaine. "'The Quagmires of Necessity': American Anarchists and Dilemmas of Vocation." *American Quarterly* 34, no. 5 (Winter 1982): 503–23.

McKinney, Cait. *Information Activism: A Queer History of Lesbian Media Technologies*. Durham, NC: Duke University Press, 2020.

McMillian, John. *Smoking Typewriters: The Sixties Underground Press and the Rise of Alternative Media in America*. New York: Oxford University Press, 2011.

Media Foundation for West Africa. "Arsonists Destroy Pro-Gbagbo Printing Press." April 27, 2011. https://ifex.org/arsonists-destroy-pro-gbagbo-printing-press/.

Menzel, Annie. "Minor Perambulations, Political Horizons: Comments on Kathy Ferguson's 'Anarchist Women and the Politics of Walking.'" *Political Research Quarterly* 70, no. 4 (2017): 728–34.

Meredith, Isabel. *A Girl among the Anarchists*. London: Duckworth, 1903.

Mesnil, Jacques. *Joseph Ishill and the Oriole Press*. Translated by Rose Freeman Ishill. Berkeley Heights, NJ: Oriole, 1958.

Monk, Craig. "Emma Goldman, Mother Earth, and the Little Magazine Impulse in Modern America." In *"The Only Efficient Instrument": American Women Writers and the Periodical, 1837–1916*, edited by Aleta Fainsod Cane and Susan Alves, 113–25. Iowa City: University of Iowa Press, 2001.

Moran, Jessica. "*The Firebrand* and the Forging of a New Anarchism: Anarchist Communism and Free Love." Anarchist Library, Fall 2004. https://theanarchistlibrary.org/library/jessica-moran-the-firebrand-and-the-forging-of-a-new-anarchism-anarchist-communism-and-free-lov.

Moran, Jessica. "To Spread the Revolution: Anarchist Archives and Libraries." Anarchist Library, May 2016. https://theanarchistlibrary.org/library/jessica-moran-to-spread-the-revolution-anarchist-archives-and-libraries.

Morris, Brian. "Guest Editorial: Rudolf Rocker 1873–1958." *Anarchist Studies* 20, no. 1 (2012): 11–21.

Morris, William. *The Collected Works of William Morris*. Vol. 9. London: Longmans Green, 1911.

Morris, William. "A Note by William Morris on His Aims in Founding the Kelmscott Press." Kelmscott House, Upper Mall, Hammersmith, November 11, 1895. William Morris Society in the United States. https://archive.org/details/ANoteByWilliamMorrisOnHisAimsInFoundingTheKelmscottPressTogether/mode/2up.

Morton, James F. "Shall We Have an Eight-Page Paper?" *Free Society* 6, no. 31 (June 17, 1900): 2.

Morton, James F. "What Can You Do for Free Society?" *Free Society* 6, no. 32 (June 24, 1900): 2.

Morton, James F. "What Can You Do for the Propaganda?" *Free Society* 6, no. 33 (July 1, 1900): 2.

Moses, Jonathan. "Texture of Politics: London's Anarchist Clubs." *RIBAJ: The RIBA Journal*, December 1, 2016. https://www.ribaj.com/intelligence/the-texture-of -politics-london-s-anarchists-clubs-1882–1914.

Murray, Simone. *Mixed Media: Feminist Presses and Publishing Politics*. London: Pluto, 2004.

Nail, Thomas. "What Is an Assemblage?" *SubStance*, issue 142, 46, no. 1 (2017): 21–37.

Nelson, Bruce C. "*Arbeiterpresse und Arbeiterbewegung*: Chicago's Socialist and An-archist Press, 1870–1900." In *The German-American Radical Press: The Shaping of a Left Political Culture, 1850–1940*, edited by Eliott Shore, Ken Fones-Wolf, and James P. Danky, 81–107. Urbana: University of Illinois Press, 1992.

Nettlau, Max. "Albert Libertad." *Freedom* 12, no. 236 (December 1908): 90.

Nettlau, Max. "Anarchist Communist Conference." *Freedom* 12, no. 122 (Janu-ary 1898): 85.

Nettlau, Max. "The Early Days of Freedom." *Freedom* 9, no. 26 (December 11, 1948): 2.

Nettlau, Max. "Mutual Toleration versus Dictatorship." *Freedom* 35, no. 385 (July 1921): 42–44.

Nettlau, Max. "Tom Keell." *Spain and the World* 2, no. 37 (July 15, 1938): 2.

Neumann, Caryn E. "Elijah Lovejoy." *The First Amendment Encyclopedia*, 2009. https://www.mtsu.edu/first-amendment/article/1441/elijah-lovejoy.

"News and Notes." *Free Society*, no. 3 (November 28, 1897): 5–8.

"News from Everywhere." *Free Society*, no. 3 (November 21, 1897): 7.

"News from Nowhere." *Free Society*, no. 1 (November 14, 1897): 7.

New York Academy of Medicine Library. "Bertha Johnson Collection, 1848–1956." Accessed October 16, 2021. https://www.nyam.org/library/collections-and -resources/archives/finding-aids/ARJ-0003.html/.

"Notes." *Freedom* 5, no. 55 (June 1891): 46.

"Notes and Comments." *Free Society* 5, no. 19 (March 19, 1899): 2.

"Observations and Comments." *Mother Earth* 9, no. 8 (October 1914): 243–53.

Offen, Karen. *The Woman Question in France, 1400–1870*. Cambridge: Cambridge University Press, 2017.

O'Hagan, Andrew. *Our Fathers*. San Diego, CA: Harvest Books, 1999.

Oliver, L. S. "Sentiments." *Free Society* 6, no. 16 (March 4, 1900): 3.

Olson, Joel. "The Problem with Infoshops and Insurrection." In *Contemporary Anarchist Studies: An Introductory Anthology of Anarchy in the Academy*, edited by Randall Amster, Abraham DeLeon, Luis A. Fernandez, Anthony J. Nocella II, and Deric Shannon, 35–45. London: Routledge, 2009.

Ong, Walter J. *Orality and Literacy*. New York: Routledge, 1982.

Online Etymology Dictionary. S.v. "letter." Accessed October 18, 2021. https://www
.etymonline.com/word/letter.

"The Opening of Marsh House." *Freedom* 29, no. 311 (March 1915): 17.

Osorio, Jamaica Heolimeleikalani. "On the Front Lines of Mauna Kea." *Flux: The Current of Hawai'i,* July 23, 2021. https://fluxhawaii.com/maunakea-movement/.

Osorio, Jamaica Heolimeleikalani. *Rise Like a Mighty Wave.* Minneapolis: University of Minnesota Press, 2021.

"The Other Side." *Free Society,* no. 8 (January 2, 1898): 2.

Otway, Fiona. *Kiss the Paper.* Accessed October 18, 2021. http://www.fionaotway
.com/projects.html.

"Our Exchange List." *Freedom* 5, no. 52 (March 1891): 8.

"Our Printing Office." *Freedom* 4, no. 47 (October 1890): 44.

"The Outlook." *Freedom* 8, no. 84 (January/February 1894): 1–2.

Overbeck, Charles. *The Tramp Printers: Forgotten Trails of Traveling Typographers.* Portland, OR: Eberhardt, 2017.

Pakieser, Andrea, ed. *I Belong Only to Myself: The Life and Writings of Leda Rafanelli.* Oakland, CA: AK Press, 2014.

Panagia, Davide. "On the Political Ontology of the Dispositif." *Critical Inquiry* 45 (Spring 2019): 714–46.

Panagia, Davide. *Rancière's Sentiments.* Durham, NC: Duke University Press, 2018.

Parikka, Jussi. "Erased Dots and Rotten Dashes, or How to Wire Your Head for a Preservation." In *Media Archaeology: Approaches, Applications, and Implications,* edited by Erkki Huhtamo and Jussi Parikka, 211–38. Berkeley: University of California Press, 2011.

Parikka, Jussi. *Insect Media: An Archeology of Animals and Technology.* Minneapolis: University of Minnesota Press, 2010.

Parikka, Jussi. *What Is Media Archaeology?* Cambridge, UK: Polity, 2012.

Parry, Richard. *The Bonnot Gang: The Story of the French Illegalists,* 2nd edition. Oakland, CA: PM Press, 2016.

Parson, Sean. *Cooking Up a Revolution: Food Not Bombs, Homes Not Jails, and Resistance to Gentrification.* Manchester: Manchester University Press, 2019.

Parsons, Lucy. "The Ballot Humbug." In *Lucy Parsons: Freedom, Equality and Solidarity,* edited by Gale Ahrens, 95–98. 1905. Chicago: Charles Kerr, 2004.

Parsons, Lucy. "The Case of Sex Slavery." *The Firebrand* 1, no. 1 (January 27, 1895): 3.

Parsons, W. H. "Interview September 16, 1887 in Norfolk, VA." In Albert Parsons, *Anarchism: Its Philosophy and Scientific Basis as Defined by Some of Its Apostles,* 188–93. Chicago: Mrs. Lucy Parsons, 1887.

Passet, Joanne E. "Power through Print: Lois Waisbrooker and Grassroots Feminism." In *Women in Print: Essays on the Print Culture of American Women from the Nineteenth and Twentieth Centuries,* edited by James P. Danky and Wayne A. Wiegand, 229–50. Madison: University of Wisconsin Press, 2006.

Passet, Joanne E. *Sex Radicals and the Quest for Women's Equality.* Urbana: University of Illinois Press, 2003.

Patten, John. "Islands of Anarchy: Simians, Cienfuego, Refract, and Their Support Network." Kate Sharpley Library. Accessed October 30, 2021. https://www .katesharpleylibrary.net/dnckhs.

Peace Pledge Union. "Joan Beauchamp." The Men Who Said No—Conscientious Objectors 1915–1919. Women Working for Peace. Accessed October 18, 2021. https://menwhosaidno.org/context/women/beauchamp_j.html.

Peterson, William S. Introduction to *William Morris, Master Printer,* by Frank Colebrook, vii–x. Council Bluffs, IA: Yellow Barn, 1989.

Pluetzner, C. "A Summer Outing." *Free Society* 7, no. 28 (August 11, 1901): 3.

Plummer, Ken. *Documents of Life 2: An Invitation to a Critical Humanism.* London: Sage, 2001.

Porter, David. *Eyes to the South: French Anarchists and Algeria.* Oakland, CA: AK Press, 2011.

Porter, David, ed. *Vision on Fire: Emma Goldman on the Spanish Revolution.* Oakland, CA: AK Press, 2006.

Porter, Dorothy, ed. *Early Negro Writing, 1760–1837.* Boston: Beacon, 1971.

"Press Censorship." *Free Society,* no. 6 (December 17, 1897): 8.

"Press Maintenance Fund." *Commune* 1, no. 3 (July–August 1923): 28.

"The Propaganda." *Freedom* 12, no. 130 (September 1898): 63–64.

Protevi, John. *Political Affect: Connecting the Social and the Somatic.* Minneapolis: University of Minnesota Press, 2009.

"The Publications of Joseph Ishill." In *The Oriole Press: A Bibliography,* edited by Joseph Ishill, 115–16. Berkeley Heights, NJ: Oriole, 1953.

Quail, John. *The Slow Burning Fuse: The Lost History of the British Anarchists.* London: Paladin Books, 1978.

Rainer, Dachine. "Holley Cantine, February 14, 1916–January 2, 1977." In *Drunken Boat: Art, Rebellion, Anarchy,* edited by Max Blechman, 177–85. Brooklyn, NY: Autonomedia, Left Bank Books, 1994.

Rancière, Jacques. *Aisthesis: Scenes from the Aesthetic Regime of Art.* Translated by Zakir Paul. London: Verso, 2013.

Rancière, Jacques. *Dissensus: On Politics and Aesthetics.* London: Continuum International Publishing Group, 2010.

Rancière, Jacques. *The Nights of Labor: The Workers' Dream in Nineteenth-Century France.* Translated by John Drury. Philadelphia: Temple University Press, 1989.

Rancière, Jacques. *The Flesh of Words.* Translated by Charlotte Mandel. Stanford, CA: Stanford University Press, 2004.

Rancière, Jacques. *The Philosopher and His Poor.* Edited and with an introduction by Andrew Parker. Translated by John Drury, Corinne Oster, and Andrew Parker. Durham, NC: Duke University Press, 1983.

Rancière, Jacques. *The Politics of Aesthetics.* Translated by Gabriel Rockhill. London: Bloomsbury, 2004.

Ray, Angela G., and Paul Stob. Introduction to *Thinking Together: Lecturing, Learning and Difference in the Long Nineteenth Century*, 1–22. University Park: Pennsylvania State University Press, 2018.

Ray, Angela G., and Paul Stob, eds. *Thinking Together: Lecturing, Learning and Difference in the Long Nineteenth Century*. University Park: Pennsylvania State University Press, 2018.

Ray, Rob. *A Beautiful Idea: History of the Freedom Press Anarchists*. London: Freedom Press, 2018.

Reid, John Cowie. "Gerald Manley Hopkins." *Encyclopedia Britannica*, July 24, 2020. https://www.britannica.com/biography/Gerard-Manley-Hopkins.

Rentschler, Carrie A., and Samantha C. Thrift. "Doing Feminism: Event, Archive, Techné." *Feminist Theory* 16, no. 3 (2015): 239–49.

Replogle, Georgia. "Pointers." *Egoism* 2, no. 8 (December 1891): 1.

Replogle, Henry. "New Papers." *Egoism* 3, no. 25 (June 1897): 3.

Review of *Emma Goldman: Political Thinking in the Streets*, by Kathy Ferguson. *KSL: Bulletin of the Kate Sharpley Library*, no. 74–75 (August 2013). https://www.katesharpleylibrary.net/f7m1kv.

Richards, Vernon. "Printers We Have Known: 1936–1986." In *Freedom: A Hundred Years, October 1886 to October 1986*, edited by the editors of *Freedom*, 28–29. London: Freedom Press, 1986.

"The Rise of the Movement in America." *Freedom* 15, no. 155 (February 1901): 10–11.

Ritchie, Ward. *Of Bookmen and Printers: A Gathering of Memories*. Los Angeles: Dawson's Book Shop, 1989.

Rocker, Fermin. *The East End Years: A Stepney Childhood*. London: Freedom Press, 1998.

Rocker, Rudolf. "Behind Barbed Wire and Bars: Recollections of My English War-time Imprisonment." Queen Mary University Library Archives, London. Introduction dated July 1924, Berlin.

Rocker, Rudolf. "The Lifework of Joseph Ishill." Translated by Markus Faigle. Honolulu, HI: 2020. Original German, "Das Lebenswerk von Joseph Ishill." Rudolf Rocker Papers, International Institute of Social History, Amsterdam.

Rocker, Rudolf. *The London Years*. Translated by Joseph Leftwich. Oakland, CA: AK Press, 2005.

Rocker, Rudolf. "Pages from an Autobiography." In *The Oriole Press: A Bibliography*, edited by Joseph Ishill, xv–xxvi. Berkeley Heights, NJ: Oriole, 1953.

Rodrigues, Edgar. "Edgard Leuenroth, 1881–1968." Translated by Paul Sharkey. Kate Sharpley Library. Accessed October 18, 2021. https://www.katesharpleylibrary.net/m63zpn.

Rowbotham, Sheila. *Dreamers of a New Day: Women Who Invented the Twentieth Century*. London: Verso, 2011.

Rowbotham, Sheila. *Rebel Crossings: New Women, Free Lovers and Radicals in Britain and the United States*. London: Verso, 2016.

Roy, Beth. "Goody Two-Shoes and the Hell-Raisers: Women's Activism, Women's Reputations in Little Rock." In *No Middle Ground: Women and Radical Protest*, edited by Kathleen Blee, 96–132. New York: New York University Press, 1998.

Roy, Rob. *A Beautiful Idea: History of the Freedom Anarchists.* London: Freedom Press, 2018.

Rumble, Walker. "From the Shop Floor to the Show: Joseph W. McCann, Typesetting Races, and Expressive Work in 19th Century America." *Journal of Popular Culture* 32, no. 1 (Fall 1998): 87–101.

Rumble, Walker. "A Showdown of 'Swifts': Women Compositors, Dime Museums, and the Boston Typesetting Races of 1886." *New England Quarterly* 71, no. 4 (December 1998): 615–28.

Rumble, Walker. *The Swifts: Printers in the Age of Typesetting Races.* Charlottesville: University of Virginia Press, 2003.

Ryley, Peter. *Making Another World Possible: Anarchism, Anti-capitalism and Ecology in Late 19th and Early 20th Century Britain.* New York: Bloomsbury, 2013.

"Salutary." *Free Society,* no. 1 (November 14, 1897): 4.

Sander, David. *Wood Engraving: An Adventure in Printmaking.* New York: Viking, 1978.

Sartwell, Crispin. "Priestess of Pity and Vengeance." In *Exquisite Rebel: The Essays of Voltairine de Cleyre,* edited by Sharon Presley and Crispin Sartwell, 3–15. Albany: State University of New York Press, 2005.

Scott, James. *The Art of Not Being Governed.* New Haven, CT: Yale University Press, 2009.

Scott, James. *Two Cheers for Anarchism.* Princeton, NJ: Princeton University Press, 2012.

Scott, Paul. "Some Personal Reflections." In *Modern School of Stelton, Twenty-Fifth Anniversary, 1915–1940,* 13–14. Stelton, NJ: Modern School, 1940.

S. D. "Peppery Pot." *Free Society* 5, no. 48 (October 15, 1899): 1.

Selbuz, Cemal. "Biography of Armenian Anarchist Alexander Atabekian." Anarchist Library, July 2006. https://theanarchistlibrary.org/library/cemal -selbuz-biography-of-armenian-anarchist-alexander-atabekian.

Senta, Antonio. *Luigi Galleani: The Most Dangerous Anarchist in America.* Translated by Andrea Asali with Sean Sayers. Chico, CA: AK Press, 2019.

Seymour, Henry. "A Battle for Freedom." *Free Society,* no. 37 (July 24, 1898): 1–2.

Shaffer, Kirwin R. *Anarchist Cuba: Countercultural Politics in the Early Twentieth Century.* Oakland, CA: PM Press, 2019.

Shaffer, Kirwin R. *Anarchists of the Caribbean: Countercultural Politics and Transnational Networks in the Age of U.S. Expansion.* Cambridge: Cambridge University Press, 2020.

Shahn, Ben. "Love and Joy about Letters." In *Ben Shahn,* edited by John D. Morse, 143–63. New York: Praeger, 1972.

Shapiro, Michael. *Punctuations: How the Arts Think the Political.* Durham, NC: Duke University Press, 2019.

Shaw, Nellie. *Whiteway: A Colony on the Cotswolds.* London: The C. W. Daniel Company, 1935.

Shpayer-Makov, Haia. "Anarchism in British Public Opinion, 1880–1914." *Victorian Studies* 31, no. 4 (Summer 1988): 487–516.

Shulman, Alix Kates. "Emma Goldman's Feminism: A Reappraisal." In *Red Emma Speaks*, edited by Alix Kates Shulman, 3–19. Amherst, NY: Humanity Books, 1996.

Slaughter, Kevin. "The First American Egoist Journal." In *Egoism: The First Two Volumes, 1890–1892*, edited by Kevin Slaughter, 3–6. N.p.: Union of Egoists with assistance from Underworld Amusements, 2017.

Slifer, Shaun. *So Much to Be Angry About: Appalachian Movement Press and Radical DIY Publishing, 1969–1979*. Morgantown: West Virginia University Press, 2021.

Slifer, Shaun, and Ally Greenhead. *Ross Winn—Digging Up a Tennessee Anarchist*. Pumpkin Hollow, TN: Fifth Estate, 2004.

Smith, Jessica. "The Papers of Peter Good: An Accrual to the Dave Cunliffe Archive." *Rylands Blog*, May 14, 2019. https://rylandscollections.com/2019/05/14/the-papers-of-peter-good-an-accrual-to-the-dave-cunliffe-archive/.

Sobchack, Vivian. "Afterword: Media Archaeology and Re-presencing the Past." In *Media Archaeology: Approaches, Applications, and Implications*, edited by Erkki Huhtamo and Jussi Parikka, 323–34. Berkeley: University of California Press, 2011.

"Solidarity an Aid to Liberty." *Freedom* 26, no. 273 (January 1912): 97.

Spataro, David. "Against a De-politicized DIY Urbanism: Food Not Bombs and the Struggle over Public Space." *Journal of Urbanism* 9, no. 2 (2016): 185–201.

Springer, Simon, Jennifer Mateer, Martin Locret-Collet, and Maleea Acker, eds. *Undoing Human Supremacy: Anarchist Political Ecology in the Face of Anthroparchy*. Lanham, MD: Rowman and Littlefield, 2021.

Standard, Paul. Paul Standard to Joseph Ishill, February 21, 1945. In *The Oriole Press: A Bibliography*, edited by Joseph Ishill, 373–76. Berkeley Heights, NJ: Oriole, 1953.

Stanley, Liz. "The Epistolarium: On Theorizing Letters and Correspondences." *Auto/biography* 12 (2004): 201–35.

Stansell, Christine. *American Moderns: Bohemian New York and the Creation of a New Century*. New York: Henry Holt, 2000.

Stansky, Peter. *Redesigning the World: William Morris, the 1880s, and the Arts and Crafts*. Princeton, NJ: Princeton University Press, 1985.

Steinberg, J. Review of *Women and the Revolution*, by Ethel Mannin. *Spain and the World* 2, no. 36 (June 24, 1938): 4.

Streeby, Shelley. *Radical Sensations: World Movements, Violence, and Visual Culture*. Durham, NC: Duke University Press, 2013.

"The Sudden Death of G.H. Exall." *Freedom* 26, no. 279 (July 1912): 56.

Suriano, Juan. *Paradoxes of Utopia: Anarchist Culture and Politics in Buenos Aires, 1890–1910*. Translated by Chuck Morse. Oakland, CA: AK Press, 2010.

Swain, Dan, Petr Urban, Catherine Malabou, and Petr Kouba, eds. *Unchaining Solidarity: On Mutual Aid and Anarchism with Catherine Malabou*. Lanham, MD: Rowman and Littlefield, 2022.

Swanson, Jo. Preface to *Hungry for Peace: How You Can Help End Poverty and War with Food Not Bombs*, by Keith McHenry, 8–11. Tucson, AZ: See Sharp, 2012.

Taddei, Dino. "Alberto Moroni, the Gentle Anarchist." Translated by Paul Sharkey. Kate Sharpley Library. Accessed October 18, 2021. https://www.katesharpleylibrary.net/69p94t.

Tamboukou, Maria. "Epistolary Lives: Fragments, Sensibility, Assemblages." In *Palgrave Handbook of Auto/Biography*, edited by Julie M. Parsons and Anne Chappell, 157–64. London: Palgrave Macmillan, 2020.

Tamboukou, Maria. "Interfaces in Narrative Research: Letters as Technologies of the Self and as Traces of Social Forces." *Qualitative Research* 11, no. 5 (2011): 625–41.

Tamboukou, Maria. *Sewing, Fighting and Writing: Radical Practices in Work, Writing, and Culture*. London: Rowman and Littlefield, 2016.

Tarrida del Mármol, Fernando. "Anarchism without Adjectives." Translated by Newster McNab. *La Révolte* 3, no. 51 (September 6–12, 1890). https://theanarchistlibrary.org/library/fernando-tarrida-del-marmol-anarchism-without-adjectives.

Tcherkesoff, W. "Friend and Comrade." In *Peter Kropotkin: The Rebel, Thinker and Humanitarian*, edited by Joseph Ishill, 23–26. Berkeley Heights, NJ: Free Spirit, 1923.

Terborg-Penn, Rosalyn. *African American Women in the Struggle for the Vote, 1850–1920*. Bloomington: Indiana University Press, 1998.

Tetenbaum, Barbara. "10 Steps to Perfect Typesetting." Letterpress Commons. Accessed May 2, 2022. https://letterpresscommons.com/setting-type-by-hand/.

Teves, Stephanie Nohelani. *Defiant Indigeneity: The Politics of Hawaiian Performance*. Chapel Hill: University of North Carolina Press, 2018.

Thomas, Edith. *Louise Michel*. Montreal: Black Rose Books, 1980.

Thompson, E. P. *The Making of the English Working Class*. New York: Vintage Books, 1963.

Thompson, E. P. *William Morris: Romantic to Revolutionary*. London: Merlin, 1955.

Thrift, Samantha. "Feminist Eventfulness: Boredom and the 1984 Canadian Leadership Debate on Women's Issues." *Feminist Media Studies* 13, no. 3 (2011): 406–21.

Tochatti, James. "Between Ourselves." *Liberty: A Journal of Anarchist Communism* 1, no. 1 (January 1894): 4.

Torres, Anna Elena. *Horizons Blossom, Borders Vanish: Anarchism and Yiddish Literature*. New Haven, CT: Yale University Press, 2022.

Travis, Trysh. "The Women in Print Movement: History and Implications." *Book History* 22 (2008): 275–300.

Tsing, Anna Lowenhaupt. *The Mushroom at the End of the World: On the Possibility of Life in the Capitalist Ruins*. Princeton, NJ: Princeton University Press, 2015.

Tuchman, Barbara. *This Proud Tower: A Portrait of the World before the War, 1890–1914*. New York: Macmillan, 1966.

Tucker, Benjamin. Benjamin Tucker to Joseph Ishill, May 1, 1934. In *The Oriole Press: A Bibliography*, edited by Joseph Ishill, 380–81. Berkeley Heights, NJ: Oriole, 1953.

Tucker, Benjamin. Benjamin Tucker to Joseph Ishill, January 3, 1935. In *The Oriole Press: A Bibliography*, edited by Joseph Ishill, 382–83. Berkeley Heights, NJ: Oriole, 1953.

Tucker, Benjamin. "On Picket Duty." *Liberty* 5, no. 20 (May 12, 1888): 1.

Tucker, Benjamin. "On Picket Duty." *Liberty* 8, no. 24 (November 21, 1891): 1.

Tucker, Benjamin. "Pointers." *Egoism* 2, no. 6 (October 1891): 2–3.

Turcato, Davide. "The Other Nation: The Place of the Italian Anarchist Press in the USA." In *Historical Geographies of Anarchism: Early Critical Geographers and Present-Day Scientific Challenges*, edited by Federico Ferretti, Gerónimo Barrera de la Torre, Anthony Ince, and Francisco Toro, 40–64. London: Routledge, 2018.

Turner, J., A. Marsh, and T. H. Keell. "A Call for Action." *Freedom* 20, no. 208 (July 1906): 21.

Tusan, Michelle Elizabeth. "Performing Work: Gender, Class and the Printing Trade in Victorian Britain." *Journal of Women's History* 16, no. 1 (Spring 2004): 103–26.

Tygiel, Jules. "Tramping Artisans: Carpenters in Industrial America, 1880–90." In *Walking to Work: Tramps in America, 1790–1935*, edited by Eric H. Monkkonen, 87–117. Lincoln: University of Nebraska Press, 1984.

US Department of Justice. *Investigation Activities of the Department of Justice*. Letter from the Attorney General, November 17, 1919. 66th Congress, 1st Session, Senate, Doc. No. 153. Washington, DC: Government Printing Office, 1919.

"A Use for Anthropometry." *Freedom* 10, no. 102 (February 1896): 66.

U.S. History. "The Sack of Lawrence." Accessed October 18, 2021. https://www.ushistory.org/us/31c.asp.

Vallance, Margaret. "Rudolf Rocker: A Biological Sketch." *Journal of Contemporary History* 8, no. 3 (July 1973): 75–95.

Voline. "Anarchist Synthesis." In *Anarchism: A Documentary History of Libertarian Ideas*, edited by Robert Graham, 431–35. Montreal: Black Rose Books, 2005.

Waisbrooker, Lois. "Just a Question." *Free Society* 5, no. 5 (December 11, 1898): 3.

Waisbrooker, Lois. "The Standard of Judgment." *Free Society*, no. 10 (January 16, 1898): 3.

Waisbrooker, Lois. "Why Is It So?" *Free Society* 5, no. 12 (January 29, 1899): 1.

Walker, Edwin. "Kansas Liberty and Justice." *Lucifer, The Lightbearer* 4, no. 29 (October 15, 1886): 2. Written from Cell 2, the Jail, Oakaloosa, Kansas, October 9, 1886.

Walter, Nicolas. *The Anarchist Past and Other Essays*. Edited by David Goodway. Nottingham: Five Leaves, 2007.

Walter, Nicolas. "Lilian Wolfe, 1875–1974." In *Freedom: A Hundred Years, October 1886 to October 1986*, edited by the editors of *Freedom*, 23–24. London: Freedom Press, 1986.

Walters, John L. Introduction to *The A–Z of Letterpress: Founts from the Typography Workshop*, by Alan Kitching, 7. London: Lawrence King, 2015.

Ward, Bessie. "Daisy Lord and Others." *Freedom* 12, no. 236 (December 1908): 91.

Ward, Colin. *Anarchy in Action*. 2nd ed. London: Freedom Press, 1996. https://theanarchistlibrary.org/library/colin-ward-anarchy-in-action.

Ward, Colin. "Notes of an Anarchist Ex-editor." *Z-Revue*, no. 1 (1975): 18–20.

Ward, Colin. "A Self-Employed Society." Accessed May 2, 2022. http://www
.theyliewedie.org/ressources/biblio/en/Ward_Colin_-_A_SELF-employed
_society.html.

Ward, Colin, and David Goodway. *Talking Anarchy*. London: Five Leaves, 2003.

Ward, Dana. Anarchy Archives homepage. Accessed October 18, 2021. http://
dwardmac.pitzer.edu/Anarchist_Archives/.

Ward, Dana. "Proudhon: A Biography." Anarchy Archives. Accessed June 26, 2022.
http://dwardmac.pitzer.edu/Anarchist_Archives/proudhon/wardbio.html.

Wexler, Alice. "Interview with Fermin and Ruth Rocker." July 1985, London.
File #593, Rudolf Rocker Papers, International Institute of Social History,
Amsterdam.

W. H. "News at Home and Abroad." *The Torch* 2, no. 2 (July 1895): 20.

Whitehead, Alfred North. *Essays in Science and Philosophy*. London: Rider, 1948.

Whitehead, Andrew. "Dan Chatterton and His 'Atheistic Communistic Scorcher.'"
Libcom.org, August 23, 2006. https://libcom.org/libray/-dan-chatterton
-scorcher-london-communist-atheist.

"Who Is Guilty?" *Freedom* 20, no. 208 (July 1906): 1.

Wieck, David Thoreau. "The Negativity of Anarchism." *Interrogations: International Review of Anarchist Literature*, no. 5 (December 1975): 1–31. http://
quadrant4.org/anarchism.html.

Wilkinson, Lily Gair. "Women in Bondage." *Freedom* 27, no. 288 (April 1913): 26–27.

Wilkinson, Lily Gair. "Women in Rebellion." *Freedom* 27, no. 289 (May 1913): 34.

Wilkinson, Lily Gair. "Women's Freedom." *Freedom* 27, no. 290 (June 1913): 46.

Wilkinson, Lily Gair. "Women's Freedom (Con)." *Freedom* 27, no. 291 (July 1913): 55.

Wingert, Dorothy H. "Gems of Printing Yield Fame, Not Fortune, for Typographer in Berkeley Heights." *Elizabeth Daily Journal*, October 16, 1956. Reprinted
by Joseph Ishill. Berkeley Heights, NJ: Oriole, 1958.

Wingrove, Elizabeth. "The Agony of Address." Unpublished paper, Department of
Political Science, University of Michigan, 2008.

"Women's Burden." *Freedom* 27, no. 290 (June 1913): 45.

Woodcock, George. *Letter to the Past: An Autobiography*. Toronto: Fitzhenry and
Whiteside, 1982.

Wright, John Buckland. John Buckland Wright to Joseph Ishill, June 22, 1933.
In *The Oriole Press: A Bibliography*, edited by Joseph Ishill, 386–88. Berkeley
Heights, NJ: Oriole, 1953.

Yeoman, James Michael. *Print Culture and the Formation of the Anarchist Movement in Spain, 1890–1915*. London: Routledge, 2020.

Zimmer, Kenyon. "American Anarchist Periodical Circulation Data, 1880–1940."
2014. Accessed June 23, 2022. https://www.academia.edu/7715169/American
_Anarchist_Periodical_Circulation_Data_1880_1940.

Zimmer, Kenyon. "Faces of the First Red Scare." December 31, 2019. http://
kenyonzimmer.com/red-scare-deportees/.

Zimmer, Kenyon. *Immigrants against the State: Yiddish and Italian Anarchism in
America*. Urbana: University of Illinois Press, 2015.

INDEX

Daniels, Viroqua, 33, 158, 266n179
Davies, Agnes A., 44, 235n26, 242n147
De Cleyre, Voltairine, 127, 130, 150, 193; in "American Notes," 150, 152, 262n88, 268n222; in "Between the Living and the Dead," 267n197, 267n200; in *Freedom*, 139, 152–53; in "Free Society," 56, 148, 158, 164; on Jo Labadie, 76–77; in *Mother Earth*, 151, 172; on the Paris Commune, 151; poetry of, 97–98, 106; social sketches by, 175–76, 177, 266n179
DeLanda, Manuel, 5–6, 16, 86, 88, 146, 169
Deleuze, Gilles, and Félix Guattari, 3–4
Derzanski, Barnett, 42, 217, 220
Dinowitzer, Lillian Kisliuk, 126
Dinshaw, Carolyn, 124, 128, 132–33
direct action, 202, 206, 214
Dolgoff, Esther, 126
Dolgoff, Sam, 57, 126
Drinnon, Richard, 83, 143, 267n197
Drucker, Johanna, 63–65, 78
Duff, William, 78, 165
Dumartheray, François, 43

Eberhardt Press, 23, 73, 23
editors, x, 7, 9, 11, 62, 108, 130–32, 139; of *The Adult*, 154; of *L'Adunata dei Refrattari*, 79; of *Age of Thought*, 218; of *The Agitator*, 47, 165, 218, 237n7; of *L'Agitatore*, 154; of *Anarchy*, 131; of *Arbeiter Fraynd*, 90; of *L'Aurora*, 217; of the Black press, 195–96; of *The Blast*, 79, 142; of *Cahiers de l'Humanisme Libertaire*, 219; of *Clothed with the Sun*, 37; and compositors, 29, 39, 41, 42, 43, 187; of *Cronaca Sovversiva*, 16; of *Cultura Obrera*, 217; of *The Demonstrator*, 218; of *Egoism*, 25, 37–38, 221, 228; of *The Egoist*, 218; of *The Firebrand*, 33, 46, 140, 152, 154; of *Foundational Principles*, 37; of *Freedom*, 15, 44, 76, 104, 131, 165, 171, 217–23; of *Free Society*, 52, 139–41, 152, 158–60, 162, 171; of *Freie Arbeiter Stimme*, 79; of *Freiheit*, 220; of *Germinal*, 90; of *Herald of Revolt*, 215; of *L'Humanité nouvelle*, 19, 143; Joseph Ishill as, 1, 14, 48; of *Khleb I Volia*, 218, 222; of *Liberty*, 37–38, 53, 222, 268n215; of *Liberty: A Journal of*

Anarchist Communism, 46; of *The Little Magazine*, 37, 215; of *Lucifer, the Lightbearer*, 31, 49, 181, 218, 222, 268n222; of *The Modern School Magazine*, 23, 57, 142; of *Mother Earth*, 79, 142–43, 147, 165; of *The Mutualist*, 218; of *New Order*, 218; of *News of No Importance*, 66; of *The Open Road*, 78; of *Our Age*, 37; of *The Phoenix*, 217; of *Prison Blossoms*, 47; of *La Protesta Umana*, 217; of *La Questione Sociale*, 42, 216, 217, 223, 226; of *The Raven*, 145; of *Retort*, 217; of *Road to Freedom*, 18, 79, 149, 165; of *La Scopa*, 220; of *Spain and the World*, 80, 146; of *The Syndicalist*, 216, 218; of *Les Temps Nouveaux*, 19; of *The Torch*, 37; of *Why?*, ix, 46; of *The Word*, 215, 219
Egoism, 25, 37–38, 42, 70, 221, 228
Enckell, Marianna, 11
engravers, 28, 29–31, 221, 225, 227–28, 238n40
Entangled Roots Press, 33, 61, 231
epistles, 3, 8, 189
epistolarium, 85, 86, 120, 250n14
epistolary/epistolarity, 112, 120, 187; doubleness of, 102–8; future orientation of, 121; incompleteness of, 88, 112, 114; network of, 94, 99, 106–8, 129; practices of, 10, 129, 147, 187; in radical politics, 3, 20, 214; relations of, 3, 15, 19–20, 83–88, 94–96, 100–101, 119, 125; temporality of, 88; women's, 96–100, 121. *See also* Tamboukou, Maria
Estevé, Pedro, 33, 39, 42, 217, 226
external reader, 10, 108–9, 112, 114, 115, 118–19, 121

Farmelant, Randie, 210, 212
fascism, 16, 20, 91, 103, 117, 125
Faye, Jules Remedios, 23, 49, 60, 65–67, 231
feminism: and anarchism, 2, 131, 133, 140, 188, 193, 195; letters in, 83; newsletters in, 127, 209–11; personal is political in, 88, 112, 114, 148, 158, 178; in printing, 35, 241n105; and spiritualism, 181, 268n222
feminist bookstore movement, xi, 13, 188, 200, 208–13
feminists: experience of, 109; and *Freedom*, 158, 175; and *Free Society*, 158–60, 162; as

information activists, 100; and inter-
sectionality, 190, 198, 270n17; Marxist,
198; and *Mother Earth*, 19, 142, 144, 158;
publications of, 115, 127, 272n67
Ferrer, Francisco, 89, 154, 197, 216, 219
Ferrero, Vincenzo, 42
Fessenden, Sarah, 201–2, 203, 214, 273n109
Finch, Bob, 45, 217
Firebrand, The (London), 3
Firebrand, The (Oregon), 33, 43, 138–41, 152,
163, 191, 220, 261n41; office of, 56; print-
ers at, 46, 218; and Walt Whitman, 154
Firebrand, The (Ross Winn), 47, 223
Fitzgerald, Eleanor "Fitzi," 142, 156, 165,
221n127
Fontanilla Borrás, Antonia, 36, 216
Food Not Bombs, 13, 188, 200, 201–6, 210,
212–13, 273n109
Fox, Jay, 47, 52–53, 226, 268n215; as distribu-
tor, 165; as printer, 4, 60, 218, 237n7
Frank, Herman, 79
Free Association, ix, xi
freedom: in anarchism, 2, 71, 130, 131, 143–44,
149, 154, 179–80; creative, 13; in daily life,
22, 184; and enslavement, 190, 192–98,
271n46; at the Mauna, 207, 208; in printing, 32, 79, 89; as process, 189; sexual, 138,
226; women's, 158–59, 173–75, 177
Freedom, x, 3, 79, 127, 138–39, 144–45, 147;
"American Notes" in, 150, 152, 262n88,
268n222; appearance of, 70–73, 75,
77–78; arrests at, 50, 154; classic essays
in, 149; current events in, 150–51;
distribution of, 139, 165; editors of,
15, 44, 76, 104, 131, 165, 171, 217–23;
exchanges in, 166–67, 169; fundraising
in, 164, 264n150; gender and sexuality, debates on, 157–58, 263–64n124; in
global network, 146; individualist vs.
communist debates in, 155–56; letters
to the editor in, 163, 269n229; as little
optical machine, 77–78; local reports
in, 161–62; masthead, *72*; memory of
anarchist events in, 151–52; Morris's
influence on, 55; poetry in, 148; poor
attendance for meetings at, 18; presses
of, 46, 52, 60, 62; printshops of, 56; as
public space, 164–65; slavery, language

of, in, 197–98; social sketches in, 172–75;
speaking tours in, 152–53; strikes in, 153;
think pieces in, 178, 182–83, 266n179;
typesetters for, 26, 39, 42–46, 57, 217–20,
222–23, 242n144; value of, 127–28, 131;
and working class, 145–46; and World
War I, 33, 115, 146, 156–57
Freedom Bulletin, 42, 227
Freedom Press, 43, 46, 52, 60, 101, 131,
145–46, 157
Free Society, 138–42, 145, 147–48; appearance
of, 70–73, 144; arrests in, 153–55; classic
texts in, 149; current events in, 150–51;
debates about printing in, 52–53; distribution of, 165, 264n142; editors of, 52,
139–41, 152, 158–60, 162, 171; exchanges
with, 166, 169; fundraising in, 163–64;
Emma Goldman, letter to, 6; individualist vs. communist debates in, 155–56;
letters to the editor in, 162–63; as little
optical machine, 77–78; masthead, *71*;
memory of anarchist events in, 151–52;
men writers for, 263n123; office of,
56; poetry in, 148–49; as public space,
164–65; raid on, 49; sexuality and
gender, debates on, 157–60; speaking
tours in, 152–53, 262n91; strikes in, 153;
subtitles of, 261n41; texts in, 147, 171,
191, 268n215; think pieces in, 178–82,
266n179; typesetters for, 43, 218, 222
Free Vistas, 20, 79
Freie Arbeiter Stimme, 79, 167
Fulton, Edward, 76, 218, 226; on individualist vs. communist debates, 156; printing
by, 31, 39, 42, 56; on tramping, 40;
writing by, 42
Furst, Alice Baker Greystone, 99, 253n70

Galleani, Luigi, 16–17, 30, 152, 225
Galloway, Alexander, 186–87
gender and sexuality, 25, 36–38, 131, 155,
157–60, 198, 246n240, 259n6
genre, 4, 84, 170; of letters, 100, 108; mixed,
11, 133, 137, 148, 170–71, 176–78, 265n177
Germinal, 44, 90, 167, 220, 221
Gitelman, Lisa, 78, 84, 136, 186; on
genre, 84, 170; on presses, xi; on
printing, 25, 27, 28, 29, 42, 50–51

Goldman, Emma, ix, xvi, 20, 126, 130, 173; allies of, 19; on anarchism, 189, 195, 198; apartment of, 165; arrests of, 154, 156, 163; and art, 81; and Leon Czolgosz, 154; and *Freedom*, 139, 152; and *Free Society*, 158, 163; and Haymarket, 151; and IISH, 117; on individualism and communism, 155; and Agnes Inglis, 94–95, 107, 114, 153; and Joseph Ishill, 28, 56, 80, 89, 116, 250n2; and Bertha Johnson, 98; and Sophie Labadie, 113; letters of, 83, 162; making a living by, 133; and *Mother Earth*, x, 138, 142, 143, 145, 267n197; as orator, 152, 153, 162, 260n29; on police spies, 19; on race and slavery, 193, 194, 196, 270n31; on rank and file, 6; on sexuality, 157–59, 263n117; and the Spanish Revolution, ix; suitcase of, 214; on violence, 17; and Ross Winn, 47; on World War I, 156

Good, Peter, 32, 49, 56, 59, 231, 239n59
Goodfriend, Audrey, 126
Goodman, Paul, 126, 146, 170–71
Goodyear-Kaʻōpua, Noelani, 204, 206
Goyens, Tom, 18
grapheme, 3, 8, 13, 186
Grave, Jean, 19, 55, 56, 149, 156, 168, 218
Greeley, Horace, 29, 52
Green, Joseph, 65–66, 231
Greenidge, Kerri, 195–96
Greenway, Judy, 158, 259n6
Greenwood, Laura, 205, 268n215
groups, anarchist, ix, x, 7, 18, 19, 36, 62, 200
Guabello, Adalgisa, 36, 218
Guabello, Alberto, 36, 218

Halberstam, Jack, 15, 134, 180, 189
Hall, Bolton, 162, 168
Hamon, Augustin, 19, 143
handpress, 43, 46, 80, 221; of Peter Good, 32; of Joseph Ishill, 62; of Johann Most, 60; of Lois Waisbrooker, 223; of Ross Winn, 56; of *Why?*, 31. *See also* presses
Harman, Lillian, 36, 49, 80, 98, 152–54, 218, 226, 228
Harman, Moses, 62, 80, 154, 181–82, 218, 222, 268n222, 269n225; teaching Lillian, 31, 36, 226

Harney, Stefano and Fred Moten: fugitive public, 11–12, 134–35, 171; radical study, 11, 12, 135–37, 184, 189; undercommons, 8, 51, 115, 134, 148, 180, 183–84, 189
Hartman, Saidiya, 190, 194–95, 196, 271n45, 271n46
Hartmann, Sadakichi, 142, 172, 176–78, 265n177, 266n179, 267n204
Havel, Hippolyte, 18, 139, 142, 165
Hayles, N. Katherine, 26, 48, 73
Haymarket, 11, 16, 39, 151–52, 160, 226
Haywood, Angela, 60
Haywood, Ezra, 60, 246n240
Hicks, John Edward, 28, 29, 33–34, 40–41, 52
Hirschauge, Eliezer, 39, 42, 218, 226–27, 241n112
Hogan, Kristen, xi, 209–11
Holmes, Lizzie, 139, 198, 263–64n124; on change, 180–81; on creativity, 14–15; on emotion, 178–80, 268n215; on Haymarket, 151; on women's rights, 159–60
Holmes, William, 151, 263n123
Home Colony, 19, 161, 226; printers in, 4, 52, 60, 165, 218, 221, 226, 268n222
hot spots, 102, 110
Hoyt, Andrew, 6, 7, 30
Hsu, Rachel, 142, 157
Hughes, Laura, 9, 116, 124
Hull, Moses, 86, 98
Humphrey, John J., 45, 217, 218
Huzarski, Dina, 226

IISH. *See* International Institute of Social History
Inglis, Agnes, 19, 20, 94, 95, 227; in assemblages, 2, 4, 6, 88; and Emma Goldman, 107, 113, 153; and Haymarket, 152, 262n87; and hot spots, 101–2, 110–11; and Joseph Ishill, 1–2, 31, 60, 185; and Bertha Johnson, 70, 86–87, 96–100, 101–2, 103, 106, 121–25, 258n193; and Tom Keell, 104–5; and Labadie collection, 95–96, 99, 106, 111, 113–15, 117, 126–28, 185–86; and Sophie Labadie, 113; making a living by, 96, 133, 252n52; and Max Metzkow, 105–6, 228; poetry of, 125, 126, 128; and the scholars who

will be coming, 127, 187; and Pearl Johnson Tucker, 86–87, 96–97, 98–100, 126;
and Lilian Wolfe, 101–2, 110–11, 126, 127
ink, 50, 75, 120, 166; interactions with paper
of, 9, 15, 34, 59, 67, 146, 187; as life's
blood, 84; pressmen's work with, 28;
problems with, 46, 48, 66–67; smell of,
57–58; thickness of, 32, 66
interface, 186–87, 189–91, 200, 214
International Institute of Social History
(IISH), xii, 86, 88, 113, 115, 117–18, 119
intersectionality, 12, 188–90, 270n17; in anarchism and feminism, 2, 178; in black
theory, 189, 191, 196, 198
Isaak, Abe, 56, 158, 218, 263n123; arrest of,
49, 154; as editor, 139, 140; and linotype,
52–53; printing by, 43
Ishill, Anatole, 31, 89, 218
Ishill, Joseph, 23, 39, 66, 90, 218, 227, 228;
and Alexander Berkman, 79; books,
alleged theft of by, 102, 110, 112, 255n134;
colophons of, 69; as connector, 4, 6, 15,
101; dreams of, 21–22, 56, 82, 125; education of, 28; employment of, 39, 42, 92,
133; and engravers, 29–31, 32, 68–69,
228, 238n40; as fine printer, 14, 19,
21–22, 48, 75, 77–81, 116–17; and future
of anarchism, 125–26; and Emma
Goldman, 56, 81; and Agnes Inglis, 1–2,
20, 60, 96, 185; and Bertha Johnson, 98,
99, 102; and Thomas Keell, 15–16, 18,
265n162; and letterpress today, 34; and
letters, 1–2, 13, 83, 86–88, 101, 250n2;
and library holdings, 115–17, 256n153;
love of nature by, 21–22; and William
Morris, 75–76; *Open Vistas, 74*; page
layout by, 68–70, 73–76; printery of, 56,
57–58, 61–62, 92, 240n77; and Rudolf
Rocker, 14, 83, 84, 88–94, 103, 108,
118–120, 125–126; as teacher, 29–31, 39,
89; and Martin Thorn, 66; and tramping, 40; and Benjamin Tucker, 89, 97;
and Pearl Johnson Tucker, 101–2, 110,
249n327; as writer, 42, 129–30
Ishill, Rose Freeman, 79, 89, 92, 228; illness
of, 93–94, 108, 118–19; and Joseph Ishill,
113, 227, 249n327; poetry of, 69, 89, 93,
227; on press, 57–58, 240n77

Jackson, Holbrook, 55, 56
James, C. L., 149, 168, 194, 263n123
Jerauld, Nellie, 140, 158–59
job printer, 22, 27, 42, 62, 92
job shop, x, 22, 37, 42, 89
Johnson, Bertha, 86–87, 96–97, 98, 99–100,
216, 227, 252n53, 258n193; as archivist,
110–11, 124; and Belle Chaapel, 101–2,
110; death of, 258n188; on filaments, 5,
99, 112; on fine printing, 70; friendship with Agnes Inglis, 106, 121–25; on
future scholars, 127; typewriter of, 114,
256n143
Joseph A. Labadie Collection, xii, 1, 86–87,
117–18; Emma Goldman's visit to,
107; Agnes Inglis in, 96, 98–99, 105–6,
115, 127, 185; Agnes Inglis's poem to,
128; and Bertha Johnson, 111, 124; and
Sophie Labadie, 113; and Pearl Johnson
Tucker, 111
Joseph Ishill Papers, xii, 86, 88, 115–16,
117–18
journals: accounts of arrests in, 49–50, 137,
140, 153–55; beauty of, 21–22, 30, 55,
61, 72, 78–81, 129; blackness in, 12, 189,
190–98, 259n7; as centers of anarchism,
x, xii, 84, 130–31, 135–37, 147–48, 186,
234–35n8; children's, 31, 60, 62, 166, 222;
circulation of, 7–8, 25, 51, 139, 141, 143,
147–48, 162; classic texts in, 11, 12, 28, 39,
130–31, 136, 137, 149; current events in,
137, 138, 141, 150–51; debates in, x, 52, 72,
136, 137, 155–60, 163, 264n145; distribution of, x, 6–7, 16, 96, 133, 139, 152, 165;
engravers of, 28, 29–30, 31, 221, 225, 227,
228, 238n40; exchange of, 11, 16, 137, 139,
142, 143, 166–69, 265n162; fundraising
for, 43, 62, 136, 160, 163–64, 264n150,
264–65n151; genres of writing in, 11–12,
136–37, 147–48, 170–84, 265n177; goals
of, 4, 26, 52, 143, 147, 188–89, 228; humor
in, 2, 76, 138–39, 145, 161–62, 228; lecture
tours in, x, 71, 141, 149–50, 152–53, 163,
260n29, 262n91; letters to editor in,
6, 84, 137, 140, 146, 156, 158–59, 162–63;
as little optical machines, 26–27,
72–73, 78, 179; local reports in, 11, 136,
137, 150–52, 160–62, 165, 169, 262n91;

undercommons: anarchist, 8, 20, 26, 81, 86, 147, 180, 198; debt in the, 134–35, 157; emergence of, 14–15, 180; hapticality in the, 148, 183; radical study in, 11, 189; and Rancière, 51, 81, 134

Union of Russian Workers, 216–22

unions, 3, 10, 28, 33, 41, 55, 135, 142; apprenticeships in, 35, 38–41, 43, 89, 226–27; coverage of, in journals, 150, 153, 160; linotype, as affecting, 51; men in, 34–35; in picnic culture, 160; printing in, x; reformist, 153, 197; sexual metaphor for, 182; typographical, 29, 34, 38–40, 42, 228; women in, 35–38

Van Scheltema, Annie Adama, 113, 117

Voline, 189, 198, 225

wage slaves, 12, 192–94

Waisbrooker, Lois, 37, 80, 158; on race, 193, 194; and spiritualism, 98, 160, 181, 223, 268n222; think pieces by, 178, 181–82, 193

War Commentary, 43, 127, 146, 229

Ward, Colin, 45, 127, 131–32, 144, 178, 223

Warren, Josiah, 28, 118, 223

Whitehead, Alfred North, 109, 113, 115, 255n136

Whiteway Colony, 60, 156, 217, 219, 220, 222, 227

Whitman, Walt, 162; and enchiridion, 77; poetry of, 5, 148, 149; as printer, 29, 65–66; "A Woman Waits for Me," 140, 154

Why?, ix, 31, 46, 106, 126, 216, 221

Wieck, David, ix, xi, xii, 126, 190

Wilkinson, Lucy Gair, 158; social sketches by, 172–77, 190, 192–93, 266n185

Wilson, Charlotte, 144, 228

Wingrove, Elizabeth, 85, 87–88, 110

Winn, Gussie, 47, 56

Winn, Ross, 47, 56, 223, 263n123

Wolfe, Lilian, 229; arrest of, 50, 154, 222; correspondence with Ishill, 16; at *Freedom*, 111–12, 217, 220; and Tom Keell, 105, 227; on letters and libraries, 101–2, 110–12; at Marsh House, 164–65; at Whiteway Colony, 60; on World War I, 156–57; and young comrades, 126, 127

women: as archivists, 113–14; Black, 190, 196; domestic work by, 57, 158, 163; farm labor of, 121–24; in feminist bookstores, 209–12, 213; and the future, 126–28; as information activists, 100, 113, 186; letters of, 87, 96, 100, 102, 121; libraries of, 110–12, 114; at Maunakea, 206, 213; organizing workers, 153, 180; in patriarchy, 121, 181–82, 263–64n124; as printers, 34–38, 53, 240n77; and rank-and-file, 6, 111; rights of, 37, 86, 160; as sex slaves, 172, 192–93; as workers, 182, 186, 263–64n124; as writers, 11, 131, 137, 140, 157–60, 171–75, 178–83, 192–95

Woodcock, George, 43, 144, 223

Word, The, 101, 246n240; printing of, 46, 57, 58, 60, 61, 215, 216, 219–20

World War I: amnesty for antiwar protesters after, 20, 94–95; effect on anarchism of, 125–26, 146, 102; internments during, 92, 229; raids during, 50; split among anarchists over, 33, 115, 144, 155, 156–57, 227

Wright, John Buckland, 31, 238n40

Yarros, Victor, 128, 223, 259n213

Zimmer, Kenyon, x, 2, 7, 162, 234n3, 235n8